M000100979

THE UNITED STATES TENNIS ASSOCIATION

THE UNITED STATES

TENNIS ASSOCIATION

Raising the Game

WARREN F. KIMBALL

Foreword by Dave Haggerty
With the assistance of Lorna Skaaren

UNIVERSITY OF NEBRASKA PRESS
LINCOLN AND LONDON

Library of Congress Cataloging-in-Publication Data

Names: Kimball, Warren F., author.
Title: The United States Tennis Association: raising the game / Warren F. Kimball; Foreword by Dave Haggerty; With the assistance of Lorna Skaaren.
Description: Lincoln, Nebraska: University of Nebraska Press, 2017.
Includes bibliographical references and index.
Identifiers: LCCN 2017016285
ISBN 9780803296930 (hardback: alk. paper)
ISBN 9781496204639 (mobi)
ISBN 9781496204646 (pdf)
Subjects: LCSH: United States Tennis Association —History. Tennis—United States—History.
BISAC: SPORTS & RECREATION / Tennis.
SPORTS & RECREATION / History.
Classification: LCC GV997.U55 K55 2017
DDC 796.3420973—dc23
LC record available at https://lccn.loc.gov/2017016285

Set in Minion Pro by Rachel Gould.

For Jackie (1938–2009), one of
the founding mothers

To Sally, who took up the burden

In a different way and for their
deep involvement in the project,
to Judy Levering, Lee Hamilton,
Alan Schwartz, George Gowen,
and Marshall Happer

CONTENTS

ILLUSTRATIONS

FOREWORD

Dave Haggerty

I am honored that Warren Kimball asked me to write the foreword for his history of the USTA—the United States Tennis Association. I have known Warren Kimball for over thirty years, and of course, tennis was the connector. I was a junior playing tennis in the Philadelphia section of Middle States when I first became aware of Warren. He was already on his way to becoming a big wig in the United States Tennis Association and Middle States Section.

Warren has an extensive and intimate knowledge of the USTA on many fronts including president of USTA Middle States, USTA Davis Cup Committee cochair, and four years on the USTA board of directors.

At my first board meeting when I joined the USTA board of directors in 2007, I learned that there was a USTA history project that was under the direction of Warren Kimball, a long-serving volunteer and noted historian and archivist.

I was a longtime USTA member who joined when I was six years old (back then it was the USLTA—United States Lawn Tennis Association) and soon began playing sanctioned tournaments. Eventually I spent over thirty-five years in the tennis industry working for many of the top tennis brands. Nevertheless, I became aware that despite my "intimate" knowledge of tennis, I had absolutely no understanding of the history of the USTA. This intrigued me, and I began to look for a way to gain a greater understanding of the governing body, the organization responsible for growing, promoting, and developing tennis in the United States.

When I was USTA president, I said that at times the USTA was perceived as the eight-hundred-pound gorilla that "mandated" or "dictated" its vision of what was best for American tennis. But there is also the other side of the coin where the USTA does so many positive things to grow the diversity of tennis, bringing it to juniors who never would have the opportunity to learn the life lessons that only tennis can teach, and administering and coordinating tournaments and league competition for seven hundred thousand players annually through its seventeen sections, states, and districts.

When I asked Warren to send me the manuscript, I wasn't sure that the history of the USTA would be of interest to a wide audience. I spent the next few days reading the story and found myself becoming more immersed in the history, discovering how little that I knew about an organization that I had the honor of serving for ten years on the board of directors and as the organization's fifty-first president.

Warren Kimball's *The United States Tennis Association* is an intriguing and compelling story that will appeal to a large number of tennis enthusiasts, not only volunteers, staff, and members involved with the USTA in a district, section, state, or national role but also the international tennis community, which will discover some inside information about one of the largest and most influential national tennis federations in the world and more importantly will enjoy a compelling narrative. Moreover, it connects the history of the USTA with the broader thrust of U.S. history. It's a good read.

Kimball takes us from the beginnings of lawn tennis in America in October 1874 and becomes even more engaging as you move through the evolution of the USTA in a delightful tongue-in-cheek story-telling way that draws you in and guides you through the USTA at its finest (and occasionally less than finest) moments.

You will discover behind-the-scenes facts that help illuminate some of the major moments and decisions in tennis such as the evolution of the National Championships from an amateur event to becoming the U.S. Open that included professionals, one of the times of tension and seminal change that have made the great sport of tennis even greater. The efforts and impact of the USTA and some of its leaders internationally are a thread throughout the book. The matter of balance between the sections and national organization is explored carefully, with persuasive evidence.

I am confident that you will get the same high level of satisfaction and understanding about the history of the USTA that I have gained through this outstanding book that Warren has penned for us!

PREFACE

Is tennis a sport? Not according to comedian George Carlin who said it's just playing ping-pong while standing on the table. In a gentle, symbolic way, this book connects the first recorded lawn-tennis players in America, Ella Bailey, Martha Summerhayes, and their unknown partners (I assume they played doubles since that was the more popular game when lawn tennis was developed), with the United States Tennis Association's most successful current membership program, the USTA Leagues. We do not know for certain how our wonderful game got to Camp Apache in the Arizona Territory in autumn 1874, but we do know that is where and when Ella Bailey and Martha Summerhayes played. So women and the American West were at the very root origins of lawn tennis in America, whatever the assumptions, claims, and conceits of my New England forebears.

A century later, five people—four women and one man, among them my late wife, Jackie Kimball—initiated local tennis league programs that grew dramatically into the Association's most innovative and successful growth initiative. Once again, women were at the root origins of a movement that grew the game like nothing else before or since.

The woman at the root of this book was that same Jackie. Without her insistence that I take on the project, and without her prodding and encouragement in equal and needed doses, I would have floated off gently into retirement, writing occasional book reviews or essays about Franklin Roosevelt or Winston Churchill and playing tennis to my heart's content. I confess I connect with Dr. George Sheehan, a cardiologist, writer, and runner who told journalist Rich Koster that life is just a place to spend time between races.[1] I just prefer that six letter word, "tennis."

After Jackie's death, my wife Sally has been as intensely supportive and understanding as Jackie had been. Anyone who would sit, listen, and comment on my reading aloud of a draft of the entire manuscript during a four day train ride across southern Canada, is very "special." I am truly a fortunate man.

The United States Tennis Association (USTA), the United States Lawn Tennis Association (USLTA), the United States National Lawn Tennis

Association (USNLTA), all are names for the same thing—what I prefer to call the Association. "Association" is not only less cumbersome and easier on the ear, it is more accurate. "Association" implies free, voluntary action; and membership in the United States Tennis Association is just that. Moreover, it connotes a sense of mutual benefit and purpose, again hallmarks of the volunteers who created the Association and of the unique combination of volunteers and professionals who have led it into the twenty-first century.

This book began in the mind of another woman, former USTA president Judy Levering. The first female president (1999–2000) and thus someone who was by definition not part of any old-boys club, she struggled to understand why the Association did what it did, why it was organized as it was, and what the past had to teach us. Her proposal for an institutional history of the Association, supported by the then executive director, Rick Ferman, generated an imaginative proposal from writer and journalist Roger M. Williams, that lay fallow in the aftermath of what was perceived as a financial crisis in the late 1990s. Not until Lee Hamilton became the Association's executive director in 2002 was the idea revived. Most who read this will not care about such acknowledgments, but they should, for without the support of such people, particularly that of Alan Schwartz, Association president from 2003 through 2004, as well as Gordon Smith (executive director, 2007–) and Rick Rennert, the Association's director of publications. Without them and the cooperation of tens of dozens of USTA volunteers and professional staff, a good number of whom I interviewed, this book would not exist. The USTA family, volunteers and staff (and former staff), was wonderfully positive and helpful. With only a few exceptions, none blew me off by not responding to questions or a request for an interview.

And it was a woman, Lorna Skaaren, my research assistant and now friend, who patiently enabled me to write all this. Without her good-natured dedication and hard work, this project would not have come to fruition. She did the heavy lifting in the USTA Archive, dug out hard to find books from various libraries, poured over newspaper reports, photocopied reams of material (temporarily creating the Albany annex of the USTA Archive), and offered valuable advice on how to organize my writing. Any historian looking for the ideal research assistant and project partner should give her a call.

Establishment of a USTA archive and records management system was indispensable to the writing of this study, to any future histories of the Association, and to the capability of the USTA to respond accurately to legal and informational requests. In 2002 when I was considering taking on this project, I asked to take a look at the Association's records. I was appalled to find them stored, unprocessed, in a big unheated and not air-conditioned garage (warehouse), full of silverfish chewing away and mice comfortably snuggled up to minutes of the USTA board and executive committee. I told Lee Hamilton that I could not even consider writing a history without having those records preserved and managed. He agreed and hired a consultant I had suggested, (Deborah Shea of the Winthrop Group headed up the study) who recommended just the right medicine. Our proposal to the USTA board stated that the consultant's report offered a number of disturbing findings, two of which needed immediate attention: there were no procedures to manage records, and storage conditions were grossly inadequate and so substandard they invited disaster. We continued:

> Our unanimous and emphatic conclusion is that the United States Tennis Association, a two hundred million dollar corporation and the National Governing Body of Tennis in the USA, can no longer afford to manage its records as if it were a Mom & Pop store. Not only is that unprofessional, but it creates serious risks that could be minimized if not eliminated by a proper Records Management System. (The great difficulty experienced in compiling the necessary records for a recent bond refinancing is a very disturbing case in point.)[2]

An archive now exists, excellently professionalized by its first archivist, Tom Norris, who deserves recognition for his enthusiastic support of this history project. His gathering of key records led me (and Lorna Skaaren) in the right direction. The delays in finishing this manuscript were personal to me, not due to a lack of accessible records. Since Tom Norris departed for the Left Coast, Brent Staples in the archive has been wonderfully helpful, despite competing demands on his time.

Transparency requires that I disclose my connection with the USTA. I was fortunate enough to choose a career as a historian and privileged to serve two terms on the Association's national board of directors during a nearly thirty-year volunteer career. That said, the volunteer and staff leadership of the USTA has made no attempt to influence what I have written. We agreed at the outset that this would be an institutional history of the Association, not a book about the game of tennis replete with descriptions of famous matches. I teased them all that I might not include the final score of a single match (I provided scores for only three). Only if a tennis match affected the trajectory of the Association would I dwell upon it, for example, the case of the exhibition between Billie Jean King and Bobby Riggs, a contest that was much more about winning equality than about winning on the court. My work has been done on a contract basis but fulfilling that contract called for a completed manuscript, not a manuscript acceptable to the USTA leadership. I have great affection for the Association and have close personal relationships with many of its members, but I have called 'em as I see 'em.

Why this book? Two observations about the Association piqued my curiosity. First, how did an organization formed by a very small group of white men, in white outfits, from whites-only private homes and country clubs, whose concern was simply to standardize the rules of lawn tennis become in less than a century and a half a not-for-profit national sports governing body with an annual revenue of well over three hundred million dollars? Second, how could an organization of over three-quarters of a million members (as of 2016) function effectively while governed and led by a unique and curious and cumbersome combination of volunteers (local, state, section, regional, and national) and paid professionals (who arrived on the scene earlier than most USTA members realize)?

When I began this project in 2005, I browsed every book about tennis I could get my hands on, trying to get my arms around the history and character of the United States Tennis Association. As I skimmed one pleasant, chatty, if inconsequential book about professional tennis at the top and getting there in the 1990s, I was struck that the only mention I could find of the USTA was a job description, as in USTA coach.[3] Whatever one may think of the USTA, of its role in American tennis from top to bottom and back up again, it is not so niggling as to be ignored.

This study takes the unfashionable perspective of history from the top. There are numerous occasions when pressure from below forced the Association leadership to respond. Perhaps the most striking and powerful were demographic shifts—the rise of the west—that forced changes in governance. Similarly powerful was the sectional revolt in 1999 against state alignment. But whatever the pressure from below, changes were made at or near the top. The USTA has exercised top-down governance (is there another kind?) since its formation. There is no other way to understand its history except from the top, down.

An epigram over the entrance to the U.S. National Archives reads "past is prologue." I would suggest that, in the case of the USTA, "past is present." The rules, regulations, structures, assumptions, and habits of the past and present are strikingly consistent with one huge exception.

Enough money! I know John D. Rockefeller once quipped that there's no such thing as *enough* money. But the remarkable success of the U.S. Open after open tennis came about, certainly provided the Association with something close to enough money.

A caveat (which is what prefaces are for): I am an endnote junkie. Without shame or apology, I pack all sorts of extra and slightly extraneous information into the endnotes. They can easily be ignored. But for Association devotees, the discursive notes may make good reading.

Authors are allowed to air pet peeves in their preface. Here's mine. Other than the official records of the Association's various committees and meetings (records that become less informative after incorporation in 1973), the single most valuable, even invaluable, source of information up through 1950, are the pages of *American Lawn Tennis*, a magazine invented and nourished for forty years by the efforts of one man, S. W. Merrihew. The index to this book will lead you to his contributions. Suffice to say he was an honest, dedicated devotee of lawn tennis, and a candid yet always courteous critical analyst of the doings of the US(NL) TA. He was revered by most everyone in the game, with the possible exception of Julian Myrick. Pops Merrihew belongs in the International Tennis Hall of Fame. It is a disgrace that he is not. Why not? There is no United States Tennis Hall of Fame yet! Why not?

A special note. There was no one more supportive of this project than the late Henry Talbert. Henry was a friend. We played singles (he was better, but I never admitted that to him) at various courts around Princeton, New Jersey, where he began his long and productive career with the USTA, initially at the E&R office in Princeton, later in White Plains, New York, at the Association's headquarters, then a decade as the much-loved executive director of the Southern California Section. Henry was gentle, soft-spoken, and rarely argumentative (even on line calls). But he had strong opinions, firmly held. In my many years as a national volunteer, I frequently sought his advice. Had I done so more often I might have been better-off. Henry was a lot faster getting the job done that I have been (a low hurdle). Shortly after I began this history, he put together a small group of former E&R personnel for the purpose of preserving their joint history. In 2005 he sent me an early draft of that history. It is very special, and I have deposited it in the USTA Archive. It comforts me that the support of that good man for this history was not in vain.

All seventeen USTA sectional offices tried and occasionally succeeded in finding useful information about their historical relationship with the national Association. But their focus is largely on the here and now, leaving history to the national body. That is, perhaps, a bit of an insight into the national-sectional dynamic.

We (Lorna and I) wish to thank and acknowledge institutions as well as individuals who made significant contributions and/or helped us along the way: Judge Robert Kelleher; Donn Gobbie (then a graduate student at Purdue University finishing a history of the Virginia Slims Circuit and a fact-checker for Billie Jean King); Peter Davenport (for access to the Joanna Davenport papers); Barbara Travers (at the International Tennis Federation); Troy Gowen (senior archivist) and Meredith Miller Richards (librarian) at the International Tennis Hall of Fame; Becky Risher (former speechwriter for the USTA); Nellie Nevarez and Patty Reber (USTA executive director's office); David Smith (Writers' Services Librarian) at the New York City Public Library; Mary Redmond (special liaison) at the New York State Library's Fischer tennis collection (St. John's University Library); Gerard Belliveau (head librarian) at the Racquet and Tennis Club in New York City; Bob Garry (longtime Association chief financial officer),and the Theodore Roosevelt collection in the Houghton Library (Harvard University). A very special thank you to the Citadel—its librarians and especially the chair of the history department and now dean of Humanities and Social Arts Sciences, Bo Moore—for its indispensable help.

The professionals at the University of Nebraska Press have been patient and positive: Rob Taylor who signed me up and has been the project editor; Courtney Oschner, who must dearly hope that she never again has to take a manuscript written in WordPerfect and reformat it for the UNP computer and who walked me through the cumbersome, bureaucratic process of getting permissions for illustrations; Brian King my world-class copyeditor who kept us on schedule; Ann Baker an uncompromising (thankfully) design and production manager who cut me some breaks from the bible (the CMS—what I called Turabian); and the UNP team that designed the best doggone book cover I could have hoped for.

My readers receive the usual absolution from sin and guilt for my mistakes. Richard Hillway, a tennis historian himself, has read the entire manuscript finding more errors of fact than I care to admit. So has George Gowen, long-time USTA general counsel and loyal Davis Cup fan, who scoured his memory and personal files, finding all sorts of information and documents otherwise not accessible. His contribution to the final chapters was unique and essential. After all, he was there. Alan Schwartz read it all and provided extensive documentation (now in the USTA Archive) and intelligent, candid comments. Likewise Judy

Levering, who also read the manuscript. Jane Brown Grimes also read and commented on the manuscript. Professor Charles C. Alexander, Jim Chaffin, Mike Mee, Marshall Happer, and the late Lee Hamilton all commented helpfully, sometimes extensively, on significant portions of my drafts. Of the former executive directors I contacted, Don Conway, John Fogarty, and Marshall Happer were wonderfully forthcoming with documents and comments. Rick Ferman initially provided useful feedback, but then chose not to respond.

A thank you to the amazing research historians digging out evidence about the early years of tennis: Attila Szabo, Geoff Felder, and especially Richard Hillway. A special acknowledgment to the late Frank Phelps, who provided Lorna Skaaren and Tom Norris access to his valuable private collection of historical tennis documents for those early years.

Throughout the writing I have kept in front of me the sardonic advice of Philip Hawk, physiological chemistry professor, well-published scientist, tennis rebel with a cause, president of the West Side Tennis Club in the 1930s, and author of a whimsical look at American tennis prior to the Second World War: "The tennis fan has doubtless often been disappointed when he expected to find an article on tennis of interest, to learn, all too late, that it was a report of the Amateur Rule Committee or a dissertation on the proper way to apportion the funds of the United States Lawn Tennis Association to the various sections. The association must of course get these things off its chest in the usual, formal, dignified, highly efficient manner. However, they are of slight interest to the average tennis fan and club member."[4] I have written with the hope that my work squares that circle, being "formal, dignified, highly efficient," but at the same time, of more than just "slight interest to the average tennis fan."

Note on Citations

The names of the USTA as well as its sections used in the text are as they were at the time of the reference. The same is true for the sectional boundaries. For example, in 1917, the section composing Illinois, Iowa, Kansas, Michigan, Missouri, Nebraska, and Wisconsin was known as the Western Section; now USTA Midwest. That information can be gleaned from the various USTA "Annuals" and *Yearbooks*, available on CDs produced by the USTA Archive.

Citations are not provided for general information about tennis records, committee memberships, and similar data that can be found easily in the various annuals and yearbooks published by both the Association and private publishers. Amounts of money numbers are routinely rounded off to the nearest hundred or thousand. Historical currency values (buying power) are calculated using http://futureboy.us. Periodicals cited may be found in the USTA Archive unless otherwise indicated. Manuscript and records collections cited without indication of the archival location are found in the USTA Archive, White Plains, New York.

1

ORIGINS

The Major and the Ladies

> "After a day or two, I went over to see what Mrs. Bailey had done. To my surprise, I found her out playing tennis."
> MARTHA SUMMERHAYES, October 1874

Who invented tennis, lawn or otherwise? In America's rule-bound society, what often matters is not so much the game, but the rules and structure of the game. People have hit objects (balls?) over obstacles (nets?) for eons. It might be pushing things a bit to claim the Greek god Apollo played lawn tennis, though that is the conceit found in the foreground of the oil painting *The Death of Hyacinth*, done by Giovanni Battista Tiepolo in 1752–53, over a hundred years before "lawn tennis" appeared on the scene. A sagging net in the background, a strung wooden racket and three balls—equipment that looks much like that of early court and lawn tennis—lay on the ground next to the body of Apollo's lover. (See gallery, image 1.) All that prompted one wag to suggest that either the racket was flung across the net, John McEnroe style, killing poor Hyacinth, or that Apollo had a "killer" serve.[1]

What came to be called "court tennis" (later "real tennis") evolved from an earlier ball game played around the twelfth century in France. Called *palla*, *pallacorda*, fives, pelota, or handball, it involved hitting a ball with a bare hand and later with a glove. Whether it started with monks in their cloisters or on medieval city streets and squares, such games became popular and spread across Europe. By the sixteenth century, rackets had appeared, and the game moved to indoor playing areas with somewhat regularized rules. A landscape painting dating to 1538 depicts two men hitting an object over a net using some sort of rackets on what appears to be a sand court boxed in by walls that may have been in-play.[2] In the late 1560s, the brother of French intellectual and essayist, Michel de Montaigne, died after being hit in the ear by a "tennis" ball (which suggests a much harder ball than what is used today). Whether or not the Italian

Renaissance master, Caravaggio, killed a tennis opponent in 1606 as some contemporaries accused, there is no question that a form of tennis was being played in Italy at that time. A Venetian ambassador reported in 1600 that there were 1,800 courts in Paris alone. Courts were "erected" at various universities including Cambridge, where the poet John Milton may have played. They were built near many European palaces including the Louvre in Paris and, most famously, Hampton Court in England—hence the connection with King Henry VIII, whose second wife, Anne Boleyn, was watching a court-tennis match when she was arrested. Shakespeare mentions the game in act 2 of *Henry V* when Henry challenges his cousin, the Dauphin (heir to the French throne), to a court-tennis match with France as the prize.[3] No wonder the sport gained the label, the "Game of Kings." Frederick, Prince of Wales died after being struck by a tennis ball in 1851; at least two kings of France reputedly died playing tennis; while a third, Louis XVI, had a very bad tennis day on June 20, 1789. That was the game's most (only?) revolutionary moment, for the French Third Estate (commoners) defied the king by proclaiming the famous Tennis Court Oath (Le Serment du Jeu de Paume). Because tennis was so closely associated with the nobility (the leisure class), selection of the Royal Tennis Court at the Versailles Palace for the statement was calculated defiance of the Crown. The oath turned out to be the declaration of the French Revolution—and eventually it was game, set, and match for the commoners. Tennis nearly disappeared in revolutionary France, but continued to grow in popularity elsewhere. Something called "field tennis" appeared in England by the end of the eighteenth century, when it was described as a challenge to the popularity of cricket. By the 1860s, various adaptations of court tennis had moved outdoors, and there were desultory attempts to make up rules. But such rule making "never traveled," leaving the court wide open (so to speak).[4]

But what really matters for lawn tennis is how it became structured with standardized rules, and why. The broad answer is organization, but there is a bit of story behind all that.

The story starts with Major Walter Clopton Wingfield. Born in 1833 Wingfield became a "career" British cavalry officer in the Kings Own 1st Dragoon Guards and spent ten years on active duty (India and China, of course—this was the Victorian Era of the British Empire) before retiring to take up his true calling, being of the landed gentry (minor aristocracy) and a professional dilettante. Unlike many of that class who suffered from a persistent shortage of ready money, Wingfield seems to have been financially secure, although "well-off" might be a bit of an exaggeration. Photographs routinely show him with a full beard and moderate handlebar moustache, like a true aristocrat of the Victorian-Edwardian era. (See gallery, image 2.) A family castle (or perhaps a "folly") in Suffolk, a mad (mentally ill) wife, membership in the right London clubs—he seems to have stepped from the pages of a Victorian novel. He "invented" a better bicycle, wrote a book titled *Bicycle Gymkhana and Musical Rides*, founded and became Supreme Don of a gourmet society (perhaps inspired by Edward, the quite ample Prince of Wales), and became a member of the Royal Victorian Order for his longtime service to the royal family particularly as a Gentlemen-at-Arms, and . . . he produced the first written set of rules for lawn tennis, at least the first set that "traveled."[5]

I take one writer at his word when he claims that tennis was "a Wingfield heirloom," a centuries-long presence in the family. It seems that in the 1430s an early ancestor of Major Wingfield, one John Wingfield, was for a time the host and jailer of Charles d'Orleans, who had been captured by the English at the battle of Agincourt (1415). Charles, in line for the French crown, enjoyed the enforced hospitality of various of the English nobility for twenty-five years, a time he spent writing poems (he is sometimes referred to as the father of French lyric poetry) and playing his favorite game, *jeu d'paume* (handball). While comfortably ensconced in Wingfield Castle, he wrote a lyric poem about that game. Major Walter Wingfield, nearly 450 years later, allegedly thought of that poem (with its "evocative refrain 'Naught fear I but Care'") when he "christened his embryo, 'Lawn Tennis.'"[6]

The creation of a set of written lawn-tennis rules, generally conceded to be the first written rules for the game, is Wingfield's one true claim to fame. To distinguish his game from court tennis, played by kings and courtiers in whatever often bizarrely shaped large hall was available, Wingfield gave it a proper name—Lawn Tennis, although even that nearly fell prey to Victorian England's obsession with classical Greece. Wingfield tried to name his game "Sphairistiké," Greek for playing ball, leading to jokes about playing "sticky."[7] Fortunately, sticky didn't stick. "Lawn" disappeared from the United States Tennis Association's name in 1975, in an obvious, and quixotic, attempt to escape the country-club image that came with the game's roots in croquet and cricket clubs, whose members were often of the leisure class ("a beneficiary" is how one well-to-do USTA president referred to himself[8]). But the preoccupation with rules that began with the major, survives intact in the USTA of the twenty-first century.

Then there is the tendentious dispute over who brought the first set of Wingfield's lawn-tennis game to America or, more properly, to the

Americas. His first edition of *The Major's Game of Lawn Tennis*, probably published in February 1874, but perhaps in December 1873,[9] proclaimed: "The game is in a painted box, . . . and contains Poles, Pegs, and Netting for forming the court, 4 Tennis Bats, . . . a bag of balls, a Mallet [presumably to strike the poles and pegs], and Brush, and 'Book of the Game.' It can only be obtained from the inventor's agents, Messers. French and Co., . . . Price Five Guineas." Just stating the price in obsolete guineas was an appeal to upper-class sensibilities.[10]

Whether or not that allowed time for one Mary Outerbridge to be the first person to bring one of Wingfield's tennis sets to the United States depends upon one's faith in the accuracy of passenger lists for that year, in the memories of early players, and in the recollections of her younger brother Eugenius Harvey (E. H.) Outerbridge. In 1923 he regaled the then assistant secretary of war and Association president Dwight Davis (yes, the Davis of Davis Cup) with a story of how Miss Outerbridge brought the game back to Staten Island, New York, from Bermuda (where the Outerbridges were "thick as thieves") in 1874. "It is certain," he wrote, "that the first net ever put up on a club grounds was the one my sister brought from Bermuda." Whatever the smell of politics—New York versus Boston, for in a game of traditions, ownership of origination is no small asset—the truth is impossible to determine. Bermuda historians have argued that Mary Outerbridge may well have brought a game developed in England by one J. B. Perera (Pereira) that he called "pelota" and renamed "lawn tennis" shortly after Wingfield's book on lawn tennis appeared. Either way, the Outerbridge claim is hotly contested by tennis historians.[11] Nor is Mary Outerbridge the only contender for the title of having played "the first set of lawn tennis . . . in the country." For the first five decades of lawn tennis in America, those writing about the game assumed that James Dwight, a sometime physician who much preferred lawn tennis to doctoring, played the Major's game in the summer of 1874 on a lawn at the home of William Appleton in Nahant, Massachusetts.[12] But as with the publication date of Major Wingfield's first book and with the date when Mary Outerbridge brought a lawn-tennis set to Staten Island, the problem is that Dwight himself offered two different years, 1874 or 1875, for that "first" game, with the latter year most likely the correct one. All that, despite Dwight's famous attention to detail, particularly tennis rules, demonstrated during his twenty-one years as president of the United States National Lawn Tennis Association—the longest serving president, by far, in the Association's long history.[13]

But the most compelling and engaging and persuasive "first" story is that of one Martha Summerhayes. (See gallery, image 26.) Her recollections have solid dating, whatever the other questions raised. An army officer's young wife, she mentions tennis being played in Camp Apache in the Arizona Territory in early October 1874! Her memoir, constructed from old letters and papers, is clear, if lacking in detail:

> The question of getting settled comfortably still worried me, and after a day or two, I went over to see what Mrs. Bailey had done. To my surprise, I found her out playing tennis, her little boy asleep in the baby-carriage, which they had brought all the way from San Francisco, near the court. I joined the group, and afterwards asked her advice about the matter. She laughed kindly, and said: "Oh! you'll get used to it, and things will settle themselves. Of course it is troublesome, but you can have shelves and such things—you'll soon learn," and still smiling, she gave her ball a neat left-hander.[14]

Mrs. Ella Bailey may well have been the game's first possessor of "a neat left-hander," but Martha Summerhayes reinforced two facts: first, that the game was already popular in the United States in autumn 1874, and second, that women played from the outset. The problem is, what game and where did it come from? "Lawn" tennis did not require a lawn (it is hard to imagine a finely groomed, green lawn at Camp Apache, located in the high plains of east central Arizona, despite its location on the White River). Like the "foot" in American football, lawns were part of the game's name, not integral to the sport. Even the Major had referred to setting up a court "on a lawn, on ice, or in any suitable sized space either in or out of doors." "The ground need not even be turf," he wrote, "the only condition is, it must be level." Ice may not have been used for serious tennis, at least not until 2008 when some Russian polar experts slid around in a doubles match on snow-covered ice (see gallery, image 3), but the Wedgemere Club in Winchester, Massachusetts, which existed only from 1886 to the early 1890s, "had two cinder and four grass courts."[15] Californians were playing lawn tennis on dirt courts at least by 1881 and on "cement" and probably asphalt by 1887. As tennis grew in popularity, cold-weather clubs laid boards over their dirt ("clay") courts to allow winter play. Since Summerhayes later wrote of tennis in San Francisco and Nebraska, one assumes she referred throughout to the same game—the Major's game—as that was the only one we know of that "traveled" to the United States. But how did it get to that isolated army camp on the high plains of east central Arizona?[16]

The answer would seem to be England via San Francisco. The Summerhayes had been in the Bay Area, presumably at Camp Reynolds on Angel Island in San Francisco, which served "as a staging area for troops serving in campaigns against the Apache, Sioux, Modoc [all mentioned in Summerhayes's memoir], and other tribes of First Americans. By 1876 this was a busy camp with over two hundred soldiers and a complete village including a church, bakery, blacksmith, shoemaker, laundry, barber, trading store, and photographer."[17] The description left out only one thing—tennis courts, something Martha Summerhayes mentions when she visited there in 1880. But how on earth could the Major's game have gotten to San Francisco in time for Mrs. Bailey to bring it to Arizona and crank "a neat left-hander" in October 1874? The answer is most likely from England by sea, brought either by someone in the British consulate or a London merchant. The game had achieved speedy popularity in England early that year and could well have arrived in San Francisco by August 1874, when the Summerhayes and the Baileys were there.

So let me offer a new entry into the list of contenders for "first" lawn tennis player in the United States, either Ella Bailey and her partners on the court or the English diplomat or trader who brought the game to San Francisco—before it arrived in New England and New York.

Whatever the truth of the Major, Martha, and Mary, the reality is that lawn tennis arrived in the United States in the mid 1870s separately and independently in at least six different places. The first formal lawn-tennis club in the Americas seems to have been formed in 1876 in New Orleans, after English merchants in the city on business brought the game over with them. But whether the first lawn-tennis court in the Americas was set up in San Francisco (my best guess), in Nahant, Massachusetts (north of Boston), or Staten Island, New York, in Canada, or even at Camp Apache in the Arizona Territory, or elsewhere—all possibilities—the game quickly became popular with the leisure class, on army posts, and wherever British merchants and diplomats traveled, which in the nineteenth century was everywhere.[18]

To return, briefly to the Major, why did he take out a patent on "a new and improved portable court for playing the ancient game of tennis"? No mention of his rules, but they came two days later. One early historian of the game dismisses Wingfield contemptuously. In the midst of Victorian England's sports craze, "He saw, clearer than anyone else, that the inventor of a new game could make a fortune from the sale of patented sets. . . . The commercial angle was always foremost in his mind. It was all very well to borrow implements [rackets], tools [the net], and scoring systems from established games. But there must be something new and ingenious about *his* game which would give him patent rights."[19] Hence the hourglass shape of the court, an original name ("Sphairistiké" or Lawn Tennis"), and "rackets" scoring (1, 2, 3, 4) rather than the arcane current system of scoring by 15s—sort of.

Major Wingfield's Patent

The Major's original patent hangs in the Museum of the International Tennis Hall of Fame at the Casino in Newport, Rhode Island. Whatever Wingfield's reasons—fame, fortune, control, or just plain Englishness—he requested and received a patent (No. 685) for his "Invention of 'A New and Improved Portable Court for Playing the Ancient Game of Tennis'" on February 23, 1874. A century later, when tennis historian George Alexander wrote his 1974 book on Wingfield and the early days of lawn tennis, the original patent given to Wingfield had disappeared. Alexander had gotten Stan Malless, Association president 1974–76, interested in the Wingfield story, and Malless set out on a search for the patent. Wingfield's heirs had hung it on the wall of their country home, but during the war (presumably the Second World War) some British officers billeted there apparently took the patent with them when they left. Eventually, Malless learned of, or was contacted by, a Chinese art collector who had found the patent in an antique shop in Berlin. Malless asked for the price, the art collector responded one million dollars! Staggered, Malless pursued the patent, finally getting a price of five hundred thousand dollars. Too steep replied Malless. When Malless threatened the art collector to prove true ownership or go to court, the art collector responded, "Court where, in China?" Met with repeated threats of court action, the collector dropped the price. One hundred thousand, then fifty thousand dollars. Malless assessed the situation, concluded that he could afford that price and that the collector was approaching the point where he could sell it elsewhere—and the deal was made. Malless then loaned the patent to the ITHF where it hangs today.[20]

Whatever the Major's motives in applying for a patent, his lawn tennis "boxes" sold quite well, and the game quickly became popular. "Lawn" tennis began in England where there was an ample supply, even overabundance, of well-groomed croquet lawns. Like croquet, lawn tennis was for England's leisure class, but with a difference. Tennis appealed to the same Victorian commitment to a vigorous lifestyle that made Baden-Powell's Boy Scouts spread like wildfire. Moreover, croquet was declining in popularity. A number of cricket and croquet clubs took up lawn tennis, including a relative newcomer, the All England Croquet Club. It might be a bit over the top to claim, as one historian does, that the All England "kidnapped lawn tennis as a means of eking out the resources of a diminishing treasury," but the club did begin using a revised version of Wingfield's rules in 1875. However, it soon substituted its own regulations in the process eliminating (with malice aforethought?) what seemed unique to Wingfield's patent. By 1877 revenue from tennis to the renamed All England Croquet and Lawn Tennis Club (today generally referred to simply as Wimbledon) exceeded that earned by croquet. If the purpose was to make "money for the All England Club [then] it did its work well." From that moment tennis was "commercialized." Certainly the club moved quickly to offer a (self-proclaimed) championship tournament. The story of All England's struggle with England's Lawn Tennis Association (finally created in 1888) for control of lawn tennis is for another book, but it cannot be mere coincidence that the United States National Lawn Tennis Association had been created only a few years earlier for the same purpose—to standardize and control the most important part of the game, the rules.[21]

In the long run, the Major won a lovely little victory at the All England. The only "bookable" restaurant (and the only one with "waitresses") on the grounds at Wimbledon during the championships is, as of 2016, The Wingfield.[22]

One of the characteristics of organized tennis, from Major Wingfield to the present, is the sense of turf, of control, of commercial opportunity, or in that wonderful phrase of the upholders of "pure" amateurism, something that "capitalizes tennis prowess."[23] That sense shaped the institution and purpose of the USTA from start to present. It would ensure that its rules were national; it would spell the slow but inevitable decline of "pure" amateurism and the establishment of "open" tennis; it would profoundly affect the development of the Association's governance structure; it would create the three-hundred-million-dollar corporation that is the United States Tennis Association in 2017.

2

THE FOUNDING GENTLEMEN

1877–1913

> "A complacent and confident Eastern seaboard upper class," "universally recognized as the supreme . . . authority in all tennis matters in this country."
> JOSEPH CLARK, 1889, and an observer

The most important lawn tennis tournament in USTA history came even before the Association's founding in May 1881. The contest, billed as a national championship, began on September 1, 1880, at the Staten Island Cricket (and Base Ball) Club—the club of Mary Outerbridge and her family. It came at the suggestion of Eugenius Harvey Outerbridge, Mary's younger brother, and attracted players from Canada, Bermuda, and England, as well as the best of the American Northeast. It may be, as one tennis historian suggests (without offering any evidence), that there was a rivalry between New York and Boston over leadership in lawn tennis, but whatever the reason (probably just plain competitive juices) the Staten Island Cricket Club offered a challenge—the first national championship![1]

A series of rule changes in England—switching from Wingfield's game to the Marylebone–All England rules—had translated into confusion in America. By Boston standards the net at the Staten Island site sagged precipitously. A contemporary sketch of the matches showed the court as rectangular, not the hourglass shape of the Major's original rules, which had been used on the earliest American layouts. The tennis balls were noticeably lighter, "two-thirds the size" of the balls the visiting Bostonians were used to, though their protests were dismissed when the tournament organizer pointed out that the word "Regulation" was stamped on the balls.[2] Initially none of the players seem to have questioned the authority for that argument-ending word. But that protest would come a few days later from two entrants from Boston, James Dwight and Dick (R. D.) Sears.

Dick Sears would later win the first seven Association national men's singles championships and six of the first seven doubles national championships, five of them with James Dwight. But things did not go their way when they traveled down to Staten Island. Newspaper reports indicated that the disparity between the balls used in Boston (Nahant) and Staten Island prompted Dwight to withdraw from the singles competition but little matter since doubles was then the more popular game.[3]

Lawn tennis was growing with unexpected speed and in unexpected directions. In 1877 at the same Staten Island Cricket Club that would host the "first" national championship three years later, the increasingly run-down condition of its facilities prompted "the most interested married men and most energetic single ones" to call "in the assistance of their wives and sisters." Who called in whom may be questionable, but within a decade the Ladies' Club had over two hundred members. A few years later, when that club offered the "first" national championship for men, there were, according to the *New York Times*, "some interesting practice-matches among the ladies." That remarkable interest and growth, echoed in other clubs, would not prompt Dwight and his colleagues to include the ladies in their Association hierarchy. It was after all the 1880s when women were routinely excluded—"liberated" was the preferred male word choice—from the burden of management and politics. In 1889 the Association graciously extended "its protecting wing to the Lady Lawn Tennis players of the country."[4] But their time would come.

Perhaps the most offbeat indication of the growing popularity of lawn tennis was a newspaper report in 1878 that the game was played at Gilmore's Garden, soon renamed Madison Square Garden, after "clearing away the rubbish left by [P. T.] Barnum's circus." (One can only speculate on what constituted circus "rubbish.")[5] In June 1880 the *New York Times*, reporting on the growth of lawn tennis, stated that "more than 10,000 tennis sets have been sold in this City to be forwarded to all parts of the country." Whatever "all parts of the country" meant to a New York newspaper, clearly tennis was gaining in popularity. In southwest Ohio, for example, the Cincinnati Tennis Club was founded that year. Two months later in an article obviously provided by the Staten Island Cricket Club, the newspaper announced arrangements for a "grand national championship tournament." The column included information about the rules (Marylebone/All England), including the requirements on the diameter and weight of the balls. "Regulation covered balls . . . can be obtained on the grounds." The singles champion would be awarded "a prize valued at $100," no small sum in those days.[6]

James Dwight and Dick Sears did not arrive from Boston until September 7 when the doubles (four-handed) matches began. Dwight protested the size and weight of the balls "the moment he arrived on the grounds." Despite a ruling by a visiting English player (reputedly "the champion of America in the singles games"), Dwight made a formal protest, but to no avail. So they played on. "Dwight did some splendid batting," wrote a reporter more familiar with cricket, but as he had thrown "a cloud upon the tournament by his grumbling," he got little support from spectators. Then Sears and Dwight were defeated in the second round of doubles play by local talent from Staten Island. Still "grumbling" a decade later, Dwight wrote, "We were forced to play with balls much under the regulation size and weight."[7]

Since the clubs hosting matches made their own rules, the size and weight of the balls was not the only significant inconsistency in the game being played in the Northeast. The height of the net varied from 4½ to 3½ feet at the netposts, and 4 to 3 feet at the center of the net. Scoring varied from today's by 15s (sort of), to the old rackets system of games of 15 points with aggregate number of points determining the winner. Court measurements differed from club to club, although the Major's hourglass shape had largely disappeared by 1880. (See gallery, images 4 and 5.) Shortly after the "first national championship," a match at the Young America Cricket Club in Philadelphia against the Staten Island club "materially hastened the formation of an association," wrote later national champion H. W. (Harry) Slocum, when the Staten Islanders found the net to be six inches lower and the balls different than what they were used to.[8]

Those tournaments' most significant result was agreement that something should be done to standardize the rules of American lawn tennis. Even though most players competed only at their local club, interclub competition and tournaments open to visiting players demanded the same playing field for all. Whoever played the key role in organizing to create a common set of rules (both Dwight and Outerbridge claimed credit), it was an idea whose time had come.

It took a half year of planning and negotiating to arrange what turned out to be the organizational meeting of the Association. From the record, one is left to guess why it took so long. Fifty years later, at the Association's 1931 Golden Jubilee meeting, E. H. Outerbridge, the only participant at the founding meeting whose comments have survived, explained that back in 1881, "There were certain reasons, which I need not go into here, why I felt it necessary to have the program cut and dried and everything planned well in advance, including nominations for permanent officers." Outerbridge had drawn up a constitution, claiming to have consulted some of his "associates on Staten Island." For the same reasons, the agenda was set in advance. Outerbridge recalled corresponding with other tennis players that he "knew well," and that he and colleagues did "considerable buttonholing and posting other delegates" to ensure that all ran "smoothly."[9]

Whatever the arm twisting and politics, on May 5, 1881, a notice ran in the *American Cricketeer* (Philadelphia), a magazine that had begun to cover lawn tennis since, according to Outerbridge, in most cases tennis was played on the grounds of cricket clubs. The call (formal agenda) for the first meeting of what became the United States National Lawn Tennis Association was short and straightforward. The purpose was to adopt a standardized "code of rules," and to create an organization that would promulgate those rules. Clubs were invited to send representatives (one vote per club), thus establishing a precedent that would reign supreme for nearly a century. The Association was one of clubs, not individuals. Philadelphia, New York, and Boston were present in the persons who signed the call: Clarence M. Clark of Germantown (Philadelphia), E. H. Outerbridge of New York (Staten Island, to be precise), and James Dwight of Boston (Nahant). The youthfulness of the organizers and those at the meeting is striking. All were active male tennis players. Of those who signed the call, Outerbridge was twenty-one, Clark was twenty-two. Dwight was the old man of the group at twenty-nine.

The organizational or founding meeting, held at the Fifth Avenue Hotel in New York City, came on May 21, 1881.[10] The number of representatives and proxies (a procedure that one assumes was developed during the "buttonholing" process) demonstrated the popularity of the new game. Some nineteen clubs sent representatives, and some fifteen clubs were represented by proxies. Many of the names are familiar to tennis buffs some 125 years later: Staten Island Cricket, Yale University, Short Hills, Germantown, Orange Lawn, University of Pennsylvania, Myopia, Longwood. All were from the Northeast; all but a handful were from the metropolitan areas of the big three cities of New York, Boston, and Philadelphia—the exceptions being Albany and western Pennsylvania.

In a series of deftly planned moves, a committee of five took all of fifteen minutes to "draft" the constitution, and then in "a few minutes" the same committee reported out its nominations for officers and the executive committee (the equivalent of today's board of directors). "Time enough," Outerbridge commented fifty years later, "not to convey the impression . . . that it was all cut and dried and prepared in advance." ("Laughter," noted the minutes.) That both the constitution, drafted by Outerbridge, and the leadership nominations had been worked out in advance established another precedent, one that became a firm and unchanged practice for the Association: selection of the leadership by a small, secretive committee. (See appendix 1.)

The original call proposed the name United States Lawn Tennis Association, but somewhere along the line the word "National" (thus, USNLTA) was slipped in. We have no details of the negotiations and "buttonholing" that preceded the meeting, but later comments suggest that the founding fathers were concerned that other tennis organizations, particularly those outside the Northeast, might not accept the nationwide leadership role being proposed. The original call had expressed the ambition for the Association in gentle words: "It is hoped . . . that it may be as universal as possible, . . . and . . . govern the game of tennis throughout the whole of the United States." But it quickly became clear (or was so at the outset) that there was much more to lawn tennis in America than just the northeastern seaboard.[11]

General Robert Shaw Oliver, who represented the Albany (New York) Lawn Tennis Club, was elected the first president of the Association. As Outerbridge later recalled, "We didn't want to elect anybody from Boston or Philadelphia (or Staten Island) because we didn't want to have the feeling go out that any one of these three larger centers had been picked out." But in fact control remained within the "family." Oliver and the Sears brothers, Fred and Dick (Jim Dwight's doubles partner), were first cousins. Moreover, Oliver had spent time in Bermuda—that cluster of islands connected by "Outerbridges." The general (Oliver was a Civil War veteran who later became a brigadier general in the New York National Guard) began his acceptance remarks by thanking the "*Gentlemen*" for the honor conferred "upon me, or, rather, upon my club."[12] That confusion between individuals and their clubs would continue in the Association for nearly a century. Oliver served for only one year, pleading that the distance from Albany to New York City made it impossible for him to attend properly to the affairs of the Association. In 1882, the éminence grise and rightful king, James Dwight, received unanimous support for the first of his twenty-one years (1882–84, 1894–1911) as president.

The Founding Father

As befits the game's reputation before the "open" era, Dr. James "Jim" Dwight (1852–1917) was a *Mayflower* descendant from a family of prominent men. As with so many of the leaders of the Association, Dwight was a "beneficiary" who did not have to worry about money. The rheumatic fever he contracted while interning may have caused him to give up practicing medicine, but not tennis. He took up the game enthusiastically, and with Sears won five of the first seven U.S. National Doubles Championships. Dwight was the first American teaching "pro." Although he seems not to have taken money for his work, he dedicated himself to improving his own skills and to teaching the game to others. His long visits to England and France allowed him to play against and learn from English champions like the Renshaw brothers who had developed the all-court game. Top players routinely cited his instruction books, *Lawn-Tennis*, published in England and the United States in 1886, and *Practical Lawn-Tennis* (1893), as instrumental in developing their tennis skills. He was the first to use photographs to illustrate proper strokes. As one biographer put it: "By 1886 Dwight was already considered the 'father of American lawn tennis.'" Perhaps no single player had greater influence as a teacher until Bill Tilden. Dwight was famously a stickler for the rules, noted for wandering around during matches insisting that foot-faults be called. Given his experience at the "first" U.S. National Championship, he "had an almost ungovernable passion for new balls." Thus when Ernest Renshaw, umpiring one of Dwight's matches in England, intentionally handed him a box of beat-up old balls instead of new ones, Dwight reacted vocally, presumably to the amusement of those who knew the story. Dwight's stewardship of the Association proved indispensable as he guided it through membership and financial difficulties in his years as president between 1882 and 1911. (See gallery, image 6.)[13]

Rules created the Association, and rules were the focus of the initial constitution and bylaws. The 1881 organizational meeting considered "several amendments," among them a requirement that a club had to have thirty members in order to have a vote and that proxies not be allowed at Association meetings—both issues that would crop up again. But the organizers had their ducks in a row, and none of the amendments succeeded.[14] Attention focused on the matter that had brought the Association into existence—standardization of the rules and equipment of tennis. They adopted the 1881 All England–Marylebone rules, and agreed on parameters for the size and weight of the ball—the "founding" dispute. But they could not get together on designating an "official" ball, something that became a perennial problem. Instead, the meeting delegated that and most other responsibilities to the executive committee that had been established by the constitution and bylaws. (See appendix 2.)

That same day, May 21, that executive committee met and made further decisions on standardization of the rules. The details are less important than the precedents. The committee consisted of the Association officers (president, vice president, and secretary-treasurer), plus three additional members (who would soon be referred to as at-large members). The committee quickly went past the indecision of the membership (the clubs) and selected an official ball and adopted court-tennis scoring (the 15–30–40–game method used today). A month later they approved a number of rules regarding net height, ball size and weight, and various rules of play. More important, they designated Newport, Rhode Island, for the "championship of America," to be held in September 1881—the first national championship (so much for the Staten Island claim). For only five dollars, member clubs could enter four singles players and two doubles teams. Dick Sears won the singles title, but never mind.[15]

For the most part, the Association's first decades found it focused on the mechanics of the game. The engineering issues of tennis-ball manufacturing (consistency of weight, size, bounce, and durability) and finding a suitable American manufacturer preoccupied the leadership.[16] Dr. Dwight, who routinely sent letters back to the executive committee during his lengthy trips to France and England, weighed in consistently for consistency. But in 1884 he also proposed that the U.S. championship, previously reserved for players from USNLTA member clubs, be "open" to "all comers." American players, including Jim Dwight, felt they could now hold their own against their English counterparts, so why not "free trade" over "protection," as the official Association organ put it. As an aside, that same letter points to the long-standing tradition of the grueling best-of-five sets matches that set the U.S. National Championships, Davis Cup matches, and eventually the four Grand Slams apart from most tournaments where best-of-three sets came to govern. Perhaps twenty-first century Grand Slam referees and tournament directors and television executives, concerned about scheduling, might appreciate Dwight's suggestion that the opening rounds should remain best-of-three sets.

What today seems amusing trivia captured the full attention of the founders. For example, Dwight's 1884 letter also addressed problems with umpiring. As he put it: "There is a strong belief that an umpire is a second [as if in a duel] in disguise, and while he is not expected to assist his man openly, he is to be as lenient as possible toward him." One umpire, wrote Dwight, did not call foot faults on a player because "he was umpiring for him," never realizing that he was cheating.[17]

In this early era, the Association was sufficiently small and parochial enough for the clubs to govern effectively at annual meetings of the membership. But occasionally the leadership was called to task. At the annual meeting of March 1886, the executive committee received a gentle slap on the wrist for changing a tennis rule. Even though the change mirrored one made in England (and recommended by Dr. Dwight?), and had been made in good faith, the executive committee "had transcended their power." The annual meeting "informed" them "that they had been elected to execute and enforce the rules of the Association but not to change or amend them."[18] The sting was removed when the meeting approved the amendments, but the message was clear.

By the mid 1880s, the landscape was changing. Member clubs represented far away places with strange sounding names: the Cheyenne Lawn Tennis Club in Wyoming, the Denver Lawn Tennis Club in Colorado. Still, as of 1888 the Eastern Seaboard dominated, with only five of seventy-six member clubs from elsewhere. More significant was the appearance of regional championships. In 1890 Harry Slocum, a three-time national champion and later Association president (1892–93), published a history of lawn tennis that included a chapter titled "The Sectional Championships." As of 1887, he wrote, there were five such "sections"—Middle (Atlantic) States, New England, Southern States (including Washington DC), Western States (Chicago region), and Long Island. The "Southerns" were not "under the auspices of the national Association," but nonetheless Slocum included them. An 1888 report on tournaments gave results for championships of those same regions, but did not call them "sections."[19]

The Association's leadership recognized what was happening. Joseph Clark, a scion of the Philadelphia lawn-tennis establishment, became president at the February 1889 annual meeting and held office for three years during the decade between James Dwight's first and second series of terms in office. Shortly after his election Clark wrote for the *1889 Official Lawn Tennis Rules* a labored explanation of the role and awkwardly exercised authority of the USNLTA. The "object" of the founders (one of whom was Clark's brother, Clarence) was an organization "which would be universally recognized as the supreme . . . authority in all tennis matters in this country." Grander language than in the original call, and no small ambition. Sanctioning the first official national championship at the Newport (Rhode Island) Casino was the initial move. (A "sanction" meant that a tournament had been approved by the Association, would count for rankings, and would be conducted in accordance with its official rules.) Within a few years, the Association began to charge a relatively small fee for providing a sanction. The fee grew larger.

But by 1889 two contentions commanded attention. One, the site for national championships, seems petty in retrospect. But it was part and parcel of the second issue, which was control of, or at least influence over, the Association.[20]

The Newport Casino had reluctantly agreed to hold the initial national championships in 1881. Lawn tennis was a game for the elites, and Newport was at the top of the social register. The late nineteenth century was, after all, a time when keeping up with the Vanderbilts and the Astors made for homes along the Cliff Walk that would become museums dedicated to excess. According to E. H. Outerbridge, the "snippy" Newport socialites thought the tennis tournament was "an attempt on the part of rank outsiders to break into the social circle of the Casino." Some players admitted to entering the tournament just get members' privileges at the Casino for tournament week. (Entry qualifications soon ended that practice.) But, as Outerbridge sarcastically observed, Casino members "were very much aggrieved when [the tournament] was taken away from them some years later."[21] In short order others wanted to host the nationals, and the venue became a matter of dispute between Newport (i.e., Boston) and New York/Staten Island—a contentiousness that soon spread west as lawn tennis grew in popularity.

The game of tennis itself would remain the Association's primary concern for the next few decades, and that included sanctioning and regulating the national singles and doubles championships.[22] But if creation of the sections (which would eventually become the effective constitutional "owners" of the Association) is a critical step, then the 1889 Association constitution is required reading. "Sections" was a familiar word in post–Civil War America. What southerners called the War Between the States was more accurately a war between the sections, Northeast, South, and the West—that vast everything west of the Appalachians. In lawn tennis, a section soon came to mean a group of clubs playing against each other within an obvious (though initially unspecified) geographic area. (Lest the reader feel a bit confused about the seemingly random use of "Sections" and sections, associations, associate members, and the like, rest easy—the revolution of 1913 is coming and the Association's constitution will then sort things out.)

Joseph Clark described the relationship between the Association and "smaller associations" in sanguine terms. They were not rivals. Relations were "extremely cordial." They could adopt "laws, rules, or implements" that were different from those of the USNLTA. But, he argued, the connection with the national association should be more than just "sympathy"; it ought to be "membership in the central power—the National Representative Assembly or Association." Why should clubs join the Association? To help the game, to be represented in the councils that drew up the rules and procedures, and so their members could play in the Association's national championships. Heavy arm-twisting for a game that emphasized good sportsmanship.

But Clark's immediate concern was what he labeled "several recent radical changes" in the Association's constitution: changes that "reached more imposing proportions than I had intended." At the eighth annual meeting, held in New York City in February 1889, the clubs (i.e., the members) amended that document to establish two classes of membership. Class 1 was as before—member clubs that, as of 1882, had to have at least twenty individual members for their "delegate" to have a vote at annual or special meetings.

Class 2 membership was different. Five or more clubs with specific geographical boundaries could form a member association entitled to two votes plus an additional vote for every five more clubs.[23] Since clubs in class 2 associations did not have a requirement for a minimum number of individual members, the change was a bit of a Trojan horse, but the role of clubs, as opposed to individuals, remained paramount. The changes were an admission that for the Association to remain *the* national organization for lawn tennis in America, it had to be inclusive. Governance and leadership (power) had either to include clubs where tennis had grown dramatically—California, New Orleans, Chicago—or allow those regions a greater voice in the Association while giving them considerable autonomy. "A Historical Sketch," issued in connection with the Association's diamond jubilee in 1956, implied that the USNLTA had stimulated the growth of lawn tennis from the outset, but that was not the case.[24] The real fears of Dwight and his colleagues were that the game had and would continue to spread outside the reach of the Association. Whatever the impulse for power and control, their primary motive was the determination to have lawn tennis played by the same rules throughout the country.

By 1891 the subtle shift in the geography of membership had accelerated. Although only six of seventy-eight member clubs were from west of the Appalachians (none were from the South), two "association" (class 2) members, Western Pennsylvania and Pacific States, each represented a number of affiliated clubs from their immediate area. A California lawn-tennis club had been set up in 1884, the Southern California Lawn Tennis Association had appeared in March 1887, and the Pacific States Lawn Tennis Association (northern California) was established in 1890. The

1893 annual meeting recommended holding the national doubles championships in Chicago to coincide with the World's Fair. By 1894 there were member clubs in Tacoma, Washington, and Tampa Bay in Florida (though its recording secretary was in New York City), and the Southern Lawn Tennis Association had at last joined the national association as a class 2 member, representing clubs throughout much of the South. Even more significant was the infiltration of the executive committee by non-easterners. Two Chicagoans joined in 1890, and that area was represented routinely thereafter, usually by R. D. Wrenn. By 1892 a Californian had been elected to the committee.[25] Wrenn had moved up in the organization by what was, in the early days, the norm—his skill at lawn tennis—winning the U.S. national singles title four times in the mid 1890s. Once the Association allowed Jim Dwight to step down from the presidency, Wrenn took over as Association president (of course protesting all the while, in proper Victorian style, that he was not a candidate) for the next four years (1912–15). By that time, Wrenn was listed as from New York, New York, so control still rested securely among the male tennis champions from the northeastern United States—the tennis establishment—and would remain there for another decade.[26]

By the 1890s, USNLTA leaders and those who commented in various publications on the state of the game had begun to puzzle over the future of lawn tennis and the Association. At the 1890 annual meeting the delegates laid out what they considered the major issues that they faced and that would face the Association for decades to come. "The real business of the night," claimed the minutes, related to three amendments to the rules of play. But such details were not the "real business." Governance was more than just the rules of the game. In editorial comments that followed the meeting report, the *American Cricketeer* magazine commented on three challenges that the Association would face for decades to come. One, a handicap system for tennis, would not be resolved until almost a century later with the USTA League program. The early handicap systems, the curious *bisque* and its cousins, were "so complicated as to utterly bewilder one," according to the *Cricketeer* reporter. Promoting good competitive play had been an early part of the game, but it soon became apparent that good competition could exist at different levels of play. In 1883 the executive committee had recognized the obvious desire of the clubs to have "handicap tournaments"; that is, scoring that gave advantages to less-skilled players. This was nothing new to lawn tennis. Jim Dwight had given handicaps in matches played in three straight years, 1876 through 1878, twice defeating Dick Sears who was only fifteen when they played the first match. In the final match, Dwight gave Sears a handicap of "thirty and three bisques." (That was, presumably, an advantage in each game of 30–love or two points to zero, plus three points that could be claimed anytime with certain restrictions—reminiscent of the "gotchyas" of golf joke fame.) Nor is the bisque extinct, though it may be a vestigial remain. According to testimony from the founder of the Tennis Corporation of America, which builds and owns tennis clubs, the bisque handicap has been used at their clubs since 1969.[27] It would be nearly one hundred years before the Association could overcome its preoccupation with single-elimination tournaments and focus on what local clubs and a number of tennis organizations not affiliated with the USTA had long understood—team matches between players of compatible levels of play would hold great appeal and spread the game.[28]

A second challenge was amateurism. Concern about defining an amateur had appeared in the second year of the Association's existence. The 1882 annual meeting passed a bylaw that identified an amateur as "one who has never played or taught tennis for money" or who played with a professional where either a prize or a purse was given.[29] Nothing better captured the assumptions of the argument over amateurism than an 1891 article in the *Lawn Tennis Guide* that described lawn tennis as "an amusement to which the college-bred man can turn after graduation with the assurance that his opponents are not apt to be out-and-out professionals." For that writer and for most players, lawn tennis was for the elite—the "college-bred." But the game's growing popularity and commercial opportunities lay waiting in ambush.

Initially, the debate was thinly disguised as guarantees for expenses. The *Cricketeer* reported that "the Irish lawn tennis cracks," who were to tour the United States in the summer of 1890, had asked the USNLTA to pay their expenses if they came. "Not likely," was the magazine's comment. Professional—play for pay—tennis had not yet appeared, but the connection between the sport and money had already developed. Wimbledon charged one shilling to watch its first lawn championship in 1877. In 1885 the Association had arranged with the Newport Casino to receive a cash payment (two hundred dollars that first year) for the national championships tournament. By the 1890s clubs and the Association realized that hosting major tournaments could generate a profit. President Joseph Clark pointed out that long summer days were conducive to excellence in outdoor sports. They were also conducive to attracting spectators who were, even in 1889 in the age of rigid attitudes toward amateur sports, paying customers whose support made it possible for clubs to hold major tournaments. Looking ahead a bit, by the 1920s clubs would resort to subterfuges to pay top players to play in tournaments (appearance money) so as to attract a paying crowd, while the Association rarely tried to enforce its own amateurism rules. It would be a long way from there to the "open" era and the huge revenue generated for the Association by the U.S. Open Championships in the twenty-first century, but the direction was set.[30]

Level-of-play competition and amateurism were issues that could wait, but the final challenge outlined in the *Cricketeer* piece was a reprise of the complications of growth. "Tennis seems to be a very popular game," was the opening comment about California in an 1890 story about methods of scoring. The founding fathers of the Association had, from the start, insisted that it be a "national" organization, one that spoke for lawn tennis throughout the country. Of course for them, the "country" consisted of the Northeast—New England, New York, and Philadelphia—but the pressure created by the growth of the game throughout the country posed a dilemma. Moreover, regional championships were being held in what, by 1900, the Association called sections (a geographic and competitive term, not related to governance)—the Western States (Chicago and the Midwest), Middle States (New Jersey, Pennsylvania, Delaware, Maryland.), New England, Southern States, Pacific Coast, and Canada. Some, like Pacific Coast, were also Association members.[31] To remain the "national" organization, the Association had to create and maintain ties with and the support of clubs from Chicago to California to New Orleans, and everywhere in between. But those clubs wanted to play a role in making decisions, as the annual debates over the location of various national championships illustrated.

At the 1890 annual meeting, the impact of growth prompted a move to arrange for a split doubles championship of the "West as well as the East," followed by a national championship match pitting the winner at the Newport Casino against the previous year's winners. In those years the most controversial issue was selection of sites for national tournaments—men's and women's singles and doubles. Of course the "west" meant for most delegates anything west of Philadelphia, in this case Chicago was clamoring for equal treatment. Later calls for making national championships "more representative" were code language for getting larger numbers of players from the west to play, raising again the long-standing argument over always holding those championships in the Northeast, particularly at the Newport Casino, which had a stranglehold on the men's singles national championships.[32]

Sites of the National Championships

In 1881, the fledgling U.S. National Lawn Tennis Association organized the inaugural U.S. National (men's) Championships, played at the Newport (Rhode Island) Casino where it remained through 1914. From 1915 through 1921 the championships were held at the West Side Tennis Club, Forest Hills, New York. From 1921 through 1923, the Germantown Cricket Club (Philadelphia) hosted the men's tournament. It returned to Forest Hills from 1924 through 1977.

The first U.S. Women's National Singles Championship was held at the Philadelphia Cricket Club in 1887. The tournament stayed there until 1921 when it moved to the West Side Tennis Club until 1977. Since 1978, the USTA (Billie Jean King) National Tennis Center has been the site for the women's and men's U.S. Open Championships.

From 1924 on, the women's and men's singles were played at the same site though not necessarily during the same tournament. Since 1935, the women's and men's singles have been played concurrently at the same site (Forest Hills and the National Tennis Center).[33]

A precipitous drop in the number of member clubs in the mid 1890s temporarily challenged the Association's assessment of the problems of growth—and must have raised concerns about losing its national status. Issues about governance and control gave way to worries over a decline in membership (clubs). In 1895, 106 clubs and 10 associations (class 2) held memberships. That dropped to 79 clubs and 9 associations in 1896, steadily decreasing until 1902, when only 44 clubs and 10 associations belonged. With club dues at seven dollars a year, a drop of 62 memberships cut annual revenues by over four hundred dollars—approximately one-third of the Association's total revenue.[34]

Reports between 1896 and 1902 to the annual meeting from the secretary (acting like an "executive secretary") have a "whistling in the dark" feel about them. The drastic drop in member clubs and the shrinking treasury due primarily to less revenue from member club dues is never mentioned, but there is a forced optimism about tournament attendance and the possibilities of growth among youths and at the collegiate level. There were occasional veiled references to the decline. Typical was an 1898 comment: "For a so-called dying sport, the seventeenth annual meeting of the National Association brought together a remarkably enthusiastic and representative gathering of delegates, and the vigor with which the various questions were discussed showed that some at least felt that convalescence was near at hand."[35]

The reasons for the decline were not clear. Perhaps, wrote one critic, it came from "weakness in the national organization. Instead of legislating upon foot faults and how to be a spotless amateur, practical steps should be taken to encourage tennis in every locality, to incite new or obscure players to open competition."[36] In 1896, the Association's official publication solicited comments on a series of issues facing the USNLTA.[37] Although some of the topics were predictably about the rules of the game, the first priority was to find "ways and means for preserving and increasing the popularity of Lawn Tennis in America." (It would take a full century for the USTA to adopt its first mission statement: "To promote and develop the growth of tennis.") The decrease in membership prompted a plaintive call for discussion about the effect on tennis of golf's increasing popularity. Although bicycling and golf would continue to appeal to a growing number of Americans with leisure time, by 1902 tennis regained its pattern of steady growth. The short duration of the membership decline suggests that the national financial "panic" of 1893 was the more likely villain, although that subject was surely too crass and undignified for open discussion by the members of the Association.[38]

Dwight Davis—More than a Cup

Dwight F. Davis (1879–1945) learned to play tennis during summers spent on Boston's North Shore, within an easy bicycle ride of the Essex Country Club, an early USNLTA member club. Two years after picking up the game in 1894 (he turned fifteen years old that summer), he entered the nationals at the Newport Casino. He won a only a set in the preliminary round and then lost the next year in the second round to Robert Wrenn, who would eventually become president of the USNLTA. Harvard University, which Davis attended, had twenty-two tennis courts and some 790 men playing lawn tennis! His classroom performance was "horrible," but his on-court performance improved dramatically. "The Harvard Group" of young players like Malcolm Whitman, Holcombe Ward, and William Clothier not only competed with each other but were the American champions for nearly a decade. Davis won the national doubles championship (with Holcombe Ward) three times and won one singles and one doubles match in two international competitions for the cup he donated, the Davis Cup. (See gallery, image 7.) He had a distinguished career in public service, beginning with becoming public parks commissioner in his hometown of St. Louis in 1911, and ending with being secretary of war and then governor-general of the Philippine Islands in the 1920s. In his brief tenure as vice president and then president of the Association (1922–23), he again vigorously promoted tennis in public parks.[39]

Perhaps, just perhaps, tennis revived because—along came Dwight! No, not James Dwight, though he was the ongoing Association president. The other Dwight, Dwight Davis and his more famous cup appeared in 1900 and helped regenerate interest in lawn tennis. Davis, a national champion in doubles, had gotten caught up in the 1899 America's Cup yachting competition (won by the American yacht *Columbia*). That series of races caught the imagination of Americans, at least those on the East Coast who could identify with yachting. Davis, who later recalled being impressed by the way east-west lawn-tennis matches held in California had fostered good tennis and good relationships, thought that an international competition for a trophy could do the same for tennis around the world. With the assistance of James Dwight and other USNLTA leaders, as well as Richard Olney, secretary of state for President Grover Cleveland, Davis drew up a set of rules for the competition. The president of England's Lawn Tennis Association even sent suggestions. The inaugural match in 1900 between a British and an American team proved the competition an immediate success. The first match at Longwood Cricket Club near Boston drew "a well-dressed crowd" that included a good many women. Some may have been there "as a decorative ornament on the arm of a tennis loving escort," but a number were active tennis players themselves. Longwood allowed only twenty-five women out of some two hundred active members, and the ladies could play only on weekday mornings, but they played with enthusiasm despite warnings from well-meaning (threatened?) other women and men that such strenuous activity was unhealthy for females of child-bearing age.[40] Whatever it did for world tennis, it did wonders for popularizing the game, and for bolstering the USNLTA treasury.

The financial importance of Davis Cup competition grew steadily. In 1911 when England played the United States at the West Side Tennis Club (then still in Manhattan), the results, on court and at the ticket window, were rewarding. The United States won 4–1, while "the financial result was very satisfactory," in the laconic phrasing of James Dwight, chair of the Davis Cup committee. The actual profit to the Association came to some $2,700, even after deducting the West Side Club's 25 percent share and a little over $100 for entertainment of the visiting players. That in a year when the overall other revenue of the Association totaled about $5,800.[41]

But perhaps the reinvigoration of lawn tennis was a doubles game—partnering Dwight Davis with President Theodore Roosevelt. Roosevelt built the first White House tennis court, and his regular tennis games with friends and foreign diplomats were reported in the press. What he called his "Tennis Cabinet" included friends, government officials, foreign diplomats, and Frederick Remington (then in his forties)—the friend of Martha Summerhayes! Ah, the small world of lawn tennis at the turn of the century. Whatever the results of tennis diplomacy, to have the president of the United States actively playing the game was invaluable publicity. One newspaper reporter wrote that Roosevelt had set "the seal of approval" on lawn tennis. Dwight Davis and Teddy Roosevelt. Perhaps the best doubles team the Association ever had.[42]

Whatever the forces at work, by 1908 membership had risen to 102 clubs and fourteen associations. Seven of the associations were colleges or "interscholastic"—six of the seven Ivy League schools plus Bowdoin College in Maine—while the Intercollegiate Lawn Tennis Association represented eight other colleges. Six associations were regional: Southern, Pacific States, Ohio, Western (Chicago area), Inter-Mountain, and East Jersey. But only thirteen of the clubs were outside the Northeast (i.e., west of the Appalachians and south of the Mason-Dixon line), although the regional associations represented a wider and more western swathe of territory. Nevertheless, the Northeast remained, in the words of one historian, "lawn tennis country."[43]

Of course that growth related to only a handful of Americans. Tennis was still very much a game for the "leisure class," not the game of some five million frequent players and another twenty-one million occasional players that it would be a century later. Tennis clubs were expensive to join, and membership was largely reserved to those who fit into the same social class—what one sociologist and tennis historian called the "national upper class." Those barriers of class, wealth, and family name ensured that lawn tennis at the end of the nineteenth century—whether played on grass, asphalt, or concrete—was limited to a handful of participants. It is impossible to offer more than a guess as to the number of people who played at that time, particularly in the absence of individual membership figures for lawn-tennis clubs. But assuming clubs averaged some fifty tennis-playing members (a generous estimate), the roughly one hundred clubs that were Association members in 1895 would have had about five thousand tennis players. No one knows how many played at non-member clubs, in public parks, and backyards. The story of Martha Summerhayes at Camp Apache in Arizona suggests that lawn tennis had escaped the confines of class to some degree, but there is no way to develop a reasonable estimate of numbers. Despite dubious reports of the sale of ten thousand tennis sets back in 1880, the game appears to have remained the choice of relatively few.[44]

Nor were social and economic class or ethnicity the only limiting demographics for the Association. Lawn tennis in this early era was dominated by the young. Contemporary accounts routinely point to the youthfulness of players, and much of the USNLTA leadership bore that out. Although James Dwight as president saw three generations of players come and go, creating a backlog of vice presidents waiting in the wings (most of whom never got to center stage), for the first three or four decades the executive committee was dominated by young, active tennis players, mostly champions and top competitors. Dwight Davis, for example, gained selection to the Association's executive committee in 1900 at the ripe old age of twenty-one—after being runner-up in the singles nationals in 1898 and national doubles champion in 1899. He had the qualifications the Association assumed: money, social status, being an active player with championship trophies. He had been born in St. Louis, but summered in New England on the North Shore, "lawn tennis country," and a Harvard education had established his credentials as a northeasterner. There were exceptions, particularly for current champions, to the age pattern. William Larned combined talent with "advancing" age; he was a comparatively ancient thirty-nine years old in 1911 when he won his seventh national singles title, fifth in a row.[45] But players from this early era were quick to complain about members of the executive committee who were no longer active players, even when they were former champions. As late as 1916, the *New York Times*, predicting that the forty-eight-year-old vice president, Richard Stevens, would be replaced, reported that the change was "in accordance with the policy of intrusting the control of the National Association to younger men." That was belied a bit when his thirty-six-year-old supposed replacement was not nominated for vice president.

Association publications and minutes in this era routinely added the prefix "champion" or "former champion" (as in "former champion Wrenn"), revealing the premise from which the Association operated in the early days—champions mattered. The Association was run by champions, and its purpose was to regulate and promote championship play. At the turn of the century, meetings continued to focus on things like "the momentous question of sending a team abroad for the Dwight F. Davis trophy."[46] But such routine business was the calm before the storm. By the end of that first decade of the twentieth century, assumptions about northeastern leadership faced growing challenges.

In 1904 just as the Association pulled out of its membership doldrums, disputes over governance, then called "representation," surfaced when clubs in Boston and New York engaged in a small, initially regional, tug of war. Tennis players in those two cities plus Philadelphia had long vied for leadership, with the prize the selection of sites for national championships, particularly the men's singles, which had been held at the Newport Casino annually since its inaugural in 1881. New York newspapers reported complaints that "the Boston crowd" ran the USNLTA to their own liking, using proxies to maintain control. New Yorkers spoke, perhaps disingenuously, of the need to have all parts of the country represented on the "Board of Directors" [*sic*] and even of "organizing a new and distinct National" governing body. Others in the "west" took up the call for greater representation. The Association enlarged the executive committee to accommodate a couple of members from outside the Northeast, but that token gesture did not quiet the protests, though it did put some foxes into the henhouse. That skirmish foreshadowed the struggles over "representation" that would dog the Association until the constitutional changes of 1913.[47]

Perhaps some of the discontent stemmed from the assumption of privilege on the part of the executive committee. The evidence is anecdotal, but in 1906 a newspaper reported some "interesting figures" in the treasurer's report that showed a slight deficit for the preceding year. "A few members of the executive committee ate Waldorf-Astoria dinners at their meeting to the expense of $253, with a tip of [only?] $5 to the waiter. Their traveling expenses to the meeting were $260."[48] Perhaps the attendees at the annual meeting were not surprised—the minutes do not mention any discussion—but the news reporter seemed to be. In any event, that dinner and travel expense set another Association precedent that has been faithfully followed ever since.

The undercurrent of discontent among lawn-tennis players from outside the Northeast, once gentle, steadily grew stronger and more public. Newspaper and particularly tennis journals like *American Lawn Tennis* (*ALT*) carried an ever-increasing number of tactfully expressed complaints. The specific issues were not new. National rankings were criticized for not including more players and for penalizing those who could not or did not come east to play. One Californian complained, "We are too far away from the 'seat of war' to send a delegation [to meet with the Association's ranking committee] every season." "California's treatment is grotesque," observed *ALT*. "The Ranking List is still an Eastern list." Annual decisions to keep the men's singles national championship at Newport generated even more heat, as did arguments over where to hold doubles and women's nationals. Time and again the executive committee argued that the Northeast had the most clubs and the most players, but those outside that region expressed increasing unhappiness, complaining that time, cost, and distance prevented those championships from being truly "national."[49] Exacerbating the dispute was the use, and misuse, of proxies. "We see a wild scramble for proxy votes," reported *American Lawn Tennis*, and "the unedifying spectacle of an official of the association going around to clubs with the intention of 'scooping the market,' and appearing at the meeting flushed with triumph and flourishing a long list of his captives."[50] Although this distasteful display would be solved at the national level, it remained a problem endemic to the Association at the section level.

In 1908 the challenge went public as the Association leadership was forced to confront continuing calls for changes in "representation." Calhoun Cragin, a New Yorker who, for unclear reasons, sided with the reformers, proposed a major change in how clubs were represented in the USNLTA. His argument was from democracy—"tennis players . . . are not represented by delegates according to their numbers." A club of four hundred players had the same "power" as a club of only ten. President James Dwight, by then worthy of the descriptive "revered," though he was only in his mid fifties, supported the proposal to create a committee to examine the pros and cons of changes that could create "a more satisfactory system of government." But in the wonderfully vague phrasing of approved minutes, "after some discussion . . . the matter was dropped."[51] Not for long.

At the 1910 annual meeting, arguments erupted over written proxies when a New York City hotel refused to hold mail sent in advance of the meeting. As a result, proxies held by Dr. P. (Philip) B. Hawk ended up in the dead-letter office. *ALT* editor S. W. Merrihew dubbed him "Generalissimo" and found the whole episode "unspeakably funny."

Hawk, a Midwesterner from the University of Illinois in Urbana who competed in the 1909 national championships in Newport, was one of the foxes who got into the henhouse when the executive committee was enlarged to accommodate members from outside the Northeast. He chaired the Association's ranking committee and had come to New York just before the annual meeting. He was a leader of those in the west and the south who wanted to set up a clay-court national championship to be played outside the Northeast. While in New York, he raised that question. When he was rebuffed, he wrote an open letter asking for a "square deal"—expropriating fellow tennis player Theodore Roosevelt's political slogan. Hawk observed that tennis was in the midst of a "boom" and that the fastest growing regions, the west and the south, would "split" from the USNLTA unless they got what they considered fair treatment. He protested that he was not a "scrapper" who wanted to destroy the USNLTA, then went on to solicit proxies in order to protect the interests of those who were outside the establishment. He claimed that Association president Jim Dwight "favors our proposition." Dwight was most likely trying to pacify Hawk with the diplomacy for which he was so praised. But Hawk would not go away, and the loss of "national" status had long been the Association's greatest fear.[52]

Wiser heads (not necessarily old or older ones) prevailed. To offset arguments that too many "national" championships would diminish the prestige of the nationals, proponents chose deletion over dilution. They eliminated the offending word, and got together to offer the "Clay Court Championship of the United States," which the annual meeting duly approved. As the editor of *American Lawn Tennis*, S. W. Merrihew, merrily reminded all, "well did the immortal bard dwell upon the significance of a name." With sarcastic hyperbole, Merrihew described the delegates locking arms while telling their "whilom [former] opponents what good fellows they were."[53]

He Carried a Torch for Tennis

Merrihew's over-the-top description of the 1910 debate is worth quoting at length: "When it was proposed to institute a *national* clay-court championship there was a loud outcry, a gathering in hostile array and preparations for a pitched battle. A happy thought came to one of the clay-court advocates . . . and he straightaway unbosomed himself to his fellow clay-courters and impressed them with the logic of a change of nomenclature. Waving it, like unto an olive branch, at the annual meeting, opposition melted away, the hostile array executed a flank movement and marshalled itself behind the 'clay-court championship of the United States.' . . . And so an episode that had assumed national importance and bade fair to cause an immense amount of bad feeling had a peaceful ending, and the meeting took on some aspects of a love feast."

S. Wallis "Pops" Merrihew was proprietor and editor of *American Lawn Tennis*, the official USNLTA organ from 1907 through 1924. He was an accomplished tennis player, and coauthored a book on tennis with J. Parmley Paret. His commentaries on Association affairs, particularly the annual meetings, were simply wonderful. An unabashed devotee of purple prose, he used it with humor and panache. Best of all, he was an honest observer of the Association. He ran unsuccessfully for the executive committee in 1911, and in his inimitable style described the outcome: "The problem that confronted their opponents—how to eliminate Hawk and yet not have Merrihew elected in his stead, was solved very cleverly." One Sumner Hardy of San Francisco was nominated, and "administration" forces had the votes to elect him. In 1924 following a contretemps between Merrihew and Association leadership over Bill Tilden's suspension, *American Lawn Tennis* lost its designation and subsidy as the official Association organ. Fortunately for historians, *ALT* and Merrihew continued as an amusing and candid inside source until 1947. He once wrote in his magazine that he had "given his best to the game of lawn tennis" for some twenty years. Quite so.[54] (See gallery, image 9.)

That neatly split the clay-court championship apart from the more troubling matter of governance. With Hawk denied his proxies, the Association leadership could get a vote to postpone (table) a governance proposal that would have "treated the player instead of the club as a unit," giving clubs one vote at the annual meeting for every twenty-five members. The committee appointed by James Dwight to study the voting and governance structure had gone even further to hold the line against the "reformers." It recommended that the Association eliminate class 2 (association) memberships and return to the old system of one club, one vote, which would have lessened the clout of non-eastern associations. It was not adopted. Some viewed broadening geographic representation on the powerful executive committee as needed, others thought it undesirable. Newspaper reports described heated discussions at the 1910 meeting. When Hawk called for the "West and South" to have seats, R. D. Wrenn, Association vice president and heir-apparent to Jim Dwight, retorted that representation on the executive committee should "come from the East," not from "afar." One Californian argued that there should be "a member for every state."[55] But the northeastern establishment had the votes, Hawk did not have his proxies, and nothing changed—not then.

A few days after the annual meeting ended on February 5, Hawk raised the ante in an open letter to the officers of the Association, published in *American Lawn Tennis*, announcing formation of an American Association of Clay Court Players, of which he was president. Hawk denied that the new group was "*antagonistic* to the interests of the USNLTA," noting it was "of an entirely different character" since it was "an association of *individuals*, not an association of clubs." Hawk may not have been a "scrapper," but his new organization posed a direct and disturbing challenge to the USNLTA for which being the "national" association—what would later be designated the "national governing body" of tennis—was fundamental.[56]

The first page of the *ALT* write-up of the 1911 annual meeting has a wonderful caricature of "former champion" H. W. Slocum, as he "pleads for Newport" to remain as the site for the national championships. But that dispute was more symbolic than real. Where the nationals were played was less the issue than "who decides" or, more precisely, how they decided.[57] Proxies had constituted nearly half the club votes at the initial organizational meeting of the Association and had been permitted ever since. In a pre-automobile, pre-air age era, proxies made sense. Travel from the "West," which included everything from Pittsburgh to California, was expensive and time consuming. But proxy gathering was an art form, and the northeastern "proxy-procurers" were adept at the game. As Merrihew pointed out, "the administration was in control of the meeting," and it controlled the only serious issue—election to the executive committee. Hawk and Merrihew stood for election and went down to defeat.[58]

With significant reform blocked on the executive committee, the ranking committee moved to fill the breach—setting a precedent that would be followed by subsequent activist committees up to the present. According to the newspaper report, the proposal was ambitious: "To do away with a self-perpetuating body in control of the sport" by establishing staggered executive committee terms of three years. How that would achieve such a lofty goal went unexplained. With President Dwight appearing supportive, the minor reform passed.[59]

But major governance proposals stood no chance of getting the two-thirds vote needed to change the constitution. In a delightful reference that should not be lost, one reporter discussing the reform of Association governance declaimed that "the new Nationalism (another of Teddy Roosevelt's campaign slogans) of lawn tennis is either to assert itself or to be smothered."[60] But smothering was still possible—in 1911.

By that year, James Dwight had become an overpowering figure in tennis and the Association. Founder, "president-for-life," expert teacher of the game—his reputation as an unselfish promoter of lawn tennis was unsullied.[61] Whatever the regional-sectional quarrels, for him the goal was to "grow the game" and to maintain "national" standards—not northeastern control. In the summer of 1911, perhaps not coincidentally the year he retired from the Association presidency, he appointed a five man committee on representation. Only two were from outside the Northeast (Minneapolis and Los Angeles), but one of the three easterners was Calhoun Cragin, who with P. B. Hawk had been the most vocal of advocates for changing the makeup of the executive committee. Dwight had obviously concluded that reform had to come, but he was in no hurry. As in 1908 when Cragin first raised the issue to the annual meeting, the problem was the unfairness of one club, one vote. Cragin's West Side Tennis club had over five hundred members. Yet clubs with ten or twenty members had the same single vote. The Association was not ready to think in terms of individual memberships, and working out complicated formulas to create weighted votes seemed cumbersome and open to disputes. How, for example, to count the four thousand members of the New York Athletic Club, only a handful of whom played tennis? As the *New York Times* succinctly put it, the Association's constitution "is an ancient one." Various annual meetings "tinkered with" it, but it remained a document designed to govern "less than a score of clubs," not the nearly three hundred clubs that were members by 1912.[62]

The 1912 meeting seemed ready to focus on three broad issues: national ranking rules (adjust requirements so the "west" would not be at a disadvantage for not traveling east to play); complaints about abuses in collecting proxy votes from clubs that could not or chose not to attend the annual meeting; and representation reform.[63]

The Three-Ring Circus Tale

Descriptions of the annual meetings of 1911 and 1912 make them seem like a three-ring circus. In ring one "we see a wild scramble for proxy votes" from the 125 or so clubs that did not send a delegate. The victorious "proxy-procurer," who had presented "the unedifying spectacle of an official of the association going around to clubs with the intention of 'scooping the market,'" appears, "flushed with triumph and flourishing a long list of his captives."

Ring three finds the Newport Casino holding forth, displaying the banner "National Championships." The other performers jockey for position, each trying to displace Newport. Their signs read Philadelphia, New York, and even Chicago. But none are able to snatch the banner; it's not even close.

The center ring finds the ringmaster, the magisterial James Dwight, standing off to the side with his officers, aloof from the politics and seemingly concerned with minute issues in the rules of tennis. In the center of that ring young and eager delegates vigorously debate "representation." Evocative of the Roman Senate, some argue that history calls for one club, one vote. Others argue for Greek democracy—one vote for each individual (so long as they belonged to the ruling class—i.e., played tennis). Meanwhile, some four thousand members (only a handful are tennis players) of the New York Athletic Club mill around just outside the ring, wondering how their votes should be cast and counted.

The ringmaster manages to maintain law and order (using, according to Association bylaws, *Cushing's Manual* for parliamentary procedure—even more confusing than the infamous, and very confusing, Robert's Rules of Order), though it must have been like herding cats. Newport kept its banner, proxies were accepted, and voting on reform was postponed. But next year's performance was only twelve months away.[64]

It is easy to imagine how important national ranking was to these young, dedicated, and financially secure tennis players for whom tennis seemed to be the most important thing in their lives. Once again, a sense of discrimination against players outside the Northeast, where the major tournaments were played, underlay the complaints and concerns about rankings. The "best" tournaments were in the East—too far for Californians. Shortened lists of ranked players cut off those who could not play in the major events.[65]

Proxy hunting prompted predictions of a "bitterly waged" fight over their validation. The *New York Times* reported that the "administration faction" held proxies for nearly one-third of the votes. The phrasing of that report indicated the tension. Referring to a "faction" suggested serious divisions within the Association.[66] When the committee on representation reported out at the 1912 annual meeting, its report was "voluminous and difficult to follow," particularly as it offered five diverse proposals. Even Merrihew, covering the meeting in his *American Lawn Tennis*, gave up and merely reported that "after some discussion" the report was referred to a committee.[67] Same time next year!

Thus ended the founding era of the Association. From 1881 through 1912, the institution maintained the same philosophy and rules of governance. Its purpose was fixed—assure standardized rules and promote competitive play at the highest levels. It was an organization of and for tennis champions, and of and for "a complacent and confident Eastern seaboard upper class."[68] The Association had come through some hard times, but by 1912 had established a firm financial foundation with annual receipts of nearly $5,800. Member clubs approached three hundred, and member associations had grown rapidly. There had been some sporadic talk about initiatives to expand the popularity of lawn tennis, but since growth had occurred without any help from the Association, why change anything?

But organizations like the USNLTA assume that they are organic—they either grow or decline. Lawn tennis remained the game of the leisure class, but that class was not confined to the Northeast. Nor were expensive clubs and grass (turf) courts required. In fact, the climate in much of the "west" and on the Pacific Coast made grass courts impractical. But the movement of the national population westward toward California would generate change in the Association even more quickly than court surfaces. The arguments and debates of 1911 and 1912 were but a prelude to the "revolution of 1913," when the Association felt forced to give effective representation to regions outside the Northeast, lest it lose its place of pride as the "national" governing body.

3

EVOLUTIONARY REVOLUTION

1913–1922

> "I will go so far as to say that it will be mighty hard for me when I go back home, to keep the Western associations from seceding from the National Association."
>
> HARRY WAIDNER, 1917 annual meeting

Geographic "representation," which appeared to be the crucial and potentially divisive issue in 1912, seemed overwhelmed the following year by arguments over amateurism. Even the perceptive reporter from *American Lawn Tennis* (presumably Merrihew) mentioned the governance change only in passing while discussing at some length the "new and Draconian amateur rule." In the short run, that report was right. Amateurism would befuddle and perplex the Association for the next half century.

Nor did the much-criticized "proxy vote" procedure materialize as an issue, though it was more to the governance point. Clubs outside the Northeast found it difficult to send delegates to the annual meetings. Proxies were the only way in which they could have a voice in Association governance, but the political process of rounding-up proxy votes had troubled the leadership since 1881. Nevertheless, the matter never came up at the 1913 meeting, apparently because the extensive governance revisions proposed would diminish the significance of proxy votes.

Creation of sectional delegates in 1913 would eventually reshape "ownership" of the Association, although those delegates did not then, and for decades thereafter, challenge the control exercised by the its establishment. Four officers and six at-large members, when added to delegates from the three northeastern sections—New England, Middle States and Middle Atlantic—ensured that the Northeast would retain control. Delegates from the other seven sections, the "west" and the "south," would have their say even if they could not win the day—but their time would come.[1]

The committee appointed by James Dwight in 1911 to revise the Association constitution continued its work after Robert Wrenn took over as president in February 1912. It must have done its homework well, for if there were any controversies, the news failed to reach the media. By the time it reported out to the annual meeting in 1913, a consensus had obviously been reached, for that portion of the new constitution passed without serious discussion.[2] The sections (whose organizational structure, where it existed, defies description) had already agreed on their candidates for delegates, so it appears that the same kind of arm-twisting and politics that E. H. Outerbridge bragged about when the Association was first formed had once again been successful. How sections were to "nominate" and/or select delegates in 1914 remained and remains a mystery. Some sections seem to have existed only in the minds of the USNLTA delegates—and in the revised constitution. Yet what "champion" Harry Slocum (Association vice president in 1913) blandly described as "the increase in the members of the executive committee" was a done deal. Nowhere was there any mention—or thought?—of the potential fundamental change in governance created by adding delegates from the sections to the executive committee.

The revolution of 1913 was, in fact, the next step in a slow and stealthy evolution. It was the logical progression from the class 2 "association members" category created in 1889. Then Association president Joseph Clark may have sensed the potential impact when he warned of "several recent *radical* changes" in the membership categories.[3] But no one else seems to have been concerned, back then—or in 1913. Association leaders remained firmly focused on playing tennis, not governing the game. Yet the constitutional changes ensured a role in governance for the sections and engendered creation of new sections and changes in section boundaries—necessitating a clause in the constitution about "encroachment" requiring either a two-thirds vote at an annual meeting or mutual agreement regarding changes in those boundaries.

Sections had existed before then, but only as a membership class and in the geographic sense of a "region" for tournament or championship purposes. "Competition section" would be a better term. Playing the game against the best competition remained an overriding concern of the tennis players who led the Association. But as the game spread out of the Northeast, some sort of "qualifying" structure for entry into the national championships became necessary. National rankings for players generated local and regional competitions; regional (i.e., sectional) competitions generated governance issues. Starting in 1914 the constitution called for sectional associations to appoint their delegates, cautiously adding that the national Association would elect delegates if they were not nominated by the "active [i.e., dues paying] associations of the sections."[4] Competitive players, particularly in the newer sections, began to realize they needed governance and structure. How else to select a delegate who would reflect the views and majority opinion of the diverse members (the clubs) that he—always a "he" until much later—represented? Representative democracy and governance expands in both directions, so the sections themselves would inevitably imitate the national Association and become involved in all aspects of the game of tennis within their boundaries, at the same time trying to influence the national Association on matters that transcended those borders. But that was in the distant future.

That sectional organizing process may have been observed by the USNLTA executive committee, but if so it was not recorded or discussed at annual meetings early in the "teens," despite evidence that things were changing. After all, sections had developed for competitive, not governance reasons. Some sections were "inactive"; that is, not organized, leaving nomination of delegates to the national Association's executive committee, or to chance, or to local individual initiative. By 1915, the Association president, Robert Wrenn, could refer to having "communication" with the Intermountain Section regarding a recommendation for "a delegate from the section," though he noted that Intermountain "itself has been very inactive." Another speaker then noted that he thought the membership list included an Intermountain Lawn Tennis Association. "Consequently," he pointed out, "we do not elect that delegate here," but should merely accept the section's nomination.[5] A small, but important step towards autonomy for the sections.

The word "delegate" has meant different things during the Association's existence. Initially, a delegate was someone who represented a member (i.e., a club) at meetings. As described in this and the previous chapter, a formula was soon devised that assigned multiple representation to some clubs and to "association" members (one ancestor of today's sections), but all were still called delegates. After the revolution of 1913, when the geographic (competitive) sections were each allotted one seat on the executive committee (analogous to today's board of directors), those selected were referred to as delegates, as were the rest of that committee's members, and as were all the delegates sent by clubs to the annual meetings. There were delegates everywhere. As the number of sections grew, the size of the executive committee became unwieldy, and other institutions of governance and policymaking were set up. By the late twentieth century, the only "delegates" were those selected by the sections, plus one representing two clubs in Bermuda that retained club membership as a vestigial remain. But all that is a story for later chapters.

Occasionally multiple nominations came from the same geographical section. In 1916 when the Southwestern Section was inactive, two "associations," Border States (west Texas, Arizona, and New Mexico) and Texas (the rest of Texas and apparently centered in Dallas) each made a nomination for the Southwestern delegate slot, both young players, of course. Despite Wrenn's quite sensible suggestion that the USNLTA accept neither and instead tell the two associations to nominate a single candidate, the annual meeting voted to elect the candidate from Dallas (J. B. Adoue), ostensibly because Dallas was a more central location and probably because more people knew Adoue as a nice player.[6]

A governance role for the sections, what would become the most transforming change made at the 1913 annual meeting, passed muster without debate. Not so the issue of amateurism, a contretemps that would occupy, and even preoccupy, the Association's attention for the next half century. "Pure" amateurism is a phrase that troubled the Association from the outset. Its meaning is obscured by a panoply of Jesuitical definitions, practical realities, and class distinctions—all stirred by the desire of athletes to be the best they can be. The renewed Olympic movement in the nineteenth century, built on a much-romanticized image of classical Greece, is partly to blame. But it is no accident that the modern Olympic games were the work of an Anglophilic French aristocrat, one Pierre Frédy, Baron de Coubertin. Like Robert Baden-Powell in England, he believed that sports helped young people to develop the "proper" attitudes toward society and success. Play-for-pay was certainly not one of those "proper" attitudes.

But the ancient Greeks had developed the games as a diversion, as an exemplar for physical conditioning (for warriors) and as a religious offering to their gods. The Greek city-states viewed their athletes with the same kind of nationalistic pride that twenty-first-century Olympians receive. They were subsidized, trained nearly full time, paid for winning, and professional athletes in every sense of the word. The Greek games were open to all classes but only to Greeks (i.e., free men who spoke Greek). There were separate games for women and men, though the women's games were limited in scope.

But in the medieval Western world, sports became a demarcation line between the nobility and other classes—peasants, artisans, laborers, the commercial middle class. English laborers and servants were expressly forbidden in 1388 and again in 1410 to play court tennis, a game reserved for royals and aristocrats. In 1535 England's Henry VIII reserved tennis for the nobility and property owners (perhaps an admission that the untitled landed gentry were a crucial part of his political support system).

Similar restrictions abounded for other "gentlemanly" sports like rowing and lawn bowling.

Class distinction as a justification for pure amateurism had largely lost its legitimacy by the beginning of the twentieth century. The "equality of sports" became a mantra that fit the growing egalitarianism of the era. But "pure" amateurism fell back on a final line of defense. It was "unfair" to expect talented athletes who played for fun and as a diversion to compete against those who played the game for a living. The litmus test, however, was not how much time and energy one put into preparing for and playing a sport. The test was whether or not a player received payment—in money, goods, or services, directly or indirectly—for playing the game.

Amateurism was a byproduct of smug assumptions by eighteenth- and nineteenth-century aristocrats and landed gentry that earning money by commerce or labor was somehow demeaning, something done by only the "lower" classes, however much the upper classes were doing the same thing.[7] Put in raw economic terms, the rich could play tennis full time, the poor could not. There is no little irony in recalling that the death knell of amateurism in international sports came during the Cold War, when the Soviet Union and its satellites turned competitive sports into an advertising program for their way of life. "Socialism" turns out better athletes, they bragged, as they turned their players into full-time professionals and employees of the state. In the perceptive phrasing of *Time* magazine, "the creed of amateurism ill fit a world in which competition was being democratized, the popularity of sport was burgeoning, and standards of competition were rising."[8]

Indirect payments drove the guardians of purity crazy. High national rankings (about which the Association fretted and fussed a great deal) gave top players leverage. Payment for endorsement of tennis rackets was obvious. But what about payment for endorsement of other goods not related to sports? Fame as a tennis player was why such endorsements were solicited. Was that not "capitalizing" on their success playing tennis? What about payment for travel and living expenses in order to play a tournament? What about employment at sporting-goods companies? Free trips to strange sounding places with strange sounding names (England, the French Riviera, from California to the East Coast) were wonderful benefits for the major players, whose presence in a tournament draw brought in bigger gate receipts for the promoter club. The establishment of the Davis Cup as an international competition certainly raised the bar and created a dilemma for Association leaders since those matches were a major source of its revenues. How could the Americans compete (i.e., win) unless they had the best players; and how could the best players be at the top of their game if they could not travel and play other top players all the year round? Regardless of attempts to grow the game in parks and cities, amateur status required that, in the words of a *New York Times* column in 1907, "those inclined toward strenuous athletic sports," like tennis, had to be able to afford to play the top tournaments that drew the top players. Success seemed reserved for the well-to-do, not any and all the talented.[9]

When the Association "revision committee" proposed a new amateur rule in 1913, concern arose that forbidding amateurs to accept expenses would prevent sending Davis Cup teams abroad and eliminate "any California invasion [of the East Coast] each year." The committee quickly dismissed the charge, saying that the national Association and local associations could pay player expenses, since those players would bring "honor upon the club or association." A tournament committee could also give players "expenses or the equivalent." The new rule aimed at preventing players from negotiating "with an organization which pays these expenses as a business transaction" to enhance gate receipts.[10] (That before the national income tax and business deductions!) But they failed to close the huge loophole, since tournament committees were, for the most part, appointed by the very same clubs that sought greater revenue by having the best players in their tournaments. Then there was the ever-present temptation of "appearance money": cash and/or goods given to players just to get them to enter a tournament.

Socio-economic status, and the east-west division in the Association, lay openly at the root of the amateurism dispute. The *New York Times* reported that the amateur rules committee claimed to wish to put all players on an equal footing; their recommendations were not "class legislation as had been intimated." The chair of the committee, Harry Slocum, spoke to the 1913 annual meeting with remarkable candor:

> I have heard statements made in some quarters that this . . . would prevent a poor man from playing tennis. . . . I am entirely out of sympathy with any such statement as that. The aim of it is entirely in the interest of warning a man who is not so richly endowed with worldly goods that he may know exactly what standard he should adopt in his play. . . .
>
> As a matter of fact, the regulations which are contained in these simple rules are made to protect the poor man.
>
> You must remember that a question of professionalism is one

> in which a rich man is never tempted. It is the poor man, the man who is not able to spend his money with freedom . . . who may be tempted at some time to violate the rule.

Slocum remarked that the strict amateur rule reminded a magazine editor "of a man who was so straight that he fell over backward. . . . A man who falls over backward may be picked up, and he is not going to suffer very much from it, but the other man who falls the other way [crooked], his fall is irremediable. He will never resume his place among us." Slocum, a USNLTA national singles Champion (1888, 1889) and the sitting vice president of the Association must have spoken for the delegates; no one challenged his argument.

But some were unhappy with the details, particularly as they might have an impact on support for West Coast players to come east and play the major national tournaments, so the rule was tabled while another committee prepared yet another report for the next year's annual meeting. At the same time, that West Coast–East Coast travel issue once again raised the question of governance, of control of the Association by northeastern clubs. It surfaced, and resurfaced in the annual discussions and disputes about selecting locations for the various National championships, something done at each year's annual meeting.[11]

As the 1914 annual-meeting date approached, New York reporters (the meeting was routinely held in February at the Waldorf-Astoria Hotel on Park Avenue—so it was a "New York" event) anticipated "some drastic measure" that addressed excessive expenses and prizes given to players to persuade them to play a specific tournament. Davis Cup matches had already posed challenges. The cost of travel, usually to England but occasionally to places like Australia, prompted appeals for public subscriptions from member clubs. Competitive juices drove the Association's commitment to Davis Cup, but that it generated significant revenue was far from irrelevant. These were active tennis players and former champions who led the USNLTA, and they cared deeply about winning. For that to happen, the best American players had to play regularly, and that affected jobs and earnings, at least earnings outside of the world of sports.[12]

The Handkerchief Dropped

The semifinal of the 1914 Davis Cup challenge round was played at the Allegheny Country Club just outside Pittsburgh. With war in the offing, the European teams were reluctant to continue so the Association agreed that, if war broke out in Europe, the matches would halt. The oddly romantic signal would be a handkerchief dropped from the press box (which had a telegraph connection). On August 1, just as the Australasia (Australia and New Zealand) completed a sweep of Germany on the court, the handkerchief dropped.

Whatever the suspicions that the signal was purposefully delayed until the match ended, the ensuing events offered an example of gentlemen's tennis transcending wartime emotions. Two members of the 1914 German Davis Cup team, Otto Froitzheim and Oscar Kreuzer, both colonels on the personal staff of Germany's Kaiser Wilhelm, were captured as they headed back toward Germany after their losing match. Both continued to play tennis while in British prison camps, though they complained of being "poorly looked after." Merrihew sent them copies of *American Lawn Tennis* to keep them in the swing of things (so to speak).[13]

At the same time, two international events were taking place that would have a significant impact on American tennis. One was the political deterioration in Europe and the colonial world that would lead to the outbreak in August 1914 of the Great War (later re-christened First World War). However much that growing crisis was affecting the lives and fortunes of the Association's leaders, it did not penetrate the meeting room at the Waldorf-Astoria. Davis Cup matches might have posed a problem, but since the Americans had won the cup the year before, the challenge round was held in the United States—far from the "guns of August." (Australasia defeated the United States, 3–2.)

Less important for the world, but eventually more important for the Association, the International Lawn Tennis Federation (ILTF) had been formed at a meeting in Paris (where else?) in February 1913. The Association's decision about joining that new organization foundered for the next decade on the issue of designating any tournament, particularly Wimbledon, as a "world" championship, as well as on ILTF voting procedures that assigned Great Britain six votes and no other nation more than five. When President Wrenn observed that, since voting strength presumably reflected the importance of tennis in a country, "we can't quite understand why the British Isles should receive six," he pointed to a governance system that would aggravate the Association's leadership even up through the twenty-first century. The ILTF's European bias was illustrated when it became inactive during the First World War, not resuming its activities until 1919. But even then the British picked up where they had left off, refusing to give up the "world championship," which they claimed had been "perpetually awarded to Wimbledon" by the ILTF. The USNLTA continued to decline requests to join.

Issues of international politics were integrally related to the very lengthy argument over changes in the Association's rules regarding amateur status—changes that would have put the United States in harmony with the ILTF. Some delegates openly feared the International Federation would take over the Davis Cup by imposing its own definition of an amateur and disqualifying American players. Just as Jim Thorpe had just been stripped, retroactively, of his medals from the 1912 Olympics, one unnamed delegate warned that:

> unless we adopt the amateur rule which they [the ILTF] are governed by, we leave them a beautiful loophole to at the last moment cancel all of our men.... Now, we have licked these foreigners so often that they are going to take any opportunity they can to beat us, and if they cannot do it by right, they will do it by might; and if they can't do it that way, they will rule us out by rule.[14]

The delegates to the meeting rewarded his jingoism with a round of applause.

The discussion of a new amateur rule, entangled with the ILTF rules, managed to take up 70 of the 126 pages of the typescript record of the 1914 annual meeting! The delegates tied themselves into knots over issues of parliamentary procedure, particularly the president's bizarre ruling that amendments to the committee report recommending constitutional amendments could not be considered since there was a thirty-day notice requirement for constitutional changes. When they rejected the proposed amateur rules, all agreed that "it would be absurd" to apply for membership in the International Federation.[15]

That the Association had gotten things done over the preceding thirty years was testimony to the consensus-building skills of the established leadership and to the remarkably homogeneous makeup of the membership in the clubs. But the geography of the USNLTA was shifting; leadership would shift with it. While the Association remained an exclusively white, male organization, overwhelmingly composed of middle- and upper-class tennis players, the lengthy debate over amateurism, whatever its friendly tone, demonstrated that the "west" (i.e., the rest) saw things differently from the northeastern seaboard leadership.

Even shifting a tennis tournament, the eastern region doubles championship in this case, to New York from Boston, presaged future changes. Association vice president Julian Myrick, from the West Side Tennis Club in the Forest Hills community of the borough of Queens in New York City, proposed shifting the event from Longwood, near Boston, to his West Side Club. Filthy lucre raised its head when Bostonians argued that after "a long series of lean years," Longwood should keep the tournament "now that the fat years had come." Longwood, and tradition, won out 82 to 79. But both revenue and location were harbingers of things to come.[16]

Nor were national championships the only competitions that drove the Association toward structural change. With sectional boundaries quickly becoming cast in cement, concern arose about the need to make them fit natural competitive relations. For example, in 1916 players from the Middle Atlantic "district" (District of Columbia, Delaware, Virginia, Maryland, West Virginia), all part of the Middle States Section, did not normally travel to play the eastern doubles in New York (then also part of the Middle States Section). Whereas players from the Middle States and New England Sections did travel to New York for the tournament. What the Middle Atlantic players wanted was a tournament in their region ("district") that would gain the winners automatic entry into the national doubles championships.[17]

That flowed into a discussion about the western championships in Chicago and the desire of the Missouri Valley district to have a sectional championship. ("District" began as a geographic competitive description, but crept on cats' paws into common usage within the Association, despite having no formal organizational definition or function. Eventually sections formally divided into sub-units; some called "districts, others called "states" since they followed existing state boundaries. The sections managed to maintain centralized control more effectively than did the national Association.) Wrenn, who had just left the presidency (no automatic seat on the executive committee in those days for "immediate past presidents"), cautioned the delegates that awarding the Missouri Valley that championship would set a precedent for breaking up sections that had existed, at least in the constitution, "for some years." A player from the Missouri Valley made an impassioned (and long) speech defending that region's right to have a championship. The western section (Great Lakes, upper Mississippi Valley) delegate opposed the move, warning that there would be no end to the splitting up process and sections would be localized to the point that they became "practically state tournaments." The Missouri Valley got its championship, and a few years later became a separate section.[18]

Imagine being a fly on the wall at a USNLTA annual meeting in the first score of years in the twentieth century. To start with, New York's Waldorf-Astoria Hotel was a most comfortable venue. Meetings routinely started off with a caveat that they had to adjourn and meet for dinner at such-and-such time—a practice that would continue indefinitely. There were energetic debates. Rankings created a good deal of stress as did definitions of an amateur. Sites for various national and regional championships and annual meetings increasingly became controversial, as the "west" pressured the leadership for a chance to hold major events. The speeches were long, labored, and impassioned. Governance decisions (for example, creation of the sections) had major implications for the future, but that somehow those slipped past the delegates, though not the leadership.

Tennis—the game—remained the focus of the Association. Arguments over "service & lets" and "club colors" captured the attention of the delegates who were, after all, almost all young, competitive tennis players rather than bureaucratic climbers fixed on becoming important within the USNLTA structure. Should "Champions" (always capitalized in the Association mind, and minutes) be awarded special medals? What about foot faults? Could a player jump in the air when serving? More mundane were issues of club dues in arrears (loss of voting power) and endless, wordy, often silly and misinformed disputes over parliamentary procedure.

Fortunately, good humor prevailed. In 1914 a delegate from Cleveland, Ohio, pretending to be a "rube" in the big city, offered a barbed self-deprecatory argument for the National Clay Court Championships to be held at his Lakewood Tennis Club in 1916:

> **Delegate from Lakewood [Kroesen]:**
> Mr. Chairman, inasmuch it has come to a point where we are all bidding, I suppose it is up to Cleveland to take a whirl at it. (Laughter.)
>
> I have been coming on here for two or three years, just dreaming and willing to sit back and be quiet, and wait until the time would come when I should ask for it, but I will be an old man before my time comes. I am a young fellow yet, and I thought this was a good time to ask for it. I think it is absolutely wrong that the thing should come to a sarcasm about those miles, and so forth, and I do not want any of that shot at me. . . . Let us all have the chance. Now, in Cleveland, we have ten or twelve tennis clubs with approximately 140 or 160 tennis courts. We have 3,790 people actually playing in the public parks, and I dare anyone to question me. (Laughter.) It is my idea that this clay court championship is to uplift the game.

> Now, car riding from Pittsburgh to Omaha is all right for anyone who lives in those two cities; Cincinnati is a good city; they should have it. I am agreeable that it should go someplace this year, someplace next year, but in 1916, absolutely—(laughter). I want to make it clear and impressive, that I am here as a young man in 1914, was here in 1913, would have come in 1912, but I could not get here, but I want the 1916 clay court tournament for Cleveland. I demand it. You owe it to me for coming. I am sure you do not think that I appreciate coming to New York for a buggy ride for five or six years, just to hear you chatting back and forth; I am here on an errand. I wish that you all would bear it in mind that in 1916, when I get up here, that you owe me your vote. Thank you. (Applause.)

Both the speech, and the proposed venue, much amused the other delegates. Two years later, as promised, when Dick Kroesen again asked that the Clay Courts be awarded to Cleveland, the tone of his speech changed. Biting sarcasm and even bitter anger showed through. He managed to get laughter and applause, but the minutes fail to clarify whether that came from other Midwesterners or from the entire meeting. The site for the National Clay Court Championships was symbolic. The root issue was control of the Association by the Northeast. As with amateur status, the placement of national championships accentuated regional differences. In the pre-air travel era, locating a national championship somewhere west of the Appalachians made it more accessible to a wider array of players, just as paying travel expenses made championships in the Northeast more accessible to "westerners." Just "listen" to the same delegate from the Lakewood Tennis Club again addressing the annual meeting, this time in 1916:

> **Croyzon [Kroesen]:**
> May I rise to a point of special privilege. (I heard that some place) (Laughter). . . .
>
> Here is the peculiar thing with this National Association: You fellows get up and vote for a paid secretary and Mr. [Palmer E.] Presbrey gets up and tells about Boston. That is round enough. (Laughter) Mr. [Julian] Myrick tells about New York, and here is what you are doing, you are developing the upper end of the body and you are letting the Western "legs" get weaker. If you are going to have a paid secretary to educate them in the East, give us a paid assistant, one to educate them in the West. Some of you need to know it and

need to know it soon: This is an Eastern Organization, with the West dragged in. . . .

You are always talking about Boston and Philadelphia and the West Side. I care nothing about you. (Laughter) Neither do my people. (Laughter) We come here and give you our money for your liquor and your food and we listen to you, but that is not helping the game. I have heard some wonderful addresses here in the last four or five years about tennis and this sport and the grand game, and we are building it up, but it only builds up right up through this end of it, New England. Give the West a chance. . . .

You fellows here that think you are getting it, that have never been outside of Philadelphia, you do not know anything. (Laughter) You have never been any place. You would not know where Lake Wrie [*sic*] was if it was not for a map. Come on and get together and say, "let us have something for those Western fellows, let us build the game there."

We have never turned anybody out of the Middle West who was a champion. The champion must, come from Harvard, Yale or from the hard courts of California, nothing from the middle. Now someday you know you were eating an apple. There was a core you know. Some day you will be looking for the middle. Come on and give us something to build on. Do not give us the outside and tell us to get to the center. Give us the center and we will get to the outside. We will give you the players. When I tell you I had to [say] two "Hail Mary's" to get our man in the National Junior Championship this year, I am not kidding you; they did not know me and the fellow I was telegraphing to was an old chum. You have got to support the West. You might as well get it under your Bermudas now as any other time. (Laughter and Applause)

Dick Kroesen's Lakewood Tennis Club in Cleveland was awarded the 1916 National Clay Court Championships, prompting a sotto voce self-admonishment: "Now I've got it; what'll I do with it?"[19]

The great debate at the 1915 annual meeting—whether or not to relocate the national championships (i.e., the men's singles competition) from the Newport Casino, where it had been held since 1881, to the West Side Tennis Club in the Forest Hills section of New York City—was irrelevant internecine warfare for Kroesen and the "west," whatever his casual remark that they might get the national championship in twenty or thirty years. Forest Hills was as "eastern" as Newport. But it was far from irrelevant to the northeastern leadership and players. President Bob Wrenn, anticipating arguments at the annual meeting, wanted "to consult counsel on the matter." The lawyers had arrived! The "stormy" debate, which pitted the "old group" against the "so-called progressive element," focused on arguments that the tournament had outgrown Newport, both the Casino and the city.[20] Tradition was the plea made by Newport's defenders, but to no avail. Each side had its share of former "champions" who spoke out. Certainly the men's national championship had become more profitable, netting just under five thousand dollars in 1914, as opposed to less than five hundred in previous years. Moreover, the Association's treasury showed a quite comfortable thirty-thousand-dollar positive balance.[21] Supporters of the move argued that those revenues would be even larger were it held in New York City, citing very successful Davis Cup matches as evidence that large crowds could be attracted to Forest Hills. The *New York Times* concluded that "sentiment" had "been supplanted by commercialism" and that proponents of the move could "throw the stellar event open to the highest bidder." The vote was close, 119 against and 129 for the shift to the West Side Tennis Club. As important as the switch to Forest Hills was to be for the Association, *American Lawn Tennis* unintentionally put it into perspective with a long, tedious, detailed piece, "The Widespread Prevalence of Footfaults," printed in the same January 1915 issue that presented the case for Newport versus Forest Hills as the venue for the national championship. The Association was still for players, not tennis politicians.[22]

Kroesen's plea to the 1916 annual meeting for fairness referred, in passing, to decisions made about two very significant long-term matters for the Association—expanding the game, and establishment of a paid staff. Expanding the game of lawn tennis had long intrigued Association leaders, although their primary interest remained with competitive tennis at the highest level. Why? They represented a northeastern elite that played the game for pleasure. They had fun, competed, and lived up to their own goals. Why the desire to expand the game?

Part of the impulse for expansion came from their desire to validate their own commitment to tennis by bringing others into the game. But their competitive nature and their cosmopolitan connections pushed them further. Meaning what? Lawn tennis began in England. James Dwight, the Association's founding father, spent nearly a decade in England and France learning from European tennis players. For the northeastern leadership, Europe was more important than Chicago, or San Francisco, or (most certainly) Camp Apache, Arizona. Davis Cup was the most prestigious international competition, but it was Euro-centric despite a series of victories by that outpost of Englishness in the southwest Pacific, Australasia.[23] Moreover, to win the cup consistently required that the United States have a large pool of talented players, which meant growing the game at home. The larger the pool, the better the chances of getting players who would win. During discussions in 1916 of the report "Ways and Means of Popularizing and Encouraging Lawn Tennis in the United States" Merrihew pointed out that the goal was to bring players along from when they played like boys to when they played like men, and that "it certainly means that all through this great United States the game of tennis is going to grow and prosper and flourish [said Merrihew, with a flourish] as nobody ever thought of. We are practically in our infancy and by adopting this thing, you are going to make the game so that there will never be a nation in the world that can anywhere near compete with us in securing the Davis Cup."[24]

Some throw-away lines that suggest the growth of the Association and the game:

- In 1914 Association membership shot up over 50 percent without any organized effort on the part of the USNLTA, prompting the Secretary to set up a new system for record keeping. Eighty new clubs joined, bringing in some fifteen thousand tennis players and over one thousand courts—some with a grass (turf) surface but many more with "dirt."
- President "Champion" Robert Wrenn announced that California had developed a great many younger players, and that the USLTA was setting up "junior sectional tournaments." Play and tournaments on public courts in New York City prompted the Association to promote "every avenue of junior play," since thousands were playing the game "without any *club* affiliations"—an initiative that would reappear periodically during the USTA's history. (Emphasis added—clubs, not individuals were the only unit of membership.)
- The increasing size of the Association complicated the easy, informal system of presidential nominations for officers and the executive committee. Elections became more contested, prompting the 1915 annual meeting to set up a nominating committee elected by the executive committee (thus keeping it all in the family). Calls for the nominating committee to offer two candidates for each officer position failed, as they would in the future. The argument was, then and later, that candidates not elected would be hurt and

upset. Moreover, a contested election would be divisive. Whatever the justifications, single-name nominations became and remained an Association practice. By 1918 a time of increasing uneasiness in the "west" about representation, that "all in the family" approach apparently rang false. That year's annual meeting instructed the executive committee to change the procedures for selecting members of the nominating committee, and in 1919 the constitution was amended to provide for election by the annual meeting. The intent may have been to make the committee more representative, but the reality was that the nominating committee nominated its own successors. It was still "all in the family," as it is to this day.[25]

In 1916 Dwight Davis, then park commissioner in St. Louis, suggested having a championship cup for teams from public city parks throughout the country. In that same spirit the Association changed its constitution to allow public parks to join without dues or vote. As stated in 1917 constitution: "Park Associations shall consist of associations of parks, not more than one association from any one city, and approved by the Park Commissioner," although the bylaws (article 2, section 7) stated that "No player shall be allowed to enter for any match given by the Association [the USNLTA] unless . . . he is the winner of a member Park Association (Class 4) final Championship Tournament, or has played in an Interscholastic Tournament of the same year."[26] That restriction could have been an effort to maintain standards of play, but was likely aimed at closing a back door to large number of parks players displacing "proper" club members.

In 1917 the Association appointed a committee to set up a "National Umpires Association," evidence that growth could challenge the USNLTA's founding purpose—standardization of the rules and their enforcement.[27]

Concern about Association growth generated a number of initiatives. A call at the 1915 annual meeting for "a broad and comprehensive plan" to get juniors playing and improving came from Treasurer Richard Stevens. A year later a committee proposed a series of interscholastic (juniors) and boys' tournaments, each leading to a national championship held in conjunction with the national singles championships. Even for an association composed and led primarily by relatively younger men, the next generation of tennis players was important. Tennis for youngsters would remain a major organizational focus for the Association from then on. It was an easy, natural decision. The structure would be adjusted. Age groups would come. A national championship for girls began in 1918.[28] Sections and local organizations would become deeply and often emotionally involved with "junior" tennis. Whatever the delivery details (which all too often would prove to be a, if not the, major stumbling block), the Association's commitment to younger players remained and deepened, especially in later decades as it slowly came to emphasize tennis for the general public rather than just for the elite—elite players who, in this earlier era, represented the social elite.

A bit less easy and natural was the decision to establish the national office referred to by Dick Kroesen with a "field secretary" and a small staff ("one or two stenographers") located in New York in the president's office. (No one asked what would happen if the Association's president was not from somewhere near New York.) With tennis growing rapidly, the Association was concerned that the president (a volunteer) was not always available to answer inquiries and provide information about rules, regulations, and court construction. A major justification for the new office was that it could do "missionary work" and help "to popularize lawn tennis," particularly with youngsters. According to Richard Stevens (son of the founder of Stevens Institute of Technology in Hoboken, New Jersey), tennis courts were being built in "every new high school" and most recreation centers. Association leaders, as "custodians" of the game, had a new responsibility. Given a treasury surplus (twelve thousand dollars over expenses in 1915, with thirty thousand in conservative investments), they could afford a field office and staff that would cost something between four and eight thousand dollars a year. Stevens admitted that it was "a radical step" but that it seemed "the best way to help tennis is to help men who otherwise could not help themselves, and I think the establishment of a field secretary in a central office would be a big help to that end." After a round of applause, the delegates unanimously authorized the executive committee to make it happen, whereupon one wag asked if "Mr. Stevens contemplated to have that permanent office in Hoboken." He had outlined a gargantuan, even absurdly vast task for one man and a couple of secretaries. But given the eventual role of the Association's executive director—the direct descendant of the first field secretary—creation of that initial staff position was crucial. A tennis court in every high school and recreation facility was wishful thinking, but they were dreams that the Association would repeatedly try to make happen—with mixed results.[29]

If the 1916 annual meeting was a "veritable love feast," in Merrihew's purple prose,[30] the following year's meeting was "stormy." Initially the arguments focused on rules for determining amateur status, but governance lay at the root of the matter. All could agree that "professionalism" was undesirable, although clubs and associations (including the USNLTA) could pay the expenses of players who represented that club or association. But the tones of the discussions got testy over proposals from the Association leadership, predominantly from the Atlantic Seaboard, that would limit clubs from paying the expenses of players they invited to their tournament. Debates over amateurism and allocation of national tournaments continued to reveal the sharp differences between the Northeast and the "West" about both the substance of the proposed rules and the voting strength within an association that had two different membership structures. In the Northeast, each member club was represented by a delegate or by proxy votes given to some other delegate. One club, one vote—the founding governance principle. But those in the west believed that the votes of association members, which comprised the bulk of western membership, were diluted, since they cast their ballots through their association (local, state, regional, or sectional). Their argument was that four-fifths of the nation was in the west, yet they were routinely outvoted by the one-fifth from the Northeast. The northeastern establishment argued that votes should be allocated according to the number of tennis players, not the total population. Nothing came of those arguments in 1917, but that only delayed a confrontation for a couple of years.[31]

Almost from the outset, the west was a force for apparent democracy in tennis. A rigid interpretation of amateurism would limit money for expenses paid by tournaments to the best players to get them to play. As that more and more included the west, westerners lobbied to get the rules relaxed since the cost and hassle of travel to and from the west, particularly the Pacific coast, was daunting. This suggests two things: first, that Californians and other westerners were not of the wealthy leisure class in the same way as northeasterners. (After all, by the turn of the century they were playing tennis on concrete and asphalt courts, not "turf.") Second, it fits neatly with the arguments of various historians, like Frederick Jackson Turner and Walter Prescott Webb, that the democratization of American society came from the West.

Only the two-thirds majority requirement for amending the constitution prevented passage of the proposals for tightening further the definitions of amateurism that so angered western delegates like the president of the Pacific States Section, Sumner Hardy. In libertarian phrases he condemned the amateur status proposals as "undemocratic," changes that would "tend directly to intensify class feeling, caused by the possession of wealth." He rejected the "right of the national association to interfere with . . . a club's making money out of the game," and ended his circular letter with what amounted to a *So there*!: "If any proof were necessary that making money from the game is legitimate," the splitting between the Association and the West Side Club of eighteen thousand dollars earned by the national singles championship "would be conclusive." Gate receipts were brought up time and again: "The question of gate receipts is becoming such a large element that it is thought best to stop or forestall any practice which will allow Clubs to enter in partnership to make money out of the game. . . . As the receipts grew so would the demands of the players grow."[32]

The tension that arose from arguments about amateurism and allocation of national championships culminated in a naked threat from the president and delegate of the Western Section, L. Harry Waidner, to secede from the USNLTA:

> I don't know whether this meeting realizes tonight that they have started something. You have absolutely ignored the Pacific Coast Associations; the Pacific, Northwest, Southwest, the Western and far West. . . . We certainly represent more clubs than have carried the votes here tonight. Now either the East have to organize in sections [i.e., geographic regions] or they have to increase the voting power of the sectional associations, and I will go so far as to say that it will be mighty hard for me when I go back home, to keep the Western associations from seceding from the National Association. The votes you have voted tonight—a few states in the East have voted against four-fifths of the country.
>
> We in the West won't stand for it and you might as well know it now. Then after you had the nerve of taking the sectional doubles away from us, you cut us off from the clay court tournament and kept it in the East. You can keep it in the East if you want to, but we will still have some national tournaments out in our own country.
>
> I am going to move that a committee be appointed to present amendments at the next meeting, with a view of reapportioning the voting power of the country.

When another delegate jeered that he preferred "a man who loses do it gracefully," Waidner quickly retorted that he'd "never been never been accused of being a poor loser yet, and the reason we lost tonight is because the whole apportionment of the voting power is not right."[33]

"Shouldn't we have a committee appointed, as Mr. Waidner suggests, to revise the constitution," suggested one delegate. "In other words, make the opinion more national. Now, are we national? That is the question that arises to my mind." Being national, being the governing body for tennis in the United States, was the reason the Association existed. The implication that the Association did not represent all of tennis in America, was deeply unsettling for the USNLTA leadership.[34]

The Association leadership neither wanted to nor could be authoritarian. It existed for its member clubs and sections, and secession threatened its very purpose. Without any recorded discussion, the delegates authorized creation of an equalization committee, with a mandate to report to the next annual meeting. It is worth noting that Waidner, despite his threat of secession, was still elected to serve on the executive committee. Civility, and perhaps politics, or perhaps the realization that Waidner was right, prevented retaliation.[35]

More Time for Tennis

With war on the horizon and serious issues of governance and amateurism before the delegates, the 1917 annual meeting focused on what, for them, really mattered—an extra hour each day to play tennis. In a move that would have evoked a smile from Benjamin Franklin, the delegates at the 1917 annual meeting endorsed a bill before the U.S. Congress:

> Mr. Garland: Whereas the delegates . . . believe that daylight saving would be of great benefit both physically and morally to the tennis players of the country, be it resolved that the Association hereby formally endorses the movement . . . for daylight saving [time], which is now before Congress. . . . An hour extra in the summer months for tennis players, is something that we all should vote for. (Applause)[36]

Whatever the growing dissent within the Association in 1917 about governance, it did not extend to the far greater national issue of the Great War. The Association had already chosen not to challenge for the Davis Cup (it would be "unsportsmanlike" to take advantage of the war). More important, there was patriotic unanimity. In February 1917, two months before the United States declared war on the German Empire, the USNLTA annual meeting passed a resolution that would, fifty years later during the Vietnam War, have been unthinkable.

> W*hereas*, our country is facing grave international difficulties, and
> Whereas, we, the assembled delegates of the U.S.N.L.T.A. representing directly or indirectly more than a million tennis players throughout the United States,

> be it resolved, That we heartily endorse the action of President Wilson in severing diplomatic relations with the German empire; that we pledge to the president and the Congress of the United States our utmost support in whatever further steps they deem necessary to maintain American rights against lawless aggression, and that to that end we pledge the services of the Association and the national organization absolutely at their disposal. (prolonged applause)

That was followed by eliminating national championship play in favor of "patriotic" tournaments with revenue going to fund Association-sponsored ambulance "sections." The ambulances were over-funded, so beyond a drop in public interest and the 1917 winners being designated the "National Patriotic Tournament" champions, the title change had little impact. But it surely indicated the attitude of the Association leadership. When its president, George Adee, went on active military duty, the Association designated vice president Julian Myrick as "acting president." No need for Adee to resign, they all agreed, since he was assigned to Fort Dix, New Jersey, near New York, in a training capacity. But just in case, Myrick had legal power of attorney.

Only a month before the United States entered the war, the Association's executive committee had voted to support proposals for universal and compulsory military service—ironically, the same conscription that the Puritan and Pietist forefathers of so many of the Association's leaders had condemned as one of the "oppressions" they sought to escape when they came to America. Myrick stated that every man had "the obligation to keep himself physically fit." Without mentioning tennis by name, he insisted that patriotism and common sense made physical fitness "better for the future of our country."[37]

A month after the U.S. Congress declared war on Germany, President Woodrow Wilson offered a wonderfully Victorian-age comment about sports during the war. Asked whether or not such activities should be continued during the conflict, Wilson wrote that it would be a "real contribution to the national defense, for our young men must be made physically fit in order that later they may take the place of those who are now of military age."

At the behest of the 1919 annual meeting, the field secretary of the Association, Paul Williams, wrote and compiled a fascinating history titled the *United States Lawn Tennis Association and the World War*. Published in 1921, it summarized all the ways in which the Association and its members were involved in the war effort. Of the book's 293 pages, only some thirty pertained directly to tennis, including a seven-page chapter titled "Historical Outline of Lawn Tennis," genially lifted from early histories. The bulk of the text consisted of accounts, many first hand, of the Association's successful efforts to fund and recruit (with army and Red Cross cooperation) two ambulance "sections" that served under combat conditions in France. Over half the book consisted of supplements and appendices that included a chronology of the war, statistics on American participation, and a lengthy listing of Association members who served in the armed forces. The "Honor Roll" of two hundred gave the names of those who "paid the supreme sacrifice"; the "Service Roll" had over ten thousand names, including a small number of women (presumably nurses). A blank page with two columns followed—labeled "Honor Roll" and "Service Roll"—"for names omitted because information was unobtainable."[38]

A photograph of the USNLTA president, Major George T. Adee, in field uniform, stood opposite the preface. The caption pointed out that he commanded an infantry battalion during combat in France. But Adee was more than just a symbol of the Association's patriotism. He also signified two important transitions within the Association's leadership.

First of all, he was re-elected president in 1918, because of what Merrihew called "a factional fight over succession." A presidential selection was contested, perhaps not for the first time, but certainly the first time it garnered media attention. Adee, who had tried to resign in 1917 because of his military service, was persuaded to stay on as president in order to avoid a contentious election struggle. With unusual blandness, *ALT* simply reported that Myrick's nomination for vice president generated opposition and that two other candidates were proposed even before the nominating committee made its report. The details are difficult to winkle out, but it appears that candidates from New England, New York, and Philadelphia—all bastions of the establishment—were challenging for the presidency. According to the *New York Times*, Myrick was seen as a representative of the "old guard," while the others were not (leaving unclear just what they did stand for). After the usual "systematic canvass for votes"—both direct and proxy—Myrick came out ahead. No issues made either the minutes or the *ALT* report. Just the vote and Merrihew's somewhat breathless description:

> The critical moment had now arrived. It was amid perfect silence that the Nominating Committee had named for vice-president Julian

> S. Myrick, and everyone waited to see if there was any other name placed before the meeting. There was not.
>
> Myrick extended his hand and Torrey grasped it amid applause. The olive branch had been extended, and the white dove of peace, thus encouraged, appeared, settled down and made himself at home.[39]

A second aspect of Adee's presidency, which began in 1916, signaled a sea change. Of the first seven Association presidents (1881–1915), three (Sears, Slocum, Wrenn) won the national singles championship, while another (James Dwight) was a runner-up. The first president (General Oliver), plus a stand-in for James Dwight when he was in Europe and T. K. Fraser, were active players but not champions. Joseph Clark won a national doubles championship. National champions mattered. They routinely appeared, however briefly, as Association officers and executive committee members; two (Dwight Davis and Holcombe Ward) became president long after their championship playing years had ended. But even before the Great War, ranked players had become more "professional" in their approach to the game, and tennis talent became increasingly less important in the selection of Association leaders. Adee played in a number of nationals but never won the championship. Julian Myrick was a good tennis player, but his name does not appear in the roll of U.S. national champions. The 1920s would be the era of Big Bill Tilden, who won seven national championships and was runner-up three times. His relationship with the national Association was, at best, prickly. The word "champion," used at Association meetings with recognition and respect for past winners, would fall into disuse.

The Great War did expose a large number of military personnel to lawn tennis. The government provided some tennis equipment at camps in the United States and abroad, and the USNLTA supported that effort with contributions. Perhaps more important, it appears (though the evidence is sparse) that lawn-tennis equipment (when provided) was made available to all, not just officers. But Association leaders were concerned that tennis might decline in popularity during the war. Acting president Myrick wrote to member clubs in December 1917 enjoining them to maintain and "intensify the club spirit" so that tennis would be protected and "membership kept up to its usual standard, both as to numbers and personnel."[40]

Perhaps the essence of the Association's attitude was captured by the field secretary, Paul Williams: "The first impulse to discard everything that was not essentially military later gave way to a realization that, after all, only a part of America's hundred million people could be in uniform. . . . but it was soon proven that sport could not be classified as 'non-essential.'"

Patriotism, practicality, and promotion of their game, lawn tennis, were the hallmarks of the Association's response to war. It appointed a representative in France (Bernon Prentice, a Red Cross official stationed in Paris and an unsuccessful nominee for Association treasurer in 1917) to be in touch with USNLTA members in France and to promote their "welfare and comfort." But initially, the war mattered most. Williams helped with a government-sponsored program called the Four Minute Men. The assignment was to speak—for no more than four minutes—at motion-picture theaters on government-prepared themes in support of the war effort. Williams organized the New York area and later commented that it was difficult "to persuade eloquent lawyers and others somewhat inclined to 'spell-bind' that four minutes included only 240 seconds."[41]

At the 1918 annual meeting, patriotic tournaments gave way to the return of national championships, though there were some who continued to believe it unseemly to have a festive tournament when Americans were facing "mutilation, blindness, [and] the great sacrifice itself" on the battlefield. But since the U.S. War Department had indicated support for holding national championships (the Association secretary, Edwin Torrey, had spoken with Newton Baker, the secretary of war), restoration of the nationals received a 155–57 favorable vote. There were lengthy and tedious discussions about changes to the "Laws of Lawn Tennis," with, of course, great attention being paid to continuing the unsuccessful effort to prevent servers from taking anything that resembled a step. Ball-testing methodologies apparently received rapt attention, and the old and unsightly "proxy vote" issue surfaced with Merrihew later revealing in *ALT* that five delegates (two of them brothers) held between them a total of 152 votes—some 75 percent of the total cast at the meeting.[42] It seemed like business as usual.

But the ongoing revolution lurked in the wings. Not all revolutions are loud and violent. Not all are a struggle between vast opposing armies or competing social forces. Sometimes the potential of a revolution is sensed before it happens. So it was in February 1918 at the annual meeting. Acting president Myrick caught a whiff of gunpowder in the air when the Committee on Equalization of Voting Power, created the previous year, reported out its recommendations. The discussion started with a reading of a letter from Harry Waidner summarizing his, and the Western Tennis Association (Section)'s concerns. Myrick collapsed the letter's argument into a few words: "Mr. Waidner's idea is that every section be organized into a sectional association, and that they in turn operate the National

Association. Of course, that would mean the whole reconstruction of the club system here in the East." The committee's report was less radical but still raised major governance questions. In its words: "a tennis club with five or six hundred members had no more say in tennis affairs than a club of twenty-five members." Myrick, surely eager to avoid an argument at a time when his nomination for vice president was being challenged, noted that the membership seemed inclined to avoid contentious issues during the war. He characterized Waidner's statements as "spirited" and noted that Waidner had "handled the system pretty hotly." After some to and fro, mainly with Merrihew, Myrick got the proposal referred back to the committee by agreeing to language that required the committee to report it out to the 1919 annual meeting. The tone is clear—Merrihew feared the proposal would be buried.[43] A bit counterrevolutionary was an amendment to the Association's constitution that called for the executive committee (the Association's key decision-making body) to include "such ex-Presidents of the Association as may be elected from year to year at the annual meeting." Presumably done out of respect for the former national champions who dominated the ranks of past presidents, the motion passed without discussion, and an institution was established. Nomination was required, but that soon became pro forma. Past presidents would play a role in policy formulation until 1973, when the Association displaced the executive committee with a management committee (later a board of directors). The past presidents did not make that cut.[44]

The "equalization" issue did not go away. A year later, the Committee on Equalization of Voting Power, which included Waidner, reported its findings. The very first sentence drew a line in the clay: "The Committee . . . begs to report, after much deliberation and thought, that there is an inequality of voting power in the National Association at the present time and that a change in the voting power must be made in the near future." The report went on to recommend that amendments to the Constitution be drafted and voted upon at the 1920 annual meeting. Though no discussion took place, one delegate (E. C. Conlin, chair of the Umpires Committee) offered a written proposal that called for individual memberships with annual dues of three dollars. Members would receive the Association's official magazine, *American Lawn Tennis*, and voting strength would be set up by states, with one vote for "each one hundred (more or less)" exercised by a delegate from a "State Association" or some similar organization. Conlin argued that this would raise greater revenue for *American Lawn Tennis* and allow it to become a "larger and better periodical." More to the point, the procedure gave "full and equal representation."[45]

A few months later, in August 1919 Myrick and the executive committee addressed the calls for "equalization." Although no one had echoed earlier threats to secede from the national Association, that ghost always lurked in the shadows. The changes Myrick supported seemed, in some ways, revolutionary. In other ways they reverted to the localism that had long characterized the curious combination of populism and conservatism that characterized American politics and society—and the USNLTA. More intriguing, and prophetic, the proposals focused on money. Crudely put, some of the proposed amendments seemed to say that we will give you (the sections) more money if you let us run the Association. What followed was reminiscent of the Great (or Connecticut) Compromise of 1787 that allowed adoption of the United States Constitution—no one was happy with everything; a majority were satisfied; a lasting union became possible.[46]

In 1919 the Association's membership list (in its constitution) began with a twenty-two page listing of direct member clubs. They came from throughout the United States. There were a few exotic names like Havana, Cuba, and Grinnell, Iowa, but the overwhelming majority came from the Northeast—the traditional home of lawn tennis. A listing of "ASSOCIATIONS: Belonging to the United States National Lawn Tennis Association" followed. It was a Mulligan stew of names, place, and categories. Eleven sectional associations—some organized, some obviously not; some clubs within those sectional associations, some not; California seeming to divide itself into northern and southern regions; state associations (Indiana, Texas, etc.); an array of city associations (Cleveland, Chicago, etc.); and various intercollegiate associations. It was, quite clearly, a governance mess—top to bottom, bottom to top.[47]

Up through 1919, dues were not a determinant of voting strength. Each member club had one vote. Dues were ten dollars per club, regardless of how many individual tennis players belonged. Active associations (composed of local clubs) paid thirty-five dollars for up to ten clubs, then fifteen dollars for every five or fraction thereof of additional clubs. Whatever the appeal of being part of an association of clubs (largely related to competition, although there social and cultural reasons), it was also a little less costly. It meant your representation at national Association meetings was not only diluted, but came through your association, not by someone from your club—but there is little to suggest that tennis players at that local level really cared about the national Association and its debates.

There were no voices for maintaining the status quo. The majority, led by Myrick, represented the Northeast, and proposed a "per capita" approach:

"Voting power and dues shall be based upon the number of individuals comprising the bona-fide membership of (1) Clubs and (2) Associations [which could be formal organized sections, or merely some clubs grouped together for competitive or social convenience]. Each (1) Club and (2) Active Association shall be entitled to one vote for each active member in good standing." Whatever the minor technical exceptions, the "per capita" plan appeared to be a concession to full representative democracy—one man, one vote. Membership was still only for clubs and associations, not individuals. But translating individual club memberships into club and association voting strength—close to participatory democracy—was expedient for the Northeast since it had more tennis players and could win votes and elections with numerical strength.

The minority report of Harry Waidner, the delegate from the Western Section who had threatened secession two years earlier, called for each sectional association to have one vote for each club within its boundaries. The rebels had seemed to have become the conservators: "A radical change based upon numerical strength of each club would result adversely to our section." But Waidner went on to offer a battle cry that the sections would later take up: "We believe the entire country would be automatically organized under a Sectional Basis if the Sectional Associations were clothed with full power and authority to regulate, supervize and completely control affairs in their territory, the National Association retaining, of course, its supervision and acting in an advisory capacity as necessary." The "expenses of the National Association were entirely out of proportion to benefits received and results accomplished." His amendments were "drafted with the idea of permitting the sectional associations to retain a larger proportion of their income from dues rather than increasing voting power."

With five members of the Equalization Committee favoring the per capita plan, and Waidner giving his "quasi-approval" while indicating he would subsequently propose ways of "enlarging the authority of Sectional Associations," the amendments went to the annual meeting. The disorganized nature of many sections caused concern and provided leverage to those proposing the "per capita" voting plan. One member accurately pointed out that sections were formed primarily "as a means to be represented in the National Doubles," not "with any idea of dividing power."[48] But approval was a done deal, and the "per capita" voting system became the rule.

The "counter-revolutionary" 1920 constitution had the appearance of being more inclined toward participatory democracy—approaching one man, one vote. But the reality was that it would preserve control of the

Association for the northeastern clubs. Voting membership was for clubs and sectional associations.[49] The active (organized) twelve sections were listed, then voting power and dues were tied together for the first time. Voting power and dues of clubs was determined by a schedule:

> 100 individual members or less, $10, 100 votes
> 101 to 125, $12.50, 125 votes

"then in regular increments of $2.50 more in dues 25 additional votes, for each segment of 25 members or less."[50]

The key provision called for all clubs to obtain membership through local or district associations, which then had membership in the appropriate geographic section. In short—clubs had to belong to their sectional association. More important for the future, local associations paid 50 percent of their dues to their section, and the sections paid 50 percent of those dues to the national Association, locking the sections into the governance structure.[51]

Once again, the northeastern clubs had won out over the rest (and the "west"), although the new system left room for the westward movement of the U.S. population to create changes in governance. At some levels, the delay proved remarkably effective and long lasting. Waidner's and Myrick's predictions came true—the Northeast would be "reconstructed" into sectional associations. Yet the first president of the national Association from west of the Mississippi did not come until 1958 when Victor Denny of Seattle begin a two-year stint.

As the Association moved into the 1920s, it could boast financial stability and steady growth of club memberships. A snapshot taken from statistics presented at the executive-committee meeting of December 1921 illustrates the point. Expenses totaled $29,200, of which a little over half was for the salary and expenses of the field secretary, Paul Williams. Davis Cup costs came to some $6,600, and the remainder went to various administrative costs, including the intriguing figure of $7 for the National Umpires Association. Revenue of $46,400 came primarily from Davis Cup matches ($19,000), and the men's national singles championship, which pulled in $14,300. The women's nationals garnered $5,200. Club, association, and intercollegiate dues brought in only $3855. In round numbers, revenue exceeded expenses by some $17,000.

The Association was growing. As the secretary reported in 1921:

> If you are not already aware of it, the fact should be made clear that the Association continues to show a healthy growth, which

> to some extent reflects the development of tennis throughout the country. I think it true that tennis in general grows more rapidly than would be shown by the addition of the new members to the U.S.L.T.A. It is apparent, for instance, that there must be a considerable increase in play before the formation of new clubs is warranted, and usually these are in existence for some time, before taking membership in this body. In 1918 the Association through its direct and affiliated membership had about 425 clubs. It now has 559 members. Fifteen new clubs were elected in 1921 and four additional applications are to be considered at this meeting. There were 12 resignations. This represents a larger net increase than in 1920.

A report of a special committee tasked to evaluate the awarding of national championships and Davis Cup matches, anticipated the search for purpose that the USTA finally agreed upon seventy-five years later in the mid 1990s, when it proclaimed a "new" mission statement—*to promote and develop the growth of tennis.* The 1921 committee, composed of former president George Adee (chair), Joseph Jennings, and George Wightman, noted that "the Constitution of the U.S.L.T.A. contains no provision stating what the purpose of the Association is. We venture the opinion that such a purpose clause would read as follows: "To 'foster and maintain lawn tennis in the United States.'" In short, to develop tennis. Stimulating interest in the game was key, and the best means was "the successful tournament" that created spectator and player enthusiasm, "all of which is reflected in the public press." The ingredients for success?—the best players available, a large and enthusiastic audience, adequate facilities, and good management.[52]

Mentioning Davis Cup leads to a compelling segue. According to the Black Tennis Hall of Fame website, in 1921 Dwight Davis, then vice president of the USLTA, served as an umpire at the American Tennis Association (ATA) national semifinals. There is no background information about how that came about, but it raises some intriguing questions about Davis's motives.[53]

Missing from this history of the United States (National) Lawn Tennis Association up through 1922 is any mention of black Americans, who composed some 10 percent of the nation's population. Although black Americans played tennis almost as soon as the game came to the United States—Tuskegee Institute, an all-black college, began holding tournaments in the mid 1890s—any discussion of black Americans and the USNLTA in this early era belongs in a box—for that's where African Americans were, within American society and within the tennis world. Arthur Ashe missed the point when he suggested that black Americans were excluded from the USLTA because "tennis was clearly associated with the upper-socio-economic classes." Race and color mattered, regardless of socio-economic class. The ATA had been formed in 1916 when over a dozen representatives from tennis clubs for blacks met in Washington to form their own tennis organization. In the words of the ATA website: "several black leaders were determined to cultivate an appreciation for 'the gentlemen's game' among people of color." Among the founders were three men who held the title of "Doctor," obvious representatives of an upper socio-economic class—of blacks. Yet they and their clubs could not join the USNLTA.[54]

Association records before the Second World War provide little evidence of how black Americans were treated, or even thought of. Formation of the ATA prompted no discussions or even a mention in the executive committee or annual meeting minutes. No one spoke for bringing young black athletes into national or Davis Cup competition, even though that might have enhanced chances of winning. Race was more important. Despite African American tennis players on teams at a number of Ivy League colleges, the executive committee voted unanimously in February 1922, not to admit Howard University, a traditionally black college, as a member club (see box), then quickly took up the apparently far more pressing matter of distribution of the "Honor Roll" book (presumably Paul Williams's history of the USNLTA in the Great War), which had sold very few copies—the publisher had gone bankrupt with seven hundred copies on hand and would sell them for next to nothing.[55]

A few months later, during a discussion about allowing industrial leagues to be "allied" (non-voting, non-dues paying) members, someone asked what would happen if an industrial league had a very fine "negro" tennis player who applied for entry into the Association's national championship? The immediate response: "He would not be accepted." The matter was referred to committee. Then, in September 1923, after then president Davis merely read a question about the matter, George Wightman moved that the question be taken off the table (not discussed). The motion carried without comment and the subject was buried.[56]

American tennis players and teams competed against blacks and others of color played on foreign teams, but not in the United States. For example, in 1924 just two years after the Howard University decision, a U.S. team played a Jamaican Lawn Tennis Association team that included B.

M. Clark, a black player with "brilliant ground shots." The match was, of course, played in Jamaica, far from the land of Jim Crow laws.[57]

Membership for Howard

MYRICK: We have a request from Howard University for membership in the U.S.L.T.A. This is a negro university down in Washington.

R. N. WILLIAMS: I move that they be asked to join the America Tennis Association which is a negro organization.

STEWART: We had this thing come up in Chicago. A colored club with very good courts applied for membership in the Western Association. The application was received and we sent somebody out to look over the grounds and situation, and it seemed to be in what we term the "Negro Belt." We asked one of their members to appear. We told him we would take it up and report to him later. We decided in view of the fact that they would be able to enter any tournament in the country that their application should be turned down. They had a perfect right to enter the Public Park Tennis Association. We cancelled two tickets they bought to go to our Annual banquet.

MYRICK: Why not do as Mr. Williams suggested? Tell them they probably should have written to the American Lawn [*sic*] Tennis Association.

LEECH: Could we possibly refer it to the Membership Committee and let an indefinite period pass?

P. B. WILLIAMS: So far as the American Tennis Association is concerned, the secretary of that organization came into the office and he asked me what the attitude of this association would be if they applied for membership. I told him I would never make application. I told him southern clubs would "see red" on that. I told him there would be no chance in the world of a club of negros [*sic*] getting membership in the Association.

STEWART: I move that their application be refused.

Carried.

"It was suggested that a letter be sent to the various sectional associations advising them of the action of this Association and saying that this establishes the policy of the Association toward a club of this kind.

Carried.[58]

Of the speakers at that unhappy meeting in 1922, Norris "Dick" Williams was a Swiss-born U.S. national singles champion (1914, 1916), a survivor of the *Titanic* sinking and a Philadelphia resident; Carleton Y. Smith was a Southern Section champion from Atlanta; J. C. Stewart was from Chicago; A. Y. Leech was from Washington DC. All were young, active players. The dialogue in the executive committee minutes makes evident that they felt uneasy about their decision. Searching for a scapegoat, they blamed it on the "southern clubs." The patriotic posturing that had characterized the Association's conduct during the First World War contrasts jarringly with Jim Crow laws, lynchings sanctioned or at least ignored by law enforcement, the Chicago race riots (arguably the worst in U.S. history), and hypocrisy.[59]

Which brings us back to Dwight Davis officiating at the 1921 ATA national championships. Why would a man who would become USLTA vice president the following year, and then president; a man who would in 1924 be appointed assistant secretary of war and then secretary of war by President Calvin Coolidge; a man whose political base was St. Louis, Missouri, a racially divided city; why would this distinguished businessman get involved with an all-black tennis association? Davis did not become USLTA vice president and thus member of the executive committee until after that committee's decision not to admit Howard University. Nor was Davis present at the annual meeting in February 1922 that elected him association vice president. Nothing in the record suggests that he opposed or supported the decision not to admit Howard University, though he was present when the executive committee assumed that no "negro" could enter the national championships. A logical speculation would be that the ATA asked him to officiate, and Davis accepted—perhaps with St. Louis voters in mind. It is possible that the Black Tennis Hall of Fame website is incorrect. But the Association's attitude was clear. A punch line from a quite unfunny joke told publicly at the 1922 annual meeting offers the clearest expression of the attitude of Association members toward blacks: "A little nigger newsboy who happened to be standing around said, 'Mrs., he ain't no doctor; he is a collector of internal revenue, and he can get money out of anybody.' (Laughter)."[60]

Exclusion of "colored" players continued until shortly after the Second World War, despite occasional public protests. In 1929, the National Association for the Advancement of Colored People (NAACP) complained about the exclusion of black players from the national championships for juniors being played in New York City. The USLTA's executive secretary rejected the request, blandly accepting de facto segregation: "In pursuing this policy, we make no reflection upon the colored race, but we believe as a practical matter, the present method of separate associations for the administration of the affairs and championships of colored and white players should be continued."[61]

The USLTA could not change segregation, even if it had wanted to—though it could have offered some small challenges. It was stuck in the box, whatever the efforts of Merrihew and *ALT* to remind them and other Americans that there were talented athletes playing tennis who could not join USLTA member clubs. Despite discrimination in the tennis world (largely based on race, though private clubs routinely discriminated against Jews and other ethnic groups), the pages of *American Lawn Tennis* routinely carried reports of ATA championships throughout the twenties and thirties, with photographs and reporting. That was the doing of Merrihew, not the Association. It was he who in 1923 caught the beauty and promise of sports in an era when racial, social, and gender prejudice were routine and unchallenged:

> Lawn tennis can be played indoors as well as out, and under artificial light as well as under the glare of the sun. It rises superior to race, or rather it attracts every race of people; and their games are along lines that harmonize with racial characteristics. Once the sport of two or three white races, whose members went on the court clothed in rigorously conventional apparel—flannels and other garments to match—we now see players brown, yellow and even black, garbed in every degree of picturesqueness and simplicity; we have even heard of courts where a breech cloth is the sole article of attire. In short, in our present-day game of lawn tennis clothes do not necessarily make the man, or woman.[62]

The Association entered the 1920s with a slightly shortened name, a decision that, if nothing else, made life easier for newspapers and book publishers. Many will vaguely recall that the Association dropped "Lawn" from its official name some time after the Second World War. That was, in fact, done in 1975, and then only after a number of tries. But few recall that, from the USTA's founding in 1881 until 1920, its official name was the United States *National* Lawn Tennis Association. It was adamant about maintaining recognition as the "national" arbiter of tennis, for that was the very reason behind its formation—to establish standardized, national rules.

Cutting the "Lawn" (out) would be done later as a conscious effort to get away from the elitist, country club image that reflected the Association's original makeup. But dropping "National" came for more mundane reasons. United States National Lawn Tennis Association was simply too long and cumbersome. Even the abbreviation, USNLTA, was a letter too far.

Some took the opposite tack, arguing that "National" was a key aspect of the Association while "Lawn" was superfluous. A few delegates even suggested dropping "United States," but that proposal gained no traction. (Perhaps they wondered if calling it *The* National Lawn Tennis Association would have prompted an arched eyebrow from the English who assumed exclusive rights to such imperiousness. Everyone who mattered knew that "The" in front of almost any organization's name—as in *The* Historical Society—meant it was British, with the words British or English redundant.)

S. Wallis Merrihew, editor of the Association's official "organ," *American Lawn Tennis*, brought both grammar and history into play. He had written in his magazine that "United States" and "National" mean the same thing. Speaking to the 1920 annual meeting, he predicted that taking "lawn" out of the title would probably happen, but the time was not right. He pointed out that "the game we play is not tennis at all" but rather lawn tennis, "a much younger game," one that is "entirely separate and distinct" (thanks to the rules drawn up by Major Wingfield) from older games—alluding to "court" and "real" tennis. But it was time to remove "National" from the title page. The delegates agreed and the word was taken out, though it remained in the official short name for the Association, as in "National Association."[63]

There were other loose ends to tie up. The politics of ILTF membership came up in 1922 following a default by England in the Davis Cup competition, something that other nations criticized. The record is vague, though news reports indicated it related to British insistence that only winners of the Wimbledon tournament were "world's champions." Somehow, that event seemed to smooth the path for U.S. membership in the ILTF. The executive-committee minutes for September 1922 note that the French were "most anxious to have the United States in the Federation." Details aside, the British backed down on their claim that Wimbledon constituted the world championship in tennis, and the USLTA voted to join the Federation. The All England Club's reaction is not recorded. Whatever the internal politics of the ILTF, Merrihew was right when he pointed out that something many regarded as a dream had become a reality—"lawn tennis will be played in the same manner all over the world." Somewhere, James Dwight was smiling.[64]

Changes in governance did not solve the issue of amateurism, one that would preoccupy, even obsess the Association's leadership for the next four decades. They could not square the circle. Definitions of amateur status that would avoid the inevitable descent into "crass commercialism," would at the same time cripple the ability of the Association to foster growth—which in their terms meant more and better competitors. Talent required development of skills, and that took playing regularly against the best players—something champions have endorsed consistently throughout the history of American tennis.[65] To get the best players together meant bringing east to west, and everywhere in between. Winning the Davis Cup demanded the best talent, and winning was what Association leaders were there for. The much-touted growth program for juniors was justified as the way to develop the best players, not as the way to develop a recreational sport for the masses. Despite the efforts of Dwight Davis and others to generate public play in city parks, winning championships—sectional, national, and international (Davis Cup)—remained paramount.

Big Bill (William T.) Tilden won the first of his seven national singles titles in 1920. Added to finishing runner-up three times and his five national doubles championships, three wins at Wimbledon, and an extraordinary Davis Cup record that included a run of thirteen straight singles wins, he dominated men's tennis in the twenties.

That star status presented the Association with intractable challenges. Member clubs that sponsored tournaments wanted, nay insisted, that Tilden be allowed to enter. Tilden himself, a frustrated actor and theater buff who poured his family assets into the theater, tried to use his fame to make fortune—or at least to make money from writing about tennis.[66] But making money from tennis, even just writing about it, violated the amateur rules. The USLTA was betwixt and between. It wanted, even needed, Tilden to play in its tournaments. He generated gate receipts and media interest; he won national and international titles. He, and others like him, generated the money that the USLTA was coming to depend upon. Nevertheless, Association leaders were committed to maintaining the sanctity of "pure" amateurism. A report written in 1921 asserted that "gate receipts as such are not an end in themselves."[67] Easy to say.

4

THE MONEY

The Twenties and Thirties

> "The game is the thing and deuce take the profits."
> ROBERT HYSON, April 20, 1937

The Tilden wars dominated media coverage of tennis and preoccupied the USLTA in the 1920s, but they illustrated rather than shaped the Association's development. Commercialization of the game of lawn tennis had begun well before Bill Tilden challenged the amateur rules. Tournaments cost money to host, and clubs charged players entry fees and spectator admission fees to offset expenses—balls, prizes, refreshments, etc. That revenue stream also offered a way to pay for club improvements, making the club more attractive for both tournament players and members. A self-reinforcing process inevitably developed. Spectators were attracted by the chance to watch the best players. The best players were attracted by the quality of competition and also by the appeal of the facility, by the grandness of the (nonmonetary) prizes, and by the prestige of this or that championship. But as time went on, with the best players found from California to Boston and everyplace in between, expenses paid for travel and accommodations became a key to getting players who would attract paying customers; and expense money was wide open to abuses. As one teaching pro quipped in 1926, if he had understood how much he could make in amateur tennis, he would not have become a professional.[1] Even the Association was caught in the bind. The national championships (which routinely referred just to men's singles) did not have to resort to expansive expense payments to attract players, but clubs with great champions as members found it expedient to pay their expenses—and then some. Loyalty perhaps, to a member and friend, but also a way to ensure that those of their players that fans would pay to see did not join a more forthcoming club. Thus the Association found itself trying to cope with its own member clubs in order to enforce the USLTA's rules about amateurism.[2]

Early defenses of amateurism had emphasized that lawn tennis was a gentleman's game, not a means of earning a living. Competitors played for the joy of competition, not money. Early national champions complained that playing tennis as a full-time occupation would give challengers an unfair advantage (even though many of the "gentlemen" did little else but play the game). But as the growth of the tennis changed the Association's governance structure and class identity, it brought increasing numbers of less-wealthy players to the courts. Programs like Dwight Davis's public-parks tennis were part of that process.

Ironically, the growing "professionalism" of tennis was paralleled by the Association's own leadership. "Professional" managers and administrators like Julian Myrick (a successful insurance broker who was acting and elected president for five years) began to displace the former champions and high-quality tennis players who had led the Association since its inception. After 1919 and through to the present, only two former national champions became president of the Association: Dwight Davis (doubles) and Holcombe Ward, who won the national singles title in 1904 and who was the last such champion to become president. Ward held office for eleven years (1937–1947), in good measure because of the Second World War, and because he had been an immovable opponent of any compromise on amateur rules. He illustrated one of Bill Tilden's long-term effects, which was to build up intense antipathy and stubbornness among Association leaders in the wake of the media mocking the USLTA's arguments. In any event, Ward's presidency illustrated a major change in the demographics of the Association's leadership. When Ward was elected, he was about to become sixty years old, a far cry from the tennis-playing young men who created and ran the Association for nearly four decades.[3] (See gallery, image 15.)

In one sense, Tilden should have been the perfect USLTA leader. He was, in the words of his biographer, "a Philadelphia patrician of intellectual pretension," which fit the mold.[4] He was smart, though by all accounts he was self-centered and argumentative to the point of being obnoxious—witness his performances at Association meetings where he challenged his ranking or was "on trial" for violations of amateur rules. Yet, despite Tilden's six straight national singles championships, he never received consideration for a leadership position. He was everything an Association president was not supposed to be. He was a professional player (unofficially), he was a showman, he exhibited no interest in the Association's business (except when he was accused of violating amateur rules), and he was a homosexual (although that goes unmentioned in the contemporary USLTA records). There is great irony in the fact that a gay man changed the public image of men's tennis from an "effete" and "sissy" sport to one of power and strength.[5]

But, the Association's battle with him went beyond just a clash of personalities, or even disagreement about the "principle" of amateurism. Change was the issue. The amateurism that Tilden challenged was more than just the sullying effect of "crass commercialism"—making money off of tennis skills. Tilden stood for a fixation on tennis, a professionalism beyond money (however important the money was to him) that frightened what had become the old guard. Bill Tilden epitomized the changing dynamics of American tennis and the USLTA.

His war with the USLTA is an oft-told story. Sportswriter and author Frank Deford took it biographically, within the context of Tilden's personality. Tennis historian Arthur Voss described the conflict in a traditional narrative style within the context of tennis in the 1920s. Both came to the same conclusions. Tilden was a royal pain in the neck. USLTA leaders had a very deep and sincere commitment to a narrow, blinkered concept of amateurism that guaranteed they would look silly and hypocritical. That, added to the very obvious personal animus toward Tilden, made the Association look like a bunch of petty, stubborn, old stuffed shirts. After all, Tilden was a popular hero.

He had been a thorn in the Association's side almost from the outset of his success on the court. He won his first national championship in 1920, having been runner-up the two previous years. In 1922 he was associated with a fund-raiser exhibition tournament for "Devastated France," a cause the USLTA had supported. Whatever the unconnected details of Tilden's financial connection with a Bancroft tennis catalogue, he had put the Association between a rock and a hard place. A subcommittee determined that the matches did not violate amateur status rules, but Julian Myrick, clearly a hard-liner on amateur issues that concerned Tilden, referred that decision to another subcommittee that he would later appoint.

Throughout the 1920s, Tilden nickeled and dimed the tennis world, and the Association, with an endless array of schemes to get more than just expenses for playing tennis before adoring, enthusiastic galleries. He routinely insisted on traveling first-class. Trips to Canada, the Caribbean, Europe—everywhere, drove the USLTA to distraction. Clubs (that is, promoters) insisted on Big Bill being in the draw. The details are tedious, as Association leaders squirmed to find ways to preserve their vision and version of amateurism without losing Tilden for Davis Cup, the nationals, or other major tournaments. At every meeting of the executive committee in this era, it was Tilden did this, Tilden did that. His footprint is everywhere. His decades of fighting the USLTA are well chronicled.[6] But what about the effect of those battles on the Association itself?

Open warfare broke out in 1924, after the Association adopted a rule prohibiting players to write for pay about tennis, particularly about tournaments in which they were playing. Tilden claimed he had been a writer before he was a famous tennis player and challenged the Association's rule. When Ward, chair of the amateur rules committee, labeled Tilden a "bad influence," the tennis champion took public umbrage and resigned from Davis Cup competition since he was an "evil influence in the game." Association leaders were obviously distressed. Whatever the details, which decided nothing, the remarkable aspect is that Tilden had the support of the sections. In George Wightman's words: "We are in a situation where the Tennis Clubs don't trust us; they don't believe in us; they don't respect our judgment." Wightman staunchly supported the player-writer rule but warned that a vote on strict interpretation of the rule would lose by a wide margin. He offered no reason why the sections would so resoundingly repudiate their national leadership, but the answer is evident: the great stars of lawn tennis were what drew fans and supporters (sponsors would come later) and thus paid the bills for tournament costs, for ever-nicer prizes, and for the clubs' own operations.[7]

An early casualty of the Tilden wars was S. W. Merrihew and *American Lawn Tennis*. In 1924 the Association discontinued Merrihew's contract to publish *ALT* as the USLTA's "official organ." The ostensible reason was that the magazine had limited circulation and that the Association could get wider distribution at less cost by publishing its own "official" magazine. No hard figures were offered. No bottom line was given.

But the strong, obvious undercurrent was that Merrihew did not reflect "official" Association positions in the magazine. Merrihew had sided with those who believed the new amateur rules were impractical and unfair, particularly the prohibition against players writing about tennis for money—a prohibition aimed directly at Bill Tilden. Those who argued for ending the relationship with *ALT*, particularly Myrick and Ward, were the ones most adamantly opposed to any compromise on the amateur controversy. Back in 1916 the executive committee had required "proper supervision" for *ALT*, but that had not worked. Myrick, by 1924 a past president, disingenuously claimed that discontinuing "official organ" status for *ALT* had "nothing to do with being against Merrihew." Myrick accepted "that Mr. Merrihew has done a great deal for tennis," adding nastily "but I think he has made a comfortable living out of it." Rather the problem was that "for a great many years the Association has been without an official organ." Myrick and prior presidents had argued with Merrihew about articles that were not "compatible with the ideas of the executives of the Association." Merrihew's response had been, "It is my magazine. It is not an official organ." When someone suggested it be taken up at the annual meeting scheduled for later that day, Myrick quickly intervened with a brusque "This is an executive matter."[8]

A few argued from practicality: "we could not publish a magazine that would compete with *American Lawn Tennis* or that anybody would pay us money for during the next three years. . . . I think *American Lawn Tennis* is a darned good paper. I think it fills the need or the demand for a tennis paper." But to no avail. The prediction that an Association publication would not be successful proved on the mark. In 1929 the Association's *Official Bulletin* cost over $26,500 against revenue of $10,500 and apparently died a quiet death from lack of subscribers.[9]

Other than some momentary embarrassment when someone on the executive committee leaked news of the decision to Merrihew before he received formal notice, the deed was done. Within a few weeks, the Association had begun its still on-going search for an effective communications vehicle that faithfully reflected "the ideas of the executives of the Association" and, at the same time, was popular with the rest of the tennis world. As an article in *American Lawn Tennis* (probably written by Merrihew) put it a few years later: "how galling it must be to an editor to know that he is comitted [*sic*] to the support of every policy and act of a governing body, as well as to being 'neutral' during any discussion of policy."[10] Both Merrihew and the magazine survived for almost thirty more years, and *American Lawn Tennis* remained what it had always been, a staunch advocate of tennis and a gentle and informed critic of the USLTA.[11]

The player-writer dispute brought on the special committee of seven, and the next chapter in the saga. Tilden managed to make the USLTA an object of ridicule. Merrihew's disaffection was only the start. Newspaper reporters and magazine writers consistently, if gently, depicted the Association as behind the times, as unrealistic. The fundamental issue was that top tennis players earned a good deal of money, but that money went to clubs and the Association, not to the players. Even indirect revenue for things like endorsements of tennis products or writing articles about play at tournaments was deemed a violation of amateur status. Paying expenses for tournament players created a huge loophole as clubs and promoters sought to benefit. In the words of one sectional president: "expense accounts . . . have grown to such proportions that many players are living off the game."[12]

At the same time, true professionalism reared its (ugly, to the Association) head. On August 2, 1926, promoter C. C. (cash and carry) Pyle, announced that he had signed Suzanne Lenglen to a professional contract. Though he mentioned no amount, a New York newspaper headline read: "Suzanne Lenglen Becomes a Professional; Is Coming Here Next Month for $200,000 Tour."[13] It was a spectacular coup.

The French champion was both a court and a media star. In the words of one tennis writer, "Suzanne Lenglen drank, swore and had lovers by the score—and played tennis incomparably, losing once in seven years."[14] Promoters, clubs, and national tennis associations loved her, for like Tilden she earned them large sums of money. Tilden claimed to have turned down an offer from Pyle, but two months later, Pyle announced that he had signed "the greatest male tennis player in the world," Vinnie Richards. Richards had just earned a ranking as the top American male player, displacing Tilden who had held that ranking for the previous six years. The two national associations, the French Tennis Federation and the USLTA, ignored how much Lenglen and Tilden had earned for the associations and local tennis clubs, and took away their ranking. Wimbledon took away Lenglen's honorary membership, yet the Nice (France) Tennis Club refused to cancel her membership. Loyalty to a member and friend perhaps, but also likely a statement about her value to the club.[15] (See gallery, image 11.)

Lenglen toured throughout the United States, even traveling to Havana, Cuba. Her North American career ended with the tour in February 1927, but the money (one estimate was $100,000) she made remained as a warning to the USLTA and as a beacon to other tennis stars who thought their dedication to the game and hard work deserved more than just a pat on the back. A highly ranked Californian named Mary Browne, who turned pro to become Lenglen's regular foil on the tour, perceptively predicted that professional tennis "will eliminate commercialism from amateur tennis and end the bickering" that went on within the USLTA. The new fans, she said, would be "the masses rather than the classes."[16]

The finale of Tilden versus the USLTA came with the 1928 Davis Cup competition in Europe. Once again Tilden confronted the Association solons about writing for pay about tennis tournaments he played in. The records of the joint meeting of the executive, Davis Cup, and amateur rules committees on July 17, 1928, contain fifty pages of discussion about Tilden's violation of the "tennis writing" rule! They likened themselves to doing the work of a "grand jury"—that is, bringing in an indictment, for there was little doubt of Tilden's violations. But with the Association president, Samuel Collom, and the Davis Cup committee chair, Joseph Wear, on their way to Europe, that decision could create problems. As ever, Myrick cut to the chase, saying he wanted to "tie the hands" of the president and Wear once the joint committee voted to remove Tilden from the Davis Cup team as both captain and player. As the "boss" put it, "for God's sake let's make the attack and say we don't propose to stand for this kind of behavior any longer."[17]

Tilden's suspension prevented him from playing in the first Davis Cup match in Italy, but the American team won without him and moved on to the challenge match against France, the 1927 winner. As the USLTA put it in the first edition of its official 1972 encyclopedia: "It was unfortunate that the team did not lose to Italy, and then the whole matter would never have arisen."[18]

"The matter" was the reaction of the French to the decision of the special committee, a decision that caught Collom and Wear unawares. The French Federation, with a new stadium (Stade Roland Garros) to pay for, was concerned about the effect of Tilden's absence on attendance. French players spoke of refusing to play unless they could compete against the best American. The press, solidly on their fellow-reporter's side, added fuel to the fire. Wear, insulted and angry, resigned as chair of the Davis Cup committee, telling those in New York that their action "is incomprehensible to competing nations and makes us ridiculous in their eyes. The lack of consideration shown for Collom and myself is beyond understanding." From Paris, Collom spent $1,950 to talk by telephone to Myrick and other "ringleaders," who stuck to their guns. Then the diplomats intervened. The French protested through their ambassador in Washington as well as to the American ambassador to France, Myron Herrick. Rumor had it that even President Calvin Coolidge raised questions about the USLTA's action; certainly the State Department made an appeal to lift the ban.

Presidents: United States and USTA

Two USTA presidents, Robert Oliver and Dwight Davis, served as assistant secretary of war. (Neither started a war, either internationally or within the USLTA.) Oliver held office during the administrations of both Teddy Roosevelt and W. H. Taft (1903–1913). Davis served Presidents Warren Harding and Calvin Coolidge from 1923 to 1929. The 1920s saw a return of the close relationship between the White House and the Association, although Roosevelt's "tennis cabinet" was not resuscitated. A steady array of cover photos in *American Lawn Tennis* showed Washington big shots (politicians, not guys with great forehands) with Association leaders—always including Davis. Harding and Coolidge, as well as Secretary of State Frank Kellogg appeared, none dressed in tennis togs, as Teddy Roosevelt had cautioned against. Since Davis served in the administrations of those presidents, becoming secretary of war and ending up as a very creditable governor-general of the Philippines for President Herbert Hoover (after flirting with a run for the Republican presidential nomination in 1928), the connection between official Washington and the USLTA in the 1920s obviously ran through Davis.

It is hard to find any substantive advantage for either the Association or for American tennis in that chumminess, nice as it was for the USLTA leadership to rub elbows with the movers and shakers of the nation's capital. Still, it likely helped build the impression that the Association was, informally, the "governing body" of tennis in the United States.[19]

Eventually the pressure convinced Collom to reinstate Tilden, but just for that event. Myrick and the executive committee wanted Wear to withdraw his resignation, then endorsed Collom's decision to put Tilden back on the Davis Cup team. An embarrassed George Wightman, elected to the executive committee as a former president, resigned, upsetting members. He gave no reason, but an interview in a Boston newspaper made it clear that it was because of the Tilden fracas—Wightman thought the Association made a mistake in reinstating Tilden.[20]

The entire affair made the Association look, and feel, foolish. The French retained the Davis Cup. 4–1, with Tilden's victory at first singles the only American point. In early August, after Tilden returned to the United States, the Association put him on "trial" (the USLTA's word). They could not "bring in the guilty party" since Tilden refused to attend, labeling the word "trial" as "very amusing," and choosing instead to present a monologue at a Boston theater. The French Davis Cup team sat in the audience. The six-month suspension that followed was lifted in 1929 at which point the affair sunk to low comedy. In February, "Peace and Progress" was the announced theme of the 1929 annual meeting and even Merrihew warned against repeating "the happenings at Paris last summer." Within a month, the USLTA began an advertising campaign announcing that Tilden would be writing on tennis exclusively for the Association's official publication.[21]

Tilden's motives in challenging the Association were hardly principled, although becoming a professional seemed distasteful to him. He lied, cheated, and acted as if he were above the rules. But he also challenged the USLTA's control of the players as no one else would for decades. Big Bill may have turned down Pyle's offer of $50,000 for a year-long tour, but realizing he could not win the Davis Cup alone (the best American players, Vinnie Richards and Ellsworth Vines, had turned professional), and facing continued squabbling with the USLTA, he joined the pro circuit in 1931.[22]

In 1933, too late to influence the player-writer argument, Merrihew found a powerful quote to back his position. Even as the Tilden wars were fading into history, he dug out a to-the-point pronouncement from the late "founding father," James Dwight: "I suppose that all newspapers prefer to have a reporter understand the games or games that he reports. I see no reason why he should be disqualified on that account. . . . it does not seem to me an honest interpretation of the [amateur] rule." But quoting from scripture rarely convinces the convinced.[23]

The Tilden wars served to illustrate the tensions created in the 1920s by the growing professionalism in lawn tennis. Champions had to make an overwhelming commitment to play the game year-round, whether for pay or not. An increasing fan base and media interest, plus larger facilities and stadiums combined to bring the game to a different level and to a different audience. By the end of the decade the Association was led by experienced business managers rather than wealthy dilettantes. Money had long been the indispensable tool for individual success, but revenue had become the indispensable tool for organizational success. That all threatened the ideal of amateurism.

Perhaps the most devastating attacks on the USLTA and amateurism during the twenties came from three magazine articles. In October 1924 the *Atlantic Monthly* printed a piece by Merrihew. After an awkward discussion of amateurism, he managed in a few quick phrases to capture the essence of the argument: Tilden's "receipts come from writing, not from play, and they are a measure not of his tennis skill but of his literary skill and industry." He derided the notion that "all profits from the sport violate amateurism" by pointing to "other tennis players actively interested in the manufacture of tennis equipment."

Then, in early 1927 the *North American Review* published a biting attack by sportswriter Fred Hawthorne, "Commercialization of Tennis." His romantic image of earlier lawn tennis players competing with enjoyment and skill contrasted starkly with the picture he drew of "tennis machines" with "faces set in grim lines" who followed "the circuits" for eight to ten months a year. People like C. C. Pyle had "turned amateur tennis upside down." Presciently he concluded that whether or not the professionals could make enough money to stay around probably depended on creating an "open" championship that put the very best amateurs on court against the very best professionals—something he saw as an exciting competition.

But the winning entry in the essay contest was the 1929 assault on "The Lawn Tennis Industry" by John Tunis. He went over the top by attacking Julian Myrick with a vengeance, arguing stridently that "Tzar" Myrick benefitted financially from his volunteer leadership of the USLTA with the extensive publicity, the photographs, the press releases, all contributing to his success as an insurance agent. But Tunis's main argument was against "Shamateurs"—players who spent the bulk of their time traveling all over the world to play tennis, with their tennis associations footing the bills. He concluded by accurately pointing out that the larger clubs throughout the United States depended on revenue from tournaments and tournaments that drew paying customers had to offer the best players.

Like Merrihew and Hawthorne, Tunis cast a roseate hue over images from the past, with dedicated happy amateurs playing tennis for fun and fitness. But the need to attract paying customers had changed all that. Certainly that was true for the USLTA and the West Side Tennis Club (WSTC) with its sizeable stadium mortgage. Evoking a powerful image, Tunis recalled, "I shall never forget the look upon René Lacoste's face after his victory . . . last fall at Forest Hills, when after the last point he was greeted by an avalanche of cushions from above. Lawn tennis has been democratized; but the gain is not without some slight loss."[24]

Assessing the effect on the USLTA of such broadsides is difficult. Merrihew's *American Lawn Tennis* had lost its contract with the USLTA because of his support for Tilden. But articles like those by Hawthorne and Tunis got no specific mention at executive-committee meetings. The Association would hold on to its definition of amateur status for four more decades, staunchly and emotionally in the beginning, stubbornly at the end. Track and field and the Olympics did the same, but it was still a lonely battle. Golf, clearly a "gentlemen's" game like tennis, had its "open" championships, yet the sport was not destroyed.[25] Professional competitive tennis would survive, if often on slick wooden basketball courts and for tiny purses. The analyses of sportswriters like these three would become reality, but ever so slowly. Until the "open" era for American tennis began in 1968, the Association's leadership devoted endless hours to such weighty matters, proposing a steady stream of unusable definitions of an amateur and unworkable regulations aimed at imposing those definitions, while consistently failing to enforce its own amateur rules. It proved an obsessive yet insoluble issue, one that distracted the Association from forward thinking, miring it in a romanticized past of lovely people playing tennis simply as recreation.[26]

Part of the Association's difficulties with amateur issues and the rise of professional tennis came from the International Lawn Tennis Federation. When the Federation was founded in 1913, the USNLTA did not join. That was largely because of England's insistence that the Wimbledon tournament constituted the world grass-court championship. In 1914 the Americans proposed changes slightly relaxing their own rules defining amateur status but withdrew the proposals lest they jeopardize the status of American competitors playing in Europe or threaten U.S. participation in one of its cash-cows, the Davis Cup competition. The ILTF's resuscitation after the World War I reignited USLTA concerns that the federation had limited the voting power of the largest lawn-tennis nations—Australia, Great Britain, France, Germany (the war was finally over), and the United States—to six votes per nation. The Americans thought it unfair that New Zealand, for example, had four votes and Japan two. The United States wanted to allocate votes based on the number of players in affiliated clubs. The ILTF refused—and still does.[27]

The USLTA finally joined in 1923 when the Federation (and the English) agreed not to designate Wimbledon or any other tournament as "the world championship on grass," and recognized today's Grand Slam events as the "Big Four" tennis tournaments. Harkening back to the Association's origins, *ALT* reported that what many had seen as a dream had become a reality: "lawn tennis will be played in the same manner all over the world."[28]

But joining the ILTF did not gain acquiescence for American proposals. Repeated requests, formal and informal, to allow an "open" tournament in the United States met with staunch opposition from the European nations—requests that were repeated, formally and informally, throughout the twenties and early thirties. The USLTA assumed that amateur tennis would continue to reign supreme, but that the Association would hold "occasional" and presumably profitable open tournaments for American players. Not only did it make financial sense, but there was pressure from the media and the public for matches between the best players, since many of the men (and a few women) had become professionals. But the French were adamantly opposed and the English unenthusiastic, and as they went so went the International Federation. In 1930 the Germantown Cricket Club in Philadelphia, experiencing serious financial difficulties, asked for permission to hold an open tournament, but the Association's executive committee agreed that it needed ILTF authorization.

When, in the 1920s, the International Federation rejected mixed amateur and professional play, it and the other amateur tennis federations surrendered authority over the professional game. The Grand Slam nations had the most desirable facilities and most famous tournaments. That gave them leverage and delayed the inevitable. But some forty years later, the professionals would collect on that surrender and level the business aspect of the playing field.

Whether out of pique or disagreement, probably both, in 1930 the Association gave three "no's" to the International Federation. The most significant was rejection of a proposal from ILTF that it assume management of the Davis Cup competition. The executive committee gave no support to the idea, with Myrick pointing out that "if the International Federation took it over, it [Davis Cup] would become a European affair"—which is what happened when the International Tennis Federation finally gained control in 1978. The two other "no's"—one to a request to eliminate "lawn" from the International Federation's name; the other to a proposal to eliminate "love" in scoring tennis, replacing it with "zero"—were both rejected on the grounds of "tradition."[29]

International play aimed, in the minds of Dwight Davis and early Association leaders, at good fellowship, good feeling, and good tennis. What later became a curious anachronism, the International Lawn Tennis Club of the United States, was formed in 1931 for the purpose of fostering "social union and matchplay." With "clubs" in France, the United Kingdom, and the United States, members traveling abroad could arrange matches and contacts. It quietly remained a harmless example of the elitist image replete with club neckties and such that the Association came to avoid later in the twentieth century. But rancor and nationalism seemed increasingly the hallmark of Davis Cup and other international team matches. In 1926 when the USLTA failed to send its two top men to play in a French-American team competition, the French federation withheld its three top women players, including Suzanne Lenglen, from the women's draw. Tit-for-tat. In that atmosphere, it is not surprising that the Americans shied away from the European dominated ILTF.[30]

That dislike intensified early in 1933. The USLTA had again proposed an open competition where amateurs and professionals would play each other—a proposal one reporter labeled "dramatic." But the International Federation evaded the issue, creating a loophole by passing a disingenuous resolution that there was nothing in ILTF rules that "permits" such events. To top it off, the USLTA's representative at the Federation meeting warned that the "overwhelming sentiment" of the other nations was firm opposition. Obviously, if the Association chose to take advantage of that loophole, the Federation would then either forbid such events or disqualify American players from other ILTF-sanctioned tournaments, including the Wimbledon and French championships. Little sense, then, to force the issue unless the USLTA reached a "positive agreement" in advance, particularly in view of the "multiple voting system" that found countries and colonies in the British and French Empires supporting their European forebears—potentially providing 90 of 274 possible votes. Lawn tennis was, after all, dominated by the established elites. Since changing ILTF rules required a two-thirds majority, the Brits and French had a veto. The idea of creating an "American" bloc of Western Hemisphere nations was patently absurd.[31]

The Americans were outraged, claiming the ILTF had no right to dictate how any nation set up its own internal rules—precisely why the Federation avoided telling the USLTA what it could not do. National associations had the right of self-determination. California, denied any national championships, wanted an open tournament. So did Middle States, although it seems that was more to provide the bankrupt Germantown Cricket Club with a revenue-producing tournament than to defend the principle. [The convention within the US(L)TA has long been to refer to the sections by their geographic name. Eastern or ETA (capitalized) means the Eastern Lawn Tennis Association, Middle States is the Middle States Lawn Tennis Association (MSTA), and so on.] At the annual meeting, Carruthers, the immediate past president, asserted that the Association had authority to have open tournaments. The delegates bypassed the executive committee, perhaps fearing it would kill the proposal, and voted for the open tournament. Given Germantown's long history and extreme distress, no one demurred from the floor. Only Holcombe Ward, that vociferous and persistent foe of any compromise with professionals, voted against the motion. The media misinterpreted the vote as a "momentous" decision.[32] Not so.

The long discussion (a sixty-two-page transcript) made some things clear. None of the executive committee members advocated holding an open tournament without ILTF approval. The anodyne, face-saving resolution adopted by the USLTA claimed that scheduling issues made an open in 1933 impossible, but as Merrihew and *ALT* pointed out, "the plan of holding the 'open' would have been abandoned even if the International Federation had not passed its resolution." As before, the French were unalterably opposed, the British went along with them (letting them take the blame?), and the open died. The French Federation's publication, *Tennis et Golf*, condemned the very concept of an open with fustian pomposity. Good for the ILTF, it wrote, for making the Americans (and the Portuguese who supported the open proposal) "understand the sacrilege they had committed in wishing to tear down the barriers . . . between sacrosanct amateurism and base professionals." Sadly, complained the French, "that pure and disinterested amateurism . . . should also so evidently concern vulgar mercenary haggling." Equally evident and forceful was the anger that the Americans felt toward the International Federation—the European federation as some viewed it.[33]

Perhaps the 1929 women's nationals had offered a lesson about star power (professionals or not). Revenue from that tournament fell off dramatically from $11,000 to $2,000, largely because Helen Wills Moody did not play, apparently because of her recent marriage and, perhaps, the expense of traveling from California.[34] Meanwhile, the men's Nationals garnered $36,000, up substantially from $28,000 the previous year.

In 1934 the new USLTA president, Walter Merrill Hall, flatly asserted that an "Open Championship" was inevitable. Moreover, he argued, professional tennis popularized and helped develop the game. When Hall asked Bill Tilden about such a competition, the answer was "sure," but it has to be in New York City and the association of players had to share equally in the "financial returns" with the USLTA. Hall told the delegates that the money was "secondary" since the Association was in good financial shape. Later presidents would find compromise with professionals unacceptable, but in 1934 ILTF opposition remained the insurmountable obstacle.

Discussion at the 1934 annual meeting of an open was less than candid, given what had just happened three days earlier at the executive-committee meeting. One delegate mentioned that the ILTF "rather frowned on" the idea, and Carruthers vaguely hinted at the implications of that frown for American players and events. But no one blamed the International Federation and the countries that simply opposed an open tournament. Carruthers went to Europe that spring to try to convince the ILTF to permit an open in the United States, but they responded by amending their bylaws specifically to prohibit such competitions.[35]

By the mid thirties, the Association had joined the "pure and disinterested amateurism" camp, or had been co-opted into "shamateurism," depending one's point of view. It continued to insist that it had a home-rule "right" to have an open tournament but opposed "in principle" such events and in 1935 passed a bylaw that forbade amateurs from playing with or against professionals except with written approval of the International Federation obtained through the USLTA. In other words—no way José.[36]

Philip Hawk (remember him?—the rebel from Illinois back in 1910), president of the West Side Tennis Club in the early 1930s, staunchly advocated an annual open tournament in the United States. In 1937 Hawk published a whimsical look at tennis in a book titled *Off the Racket*. The villain of the piece was the ILTF, "that pompous stuffed-shirtish, organization" that banned competition between professionals and amateurs "for a 'gate,'" even while knowing the rules were routinely evaded. Who were they to dictate to the United States what it could do within its own borders? USLTA leaders rarely forgot their manners, but Hawk could not restrain from writing that it was a mystery "why a good guy like Louis Carruthers ever accepted the presidency of such an organization" as the ILTF. Perhaps. But Carruthers (who became ILTF acting chairman or president at one meeting of the federation) emphasized the need to have an effective presence at the ILTF and dismissed speculation that "a good deal of political intrigue" characterized the ILTF, though he did talk about food and drink. (Ah, those clever French.) But he was not seduced by cuisine or Cointreau. He spoke forcefully and persuasively to the ILTF about appropriate voting strength, and vigorously defended self-determination for national associations about their own regulations.[37]

Of course the "crass commercialism" so disparaged had arrived for the Association (though not in the eyes of its leadership) even before the Tilden wars. In late 1922, the USLTA opened negotiations with the West Side Tennis Club about construction of a permanent facility for both the national championships and home Davis Cup matches—the two largest sources of the Association's revenue.[38] But it was, obviously, more than just money. The prestige and the public attention that an enhanced facility would generate were seductive. Bigger was better. Olympic stadia in ancient Greece, coliseums in Rome, were all precursors of what would come. A thirteen-thousand-seat stadium in Forest Hills would lead ineluctably to a thirty-three-thousand seat tennis center in Flushing Meadows some seventy years later. Tennis was no different from other professional sports, like football and baseball, all of which built their "pyramids" in the late twentieth and early twenty-first centuries. Eventually, the venue, the "buzz" as one business innovator put it, overpowered the sport. Stands rose higher and higher. Spectators would need binoculars to see the players. But Cowboy Stadium in Dallas, Texas, was nearly a century away from the building of a stadium at Forest Hills.[39]

The West Side Tennis Club was located in an oasis of green grass and small homes inside the borough of Queens in New York City. It seemed the perfect place to locate the Association's two major events. Association leaders, themselves financially secure, recognized that money was needed if the USLTA was to expand the game they loved and played—or at least used to play. The West Side Tennis Club had hosted the Davis Cup finals in 1914, and again for three straight years starting in 1921. A fixed venue in New York, the nation's largest and most prosperous city, made sense as did permanent stands since the Association had been paying the club to set up and take down temporary seating for each event. Tennis was popular in the metropolitan area, gate receipts and newspaper coverage had been good, and New York was clearly the nation's financial and cultural center. Of course it is no coincidence that the moving force behind the stadium was Julian Myrick—the Association president, and past president of the West Side Tennis Club.

The competition was important, but money mattered, especially as the sections were asking for it. When the USLTA field secretary, Paul Williams, resigned after seven years of roundly praised service, he was replaced by Edward B. Moss, who served from 1923 through 1943, holding the new title of executive secretary, at starting salary of six thousand dollars a year.[40] The decision a decade earlier to hire a field secretary had proved successful, so much so that the sections wished to do the same, arguing they were better situated to expand the game. When, in autumn 1922, the Western (midwestern) Section asked the Association to subsidize a field secretary, the executive committee worried that helping out would prompt other sections to make the same request. Then when someone suggested letting the sections keep all the revenue from dues, Myrick made an argument that became a staple of Association rhetoric:

> There is one principle that I want to lay down and hope you will accept it and that is about making money. A lot of people say we do not want to make too much money. I agree with that sentiment but I think that the principle we want to lay down and consider is that the money we make goes back into the development of the game all over the country. The main thought of the Association is to develop the boys' and juniors' play. I think our first job is to establish that [Davis Cup] fund and not have it touched in any way. That is, for Davis Cup purposes and nothing else. After that is once established, take care of our running expenses and distribute the balance.[41]

A year later, Myrick presciently laid out the parameters of a debate that became another staple within the Association—sectional (local?) autonomy versus national direction, a debate that would become more strident as the Association's revenues grew.[42] Myrick is, as ever, worth quoting:

> I think it is largely a question of home rule. Many sectional associations want a division of the surplus money sent back to them so they can develop the game. . . . Is the National Association going to send the money back to the various sectional associations and tell them to do what they see fit with it? I mean that is my idea of the way the thing should be handled. It is up to the succeeding administrations whether they want to follow that idea or tell the associations which way the money should be spent. It is a big broad policy to be decided.[43]

Uncle Mike (Julian Myrick, 1880–1969)

If USTA president Slew Hester was the Association's (and New York City's) tennis savior in 1978 for moving the U.S. Open to Flushing Meadows, then Julian Myrick was its John the Baptist in 1922–23. It was Myrick who presided over and shepherded the arrangement between the USLTA and the West Side Tennis Club for a permanent stadium that made the Association's national championships a financial success and a fixture in New York City. Myrick implemented the Wightman Cup competition after Hazel Wightman's proposal for women's matches analogous to Davis Cup was ignored in 1919. He correctly saw it as a perfect initial competition for the new permanent facility at Forest Hills that opened in 1923.

That was, of course, the same "Mike" Myrick whose crusade to force Bill Tilden to adhere to the Association's rules of amateurism, particularly those directed at "tennis writing," eventually embarrassed the USLTA. He was the same "Czar" who would hound twenty-year old Alice Marble into playing four matches (108 games) in a single day, to the outrage of the media. His presidency of the Association lasted three years, 1920–22, though he was "acting" and very real president during 1918 and 1919.

Whatever his reputation in the 1920s as the USLTA's political "boss" (hardly a compliment), he recognized the opportunities that lawn tennis and the Association had before them. "A Sport for a Lifetime" became a USTA slogan in the 1950s and again in the 1990s, but in 1918, Myrick described tennis as "one of the few games" people could play after age twenty-five. Tennis enthusiasts from the West Coast, Chicago, Atlanta, and points in between, have argued that fixing the U.S. National/Open

Championships in New York City was, at the very least, unfair to the rest of the country, and possibly unwise. But if siting that event in New York was the best thing for tennis and the Association, as the "bottom line" suggests, then Myrick deserves the niche he has in the International Tennis Hall of Fame. Without doubt "he helped make tennis a major sport." Myrick made it into the International Tennis Hall of Fame, but as an "administrator," not a player.[44]

Concerns about keeping Davis Cup competition solvent inevitably spilled over into overall questions about the financial well-being of the Association. In December 1922, a special committee appointed earlier that year to consider the Association's "future financial policy," reported out. Putting Davis Cup aside (they recommended a reserve fund for the Cup, since profits were unpredictable, depending on who hosted ties, etc.), the national championships and membership dues were the prime sources of revenue. No one advocated raising dues, but making Forest Hills a permanent site promised to stabilize and increase proceeds. The specific proposals focused on the revenue split between the West Side Club and the USLTA, not on marketing (which would come later). Each side played hardball, with the club asking for 75 percent of the revenue and a commitment on holding at least the Davis Cup, or the men's national singles, and/or doubles championships there for at least ten years.

At that same meeting, Myrick, in a delightful understatement, pointed out that "I happen to know a little bit about both sides of the question." He went on to recommend accepting the club's position, and the executive committee did just that. Perhaps more to the point, one of those negotiators commented that "it is almost certain we will get for New York one big event for ten years or more." That is where the national-championships tournament went, and where it has remained, though it came to include the women's national championships, became an "open" competition, and eventually moved a few miles north to Flushing Meadows.[45] The first men's tournament played in the new stadium at Forest Hills was the 1923 Davis Cup final between the United States and Australia. The United States won 4–1 with Bill Tilden (of course) winning the doubles and both his singles matches.

The agreement with the West Side Club was a defining identity shift for the Association. With the decision to capitalize the Forest Hills stadium, the business of tennis moved irrevocably toward being business, not just tennis. It also assured that "amateurism" would pose even greater challenges. Inevitably, players would want a share of the profits they earned for others, including the USLTA.

The May 1923 issue of *American Lawn Tennis* contained an architect's drawing of the new stadium and an announcement of "An Opportunity—And a Privilege!" For the not so princely sum of $110, a subscriber could purchase exclusive use of a seat in the new stadium for a list of Association-sponsored events scheduled to be played there over the next ten years, from 1923 through 1932. In accordance with the deal made between the USLTA and the West Side Club, those events comprised one major event each year—at least five men's national singles championships, plus Davis Cup challenge round matches or men's national doubles championships, depending on which ones were awarded to the club by the Association.[46] Luxury boxes and National Football League "personal seat licenses" were seventy-five years away.

But all was not a bed of roses for the West Side Club. Within two years the club appealed for financial assistance from the Association pleading that construction costs, which were paid by the club, were 50 percent higher than the estimates in the 1923 contract. As a result, the club had difficulty retiring its mortgage debt on the stadium. The Association agreed to a complicated loan formula that, in essence, provided interest-free loans of up to six thousand dollars per year, depending on the club's net receipts from Association events played at Forest Hills. Repayment of the "loan" did not have to begin until 1933.

By the early thirties, the nation was in the darkest days of the Great Depression. With an increasing number of sections not paying annual dues, the Association's operating deficit for 1931 was over $9,000 (compared, for example, to an excess over expenses of $60,000 in 1927); the treasurer recommended suspending the $11,000 distribution to the sections; reserve fund bonds had depreciated by 50 percent; the Association's official magazine, *Tennis*, would be sold; the West Side Club owed the Association $42,000; and on and on. At the December meeting of the executive committee, the debate seemed more appropriate for a Wall Street bank's investment planners than for a tennis organization. And it would worsen. For example, in 1934, the executive committee approved a six-month no-interest loan of $500 to the Middle States Section because it "finds itself practically without funds at this time to undertake the activities of the season."[47]

TABLE 1. Snapshot of USTA finances (in thousands, rounded)

1931 REVENUE	
Tournaments	$42,000
Men's singles	$2,000
International matches	$12,000
Davis Cup	$5,000
Wightman Cup	$3,300
Other international	$3,700
Club membership dues	$3,300
Sanction fees	$1,700
Interest on investments	$2,400
Net revenue over expenses	$7,500
1931 EXPENSES	
Executive secretary's office	$16,400
International teams and committee	$18,140
Tennis magazine (net loss)	$10,900
General expenses	$10,000
1934 READY ASSETS	
"Free" balance	$52,000
General fund	$29,000
International play fund	$28,000
1934 REVENUE	
Accounts receivable	$24,800
Liabilities	$1,400
Operating profit	$8,000

All 1931 committee expenses, including international committees, amounted to $10,000. Source: *ALT*, April 20, 1932. The report noted that the "distribution" to sections based on the formula of twice the dues and sanction fees paid to the USLTA would be larger than an alternate scheme of 75 percent of association "profit." The distribution for 1934 was $27,000. Sources: 1934 annual meeting, 24–26, and treasurer's report, 1935 annual meeting, 2.

Nonetheless, the Association's own finances were surprisingly secure. The 1923 contract for the Forest Hills stadium had been signed for the WSTC by the club president, Louis J. Carruthers. Ten years later, the president of the club, Philip Hawk, sent a request for financing help to the president of the USLTA, the same Louis J. Carruthers. Hawk pointed out that long-term indebtedness for stadium construction was "much greater than is justified by the requirements of a sound financial structure." Those nice words barely hid the reality—that the depression jeopardized the club's bottom line. At the leadership level, the USLTA retained the friendly, clubby atmosphere that had been there at its inception. Little wonder that Forest Hills got some help. Not only was the stadium the Association's golden egg–laying goose, but it was all among friends. Whatever the coziness of relationships, the USLTA had husbanded its resources and could still help member clubs—or at least one of them. Similarly, the Association decided that, given "the condition of the Sectional Association treasuries" and in lieu of a distribution, for 1933 it would "lend" the sections what they owed in dues by not asking for the dues. It was a graceful way to provide assistance during tough times.[48]

Nor did public interest in tennis disappear under the pressure of the Depression. In July 1931 *ALT* took note of a Night Industrial League in Sharon, Pennsylvania, and of "pay courts" where players put out anywhere from seventy-five cents to three dollars for an hour of tennis.[49]

Whatever the economic pressures on the Association, internal politics continued apace. In 1929 what became a challenge to the established rotation of USLTA leaders began with a nasty fight within the Eastern Lawn Tennis Association. Ever since E. H. Outerbridge's "considerable buttonholing" in 1881, and until 1915, leaders were selected by informal agreement with the annual meeting formalizing the recommendations. As growth and expansion began to prompt occasional nominations from the floor, the national Association set up a nominating committee to prepare an election slate of officers and executive-committee members. By 1919 that nominating committee itself became self-perpetuating, proposing its own members. In 1946 President Ward criticized the nominating-committee practice of allowing individual members to select their successor. Someone asked if that were in the rules; the quick response was not in the rules but "in the rule of custom." Laughter followed. Nor were there any requirements for a geographic distribution of members (that would not come until 1948), giving an obvious advantage to the northeastern establishment.[50] Quite clearly, the nominating committee could suppress or stimulate change.

The details of the dust-up in 1929 are sketchy,[51] but a new group in Eastern not only captured the sectional presidency but, according to *New York Times* reporter Allison Danzig, spoke of challenging the slate offered for election by the national Association's nominating committee. The voting issue was whether or not Eastern's delegates to the national meeting should be instructed to vote for those recommended by the national nominating committee. Mike Myrick and Walter Merrill Hall (then president of the West Side Tennis Club and soon to be a USLTA officer) wanted them instructed. Louis Dailey, the nominee for president of the USLTA, and P(eter) Schuyler Van Bloem, the president of Eastern and former president of the West Side Tennis Club, did not. Why the differences? The leaders of both factions were all from New York and major figures within the USLTA and the Eastern Section. In any event, Eastern voted to send its delegates uninstructed to the national meeting, prompting an apprehensive national nominating committee to close its report: "We shall take no offense if our selections are not confirmed at the Annual Meeting."[52] It never came to that, but just wait 'til next year.

Whatever the roots of the discontent, Eastern's squabbles were crucial since active management of USLTA affairs came overwhelmingly from leaders living in the New York area, often men who were former presidents of that section. Of the fifteen individuals who served as Association president between 1881 through 1930, only six lived outside the New York metropolitan area—Oliver, Dwight, Sears, Clark, Davis, and Wightman. Through 1930, all three Association presidents who served but a single year (Oliver, Davis, Wightman) were from outside the New York City area. During the 1920s, '30s, '40s, four presidents of the Eastern Section became president of the USLTA (Jones Mersereau, Dailey, Ward, and Russell Kingman). That geographic stranglehold was strengthened by the close connection between Association leadership and the West Side Tennis Club—home of the national championships. Three presidents of the Forest Hills club (Myrick, Carruthers, and Hall) later became president of the USLTA (all between 1917 and 1936), and the Association's executive committee routinely had multiple members from the West Side Club.

Merrihew and *ALT* reporters, who must have known full-well what had happened in Eastern, offered a tongue-in-cheek commentary about USLTA politics with a delightful and sarcastic description of goings-on aboard the special chartered train from New York City to St. Louis for the 1930 annual meeting. The portrait has a timeless quality:

> Thursday afternoon and evening and Friday morning were busy times on the tennis special. Practically all of the dignitaries occupied drawing rooms—a few condescended to compartments, and the present writer [Merrihew?] had a lower berth, fortunately; and it was an interesting sight to walk along the car and glance into open

> doors—some were shut, however—and glimpse delegates working with their coats off and working their hardest. As one Southern gentleman put it, "You got a handshake and an absent look, and the gabfest was on again." Thrones tottered, dynasties were threatened, slates were made and unmade, the knife was inserted here and there; in short the business that was supposed to be transacted in open meeting at St. Louis was "put on the ice" on the way to that city. All this last, or most of it, is predicated on the views of these who think that the U.S.L.T.A. has long been a closed shop and now had become an oligarchy.[53]

The day before the annual meeting and Louis Dailey's election as president, the executive committee discussed the "distribution" of funds to the sections—by then a fixture of the national Association's budget. Myrick, who once stood as advocate for the primacy of the sections, now stood as the centralizer, pushing a larger reserve for the national Association. But Dailey protested that there was no reason to keep the sections poor while the Association held a "precious" $90,000 reserve for future contingencies that might never arise. He gave a preview of his acceptance speech, arguing that "the development of the game is dependent upon the enterprise of the sections. . . . Our funds should be used for that purpose." As was the norm, "the boss," Myrick, won out, arguing that the Association could well experience two or three bad years and deficits, so the reserve had to be built up while they could do so. He did not mention that the Association had run a deficit of nearly $7,700 in 1928, but presumably all knew. Politics prevailed, but the compromise distribution of $20,000 divided among thirteen sections was on the low end.[54] The discussion gave no hint that the 1929 Wall Street Crash and the growing Great Depression had any impact.

Whatever Dailey's political problems inside the USLTA, his ideas resonated. Even as he left the scene, the executive committee established a formula for determining the size of what had become the annual distribution to the sections. The pot of money to be divided according to the voting power of each section would be either 75 percent of the USLTA's net profits (overwhelmingly from events) or a so-called "minimum refund," which was twice the amount remitted to the Association for section dues and tournament sanctions. Previously the distribution had come only from the Association's net "profits." The Great Depression had cut into those profits, and the leadership wanted to establish some funding stability—keep the "the distribution on a fairly even keel." Even so, the sections received only $10,500 in 1931, $10,000 less than the previous year.

The distribution remained in that ballpark throughout the 1930s, and the formula remained in place through the 1940s.

The president of the Eastern Section, Schuyler Van Bloem, reflected the Dailey insurgents' point of view when he pointed out that the "net profit" method of calculating the distribution expressed a policy of putting international play ahead of the internal development of the game. A net profit calculation gave priority to the international game since it first deducted the considerable expenses, including foreign travel, of Davis Cup and other international teams ("to their great delight and profit" he added sarcastically).[55]

Dailey had won the initial battle in Eastern, but eventually lost the war, running aground within the Association. Elected as president of the USLTA in February 1930, his acceptance speech garnered only a few "Ohs and Ahs, with an occasional lifting of eyebrows." Perhaps most of the delegates concentrated on their drinks and food—waiting to be beguiled by the guest speaker, baseball's Branch Rickey, who proceeded to massage their prejudices with stories of honest amateurs.[56]

Dailey's address genuflected to the usual icons—amateurism, subordination (but not elimination) of commercialism by clubs, continued pressure on the International Federation for an open championship in the United States, and recapturing the Davis Cup. But the alarums should have rung when he opened with a call for distributing to the sections the responsibility and the money for developing tennis, and then closed with, "the United States Lawn Tennis Association has in the past made mistakes." Both were red flags thrown at the feet of Association leaders who had consistently moved toward control from the top. A later news report asserted that Dailey's advocacy of decentralization was popular with the "rank and file of tennis players throughout the country," making his challenge even more unsettling.[57]

At that 1930 annual meeting, an amendment to limit sectional delegates to one-year (renewable) terms on the executive committee prompted a curious discussion. Myrick argued that a two-year term made more sense since it took time to learn the ropes. Dailey, like Myrick, a former Eastern Lawn Tennis Association president, responded that sections ought to be able to select their own president to represent them on the national executive committee. With elaborate courtesy, Dailey pointed to Holcombe Ward, Eastern's delegate, who had entered into his second year of a two-year term just as the section elected a new administration. As Dailey put it, they wished "to have it in their power to put their president on the Executive Committee of the National Executive Committee."[58] Logical?

Yes. But, Dailey's protestations to the contrary notwithstanding, it was a slap in the face for Ward, a respected old warhorse.

Whatever the rumblings, the battle was not joined. The USLTA nominating committee slate for 1930 was elected without challenge. Then, in December 1930 Dailey announced he would not accept re-nomination as president. He stated that he was "terribly busy" and that lack of time was the "sole reason for my decision." Perhaps. His career was in real estate, and the Great Depression made that a dicey livelihood. But frustration likely played a role. He had managed to put through some reforms, including allowing executive-committee members to vote by mail when they could not attend meetings in New York—a trip too long for many. But his support for giving the sections more resources and greater autonomy was not popular with most of the Association's leaders. When Dailey died of pneumonia quite unexpectedly on February 17, 1932, a *New York Times* report pointedly commented on his "characteristic straightforwardness which proved disturbing to a number of persons connected with the game."[59]

Whatever the reasons for Dailey's decision not to seek a second one-year term, the insurgents in control of the Eastern Section were biding their time. As the 1931 annual meeting of the USLTA took up the nominating committee recommendations, all seemed to be the usual routine—nominating nominates, the annual meeting elects the committee's slate. Then, when the just-installed new president, Louis J. Carruthers, called for nominations for second vice president, the routine was broken as Eastern's president, Van Bloem, nominated from the floor the Association's secretary, Joseph Ivy of Kansas City. Van Bloem had the proxies and Ivy defeated the "regular" candidate by a solid margin of 3600 to 2200 votes. Four other "regular" nominees, including three proposed for membership on the nominating committee, likewise went down to defeat.[60]

The Eastern uprising, Dailey's policies as president, and the rejection of some of the nominating committee's recommendations in 1931, constituted a direct and unsettling threat to the USLTA leadership. (Moreover it was embarrassing since 1931 was the fiftieth anniversary of the Association's founding, observed by speeches and publication of a history.) Then, according to Ward, came reports of a "secret meeting" in September 1931, where, he claimed, "suggestions were made to eliminate not only Louis J. Carruthers," who was standing for another term as president, but the treasurer, Merrill Hall, and four other members of the executive committee. A coup d'état, or at least a *coup d'association*!

All this prompted Holcombe Ward and some other USLTA leaders to cobble together something they called the Tennis Committee of One

Hundred, with Ward as chairman (the only such formal extra-Association "political action committee" I have found—either for or against the existing leadership). The committee mobilized the troops against the rebels and won handily, in Eastern and in the USLTA.[61]

That a fight from within the Eastern Section became a national Association battle speaks volumes to the clout of the New York City region. The Committee of One Hundred aimed at gaining national support, but getting the Eastern Section under control was the key. Association leaders came largely from there, and when dissent from national policies came from New York (Eastern) tennis leaders, the USLTA paid close attention. Association and Eastern leaders were often one in the same, sitting on the executive committees of both. Dailey, by then past-president of the USLTA, seemed not too busy for tennis politics, and actively supported Van Bloem and his faction. USLTA president Carruthers echoed the words of the Committee of One Hundred, condemning the actions of a small, secret, undemocratic group who ignored their responsibilities as representatives (proxies) of the members (the clubs). As Allison Danzig pointed out in the *New York Times*, what happened at the Eastern meeting ensured that the national Association would follow "regular" procedures. How Ward and his supporters gained the upper hand in Eastern is shrouded, but he became president of the section, easily defeating Van Bloem who ran for a fourth year in office. It was "a sweeping victory for the regular ticket of The Committee of 100."[62] Ironically, none of this related to Ward's obsessions—amateurism and Bill Tilden.

The entire affair was a lesson learned for Association leaders and those who hoped to achieve leadership positions. Perhaps it was also a lesson for Association presidents. Dailey had lain low for nearly a decade as an officer, speaking out but never disrupting or challenging the majority. But when he became president he thought he could redirect national priorities and quickly found himself isolated.

In the end, civility ruled. Van Bloem remained on the Eastern executive committee for a number of years, while Joseph Ivy, the insurgents' choice as second vice president, remained in that slot for six years, though he never moved up the ladder. This time, Association leaders understood the wisdom of Winston Churchill's maxim: "In victory; magnanimity." Ward's reward would come in 1937 when he began eleven years as president of the USLTA, second only to James Dwight's twenty-one years.[63]

The growing desire of the sections to play a greater role in national governance, driven heavily by "western" reaction to northeastern dominance, cropped up during the February 1933 meeting of the executive committee, when an extensive debate took place over authority of the sections versus that of the national Association. The Eastern Section had proposed an amendment to its constitution that would let it discipline its players and members. Other sectional delegates agreed that the USLTA "should stay out of these small laundries." The final clause in the amendment proposed that the sections "have the power to suspend, expel or disbar any club or player under its jurisdiction who shall act in a manner contrary to the purpose of the Association or the welfare of the game." Holcombe Ward, president of Eastern and also on the USLTA executive committee, defended his section's position. There was no disagreement with Ward's long-standing hard-line stance on amateurism, which seemed the likely reason for the proposal, but Carruthers, Myrick, and other USLTA leaders, insisted that the Association's bylaws specifically empowered only its executive committee to determine amateur status and eligibility—designating it a "tribunal" so as to emphasize its full and final authority.[64]

When someone suggested that the situation was analogous to the relationship between the U.S. federal government and the states, President Carruthers went well beyond the specific case to present an overview of the Association's governance structure and history. He pointed to the accepted practice of "chartering" sections once they got USLTA approval for their constitutions and bylaws, which meant that Eastern's had been approved without such a new grant of authority. Then came his declaration of governing principles:

> In the first place the powers and rights of a Sectional Association which is a member of the National Association are entirely different from those of the states in the Union. Far be it for me to be drawn into an argument on states' rights here but the states had original powers. The Federal Government had but what powers the states granted it. The very opposite is true with respect to the National Association. The original organization was the National Association. *The Sectional Associations have but those powers which have been granted to them by the National Association.*[65]

Resolution of the details was unimportant—the USLTA gave approval for the Eastern proposal, on the condition that "disbar" be struck from the wording. Much more significantly, no one at the meeting challenged the political philosophy set forth by Carruthers. The national Association created and owned the sections, not vice-versa—at least in 1933.

As the sections shifted from geographic to organizational roles, the

USLTA prodded them to be on the same page with one another and the Association. The 1920 constitution required issuance of "a charter to each active association which is a direct member of the National Association, defining its limits and duties. Sectional associations shall issue a similar charter to each of their member associations." Charters required that the sections replicated USLTA procedures and policies, however much they were adapted to local and regional needs.

The Bermuda Exception

Sections as chartered members of the USLTA made direct member clubs an anachronism. How is it then that as of 2016, two clubs in Bermuda (Bermuda Lawn Tennis, and Coral Beach and Tennis) were listed by name as the only two exceptions to the rule that all clubs and organizations must be within the boundaries of a USTA section?

The answer is in the history. In the first half of the Association's existence, adjacent foreign clubs in the Caribbean, Mexico, and Canada were popular venues for tournaments that attracted the best American players. Clubs there joined the Association; no one objected. After all, they were lawn-tennis facilities, and in Bermuda's case, the Outerbridges came from there. The 1920 constitution expressly validated membership for foreign clubs with the explanation that they needed to "legalize" some clubs in Mexico and Canada that were already members. In 1922 just before some Bermuda clubs were first listed as members, the Bermuda government, working through its Trade Development Board, set up the First "Annual" Championship of Bermuda and sagely offered to pay the expenses of Americans who wanted to play. (Many of the best players, e.g., Dwight Davis, were on the USLTA executive committee.) A few of the guardians of pure amateurism grumbled and claimed that Americans were not allowed to play in unsanctioned tournaments, but common sense prevailed when other executive committee members called that an unenforceable technicality. The following year, the Bermuda clubs became "direct members"; thus tournaments could be sanctioned—hardly a coincidence.[66]

Chartered sections were a small step toward greater sectional autonomy. Each had a delegate on the USLTA executive committee, giving the sections a majority. The only "direct" member clubs (not members through a geographic section) would soon be just a few foreign clubs in Bermuda and the Caribbean—vestigial remains of an earlier era. Chartering a section was pro forma so long as that charter did not call for boundaries that conflicted with other sectional boundaries and did not contain any provisions that were in conflict with the USLTA constitution and bylaws. The chartering process seems not to have been used by the national Association for political leverage—though that would be hard to detect unless someone lost their temper in public. Unthinkable for a clubbable gentleman! It took some of the older sections a few years to rewrite their constitutions and get a charter, but by 1930 all but three of the thirteen sections were in the fold.[67] (See gallery, image 13.)

In a curious way, the development of organized, chartered sections proved unintentionally undemocratic for an Association based upon club memberships. By 1923 a number of sections had begun to cast their sectional vote at the USLTA's annual meetings as a bloc, rather than having clubs vote individually. Clubs from within the same section voting differently became increasingly rare, although occasional anomalies occurred.[68] Put two of those bloc voting sections together, such as Eastern (New York until 1927) and Western (later Midwest), and they commanded some 19,000 and 9,000 votes respectively—far more than the roughly 14,000 proxy votes the other clubs could cast. As Merrihew pointed out, the "bulking of proxies in the hands of one or more individuals" was exceeded by those sectional associations casting all their votes en masse. Among his examples was a description of "the age-old Philadelphia feud"—which pitted the large Philadelphia clubs against the other smaller clubs in the Middle States Section.[69]

Tennis remained the Association's purpose, whatever the "big issues" of amateurism, Bill Tilden, governance, and commercialization. Davis Cup, Wightman Cup, awarding of national championships, the stadium at Forest Hills, and developing greater interest in the game all occupied the attention of the leadership. The office of the executive secretary handled some of the details, but presidents and those executive committee members who lived in the New York area spent a good deal of time on the day-to-day affairs of the Association. That growing complexity required more formal procedures and governance structure and decades later expansion of the paid staff. In the 1930s USLTA leaders maintained control of national and international matters, but increasing the number of players ("growing the game" as it would come to be called), running tournaments, taking care of local details, all prompted devolution to the sections, and the sections were happy to oblige. Occasionally they had been fractious, but the basic relationship between sectional and national leadership was one of mutual support. Sections focused on local matters, leaving the "big issues" to the "big shots" in New York. As an executive committee member put it: "One of the objects of sectional associations is to relieve the National Association of details."[70] The sections might have added "and for National to provide us with the resources we need."

The Dailey insurgents did not win the day on USLTA spending priorities and the creation of a large reserve, but the complaints did not go away. Ten years later, in 1939 the Association responded to arguments that it spent too much money on the international game. A lengthy defense titled "The Business Side of Tennis," argued "that leadership in the tennis world went hand-in-hand with financial stability," so the Association did all it could to "foster our Championships and the International Matches which so helped to make them successful." By suggesting that the success of the Tilden-era Davis Cup teams made possible the construction of the Forest Hills stadium and the profits it generated, the argument conflated the success of the (men's) national championships with international play. Whatever the validity of that connection, the reality remained that the sections continued to agitate for more money. Local was more important to them than international.[71]

The Association's annual meeting had been a fixture in the Northeast from the outset. In 1922 the executive committee had quickly tabled, without discussion, a motion to hold the next year's meeting in San Francisco. But demographics triumphed. In 1926, only a handful of delegates attended the meeting—turning it into a meeting-by-proxy. In 1927, the annual meeting took place in Philadelphia—the first meeting outside New York City. Then the Association's center of gravity moved westward when the 1928 annual meeting was held in Chicago.[72]

As the Association and lawn tennis grew, so did the executive committee. In 1930 the annual meeting created an additional officer position of second vice president. Executive committee minutes for 1929 are missing, but it is safe to assume that the workload was increasing. Whether or not the move was intended to create leadership stability, it had that effect. The increased number of rungs on the ladder to climb meant it took longer before officers faced move up or move out. All this, as well as the increasing average age of the leadership, suggests an organization that had matured. By the mid 1930s the executive committee had begun to meet in cities other than New York, answering one of the long-standing complaints from the sections that travel distances often prevented their delegates from attending.[73] In 1938 at the recommendation of an ad hoc sectional advisory committee created to "bring the National Association into somewhat closer cooperation with the country at large," four "regional" vice presidents were added to the USLTA executive committee, raising the total membership to an unwieldy thirty. That the sectional advisory committee recommended they be officers suggests that the sections wanted to be included in the top tier.[74]

The 1933 annual meeting took up a raft of constitutional amendments that had been discussed and then deferred for a committee to study. Although they seemed routine, most gently expanded the rights of the sections. One ended the practice of the annual meeting electing a delegate from any section unrepresented at the meeting. Instead the section had to fill the vacancy. The sections won another small victory with a change allowing any section in good standing (i.e., that had paid its dues) to nominate candidates beyond those on the nominating committee slate so long as they met a filing date of January 10. The annual meeting also accepted the new contract for the Forest Hills stadium, one that gave the club a larger share of tournament revenue and restructured the "loan" of six thousand dollars per year and the payback terms, all in response to WSTC budget problems. Good business practices prompted a requirement that contracts be approved by the executive committee before being signed by the appropriate officer(s).[75]

Negotiations over special financial arrangements between the Association and the West Side Tennis Club would not go away and in September 1940 prompted a lengthy heated discussion by the executive committee. A special committee reported out on the finances of the long-term contract with the West Side Tennis Club, and the recommendations ruffled some feathers. With an eye to Association politics, committee chair Jones (Joe) Mersereau,[76] a former Association president but not a member of the WSTC, pointed out that the distribution to the sections (which had a majority on the executive committee) depended on the revenue from the nationals played at Forest Hills. This came after a year in which the Association had run a deficit that forced the use of reserves. Louis Carruthers, who had been present at the creation of the stadium, retorted, "if we were engaged in the trial of a case and Joe were my opponent, I should call that an inflammatory statement." The minute taker recorded "laughter," but it was an unusually direct challenge. The long and short of the report was that the WSTC had earned back 100 percent of its investment (costs of the stadium and such) and had earned a return of more than 8 percent on that investment. The report called for the Association's share of the profits to be larger than 50–50, and for all revenue from a (radio) broadcasting contract to go to the USLTA.[77] Similarly, revenue from catering (concessions), no small amount, should be reserved for the USLTA. A good portion of the report dealt with what could only be called sleight of hand (but never were, except indirectly by the Internal Revenue Service) in determining the club's expenses and depreciation.

A Glimpse of the Future

In 1939, the future became possible—though no one suspected just how expansive and profitable that future would be. The first television broadcast of lawn tennis (in the United States) was made by NBC that summer. It showed the eastern grass court championships from Rye, New York, on a twelve-inch screen, located on the sixth floor of the A. G. Spalding & Brothers store on New York's Fifth Avenue. The some fifty viewers were impressed by the novelty but complained they had trouble following the ball. It was a far cry from the "jumbo-tron" that by the twenty-first century would show matches inside Arthur Ashe Stadium to crowds gathered in the food-court area below, providing a better view than all but the best seats in the house. But in 1939 the future was there on Fifth Avenue for those with the imagination to see it.[78]

The scions of Forest Hills, many former USLTA presidents, quickly came to its defense. Beginning by routinely referring to "my friend Joe," Carruthers smoothly argued for "fair" treatment of the WSTC. As temperatures rose, it became "Mr." Mersereau. Carruthers criticized the idea that only money mattered—fair treatment was also essential. But money did matter. He hinted that the recommended changes could pose problems for other sites holding national championships, although the reality was that the men's nationals and Davis Cup matches played at Forest Hills were what paid the freight. Westside officials spoke of "nursing" grass courts that their members did not need and of potential income taxes on the profits. But in Carruthers's words, "It has been the labor of love, the labor of sportsmanship and everything that has gone into it that has made these things possible." Mersereau (rolling his eyes?) bemoaned the image of his committee as "having taken candy away from the baby and [that] we ought to feel ashamed of ourselves." And so it went on, and on, and on. Grudgingly, Carruthers finally gave the point: "Suppose you did hold it somewhere else. You would be cutting off your nose to spite your face if it was deliberately done, if fair terms weren't arranged with the West Side Tennis Club, because you certainly couldn't make the money, looking at it in a cold financial way, elsewhere that you can make at Forest

Hills." New York City was where the action was and with no other tennis stadium available there, the West Side Tennis Club had a powerful argument, one that gave it the leverage to hold on to its special relationship with the Association.[79]

A note taker wearily recorded on page seventy-four of the transcript that they "finally" referred the report back to the special committee for further study and discussions with "various clubs which are particularly interested." The closing retort came from a member of the special committee: "You are going to end up by the Association underwriting all Clubs." It was unclear why the plural "clubs" was used.

Mersereau and his committee stuck to their guns. They quickly reported back to the executive committee in time for the February 1941 meeting. Despite whinging from representatives of the West Side Club that the report had Forest Hills as its target, Mersereau argued that it had received preferential treatment for just short of twenty years with no other club allowed to bid on the nationals. Why should that club get "more liberal terms" than any other? The arguments over depreciation schedules, taxes, and profits were not the point. As Mersereau put it, "What you are doing is putting in the expense of your own plant [the WSTC facility], and that is something we are not responsible for." At that point, Carruthers, to get a word in edgewise, offered an apt quote about a speaker:

> who, too deep for his hearer's ears,
> Still went on refining, and thought of convincing,
> While they thought of dining.

Carruthers himself then went on for four pages of the transcript.

The actual report, which apparently recommended competitive bidding, was "adopted." The delegates at the 1941 annual meeting did not ask for discussion of the report and duly awarded the West Side Tennis Club the men's national singles championships for that year. Whatever the call for competitive bids, the gravitational pull of New York City—and good business sense—kept it there until 1978, and even then the tournament (however much expanded in the "open" era) just moved a few blocks away.[80]

But the overwhelming obsession of the USLTA in the decade before the Second World War was, in reality, another circus. How the Association, the media, and the players confronted "amateurism" is a classic clash of hubris. Association and ILTF policies on amateurism approached the absurd. But so did media reports and player reactions. Some random selections from the 1930s illustrate the point:

The British proposed changing ILTF rules to permit amateur players to make "action film pictures" but retain amateur status. A film company put fifty thousand dollars in escrow for Fred Perry, the top English player, while the rule change made its way through the tennis bureaucracy. Ernest Renshaw, another highly ranked British player, reportedly forgot "a suitcase full of prizes" found under the bed in a hotel room. With lovely British sarcasm, the *Morning Post* of London, commented that "it seems a novel way to strengthen the amateur game by robbing it of one of the few vestiges of amateurism."

Since national federations (like the USLTA) determined amateur status, the French professional, Henri Cochet, could play against amateurs in the Philippine Islands, but not in Australia. Routinely, reports appeared of amateurs taking "vouchers" that they could turn into cash and similar ploys.

In 1938, the Association outlawed "lump sum" payments to players for expenses. *ALT* commented that "the game has become thoroughly democratized," making the "the gate" crucial. Tournaments would "vanish," unless expenses were paid. Then there was the ludicrous debate in January 1941 over free rackets and stringing for top players. That was, for the Association, a "growing evil." A bizarre "schedule of frames and stringing allowances" prompted Myrick, still on the executive committee after two decades and no friend of relaxed standards of amateurism, to quip that the proposal "reminded me of the rules and regulations that come out of the Treasury Department" (i.e., the tax code). That meeting would have tried the patience of Job, with 111 pages of the 124-page transcript taken up with amateur status rules.

In 1941 the Association revoked the amateur status of highly ranked Frank Kovacs. Showing no little hubris, Kovacs reportedly said: "The old fossils sit around a big heaping table of food, using up some of the money I make them, and they say, 'Let's see who we can bar now?' Why try to kid ourselves about this business? I have made a fortune for the USLTA. They can't get along without me. When they barred me the game went down the sewer. And all the brass hats will have to get off the gravy train and thumb their way home."

A silly statement about volunteers who, however stubbornly and foolishly committed to doing tennis their way, did not make a living from the game. In fact, a significant portion of the revenue gained by the Association went to paying expenses for international matches like the Davis and

Wightman Cups (and travel for some of those volunteers). But Kovacs had a point.

In a 1939 article about "shamateurism," *Time* magazine ridiculed the USLTA's failed attempts to implement a "pure" amateurism policy:

> In the summer it is Sea Bright, Southampton, Newport, Rye—staying at the best hotels or draw-my-bath private homes. In the winter it is Palm Beach, Bermuda, Jamaica. In the spring Pinehurst, Asheville, Hot Springs—guests of hotel managements that occasionally offer more attractive bait for players than mere traveling expenses and $30-a-day suites. Some tournament promoters have been known to offer lump-sum traveling expenses that could take the player to Buenos Aires and back. Now & then a well-heeled promoter has even been known to get around the amateur code by making a friendly little wager—for instance, a $500 bet that the player cannot jump over his tennis racket.[81]

For the twenty years between the two world wars, the guardians of "pure" amateurism honestly, if stubbornly, thought they were saving their game. The Association struggled with Bill Tilden, complicated and petty amateur-status rules like twelve-week versus eight-week limits on play, and designating free hospitality as payment of expenses. At one point (February 1941) after another of the endless decade-long discussions about making the amateur rules on expenses effective, Holcombe Ward—the Avery Brundage of the USLTA—commented that "if you are going to have so many exceptions, gentlemen, you will have a player playing more than fifty-two weeks in the year. (Laughter)."[82] The executive committee may have been laughing with Ward, but outside the room the laughter was directed at them.

But as the thirties drew to a close, the lawyers—yes, the lawyers!—were busy saving the USLTA's future. What resulted had a profound effect on the Association's development.

When the West Side Tennis Club presented its case for continuing the subsidy it had received from the Association to support the Forest Hills stadium, the argument included a projected income-tax burden. To use the phrasing of one lawyer-historian, "the Internal Revenue Service, ever alert to new stratagems to avoid taxes," determined in 1939 that the WSTC was liable for taxes on the profits it received from the two USLTA events it hosted, the national championships and the Davis Cup matches. A tax exemption required that the club operate "exclusively for pleasure, recreation, and other non-profitable purposes." Whatever pleasure the members got from having the events held at their stadium, the profits "were in the main simply a means of carrying the expenses of the club by means of profits obtained from the public," language strikingly similar to those on the executive committee who opposed continuing to subsidize the Forest Hills club.[83]

The USLTA lawyers, particularly Lawrence Baker, a longtime Association officer, recognized the threat to the West Side Club and, apparently, to future revenues for both the Association and the sections. After two years of IRS orders, affirmations, and appeals, on August 11, 1942, the Tax Court upheld the USLTA argument, although the West Side Tennis Club lost its case and paid taxes on stadium events thereafter.[84] The IRS commissioner and Baker struck a deal whereby the IRS would designate the Association exempt as a "social club" and not file an appeal. That face-saving device moved the USLTA to the status of what would come to be called a not-for-profit organization, but did not allow it to receive tax-deductible donations. In the words of the commissioner of Internal Revenue: "You are exempt under the provisions of section 101(8) of the Internal Revenue Code."[85]

The logic of the initial IRS rulings made sense—the Association's national championship were hugely profitable. As profits from the events grew, so did IRS interest in taxing those profits. But Congress had put in a loophole, and whatever the original intent, legislators consistently refused to eliminate it. The basis for all the successful defenses against taxation of Association income rested on the 1942 decision and Baker's work. That alone would have justified his selection as USLTA president from 1948 through 1950.[86] Whatever the Association's preoccupation with "pure" amateurism, it was growing up.

5

MARKING TIME

1941–1968

> "We can't think of trying to make progress. . . .
> We haven't the sinews of war . . . we require."
> "We are merchandising amusement."
> PRESIDENT RUSSELL KINGMAN, August 1951 and January 1954[1]

With the Stukas of September, the Second World War engulfed Europe in 1939. The German attack on Poland, led by tanks and Stuka dive-bombers, quickly brought declarations of war from France and Great Britain just twenty years after their last conflict with Germany. *American Lawn Tennis* sadly observed that "in Europe, our game is dead." Initially, the USLTA, seeming to treat the war as irrelevant, merely observed cancellation of Davis Cup matches and of the International Lawn Tennis Federation (ILTF) meeting.[2]

Otherwise it seemed like business as usual for the Association over the next two years. It passed a resolution of support for little Finland standing up to the Soviet Union in 1940, while early in 1941 *American Lawn Tennis* praised passage of the Lend-Lease Act, arguing that the "Democracies" had "to face a world gone mad." The immediate concern was international play, but there was little that could be done. After all, the lawns of Wimbledon, closed for the duration of the war, had been given over to "Pig-Keeping" as its contribution to Britain's war effort. Davis Cup remained suspended from 1940 through 1945.

But even with the world at war and the Association struggling to make ends meet, it also engaged in two often emotional conflicts. The ongoing tension between "progressives" and the northeastern establishment continued as the "west" demanded greater participation in governance. What looked like democracy would win out but not without hints of secession. More emotional and heated was the threat of "creeping professionalism" versus "pure" amateurism.

The abiding concern of the USLTA remained the amateur rule, or as

American Lawn Tennis described it, the new "Amateur Law," a phrase that meant "when the War is over and lawn tennis returns to normalcy the Federation and the Davis Cup nations will be confronted with rules vastly different from anything they have known." Of course those foreign federations might not agree and conform to the new rules, the editors warned, then pointedly asserted that "the American governing body has long ceased to be a deliberative body." The comment was directed at how the amateur law had been run through the 1940 annual meeting without significant discussion (*ALT* editors did not agree with some provisions), noting that the Europeans, had they not been distracted by war, might have wondered a bit about the lack of consultation.[3]

Despite the collapse of international play during the war, Association leaders remained unhappy about the relative lack of American influence within the International Federation. Informal discussions in 1943 with a British federation official (in the United States to discuss lend-lease), resulted in talk about a joint United States–Australia––Great Britain tennis "federation." President Holcombe Ward commented that he didn't care about the same or a new federation, his complaint was that the United States had never had a member on the ILTF committee of management, and that "the voting strength is entirely out of proportion."

In a letter to the secretary of the (British) Lawn Tennis Association, Ward gave the wonderful example of voting strength for Mauritius, "a tiny island in the Indian Ocean," as greater than that of Pennsylvania, which had sixty times the area, a population twenty-three times greater, and thousands of tennis players. He went on to compare the voting strength of Uganda to that of California, Kenya to Texas, and Trinidad-Tobago ("tennis interest . . . almost negligible") to Michigan with thousands of players, and complained of how colonies gave Britain a huge voting advantage. Ward suggested that the committee of management (the ILTF governing body as of 1933) be composed of a representative from each of the nine major tennis-playing nations. He also questioned that meetings "have invariably been held in Paris," thus making it easier for European representatives to attend. (Ah, the echoes of Cleveland's Dick Kroysen and the west.) Of course Ward also lectured on amateur rules and their enforcement, conflating wartime propaganda with professional tennis: "The spirit of amateurism, like the spirit of liberty, should be guarded with vigilance; otherwise organized propaganda (signs of which have occasionally appeared in the U.S.A.) may spread." He received a predictably non-committal "will be considered" response—just as the International Federation, backed by Great Britain, has responded ever since.[4]

Japan's attack on Pearl Harbor on December 7, 1941, changed all the atmospherics but not the Association's focus. The January 1942 annual meeting did echo the resolution of twenty-five years earlier in a "rising" unanimous vote:

> we endorse the action of Congress and of President Roosevelt in their declaration of a state of war with the Axis nations; that we pledge to the President and the Congress of the United States our utmost support in whatever further steps they deem necessary to maintain American rights against lawless aggression; and to that end we place the services of the Association and its national organization absolutely at the disposal of the government.[5]

The Association went on to act largely in the same way it had during the First World War—no surprise given that Julian Myrick was acting president during 1918–19 and still an active member of the executive committee twenty-five years later. Drawing on that First World War experience, the Association committed itself to the "National Defense." Myrick summarized for the executive committee how they had responded to American entry into the war in 1917: The national championships would continue, though this time they would not be renamed "National Patriotic tournaments" as had happened during World War One. Fund raisers for the Red Cross and ambulance companies, donations of tennis equipment to military recreation facilities, and a commitment to overall physical fitness, all seemed the right thing to do.

As 1943 ended, Ward could announce that the Association had experienced a busy but difficult time. Tournament participation had dropped with so many men off to war, yet the national championships showed a six-thousand-dollar profit. Membership had also dropped, but there were still some six hundred clubs in the USLTA. Junior programs had become a priority, yet only prep schools and colleges had proper coaching. Fund-raising efforts for the Red Cross had been successful, tennis equipment had been collected and donated to the military recreation programs, and the new synthetic rubber tennis balls seemed "livelier and stronger." The "uncertainty" of wartime conditions prompted agreement not to propose a budget, yet the three reserve funds were topped off at a total of $75,000, and an excess of revenue over expenses allowed a distribution to the sections of $5,100. All that after the Association had donated $10,000 to war relief.[6]

But when Helen Jacobs, four-time winner and four-time runner-up in the women's national singles championship, suggested that the USLTA allow amateur and professional players to compete in tournaments to raise money for national defense, Ward drew the line. The first frontier of defense for Ward and the Association seems to have been amateurism, not Germany or Japan. Buried within a long (ten-paragraph) defensive letter, he declared that "We have no intention at present . . . to throw our amateur tournaments and matches open to professional players to the detriment of the game, and perhaps to its ultimate ruin." He then dismissively suggested to Jacobs that she could devote her energies to youth clinics, obviously relegating her to what he saw as the appropriate activity for a woman.[7]

Putting aside Ward's priorities, asserting that play between professionals and amateurs could lead to the "ultimate ruin" of lawn tennis revealed that the preoccupation of Association leaders with defending amateur tennis overrode all else. In a sixteen paragraph article that only summarized the August 1942 USLTA *Service Bulletin*, Ward wrote that the amateur code, built up over sixty years, "is the foundation on which the USLTA rests." It cannot be mere coincidence that Ward was president for the ten years beginning in 1937, a period that saw Association leaders switch from interest in some sort of regulated "open" competition to adamant opposition and the conviction that mixing with professional tennis could lead to "ultimate ruin."

At the same time, Ward commented that it was, perhaps, acceptable that amateur play would be "slightly less skillful." But "amateur" tennis would continue, he promised, with an expansion of lighted courts so that day workers could play at night.[8] Amateurism and finding rubber for tennis balls seemed the Association's overriding concerns. "Victory" tennis balls, made without rubber, appeared in mid 1942, although production of synthetic rubber would soon end that crisis. Junior development got its usual endorsement despite lack of a broad, nationwide program; competitive tournament play was about all there was for younger players.[9]

But patriotism and public image soon had their day. President Roosevelt's physical-fitness committee chair, rowing champion John Kelly, gave his blessing to USLTA plans to continue with national championship tournaments, while *ALT* editorialized that the Association should "cut prices to the bone" at the nationals and experiment with catering "to the proletariat." By June 1942 the Association and the army had negotiated a temporary "code" for amateurs and professionals in the service to play each other in military-sponsored tournaments. The amateur or professional status of the "soldier-athletes" was "frozen" with regard to military sports. The army did comment that it would "discourage" boxing or wrestling matches between pros and amateurs lest a "cocky recruit" try to take on Joe Louis. Unhappily, there are no reports of those negotiations in the archives or in the minutes, but the guardians of amateur purity could not have been comfortable with mixing pros and amateurs together.[10]

That unease was surely intensified as they confronted the remarkable popularity of tennis tournaments that pitted amateurs against professionals. The "code" negotiated with the military allowed "exhibition" tennis matches between top amateurs and pros to raise funds for patriotic causes like war bonds and the Red Cross. Patriotism made war bonds a popular cause, but great tennis provided the vehicle. Clearly, the public would pay to see the best play each other.

The effect on the national championships of the steady drain of top amateurs into professional ranks was exacerbated for the men by absences because of service in the military. The Association eschewed any effort to arrange leaves for the top amateurs (although Jack Kramer did get time off to practice for the national championships) and by 1943 had to shorten play to just six days.[11]

The biggest tennis story of the war, one that drove home the appeal of open tennis competition, came in late January 1944. A war bonds fund raiser at New York City's Seventh Regiment (the Silk Stocking Regiment) Armory brought in six thousand paying customers and raised over $2.7 million; $35 million in today's dollars—not until the 1980s would a tennis event bring in such money. The most appealing of those matches pitted the first Grand Slam winner, Army Air Force lieutenant Don Budge, who had turned pro in late in 1938, against a young Coast Guard cadet who, as runner-up in the 1943 wartime national singles championship, made the Association's yearbook as "Seaman Kramer." (In 1946 that same Jack Kramer won the first of his two U.S. national singles titles.)[12] Alice Marble, who had become a professional in 1941, played British star Mary Hardwick, then they joined Budge and Kramer in mixed doubles. The crowd loved it. The same headliners met again in March for a Red Cross fund raiser, while Bill Tilden agreed to play in another Red Cross benefit in July. With a popular, winning war in progress, enthusiasm for such fund raisers was easy to generate. But pitting pros against amateurs obviously excited tennis fans, who had never made any bones about their preference for the best tennis—the pro-amateur war didn't matter. It could not have escaped the attention of Association leaders that the professionals—Bill Tilden, Don Budge, Mary Hardwick, Alice Marble—were the ones who got the headlines for entertaining the troops.[13]

Not surprisingly, in the midst the wartime flexibility Ward found it necessary in 1944 to warn players, in one of his usual long lectures, that the agreement with the War Department to allow some mixing of professionals and amateurs in the armed forces, required the "full cooperation" of all. Amateurs and professionals could play with or against each other in exhibition (fund-raiser) tournaments only so long as one of the parties was serving in the military. But under no circumstances could "civilian" professionals play "civilian" amateurs without making "the amateur player liable to disbarment from all" USLTA-sanctioned tournaments. The Association went into war deploying fund raisers and flexibility, but amateur tennis remained its mission. In mid-1944, *SMASH,* the bulletin of the Wartime Tennis Committee called for Association clubs to make one last push to raise money for the American Red Cross. The committee called for local clubs to run "American Red Cross Tournaments" with entry fees donated to the Red Cross. The heavy hand of Holcombe Ward seemed apparent given the injunction that the Association wanted to involve local players—"We do not wish to put emphasis on Exhibition matches."[14] Tennis, not fund raising was the goal. Matches with professionals raised more money, but that was tainted even with the special wartime arrangements. The "carry-on" wartime policy of continuing national championships, along with statements of support for junior tennis (largely limited to Junior Davis and Wightman Cup teams) had merely kept things going. But there were other voices.[15]

Schuyler Van Bloem, president of the West Side Tennis Club in 1945, after being president of the Eastern Section and on the USLTA executive committee, argued that the game could not "stand on tradition and precedent" as it prepared for the postwar world. Revenue was short, making the sections "poor relations" and limiting the Association's ability to build the game. The answer was obvious: obtain a larger "gate" at its tournaments and hold "at least one national open tournament per year." To draw larger crowds, the Forest Hills stadium needed extensive capital improvements, including a roof and repair of the "dilapidated" marquee. Anticipating expansion of the professional staff, Van Bloem pushed for a "public relations committee or counsel with promotion experience," which would "pay its own way" by increasing public attention and attendance. All but the roof over the stadium would come to be—and, in 2016, even the roof appeared though over a different stadium. He feared some would think his proposals too "commercialized," but in hindsight he was prescient: "Tennis, if it is to take its place as an instrument for building our post-war world, must have financial means to further its own development. . . . the game must help itself by planning and systematizing its efforts." But it would be another two decades or more before Van Bloem's call for change would take root. He and others also proposed an American Hall of Fame and National Museum of Lawn Tennis, but, despite some proposals, that has failed to materialize except as a predecessor to the International Tennis Hall of Fame.[16]

There is something both sad and bizarre that in January 1946 the Association's executive committee would consume forty-five pages of the minutes discussing how to control distribution of free tennis rackets to top amateur players (and then complain about the same problem twenty years later). Whatever the tortured nuances of choosing to allow distribution of precisely six rackets, most interesting were a series of changes in the amateur rule proposed by a delegate from New England, whose resolutions began with a combative challenge: "relations between the USLTA and the men and women tennis players are most unsatisfactory, and . . . enforcement of our amateur regulations . . . is generally regarded as the reason for the bad relationship." What followed was a series of proposed changes to the amateur rule that struck at the heart of USLTA policy. Ward grumpily refused to read the resolutions to the committee and opposed referring them to any other committee. Only after a suggestion to "just refer it to the Amateur Rule Committee and leave it there" did Ward call for a vote that sent the resolutions to their grave. "If playing for money instead of love for the game became the ruling spirit, Tennis would suffer irreparable injury," wrote Ward in a long and dense series of articles published in *ALT*. His personal dedication and efforts were beyond reproach; his creativity and imagination less so. In the favorite phrase of the newspapers, he was a USLTA "stuffed-shirt."[17]

But it was not always so benign. In April 1947, Ward, supported by the amateur rules committee, suspended the amateur status of Pauline Betz, the world's number-one woman player and winner of five Grand Slam tournaments, for "authorizing" announcements that she, and Sarah Palfrey Cooke, would play for pay. The minimum guaranty was a paltry $350 on weekdays and $500 for weekend exhibitions. In Jack Kramer's words, the action "was the closest thing to what the Olympic Committee did to Jim Thorpe. It was a crime, Pauline had not signed a professional contract."[18]

Feeling pressure from the press in the wake of the Betz-Cooke suspensions, USLTA officials complained of the difficulty of getting "substantiation for the various rumors that float about." Kramer, Gardnar (Gar) Mulloy, Billy Talbert, and Pancho Segura had been accused of taking excessive expenses but all denied doing so. Kramer, never one to gild the lily, later explained it all in his candid autobiography. He and some other players had received and split $1,500 in early 1947 to play in Daytona, Florida. Ward had asked Kramer to stop by the Association office, and handed Kramer a news clipping that said the players had gotten $2,500 to play. "Is that true, Jack?" he asked. "No sir," replied Kramer, since the amount was wrong. Technically he did not lie, but he made no apology then, or later. Kramer suspected that the Association found ways not to suspend the best players, presumably so they could play Davis Cup. He could recall only four top male players being banished. Mary Hardwick, writing in *ALT*, wondered when the Association would "do a complete job," pointing out that Kramer had stated he would probably go pro at after the 1947 season, which was all Betz had done.[19]

It was all about so little. One example among hundreds: in 1947 one Tom Brown received "prize order" vouchers for twenty-five pounds from the British Lawn Tennis Association after playing at Wimbledon. His girlfriend cashed in the vouchers, with the British association's permission and bought clothes rather than authorized tennis equipment or prizes at an authorized store. When Ward learned what had happened, he phoned Brown who returned the money when told it was a violation of the U.S. amateur rules. For ten pages of the executive committee (ExCom) minutes the discussion proceeded with excruciating detail and pettiness. While the majority found the British at fault and proposed asking them to return the twenty-five pounds so the USLTA could use it to buy a present for Brown, President Ward said that would reverse what he had told the British association. From the language it is clear that Ward stared them down. Brown got a slap on the wrist, he did not get his prize vouchers, and purity prevailed.[20] So did confusion about the amateur rules that continued to become so detailed and specific as to baffle Solomon.

In 1948, the guard changed—a little. Ward retired, or was retired, at the end of 1947. Along with testimonials to his dedication and determination was a long letter sent by the Association to tournament committee chairs, read by Ward to the annual meeting. It had the timbre of a farewell address combined with the confidence of the righteous:

> For 65 years the U.S.L.T.A. has upheld high ideals in sportsmanship and amateurism. It would seriously injure the game if the ranking players decided that amateur tennis owes them a living because of their skill and that it is smart to chisel a few extra dollars of expenses out of the clubs whose guests they are, and that they need not be ashamed of evading the rules unless they are found out. We must help the present generation of players and the next who have high ideals.[21]

Perhaps Ward missed the big picture on amateurism, as did the other Association leaders, but whatever the image of a finger in the dike, Ward was roundly and soundly praised by his colleagues for leading the Association through the lean years of the Second World War. No small challenge.

For the next decade, the reports of the amateur-rules, the scheduling, and the ranking committees dominated the Association's annual meetings. The USLTA was still all about tennis even if it was more about rules and regulations than the game itself. Scheduling and ranking quarrels were two halves of the same walnut, particularly since geography still made access to the major tournaments more difficult for West Coast players—a complaint that had prompted steady reforms, albeit ones that came too slowly for those west of the Mississippi.

But the amateur-open debate went on and on and on. The opposing arguments became mantras rather than discussions aimed at a common-sense compromise.

In 1948 Lawrence Baker finally became president after ten years in the wings as a vice president. Back in the late thirties and early forties, he had negotiated the Association's perhaps dubious tax-exempt status but was at the same time an adamant defender of amateurism, expressing concern that too many players were "living on the game through the year." Playing games with the tax code was legitimate; playing games with the amateur rules was not.[22] But by 1948 the game of tennis was capital, in the economic sense. Arguments over the "gate" were, at their root, arguments about investments and profits. Van Bloem had earlier grabbed the tiger by the tail: "Tennis, if it is to take its place as an instrument for building our post-war world, must have financial means to further its own development."[23] He was on the mark, but amateurism stood in the way. The fund raisers during the Second World War had demonstrated that there was money to be made in open competition between amateurs and professionals. But the legacy of white northeastern country-club leadership by older businessmen was too strong to overcome. Change would come but not from within until a new generation of leaders, and pressure from the outside combined to make it happen.

The most powerful outside influence would eventually be broadcast radio and television. The partnership of television and the Association that would revolutionize its finances and business philosophy is older than most would guess. It began with radio. President Franklin Roosevelt's Fireside Chats in the 1930s demonstrated the remarkable effect of the seemingly personal contact that occurred over the airwaves. Julian Myrick had preceded Roosevelt by a decade when he discussed lawn tennis in a radio broadcast in 1922, though it hardly gained a Roosevelt-size audience. In the late 1930s the executive committee wrestled with fears of commercialization versus revenue (the "Wheaties" championships).[24] By 1944 the contract for radio broadcasts, with sporting goods firm A. G. Spalding and Brothers as sponsor, brought in $17,500 for that year and in 1945 for just the men's national championships. Davis Cup was available for the Association to market. Thereafter, that figure began to fall off a little, bringing $10,000 in 1948 and just $5,000 in 1949. But the Association had hope. In 1947 the executive committee heard a report that Spalding would sponsor a radio broadcast of the semifinals and finals of the 1947 U.S. National Championships from Forest Hills. In "cheerleading" style, *ALT* exclaimed that "the program will command the air, coast-to-coast" with Harry Wismer, "the Nation's Number One sports announcer" whose voice "is like the 14-karat mark on gold."[25]

The 1939 experiment with television broadcasting of tennis had lain fallow during the war, although the technology had improved apace. In 1945 the Association received one thousand dollars for the initial television broadcasts of the U.S. National Championships and the same for Davis Cup matches. Radio broadcast rights that same year brought in ten thousand dollars—ten times as much. Television payments grew slowly during the forties. Contracts with the National Broadcasting Company (NBC) and the DuMont Television Network in 1948 for the rights to the U.S. National Championships (at the West Side Tennis Club), and the Davis Cup matches brought the USLTA $15,000—the equivalent of about $140,000 in today's dollars. As of 1949, sponsors for tennis broadcasts had become difficult to find. One report noted "advertisers not putting out this year," and NBC could not find a sponsor for the national championships television broadcast—though, presciently, the network stayed with it in the hope that a national broadcast would generate interest in the long term. Little did they know.[26]

The promise of increased financial benefits from tennis broadcasts added to the growing pressure on the amateur system. By 1953 that pressure had become a matter of concern for the sections. An ad hoc Fifteen Presidents Committee (i.e., the presidents of the fifteen sections) reported that it had studied and essentially approved existing amateur rules, though they recommended some seemingly minor changes. In essence the rules were those of the ILTF, and the Association was unwilling to challenge that body. Why? In good part because amateur status was an international matter. Not only were Wightman and Davis Cup international by definition, but the USLTA wanted good showings by Americans at Wimbledon and the other Grand Slam tournaments and had long subsidized travel for players entered in those events. (Recall Julian Myrick's anger at Alice Marble in 1934 for having "wasted" USLTA money used to send her to Europe.) Committee members commented that the USLTA seemed to be carrying the ball all alone. As the Association president awkwardly put it: "In one way, we are less liberal than the international would allow us to be"; nonetheless, "in general the report adopts the complete International Laws as our laws. We have to subscribe to them, anyhow." Some hailed adoption of the ILTF amateur rules as a breakthrough, but it soon became apparent that it was the same game, shamateurism, by a slightly different name.[27]

Not only were American tennis players "living off the game" by "negotiating" with tournaments for increased expense money (an oft-repeated complaint), but other national tennis federations, all members of the international Federation, were more relaxed in their interpretation and enforcement of the amateur rules. Perhaps what pushed the Association into supporting what President James Bishop called a "more realistic" amateur code was the threat that (in the words of Davis Cup captain Frank Shields), "Australia can hold the cup for the next ten years."[28] The infamous eight-weeks rule that attempted to limit tennis players to only eight weeks of tournament play was eliminated in 1954, by which time only the United States still had the unenforced and unenforceable rule. The exceptions had become ludicrous, especially for Davis Cup players who wanted and needed more play in order to be competitive. At the same time, there were calls for "open" tournaments from nations like Australia. Requests from "so-called touring pros for reinstatement" added to the pressure for stricter American rules since the executive committee and the Fifteen Presidents Committee staunchly opposed any easy reinstatement policy, particularly for veteran players. Becoming a touring pro was, for hard liners like Julian Myrick, a betrayal that deserved punishment, or at least banishment:

> people who turned professional, not to teach or to instruct, but to make money out of the game and to tour the country, Kramer, Sarah Palfrey, all those people now want to come in and play in the Veterans' Tournaments, and get back in the amateur game. . . . If they turn professional just to make money out of the game, they should not be permitted to come back and go into championship tournaments in years to come.[29]

Nor were clubs and promoters (often the same) helping. Not only did American clubs stretch the expense rules beyond their limits, but foreign federations like Australia required that host tournaments abroad (obviously referring to major events like the U.S. National Championships) to pay a "premium" to cover the costs of sending Aussie players. One USLTA section even made a similar request in order for a specific player from their section to participate in "various European and other tournaments." If that practice continued to grow, it could well have jeopardized the larger amateur tournaments (i.e., the nationals). Little wonder that Association leaders sought cooperation with the ILTF "to bring about some control of sanctioned international events."[30]

Nothing was too picayune to worry about. The Association had agreed that tennis professionals (apparently including teaching pros) could not be officers in sectional organizations. But could pros act as officials in matches? Sort of. The vote allowed pros to act as officials but only at a level below sectional championships. In 1954 Lawrence Baker, former president, used the tax code to buttress his own preference, pointing out that in the federal tax-exemption case the Association had stated it would maintain its commitment to being "an amateur organization." It was dubious, to say the least, that the IRS would interpret pros being officials as a violation of being "an amateur organization" since they were not being paid to officiate.

Touring professionals were likened to men who made a "career of fortune hunting, or marrying a rich widow or of becoming a gigolo or a tennis bum." Association meetings were characterized by lengthy reports about calculated misuse of funds and under-the-table payments to players, particularly in European tournaments. There was much gnashing of teeth and wailing, but no solutions except to call for international cooperation.[31]

Perhaps the most public challenge to shamateurism in tennis came with Jack Kramer's article, "I Was a Paid Amateur," published in May 1955. Even though he gave no details, the piece made clear that Kramer "took money for playing tennis—over and above expenses." Association officials were officially aghast. Although Kramer called for the Association to be the "governing body" of open tennis in America, he was "fired" as an unpaid coach of the Junior Davis Cup team (a program he had promoted). But the USLTA was not embarrassed enough to stop him from working out with the U.S. Davis Cup team that August—all this in a year when Kramer was recruiting for his pro tour top players like Lew Hoad and Tony Trabert. As ever, Davis Cup took precedence.[32]

Despite, or perhaps because of the disruptive challenge of professional tennis, the Association elevated small problems into matters of principle. Back in 1927 a lengthy debate followed a motion to remove the names of honorary Association members who had turned pro. One executive committee member went to the essence of the argument: "Don't we feel very strongly about this just now because this Pyle troop has gotten us all stirred up?" Julian Myrick pointed out that declared professionals were honest, clearly implying that those who played games (so to speak) with amateur rules were dishonest. Why take away their well-earned honorary status? The motion lost, 5–7, was referred to committee and apparently never emerged.[33]

In 1954 a special committee studying the honorary-member category, which had fallen into disuse since 1938, reported out to the executive committee. The report called for adding new names to the roll, while subtracting others:

> Your Committee [chaired by Lawrence Baker] is of the opinion that those who have won the [National] Championships, either in Singles or Doubles, since the last champions were elected should be added to this roll of honorary membership, except those champions who have subsequently become professionals, and it is our opinion that with respect to those who are presently honorary members who have since that time become professionals, recommendations should be made, after study, as to whether those who have turned professional should be removed from that roll.

The executive committee approved the nominees, although no list was included with the minutes found in the archive. No women were nominated, but the special committee did feel it necessary to consider "the question of whether or not the regulations should be broadened to include women players." The list of honorary members in the archival copy of the 1941 *USLTA Yearbook* has handwritten lines drawn through the names of players who had become professionals after being made honorary members. Bill Tilden, Fred Perry, and Vinnie Richards topped the list of strike outs. Not the first time professionals were viewed as without honor.

Drafting new rules and regulations for the honorary-member category was referred to the special committee, but no action seems to have been taken. Perhaps by 1954 a gratuitous insult to well-known professionals seemed unwise or at least impolitic.[34]

Curiously, amateur versus professional tennis never came up in the discussions about "sanctioning" an American tennis hall of fame and museum at the Casino in Newport. The idea had been bruited about for awhile, but was broached forcefully in 1946 when the Association received a report from William Fischer, founder of the Fischer Lawn Tennis Library[35] and chair of a special committee authorized in 1945 to examine establishment of a Hall of Fame and National Museum of Lawn Tennis. Costs and the uncertainties of immediate postwar America precluded any decision to build a hall of fame for the foreseeable future. But there were various suggestions. Schuyler Van Bloem proposed a "living war memorial in the form of a Tennis Museum." Hamstrung by the lack of funds, the committee recommended placing historical tablets at key locations, for example, at the site of the first tennis game on Staten Island (now a railroad freight yard); at the Newport Casino, where the inaugural national championship had been played; and at the old grounds of the Longwood Cricket Club (now a school grounds) where the Davis Cup competition began. It also recommended gathering histories and artifacts for use and display in a future hall of fame. The committee suggested that it be continued and that it expand its activities "to include all historical matters, archives and records."[36]

Nothing came of all that until 1953. Early that year, Jimmy Van Alen, a long time Newport Casino member and tennis enthusiast who had the support of the Casino's board of directors, asked the USLTA to sanction establishment of an American hall of fame in Newport, Rhode Island. The debate within the Association was never about the validity of a hall of fame but about its location and who would pay for it. The argument was that Newport was too far off the beaten track to attract many visitors. A number of New Yorkers plumped for the Fischer Library in New York City as the appropriate site and organization, but its lack of resources made that impractical. The executive committee concluded that a bird in the hand was worth two in the bush and authorized discussions with Van Alen, although the Association wanted the right to move the museum to a more suitable location. Early in 1954 it gave Van Alen a five-year option to set up "the shrine at the Casino," during which time the Association would not ask the Casino to move it to another location. Nothing was said about prohibiting professionals, many of whom had been U.S. national champions, from enshrinement. In 1957 Mary Browne, a national champion who had turned pro in the 1920s, was installed into the Hall of Fame. Tilden followed in 1959.[37]

But professional tennis was not the only challenge to tradition faced by the Association. In March 1948 a forty-year-old man lost in the second round of the USLTA national indoor championships, played at the Seventh Regiment Armory in New York City. The winner was Billy Talbert, a highly ranked player who had been twice runner-up in the men's nationals and much younger than his opponent. The loser was Reginald Weir, a well-known local player. He was an African American, a black man. That meant he likely could not meet the entry requirement of belonging to a USLTA member club—custom not legal segregation made most of New York's clubs all white. Nor were there any "Negro" member clubs since they had routinely been told to join the ATA, the American Tennis Association, the organization for "the colored people" of the United States.

The USLTA had long used persiflage on the issue of discrimination, taking an official stance that the tournament committees for each competition made all the decisions about entries. Such committees were normally selected by the host club or organization and therefore followed club rules or practices, or segregation laws that excluded blacks (more precisely, nonwhites, a legally defined status). Moreover, to enter any national championship, applicants had to be members of a USLTA club. In 1948 that rule was waived by the Association for Weir and a few others, all the while denying that such waivers set a precedent.

Back in 1929, that same Reginald Weir along with Gerald Norman Jr., another young black player, had entered the USLTA national indoor junior championship, held at that same Seventh Regiment Armory. When they showed up for their matches, they were denied access. Appeals by Norman's father and the NAACP were dismissed with the comment that, although the Association had nothing against black players, "as a practical matter" it believed separate tennis organizations "for white and colored players should be continued."[38]

In 1940 *American Lawn Tennis,* which had routinely reported on ATA championships, carried an article about its national championships at Wilberforce University in Ohio, a traditionally black school named after the English antislavery reformer. A USLTA member who attended sent in a "glowing description" of some one thousand black spectators who watched "exciting and very good" tennis. Tickets were inexpensive and, since "these individuals" did not have much money, lodging and meal costs at Wilberforce were kept quite low—two dollars per day. However grating the unquestioned acceptance of segregation, a nationwide attitude, the report was praising and positive about the sportsmanship of the athletes and the "gracious and appreciative" reactions of the crowds. "Their galleries are intelligent, attentive, spontaneous and enthusiastic," wrote the observer for *ALT*.[39] In a small, perhaps insignificant way, that language challenged stereotypes. The three top players at that tournament were the Californian Jimmy McDaniel, who had won four ATA nationals, including those in 1939 and 1940, and the other finalists those two years, Reginald Weir and Richard Cohen.

Weir again gently challenged the color line in July 1940 by playing, before a "large crowd," an exhibition doubles match against Don Budge, the former USLTA national and Grand Slam champion, who had turned pro the previous year. The site was the Cosmopolitan Club, a "leading Negro net organization" according to the *New York Times*, which did not mention that the club was located in Harlem. In the feature match, Budge defeated McDaniel, then teamed up with Weir to play McDaniel and his doubles partner at Xavier College, Richard Cohen.[40]

The USLTA took no official notice, though the executive committee privately squirmed uneasily, trying to convince black Americans that to push the envelope would "merely antagonize people." Budge was a professional while the other three were members of the ATA. Neither the USLTA's amateur rule nor its unofficial practice of segregated tennis were challenged. Eighteen months after the war ended, the Association rejected requests from the ATA that it support Cohen's application to the national championships. The ATA asked that "our American democratic ideals and way of life should be the guiding influence in your consideration," but a special arrangement by the USLTA for black players was diverted when Lawrence Baker tarred the request "as discrimination in their favor"—reverse discrimination. When President Ward suggested the request be quietly buried by referral to a study committee, Baker warned, "If you appoint a committee, the committee is going to have to report. Then you are going to have a discussion . . . [and] pressure for action on the report." For all the talk about admission based on results, and about avoiding what would later be termed "quotas" based on ethnicity (what about a reserved slot for the best Chinese player, asked Baker sarcastically), Holcombe Ward bluntly told the ugly truth: "we should continue as we do now, and allow the local tournament authorities to accept Negro entries if they wish to do so, and if they do not wish to do so, they may reject them." The Association, like most of America, refused to confront the contradiction between wartime ideals and domestic reality. Equal access was for white people.[41]

But Weir's "courtesy" appearance at the national indoors in 1948 presaged change. He and other black players had previously been permitted to enter eastern championships since the national Association evaded the membership issue by allowing the sections to decide who could or could not enter their tournaments. A few months after Weir's long-belated entry into a USLTA national championship, Oscar Johnson, a young black player, won the Long Beach Junior Open, becoming the first African American to win a USLTA-sanctioned event—fittingly, on the Fourth of July. He quickly followed that with a victory in the Association's national junior indoor championship, becoming the first black player to win a National event.

When Weir received the waiver to enter the 1948 tournament, Association executive secretary Edwin Baker emphasized that "this is not intended as a precedent-setting action." He pointed to Weir's long record of quality play but then cautioned that, although USLTA policy was to allow local tournament committees make decisions about entry applications, "this doesn't mean that Dr. Weir (who had, by then, earned a medical degree) will be in the national outdoor championships at Forest Hills, which is our real championship."

Of course not! Few near-forty-year-olds could expect to compete with the best tennis players in the country.[42] Any fool could tell that Weir's acceptance was as much a matter of skin color as were the previous refusals to grant entry. The decision to allow him to play, after rejecting his applications for two decades, clearly had approval from the Association's leadership. Alrick Man, the chair of the tournament committee, which officially made the decision, was nonplaying captain of the Davis Cup team and by definition a part of the establishment. Yet USLTA minutes for the executive committee and annual meetings during 1948-49 make no mention of what transpired. In fact, there is no mention of Negroes, colored people, African Americans or anything of the like. Not only was the waiver not a "precedent-setting action" for the Association, it was a nonevent.

Harold Rosenthal writing in *American Lawn Tennis* a few months later, bitingly mocked the USLTA: "the first Negro has played in an American tennis championship and, at this late date, there have been no reports of any worlds having split asunder as an aftermath." Rosenthal speculated as to the reasons "for the ultimate appearance of a Negro player . . . in a sport which had heretofore been divided sharply along the color line." He dismissed both gate receipts and personal pressure from Weir's friends in New York City, then failed to answer his own question.[43]

Touring tennis professionals like Don Budge never got the credit they deserved for breaking the color line in 1940, although professional tennis had a relatively low profile in the world of American sports. But seven years later, no one in the USLTA went on record publicly or in Association minutes mentioning the name of Jackie Robinson, who famously broke the color line for Major League Baseball on April 15, 1947. None of those Association leaders could have failed to recognize the impact for sports of what had happened. These were smart businessmen who cared deeply about the image of their Association. Professional baseball was hardly their role model, but by the time Weir applied to the national indoor championships, change was in the wind.[44]

Moreover, the Eastern Section, which included the New York City region, had actively challenged the de facto segregation practiced by the national organization and routinely allowed black players to participate in Eastern's tournaments and championships. Weir played in Eastern championships a number of times before getting his waiver, and only a year later both he and Althea Gibson, the top-ranked black female in the ATA, played in the same national indoor championship.[45] Eastern had long been the home section for the largest number of USLTA leaders, who could not have helped but notice. Perhaps Association leaders, cautious about any public backlash, were allowing the Eastern Section to test the waters—but there is no evidence of such wisdom.

The door would open forever in 1948 when President Harry Truman issued Executive Order 9981 desegregating the U.S. Armed Forces—arguably the most important change of legal status for black Americans since the Fourteenth Amendment eighty years earlier. Tennis and the USLTA had stuck a tentative toe into that opening door, but ever so quietly and reluctantly. The Association's position had always been that social reform was not the business of the USLTA. But the rhetoric of character building and leadership that accompanied its ardent defenses of amateurism gave the lie to that argument.

Then in 1949 the tennis skills of a twenty-two-year-old woman pushed the Association over the color line. Althea Gibson had been the American Tennis Association women's champion for three straight years, winning everything the ATA had to offer. Although that organization's leaders recognized that she was a likely candidate to put forth as qualified to play major USLTA national championships and find the competition she needed to improve, the black association had no intention of creating a "stir." Reginald Weir had broken the barrier, but that was at the 1948 national indoor championship, an event routinely held in the friendly confines of New York City's Seventh Regiment Armory. But *the* national championship was a horse of a different color, so to speak, even if it was only just across the East River in Forest Hills, home of a very private club.[46]

But while the ATA played softball, Alice Marble played hardball. Marble had a distinguished record as a tennis player, between 1936 and 1940 winning Wimbledon once and the U.S. national singles four times. Add to that six Wimbledon and U.S. national doubles championships and you have a heavy hitter. Her courage was indisputable: following her husband's death during the Second World War, Marble agreed to spy for the United

States on her former lover, a Swiss banker cooperating with the Nazis. After being shot by the Germans, she escaped Switzerland. One tough cookie.[47]

In the July 1950 issue of *American Lawn Tennis*, Marble took on the tennis establishment as well as American society. She asserted that Gibson's record warranted her entry into the women's national championships at Forest Hills, coming up in September of that year. An anonymous member of the tournament committee for the nationals (there were thirty-six members and the same Alrick Man was the chair!) told Marble that for Gibson to qualify for the Nationals, she had to play well in the major eastern tournaments during the summer, mostly "invitationals." No invite, no play; and few if any had ever allowed a black player on their courts. Describing the USLTA's duplicity, Marble wrote:

> Miss Gibson is over a very cunningly wrought barrel, and I can only hope to loosen a few of its staves with one lone opinion. If tennis is a game for ladies and gentlemen, it's also time we acted a little more like gentle-people and less like sanctimonious hypocrites. . . . If Althea Gibson represents a challenge to the present crop of women players, it's only fair that they should meet that challenge on the courts. . . . If she is refused a chance to succeed or fail, then there is an ineradicable mark against a game to which I have devoted most of my life, and I would be bitterly ashamed. . . . If the field of sports has got to pave the way for all of civilization, let's do it. . . . The entrance of Negroes into national tennis is . . . inevitable. . . . Eventually the tennis world will rise up en masse to protest the injustices perpetrated by our policy makers. Eventually—why not now?[48]

Common sense, public pressure, whispers from the USLTA leadership, who knows? On August 21, five days after receiving Gibson's application, the tournament committee announced that she "was accepted on her ability." The twenty-three-year-old became the first black American player, man or woman, to play in a Grand Slam event.[49] (See gallery, image 20.)

Gibson lost her second round match in the 1950 national championship singles to Louise Brough, the fourth seed and the current Wimbledon champion, by a 9–7 score in the third set.[50] Gibson had been ahead in that final set 7–6 when a thunderstorm forced suspension of play. The next day, after a night to think about it, Gibson lost three straight games and the match. The 1951 *USLTA Yearbook* called her performance a "remarkable feat" for the "Negro Champion." Obviously, race still mattered, and would continue to matter. Gibson was denied entrance into a number of tournaments for the next few years, and black Americans in general were still unable to join most private clubs.

Shortly after the Forest Hills event, in "An Open Letter to Althea Gibson," Marble wrote that she *now* knew who weren't her friends: "People who had called me 'Champ' since 1938 suddenly remembered I was 'Miss Marble.'" People who had greeted her with kisses "gave me a chilly handshake . . . or glared, which was even funnier. . . . They only remember a terrible article I wrote, saying a good tennis player named Gibson ought to play in the Nationals."[51]

In October 1951 *American Lawn Tennis* published a short article stating that the ATA had put "real grit" into integration by attracting "several white players" to the ATA national tournament. All anyone wanted was good tennis.[52]

In 1955 as the civil rights movement moved into its most active phase, then president of the West Side Tennis Club and USLTA first vice president (soon to be president) Renville McMann, asked Gibson to join a U.S. State Department sponsored "goodwill" tennis tour—three white players plus Gibson—an obvious attempt to offset the international image of racial discrimination and violence in the United States. But the invitation from a West Side Tennis Club president hardly meant that the club had turned over a new leaf.[53]

The private Forest Hills club continued to refuse to admit blacks, in 1959 denying membership to Ralph Bunche, a diplomat and Nobel Prize winner, as well as to his son. When Bunche made public the remarks of the club's president, Will Burglund (a "Public Relations expert"), that the rejection had nothing to do with color and that the club rejected many applications and specifically Jews, a public firestorm followed. The club offered an apology and invitation of membership, while Burglund resigned without withdrawing his remarks. Bunche refused membership because the change appeared based on his personal prestige and not on any principle of racial equality. "No Negro American can be free from the disabilities of race in this country until the lowliest Negro in Mississippi is no longer disadvantaged because of his race," he told the press. Lamely, club officials pointed out that nothing in the club's constitution or rules barred membership on the grounds of race or religion. But Abe Stark, New York City's acting mayor, began searching for ways to take public tournaments away from the Forest Hills site, five U.S. senators jointly condemned the policy, a municipal commission set up an investigation, and the press hammered away.[54]

Once again, the West Side Tennis Club had managed to get on the wrong side of the Association. But it was the style and publicity, not substance that annoyed the Association. Only a few weeks later, USLTA president Victor Denny released a public statement arguing that the USLTA had "no control" over the actions of member clubs that discriminated on racial grounds: "It is a great mistake to make a public and political issue over the right of any individual to demand membership . . . solely on racial or religious grounds." The persiflage continued.

In 1960 reacting to quite gentle ATA representations about membership, the *USLTA* executive committee agreed that "integration—if you could call it that—will come about at a normal pace, where it is approved by the Sectional Associations themselves." The local-sectional veto lived on. Witness the decision by the University of Virginia to end its hosting (since 1946) of the Association's National Interscholastic Championships. The university indicated it no longer wished to hold the event since "interest in the tournament was dropping off." But an editorial in *Sports Illustrated* suggested a different motive, asserting that "since Negroes began to appear regularly," the town folk were unhappy. True or not, the USLTA agreed without public discussion to move the tournament to Williams College in Massachusetts. The minutes for the only question inferred a backroom decision when the questioner answered his own question:

MR. MCMANN: Mr. Chairman, what has happened to Charlottesville, just as a point of information?
MR. WHEARY: They—
MR. MCMANN: Bowed out?
MR. WHEARY: Bowed out, that is right.[55]

Nor did the Forest Hills club change its way of thinking, even after the civil rights movement and legislation of the 1960s. In 1977 when the U.S. Open moved from Forest Hills to its current site in Flushing Meadows, a member of the board of the West Side Tennis Club publicly disparaged the shift warning that the neighborhood was "'95 percent . . . Negro' in fact, it was mostly white," fans would be reluctant to go there, and the local community would not work with the USTA. The board member resigned, but the attitude remained.[56]

Early in 1969 a proposed amendment to the Association's constitution called for an applicant for a sanctioned event to agree not to discriminate against any participant because of race, creed, or color. "A violation of this provision *may* result in a refusal by the USLTA to issue any further sanctions to such applicant." Gene Scott, the delegate from the Eastern Section, which had offered the amendment, asked why the constitution and rules committee had substituted the word "may" for "will." The brief discussion focused around requiring action as opposed to permitting action—a "warning" as one speaker called it. Most of those who commented preferred "will" as a stronger statement, but the vote went for the legalistic argument of Lawrence Baker and Robert Kelleher who argued that "will" would be "self executing" thus tying the hands of whatever body would make a decision. In plainer English, the USLTA supported statements against racial and religious discrimination but did not want to set up machinery to police that verbal commitment. As an organization with a number of member clubs that routinely discriminated against blacks and Jews, the inclination was to leave such matters as simple statements of good intentions.[57]

That same year, then Association president, Robert Kelleher, personally prompted and supported Arthur Ashe in his famous confrontation with apartheid South Africa by requesting a visa for Ashe to play in the South African Open, while the Association's caution continued. Not until 1974 was its first black staff member hired (by Eve Kraft, co-chair of the Education and Research Committee in Princeton, New Jersey), Henry Talbert (who went on to be executive director of the Southern California Section), yet a minority-affairs committee did not appear until 1991.[58]

Although "encouraging" nondiscriminatory play became a stated Constitutional purpose in 1979, the discretionary "may" word remained in the Association's rules against discrimination based on race, creed, color, etc. (age, national origins, sex were all added) until the 1993 standing orders. Discrimination then became "not allowed" and, by the turn of the century, the rule had teeth:

> Discrimination Prohibited. Membership and all rights of participation in the USTA, including all tournaments and other events conducted or sanctioned by it, shall be open to athletes, coaches, trainers, administrators, officials, and all other persons without regard to race, age, creed, sexual orientation, color, national origin, or sex. (USTA *Yearbook*, 2013, Bylaw 10.)

It was a long, hard haul.

To take this to a close—fittingly, tennis "the game" moved more quickly than the tennis Association; after all the game was the reason for the USTA's existence. In 1981 the ATA women's and men's singles champions were awarded automatic wild cards into the qualifying round of the U.S. Open (since rescinded).[59] Nevertheless, it would take two generations of black tennis players, from Arthur Ashe to the Williams sisters, before black Americans would feel comfortable within the embrace of the United States Tennis Association. The Minority Participation Committee was established, at long last, in 1991 with Dwight Mosley, as chair. The very creation of that committee was an admission that there had not been a level playing field. Not until 1993 would a person of color become a member of the Association's board of directors, when Mosley was elected secretary. It is no small irony that the first black (male) board officer came only four years after the first female officer, Barbara Williams.

By autumn 1998, the executive director (Rick Ferman) could "report that since 1996, the minority composition of our staff has increased by eighty-five percent. . . . [which] doubled the percentage of minorities holding professional and management positions. . . . [And of] our new minority hires in that same time period, forty-five percent have assumed professional and management positions. So the USTA today stands with 30.5 percent minority composition, and we'l1 proudly compare that to the national U.S. minority composition of 27 and a half percent. And still we have a lot more work to do in this area."[60]

Although diversity came slowly, other changes were in the wind. The suffocating effect of the Association's preoccupation with amateurism while the most famous players were becoming professionals seemed about to come to a head in 1951. *American Lawn Tennis* described new president Russell Kingman's inaugural proposals as "drastic changes" that could serve "as an antidote for the public's tennis apathy." Kingman was remarkably accomplished. An "inventor of some fifty devices and processes," he became chairman of the board of the Metal Textile Corporation, was an "amateur 'cellist of distinction," and a friend of Pablo Casals. He was not only the first American to be the true president of the ILTF, but he had two terms, 1949–50 and 1954–55, in between serving two years as president of the USLTA. He was treasurer of the Association for ten years (1937–47). Despite credentials as a member of the tennis establishment, he was a strong proponent of reforms. It may be indicative of the attitude of the USLTA leadership toward the ILTF that when Kingman died in 1959, *The Official USLTA News* made no mention of his two terms as president of the Federation even while it listed his other major tennis offices.[61]

"A European Affair": The International Federation and the Association

For over a century after the ITF was formed in 1913, only two Americans (Kingman, for two terms, and Walter Elcock) held the formal title of Federation president. Louis Carruthers was "principal/chairman, effectively president" in 1934, but that appears to have been meaningful for only the annual general meeting he attended in March 1934. Just a handful of non-Europeans have led the Federation. A number of presidents have come from France and Great Britain. Australia, then perhaps Asia's most European nation, provided five. Most of the western European nations are represented. Mighty Belgium, hardly a consistent force in international tennis play, has held the presidency six times. So much for American imperialism—until 2015 with the selection of an American, David Haggerty as ITF president (not that Haggerty is an imperialist).[62]

"Long hailed as a tennis liberal," Kingman indirectly acknowledged the growth of the professional game by calling for more attention "on the game's colorful players" and for better public and media relations. In high-flown phrases, he acknowledged that the Association's financial problems came largely from decreased public interest, which had translated into lower attendance at major tournaments. "We should more occasionally dispense with the drab academic aspects of our exterior and present tennis in more interesting, brighter, and warmer colors." Tennis was "only an amateur sport," he observed, but one "overflowing with interesting episodes."[63]

Easier said than done. It would be some forty-five years later before that call that would be echoed, and with far greater success, with the appointment of Arlen Kantarian as chief executive of professional tennis and responsibility for marketing the U.S. Open.

The perception of decline set the stage for a remarkable meeting of the executive committee in August 1951 and for the beginnings of a shift in thinking. Not only had the Association been unable to make a distribution to the sections in January, but there was deep concern that tennis was not growing as they had hoped, or so tennis equipment sales suggested. That despite the interest in the nationals and Davis Cup created by expanded radio and television coverage, although sponsors were difficult to find. The concern prompted proposals related to amateur rules that must have infuriated Holcombe Ward, still a member of the executive committee, although he said nothing recorded in the minutes. The chair of the Amateur Rules Committee reported that his group had discussed but not decided on a number of changes regarding amateur status that would allow players to compete for an entire year (not just eight weeks) and, following the lead of the ILTF, change the player-writer rule to permit competitors to write for the media about tennis matches without jeopardizing their amateur status. That after the USLTA-Tilden wars of the 1920s! Although the committee did not endorse or oppose such changes, the chairman vigorously supported them. He finished saying he did not know if his proposals would be approved, but that he would "keep on fighting for them." The minutes recorded that applause followed.[64]

The immediate problem seemed to be money. As one member of the executive committee put it, the Association had to progress and grow, or it would go backwards. Tennis needed to develop juniors and attract new players. Every "reasonable" way to raise money, money that would go eventually to the sections, should be examined closely. If it is honest and does not "interfere" with amateur issues, then the executive committee should support it. "The future is with the youngsters"—a truism that has remained the Association's mantra ever since the youngsters no longer were in charge.[65]

From the outset Association leaders were competitive—on the court and for the prestige that went with winning international championships, especially the Davis Cup, later the Grand Slam tournaments. Losing streaks, however brief, invariably brought on Cassandra-like prophecies of gloom and doom for American tennis. In 1922 Julian Myrick had argued vigorously that "the main thought of the Association is to develop the boys' and juniors' play." Thereafter, junior development initiatives punctuated the Association's existence. The discussions became more intense as professional tennis began to skim off the cream of the amateur crop (though it must have affected the other tennis nations just as much). By the late 1950s, President Ren McMann, talking about the Association's junior program in the wake of Australian Rod Laver's victory in the U.S. boys junior championship, dismissed the idea of finding promising players at an early age then keeping them together as a squad of competitors through "prep school" and college. (An idea that would surface in more sophisticated form, but with equally unsuccessful responses, in the late 1990s.) McMann's solution? The usual—study the junior development program some more.[66]

In general, the Association assumed that only the sections could effectively set up and operate junior programs, so assistance from the national organization was largely financial. Such aid normally came with "careful scrutiny," framing a question that would trouble the Association at the turn of the twentieth century—to what degree are the sections autonomous? Can the national association dictate to the sections since it is the cash cow for all? Occasionally a proposal would surface that called for national action—such as training centers and/or special programs supported by patrons' organizations. One president of the Florida section argued that "decentralized" programs could not develop "outstanding prospects on the national level." But the issue of sectional boundaries rather than competitive development always surfaced. Sections wanted their players win national championships, just as the national association wanted Americans to win international championships. Attempts to create a national structure for junior development threatened sectional autonomy, and sectional pride. It is worth noting that by 1942 each section had a specific number of "endorsements" for its junior players to enter the various national championships. The size of a section's quota was determined by its number of junior players, not by its talent pool.[67] Those who favored the endorsement system argued that it was only fair to give players from every section an equal chance. Former champions—Jack Kramer most notably—argued strenuously that the very best juniors came from areas where there was strong and extensive competition. He had in mind, of course, Southern California.[68] Eastern and Florida would soon make the same claim.

Ironically, once open tennis became a reality in the 1970s, USTA ownership of the U.S. Open necessitated that the Association promote junior development, but so that American professionals would win the major championships. So strong was the commitment that the USTA eventually made having Americans win the U.S. Open a specific goal in its strategic plan.

But junior tennis was only part of the reforms Kingman promoted. He appealed to the Association to seize the opportunity to raise revenue and to become something no one could imagine. This fell not so much on deaf ears but on ears not ready for change, especially when filtered through the mantra of pure amateurism. He went on at length about how to turn charity matches into fund raisers, but as was de rigueur in the immediate post-Ward days, paid homage to amateurism—no payments to pros—pointing out that an earlier charity match had been a "fiasco" since the professionals submitted expenses that left "little for charity." Amateur standards were more important than the game. Kingman's proposal was impractical—charity matches between primarily local players would not solve the Association's financial shortfall. Large charities, promoters, and clubs were not interested in organizing events between relative unknowns that would bring in only a few hundreds of dollars.

A smarter idea was the Tennis Educational Foundation, the "brainchild" of former president Lawrence Baker, the Association's tax expert.

The Association's tax status as a "social club" meant it did not have to pay taxes on dues and tournament proceeds, but donations were not tax deductible for the donor. The foundation, founded late in 1951 as a not-for-profit organization, could accept gifts that were tax deductible for the giver. Although it was a "nation-wide tennis patron's association," the foundation raised relatively small amounts for most of its existence and was eventually merged into the International Tennis Hall of Fame. Ironically, in 1957 Baker apparently tried to rescue his foundation by crossing the line between amateur and professional tennis. Speaking to the Professional Lawn Tennis Association he proposed that they create a committee to work with the Tennis Educational Foundation to get more people playing tennis.[69]

Kingman had created the Public Relations Coordinating Committee tasked with generating new ideas and proposals, particularly about money problems and expanding the game. In August 1951 Sidney Wood, a former Wimbledon champion (and nephew of Julian Myrick), presented a report that proposed various public-relations initiatives and that also criticized umpiring at Forest Hills and chided the club for not being responsive to player requests for improvements. That prompted a brief squabble when West Side members took umbrage. Kingman tried to throw oil on the troubled waters, insisting that everyone had great admiration for the West Side Club and that they merely had "a sincere difference of opinion," but the tension was evident. Wood's enthusiasm for creating a better image was infectious. The minutes recorded "applause" when he concluded with a plea not to restrict the growth of tennis by "keeping it in swaddling clothes for too long."[70]

Another of Kingman's suggestions had been construction of forty boxes at the Forest Hills stadium, which would raise an estimated twelve thousand dollars additional revenue for the national singles championship. The Association was finding it increasingly difficult to work with the West Side Tennis Club. Kingman reported that his proposal had been cut by the club to twenty boxes. He indirectly accused a club member of initiating a letter-writing campaign aimed at convincing others of the "infeasibility" of the boxes.

Seamlessly, Kingman moved on to describe the reaction of the Forest Hills club to a proposal aimed at helping junior players:

> In view of the Sections having no distribution last January, it was proposed that two or three well-known [amateur] players assemble at the West Side Tennis Club once each week in these youth-inspiring

> surroundings to give of their time and talent in coaching juniors by appointment from within a radius of, say, 50 or 100 miles. Talbert, Wood, McNeill and Shields agreed that two of their number usually would be on hand at about four in the afternoon, perhaps once each week. The West Side Tennis Club objected, saying that these players, most of whom are not members the West Side Club, were merely trying thus to obtain free use of the Club! . . . This was a little disappointing, but I suppose was part of the day's work.[71]

Bill Talbert, Frank Shields, Don McNeill, and Sidney Wood were all top American and international players, each of whom would later be in the International Tennis Hall of Fame. It was ludicrous to suggest that any one of them needed "to obtain free use of the Club."

Wood, reporting for his public-relations committee to the 1952 annual meeting, used phrases that would be echoed in the 2000s, when Arlen Kantarian became ringmaster of the U.S. Open:

> We went to work, first of all, with all the powers of persuasion at our command and attempted to work in some boxes in the Stadium courts at Forest Hills, feeling that if this first step were made, new faces would begin to appear on the scene, names would appear at Forest Hills that had never been there before perhaps. Celebrities would show up. That would, in turn, entice more people to come out to the tennis, not only to see the show, but also to see tennis.

For 1951 the Association received just $15,000 fifteen thousand dollars for radio broadcast rights and nothing from television. Why? According to Wood, because the television companies knew that tennis was not popular enough to get sponsors.[72]

In November 1951, *American Lawn Tennis* was incorporated into a new magazine, *The Racquet*, which covered tennis, badminton, and squash. The conflation of all racket sports into one publication pointed to the decline in popularity for lawn tennis that Kingman emphasized in his inaugural speech and to the concern that Sidney Wood expressed about the need for the Association to modernize. News in the magazine about the USLTA was reduced to mere announcements rather than the kind of analysis that Merrihew had provided for nearly four decades. In keeping with Kingman's concerns, the Association announced it would issue a mimeographed bulletin aimed at creating "closer contact between the active players and the USLTA," but the bulletin pertained to rules and procedures of the game, not to USLTA and tennis news. In October 1953, *The Racquet* was purchased by *World Tennis*. Gladys Heldman was about to step out, front and center.[73]

The retirement of the executive secretary in 1943, had left then president Holcombe Ward without management assistance. In January 1944 Myrick noted:

> we find ourselves very much as we were in the last war when the executives of the Association, not having an Association office . . . carried on the work of the Association in their own offices, and paid the costs themselves. And so in the meeting of 1914 and 1915 Richard Stevens moved the members have an Executive Secretary. . . . We must prepare for the future. I believe that Mr. Ward in carrying on next year should have someone taken in and trained to carry on the work. No executive officer who will be elected can afford to give the time and energy he has given these past years.[74]

Despite Myrick's plea, what began as a cost-saving move during the war—with Ward doing the jobs of both president and the executive secretary—lasted through 1947 and Ward's departure, finally, from the presidency. In 1948, Edwin Baker was hired as executive secretary. He remained in that post until 1967. Ward's role as volunteer and staff leader was an anomaly. Nonetheless, it demonstrated and strengthened the conviction that the volunteers could lead the Association wherever it chose to go. Professional staff were an asset; volunteers were indispensable and all that was really needed.

At mid century, the Association staff, located at 120 Broadway in New York City, consisted of the executive secretary (Edwin Baker); the accountant; the cashier, a "Miss Valentine"; and other office staff. As of October 1951 the treasurer proudly reported, they could function with just "one girl . . . a trend which your officers encouraged, even though it appears to be at variance with the policies in vogue in our Federal Government. (Laughter)."[75] *Plus ça change, plus c'est la même chose.*

Nevertheless, Association leaders were conducting lengthy discussions about hiring a paid assistant to the president, in addition to the executive secretary, primarily to promote the growth of tennis at the sectional level—an idea that had been bruited about for a few years. This came after a financially difficult year in 1951 but after the executive committee had still voted for the standard distribution to the sections of one and one half times the dues and sanction fees paid by the clubs to the sections.

The California delegate opposed the paid-assistant idea, saying they didn't need such a person since both California sub-sections (about to become full "sections") had secretaries "making a nominal salary." But despite concern about the cost (a twelve-thousand-dollar salary was proposed), no one else spoke against the proposal. They finally voted for a special study committee that would also present the idea to the sections. Clearly the executive committee would not act without sectional approval.[76]

Kingman was on the mark when he pointed to the French and British associations, which had two to four staff members working on expanding the game. "We can't think of trying to make . . . progress. . . . We haven't the sinews of war in this Association that we require."[77]

His staff proposals called for a well-paid (fifteen thousand dollars earmarked) assistant to the executive secretary, who would be provided travel money and a secretary, with the job of promoting the newly established Tennis Educational Foundation, visiting all the sections each year to problem solve, and finding advertisers for the official program used for all national championships and for a new *USLTA Bulletin*. The ambitious goal for the new hire was to bring in enough money to pay his own salary and expenses and provide the Association with money beyond that. Yet, in January 1955 the Association allocated only a maximum of $3,000 as start-up money for the foundation—much to Lawrence Baker's distress. A few years later, President Ed Turville called for an "Executive Vice President," and also set a pattern by engaging an expert as chair of a public-relations committee (who served as a volunteer). Turville warned that such appointments would require a person to spend five to ten thousand dollars of their own money. In 1966 another Association president would speak to the need for an executive director, complaining that he had been doing that job as well as being president for his two years in office. The title "executive vice president" meant different things to different people, but clearly Association presidents were feeling overwhelmed.[78]

Despite the struggle between the old guard and the young Turks, a struggle where Kingman's sympathies clearly lay with the reformers, he received nomination for a second one-year term as president (two-year terms would not begin until 1974). Kingman spoke in a tone of disappointment but not despair: "They say that wisdom comes with age, although I sometimes wonder whether that conservatism which accompanies advancing years offsets wisdom by fear of [or?] indifference to new ideas and progress in general." Noting that he had appointed some "younger talent . . . that added power which only youth can yield," Kingman praised the old-timers for their patience but clearly defended the newcomers.[79]

Kingman's concerns about a downturn for tennis were offset by other signs. Perhaps the game was falling off in its traditional northeastern home base but not in two tennis hot spots. In September 1950 the executive committee endorsed petitions from both the Southern Section and its Florida district to allow the state to become a separate USLTA section. The petition engendered "considerable discussion" at Southern's annual meeting, but then passed unanimously. Distance (Key West to Pensacola was over one thousand miles) and scheduling issues created by Florida's year-round warm weather and rapid growth (the Florida district, created in 1950, had nearly doubled in size to fifty-one clubs in just a year) were the stated reasons. It was the first large-scale "secession" in the Association's history, agreed to perhaps because Florida's tennis growth posed a threat to take over the entire Southern Section. A year later, northern and southern California finally agreed to a formal split into two separate sections, although they had been largely separate for decades. The USLTA agreed, following its long-standing policy that boundary changes had to be negotiated by the sections involved. Equally reassuring, 1951 actual revenues of $61,692 exceeded the budget by some $5,600.[80]

From there on there was a slow but perceptible shift among the national leadership toward change—change that would culminate in a degree of democratization with creation of individual memberships and eventually the democratization of the game itself with the establishment of open tennis and the U.S. Open as the national championships. The shift had many causes. Key were the financial problems of the post–Second World War era that directed Association concern toward decreasing public interest in tennis, particularly in the light of the game's growing popularity in England and Australia, which had translated into increased revenue. A string of postwar Association leaders—from Schuyler Van Bloem to Russell Kingman—had argued that the future of tennis in America lay in the hands of the USLTA and its sections, a future that could be realized only if the Association had the resources to promote the game.

Younger people like Sidney Wood began to challenge the restraints of tradition that the USLTA leadership, overwhelmingly businessmen, tried to impose. He pointed to drops of 28.6 percent in racket sales and 18.8 percent in ball sales since 1935. The Association's treasurer cautioned that in 1953 revenue from NBC came to only $12,500. "We get very little out of television" was the comment; broadcast costs (equipment etc.) were expensive—NBC paid out $100,000 that year, yet sponsorships came in at half that. Moreover, the tournament regulars were complaining about poor facilities, uncertain scheduling of tournaments and matches, and the need for a larger role for players on ranking and Davis Cup selection committees. At tournaments in Baltimore and New Jersey during the summer of 1952, top-ranked players agreed to set up an organization to work with the USLTA to improve how tournament players were treated. No formal contact with the Association was reported, but the Tennis Players League (TPL) finally appeared in December 1953 with Sidney Wood as president. The TPL called for modernization of the rules, better relations with the press, more effective public relations, and new tennis clubs and courts. Their call for reform did not include challenging the amateurism rules. Rather, the TPL called for an investigation by the Association into accusations that one well-known player had asked for "excessive expenses" from a Baltimore tournament.[81]

The TPL seems to have disappeared within a year or two, perhaps because much of its leadership was absorbed into Association committees. By 1958 a USLTA Players' Committee had been set up.[82] But the TPL constituted an interesting experiment. With its membership limited to the top amateur players, it could have become an effective pressure group—a "professional" organization for amateurs—that could improve tournament and competition conditions (court maintenance, both tournament and match scheduling, housing and amenities, etc.). All they had to do was to threaten a tournament with a boycott, and negotiations would have begun. But with most of the very best players, particularly in the men's game, moving into the professional tours, the TPL had no future. Had it offered the pros membership it could have been a very different story, but that was unthinkable at the time.

No one seems to have taken the hint dropped in the *USLTA Service Bulletin* of April 1953, which contained an article describing the relationship between professionals, both teaching and playing, and Britain's Lawn Tennis Association—printed in an official USLTA publication! Back in 1934 the professionals had asked the British association to be their governing organization, making it the governing body of both amateur and professional tennis in Great Britain, and things had remained that way ever since. Although Kingman had left office a few months before the story appeared, publishing such positive information in the early 1950s about cooperation between playing pros and the British Lawn Tennis Association has his stamp all over it. In his quiet, calm way, he looked at tennis on a far broader canvas than many other Association leaders.[83]

Allison Danzig, the tennis writer for the *New York Times*, suggested that formation of the TPL as well as a meeting of "the high brass" from clubs holding the major tournaments in the east, both stemmed from "rising mortality" of those events, particularly ones played on grass courts. Players were heading westward to the hard courts, or to Europe to play on clay, because eastern clubs failed to provide appropriate amenities for the players—accommodations, meals, and "a bit of entertainment." Perhaps what Wood had referred to in his criticisms of the Forest Hills Club. In reality, players were shopping for the best offers, and clubs were responding. The movement of top players into the professional tour went unmentioned, perhaps because Danzig was committed to amateurism as well as to grass court play.[84]

Wood continued to propose a public-relations initiative, and former-president Kingman supported him, noting that people who have run successful businesses have had full-time staff to deal with promotions, publicity, and sales, "particularly in the merchandising business, and we are merchandising amusement in this case." The repeated suggestions and the sense of an overall decline in tennis had some effect. Despite concerns about costs during hard times and suggestions that the revenue stream would not justify the expense, they set up a study committee. Not surprisingly, that report seems not ever to have been delivered.[85]

Wood's other idea was a national round-robin tournament, pitting the top ten players against each other. The Town Tennis Club in New York had applied for membership and planned to hold such a tournament. They had already gotten a local TV station (WPIX) to cover it but only if it was a "national" event. After some squirming, the executive committee agreed that the club could call it anything it wished. Part of the grand scheme was to have the tournament run constantly for most of the year with one or two matches each Monday night, although the television station would go beyond six weeks of coverage only if a sponsor was found by then. The motion passed with the clear stipulation that the USLTA was not responsible for organizing or running the event, just giving a sanction. The TPL was not mentioned, but it was the event's promoter. Sponsorship failed to develop and the round robin, which had begun in April, petered out by early summer. The event seems not to have been held again, but that the Association agreed to give it a try meant reforms were in the wind.[86]

A few years later, Sidney Wood offered Gladys Heldman—also a rebel with a cause—space in a laundry he owned as her office for *World Tennis*.[87]

Pressure for reform—streamlining the Association as one delegate put it—came from other than, and in protest against, the northeastern establishment. At an executive-committee meeting just before President Kingman left office, Gerald Misner, the newly selected delegate from the Northern California Section, took the floor in an obviously prearranged move. He needled and teased the Association for being stodgy and averse to change, reminiscent in style and substance of the "secession" speeches of nearly four decades earlier.[88] The committee must have sensed what was coming when Misner thanked Kingman for cigars and Kingman's successor, Jim Bishop (it was all first names), for a bottle of scotch, then followed with a zinger: "but when underneath our door at the hotel we found that 'Ren' McMann had arranged for this headline, 'Fog snarls city a second day,' we knew we were right at home." The laughter that followed was surely sour for the northeastern old guard.

Misner worried about relations with the press: "One thing we should do is develop a better understanding between the USLTA and the press outside of the Metropolitan area. Really, fellows, there are parts of the United States that are getting along pretty well outside of this area." But his concern was more than just press relations. "For the life of me," he said, "I don't know how we can sell the USLTA to the other forty states," setting the eight northeastern states apart. As tennis in California demonstrated, "control of the players should be within the Section itself." "Let us streamline the Association," with a little "Hoover Committee" that would "upgrade" the USLTA.[89] After proposing a committee of five—one member from each of the Association's four regions plus an at-large member—Misner entreated: "I suggest that such a committee be appointed and the delegate from each region immediately get in contact with the presidents of the various groups, the sections in his group and the various clubs, and get the answers, and get them quick." He recalled that, at the 1952 annual meeting, Kingman "made quite a plea to do this thing. I never saw a fellow more haunted in my life. You are not doing anything differently today than you did two years ago," or even back ten or twenty years, he went on. Kingman, chairing the committee, diplomatically suggested that Misner was asking that his suggestions be "reviewed" by the new administration. When Misner replied that he hoped they would be "acted on," Kingman said they would be since "they are very well taken in many instances."

In the short run, little seems to have come from Misner's pleas or Kingman's proposals—although the 1956 diamond jubilee annual meeting did take place in San Francisco, the first meeting west of the Mississippi Valley.[90] Minutes of annual- and executive-committee meetings suggest that the Association remained mired in the miasma of amateur rules and the endless squabbling over national rankings of tennis players. As President James Bishop revealingly told the executive committee in September 1954: "I have no definite or organized report. . . . We don't know what we wish to do next year." The tax issues related to the West Side Tennis Club continued to aggravate the Association, but otherwise, theirs was a charming and innocent world, but one that did not last for long.[91]

The diamond jubilee observance of the Association's seventy-fifth birthday was intended to be more than just a visit to San Francisco. The pleas of Kingman, Wood, and others had finally prompted a major promotional campaign around the celebration. President Ren McMann called for the sections to launch a major effort to popularize the game, and the executive committee authorized expenditures of twenty thousand dollars. The effort seems to have largely been a failure. Comments during executive-committee meetings as well as in official and unofficial publications expressed disappointment. The diamond jubilee overspent "a little bit," according to McMann, and "threatened to run up to fantastic figures," according to the *Lawn Tennis Library Record* (LTLR), until McMann called a halt. *LTLR* praised McMann for trying something new, gently chiding the Association that it had tried "nothing really new" since Myrick began pushing for junior programs "many years ago," but, unfortunately, the organizers failed to consult people with expertise in the finances of campaigns. Some hoped that sale of the 500,000-plus instructional ("unfunny") comic books (see gallery, image 17) and unsold copies of the jubilee history, *American Tennis*, might bring costs down to $31,000, but the jubilee would still be $11,000 over its $20,000 budget. No wonder they considered not making a distribution to the sections in 1957. But despite the treasurer's recommendation, the executive committee, dominated by sectional delegates, voted a reduced distribution of $10,000. No need to wake up the sleeping giant.[92]

Although the diamond jubilee promotion cost more than expected, McMann supported continued promotional efforts to expand tennis. He called for spreading a slogan: "'*Tennis is a sport for a lifetime.*' Let's drive that home! Start it at the grammar school and continue right up until they get to be 80." Others agreed. That slogan was, argued the *LTLR*, "the true diamond in the jubilee campaign." With proper promotion, "it may be worth all that the campaign coast."[93] Someone seems to have remembered. Some forty years later, USTA president Les Snyder used "Tennis—The Sport for a Lifetime" as the slogan for his term in office.

Throughout the 1950s executive-committee meetings were characterized by lengthy reports about calculated misuse of funds and under-the-table payments to players, particularly in European tournaments. When Kingman again became president of the ILTF, all hoped he could deal with the bad practices. But that was not to be. There was money to be made by clubs and promoters running tournaments and that drained off the cream of the amateur crop. Promotional campaigns to attract the public to tennis were expensive and could not put "fannies in the seats."[94] People paid to see the best.

All of which led directly to pressure for at least a single open tournament, though not open tennis where amateurs and professionals could routinely compete. In part the Association wished to "strengthen tennis," to get young people interested in playing the game. But constant denials to the contrary notwithstanding, the Association's financial weaknesses directed attention to the potential revenue that such a tournament could generate. The concern about revenue prompted recommendations that the national championships end on a Sunday, since NBC could not make arrangements for a Monday date.[95]

An open tournament was an old idea that had surfaced in the late 1920s. As things stood in 1957, ILTF regulations did not permit such events. The long-standing public USLTA position was in favor of national autonomy—that is, any member of the Federation could hold open tournaments. At the same time, Association leaders firmly favored keeping amateur and professional tennis separated.

In early 1957 President Ren McMann created a study committee to examine the pros and cons of an open tournament. The members included the next three future USLTA presidents (Victor Denny, George Barnes, and the chair, Edward Turville) as well as Allison Danzig of the *New York Times*. The main question—"Will an Open strengthen tennis?" A number of Association officials thought the time was right to take a "look-see" at the idea. If so, the ILTF would be asked to change its rules to allow members to decide for themselves about holding open tournaments. How would such a tournament affect the Davis Cup—still the blue chip event for the USLTA? Would an open tournament stimulate interest in tennis among American youth? The study committee was to talk to all the stakeholders—club members and officials, players (unclear if that included professionals), the press, anyone "even remotely interested in tennis."[96]

The committee's recommendations in favor of an open tournament generated a long, angry discussion. The report argued that an open tournament was the best way to correct existing abuses of expenses being paid to amateurs and, perhaps, to stem the flow of top amateurs to the pro tour. Moreover, its survey found that such an event was "overwhelmingly" popular. After some two hours of debate, the executive committee voted against the proposals, then waffled on how to announce its decision to the waiting reporters. Myrick and others who were against an open tournament stridently opposed release of the report since that would appear as an endorsement for the committee's recommendation to hold such a tournament. Danzig warned that the substance of the report would be leaked and the press would cover the story, so there was no gain in trying to keep it secret. Ed Turville, clearly frustrated, rejected proposals that his committee restudy the issue and resubmit its report, commenting that no one was willing to change their mind, so why bother? He also challenged the "caste system" where certain clubs assumed they were superior to others. "Undemocratic" he called it. "My feeling is that the pro-grass group, and the anti-open group have affected a kinship and a working arrangement, based somewhat on the assumption that they are nicer people." The Association called for larger, realistic expense allowances for amateurs, while the ILTF, seemingly disinterested in preserving any sort of effective amateur code, passed new and lower expense-payment rules. At the same time, the Federation flatly refused even to discuss open tournaments.[97]

Distrust of ILTF purposes and tactics was apparent when in 1959 the agenda of the July meeting of the Federation included four amendments to the amateur rules with the statement "Proposed by the USA." In fact, what the USLTA did was to propose "an exchange of viewpoints" on the whole array of amateur-rules discussions. Ned Potter, a regular columnist for *World Tennis*, concluded that since the honorary secretary of the ILTF was also the honorary secretary of the British Lawn Tennis Association, chicanery was afoot.[98]

As Jack Kramer pointed out, "from 1931, when Tilden turned pro at the age of thirty-seven, until 1968, when the game finally went open, virtually every player who won both Wimbledon and Forest Hills turned pro. The only amateurs who won the two major titles but failed to sign contracts were Schroeder, Vic Seixas, Neale Fraser and Manolo Santana." In other words, so-called amateur tennis—international and national—had little choice but to go open since it was excluding the best players, the players the public wanted to see. As two former presidents, Ren McMann and Victor Denny warned in 1960, "the so-called man on the street, he is for open tennis, and that is a tough situation to buck."[99]

In the late 1950s, the Association found a new ally in the battle to save amateur tennis. The U.S. Professional Lawn Tennis Association (PLTA) (for teaching pros) asked the USLTA not to relax its amateur rules and enforcement. It expressed concern at the growing number of amateur high-school and college tennis players who were taking employment as tennis instructors particularly in the summertime. Not only could that jeopardize their amateur status but argued the PLTA, the ability to play well did not ensure that a person could teach tennis well. Moreover, the practice might limit the ability of teaching pros to find jobs and lower the "economic standard" of those who make their living as qualified pros. In what was the beginning of a long relationship between the two organizations, the PLTA offered to provide the USLTA with a list of its qualified teaching professionals.[100]

Who Decides?

By the 1950s the executive committee had become large and unwieldy. Besides the four Association officers and the four regional vice presidents, each section had a delegate, there were eight at-large delegates, and a certain number (usually five) of past presidents were members—thirty-five plus people. Moreover, meetings were expensive since members came from all over the country and had their full expenses paid. In 1938 the costs and vagaries of travel had prompted ExCom meetings to be limited to two a year, one in autumn and the other just before the annual meeting. The finance and advisory committee, which would become the administrative committee, took on an unofficial role as a kitchen cabinet shortly after the war. By the 1960s the administrative committee was empowered to act for the Association whenever the executive committee was not in session. It would not be long (1971) before a management committee replaced the administrative committee, to be replaced by a board of directors in 1986. The executive committee, which had essentially managed Association affairs for nearly fifty years, became advisory, not empowered, making it largely a vestigial remain. But, as a constitutionally required body, it was treated with respect as befit the traditions of the Association. The "delegates assembly," which consisted of the official delegate from each of the sections, began in 1956 to meet informally at annual and semiannual meetings. In 1962, the delegates assembly became a required standing committee. At that time, the constitution and rules committee recommended that the president choose the group's officers, but the delegates preferred to choose their own—a hint of the independence that would come later. The president (George Barnes) and the ExCom agreed, without debate, to that change. The assembly eventually became the vehicle for expressing collective sectional opinions—recognized in the bylaws until they were revised in 1971–72.[101]

But saving amateurism did not remain the primary focus of the Association. At the annual meeting in January 1958, Victor Denny, a resident of Seattle, Washington, became the first USLTA president from the Pacific Coast. He pointed out, proudly and accurately, that a truly national leadership, one representing all regions of the United States, had at last become a reality. The westward march that had begun in earnest early in the twentieth century had come of age. Denny acknowledged speedy communications and transportation had made that both possible and desirable, but the fact was that the popularity of the game of tennis was the driving force behind the shift.

He was more than just a guy from the West Coast. Denny opened his presidency with a blunt warning that "additional finances" constituted the Association's greatest problem. He then announced the membership of the administrative committee; and the date of its next meeting, only a month later, indicating just how the growth of tennis was moving the Association toward a more streamlined leadership structure. By this time, executive committee meetings had come to focus largely on proposed amendments to the constitution, bylaws, and standing orders. Discussions would occasionally take place, but most or many of the issues had been decided at a lower committee level. Bringing the many executive committee members to a meeting was disproportionately expensive. Institutionalizing the delegates assembly was part of the process.[102]

Two initiatives characterized his efforts. First, creation of what became "individual" membership in the Association. Second, an imaginative communications effort, however short-lived.

TABLE 2. Sections' voting strength as of January 18, 1958

Eastern	15,200
Western	9,875
Middle States	8,025
New England	7,700
Southern	5,450
Southern California	4,950
Northern California	4,250
Pacific Northwest	4,150
Florida	2,775
Mid-Atlantic	2,675
Intermountain	2,125

Missouri Valley	2,125
Texas	1,625
Northwest	750
Southwest	650
Direct member clubs	175
Total votes	72,300

For the seventy-seven years following the Association's founding in 1881, the membership consisted solely of clubs. Initially it was one club, one vote. But as tennis grew and clubs multiplied, voting strength was calculated by various formulas that allocated more votes to clubs with larger numbers of tennis players. As the Association tried to help the game grow, it allowed certain club-like organizations (e.g., parks and recreation associations) to be associate or sort-of members. But the concept of clubs as the members remained. In 1956 the secretary told the annual meeting that memberships had increased by 83 to a total of 1,471—clubs, of course, not people.[103]

In January 1958 at the annual meeting just before the introduction of individual memberships (registrations) and the recalculation of sectional voting strength that followed, the credentials committee reported the voting strength for each section. (See table 2.) The traditional center of lawn tennis in the Northeast, dominated with 33,600 votes—just short of a majority. Other regions, like Chicago and the rest of the Western (later Mid-western) Section measured up with nearly 10,000 votes. What would become one of the two dominant tennis regions, the South plus Florida, garnered just over 8,000 votes—a surprisingly low number.[104]

Individual "registration," which began in 1958, was designed, in Denny's words, "to secure more fixed income for the Association" so as to provide more support for the sections than came from the semiannual distributions (semiannual by this time presumably so as to even out cash flow to the sections). The new rule read:

> All players resident in the United States who play in sanctioned tournaments of the USLTA are required to possess annual USLTA membership registration cards. The annual registration fee is $3.00 for any such player 18 years of age or more and $1.00 for any player under 18 years of age. . . . Application for a registration card can be made to a player's home Sectional Association or to the official in charge

> of a sanctioned tournament. Sectional Associations are required to submit to the USLTA $1 for each adult registration and 50¢ for each registration of a player under 18 years of age.[105]

Various voices had suggested dropping the cost to two dollars or even one dollar lest they lose participants. Others successfully argued that, in marketing terms, below five dollars was all that mattered.[106] Although the ongoing East-versus-West argument never surfaced, that the move took place during the presidency of the first westerner to hold that office was not surprising, for it seems to have represented the wishes of many in the Pacific Coast where tennis had expanded the most.[107]

It proved a breakthrough decision. By the end of 1958, the Association had nearly 13,000 individual registrants. The next year, there were some 15,000 adult and junior registrations, while the total voting strength of all the sections put together grew by four thousand votes. For the next six years, membership nearly tripled, averaging 20 percent a year to attain 34,891 in 1964. Growth then dropped off to about 7 percent a year until the 1970s, the halcyon years of the "tennis revolution" when the game temporarily became wildly popular.[108] Those numbers generated revenue, generated participation, and they generated change—though the latter took some time.

Although the leadership understood that a great many were playing tennis without belonging to a member club, the initial purpose of a "registration" fee was to raise money, not from a desire for a larger head count or because it would stimulate growth of the game.[109] In fact, members of the executive committee expressed concern that the additional cost might discourage players from entering tournaments. The move flowed from the long-standing and striking commitment of the Association leadership to fund the sections, a commitment that represented both politics and reality. While the sections may not have "owned" the Association, the national leadership came from the sections. Few, if any, national leaders did not have extensive experience either as ranked tennis players or as sectional volunteers—often both.[110]

Since each section voted en bloc (split votes were "legal" but not used), individual memberships were not democratization in the "populist" sense of one person, one vote. Rather it was more like the electoral college in U.S. presidential elections. The difference was that the Association's sections each decided how to cast their entire vote either by a vote of the sectional leadership, or by a vote of a section's "members" as defined, often quite differently, in each section's constitution or bylaws.

Individual Membership

To pull together the threads of changes to individual membership as they took place over the next fifty years: even after individual memberships (of a sort) began in 1958, the Association's voting formula did not simply count the number of individual members of each tennis club. Despite a recommendation that "Class A clubs have one (1) vote for each voting member, the Association maintained block formulas that differentiated between large and small clubs, harkening back to the 1920s and early attempts to escape the original "one club, one vote" system. In 1960 that formula called for clubs with fifty members or less to have fifty votes, with twenty-five votes for each twenty-five additional members (or fraction thereof). Commercial tennis clubs were made eligible for club membership in 1961. Not until the 1969 constitution did the block-voting calculation change to the sections having one vote for each "enrollee" (i.e., member) and one-half vote for each junior "enrollee" (under nineteen). In 1971, "individual member" became a constitutional category. As of 1972 anyone could join the Association, although member clubs retained a vote. However, sectional voting strength was calculated by the amount of dues paid (an indirect acknowledgment of individual membership), with adults paying eight dollars and those under twenty-one 21 paying four dollars (including the "official" magazine). That voting formula has remained the same up to the present (2012), even after incorporation in 1973, although the dues would go up (of course) and small details would change. The basic wording has remained the same for just short of a century: "The only voting members of the USTA shall be the Sectional Associations and Direct Member Clubs and Organizations," with the direct members category a meaningless vestigial remain from the era before active and organized sections developed in the 1920s.[111]

Denny's communications initiative came in May 1958, when the *Official USLTA News* replaced the *USLTA Service Bulletin*. With that move, the Association embarked on an unusually expansive and effective communications program. The clear, unequivocal purpose was to bring the entire membership, individual and organizational, on board with national decisions about everything from international competitions to USLTA assistance for tennis at the local level. Instead of lectures from the president and lists of fussy little rule or regulation changes, the rejuvenated newsletter offered near monthly summaries of Association decisions, reports on Association activities (summaries of executive-committee meetings, Davis Cup, junior development, the retirement of Jack Kramer as head of the pro tour, the debate over open tennis, etc.), and kept its members and "registrants" (individuals were still "registrants") well informed. Occasionally it read like a travelogue about the journeys of the president to exotic tennis venues from Paris to Rome to London, and everything in between—an image that could have engendered resentment that the dues and registration fees of members were paying for the junkets of high-placed officials. But nothing in the records suggests that reaction. It lacked entertainment value, but the news was certainly what the USLTA wanted people to know. The publication did not benefit from the kind of firm but loving criticisms of a "Pops" Merrihew, or offer deep insights into discussions among the Association leaders, but no one could complain that they did not know what was going on at the national level. From the perspective of communications professionals, it was a very smart initiative.[112]

Volunteer Committees

In 1958 a call for a committee to study revisions to the constitution, bylaws and standing orders prompted suggestions that the number of committees be cut and the size limited both for greater efficiency and to lessen costs. Even the sacred nominating committee seemed too expensive. But little came of such proposals. The problem was that people's feelings got hurt if they were not appointed or reappointed to a committee. Moreover, the sections consistently pushed for each section to have a member on each major committee. Those were dynamics that would not go away.

By the 1960s the national volunteer committee structure had taken on the size and shape that would last through the end of the twentieth century. It was, and still is, perhaps, the largest volunteer cadre of any governing body in U.S. sports. In 1962 the Association president (Edward Turville) called for "more women in important positions on Committees." By 1963 of some fifty-two committees, women were vice chair of three important ones but chaired only women's committees (Wightman Cup, various women's ranking committees, etc.). Their time was coming but with remarkable slowness for a physically active sport that had allowed women to play, though not to govern, from the earliest days of lawn tennis in America.[113]

Sometimes the media just doesn't get it. When Victor Denny became president in 1958, *Sports Illustrated* effusively wrote of a "Jacksonian revolution" where Denny appointed westerners over easterners to various committee chairs. But that ignores how traditional the Association has been from its inception. Denny was no newcomer. He had been first vice president of the Association for two years, after being president of his section for twelve years, and on the USLTA Davis Cup committee. He was a known quantity. But *Sports Illustrated* insisted "it was a revolution achieved without bloodshed or fanfare . . . when the nominating committee . . . after months of quiet backstage politicking, put up a new slate of officers . . . to succeed New Yorker Renville McMann, whose administration, like those of all before him, had been predominantly eastern. With a Chicagoan and a Floridian as his chief lieutenants, mild-mannered, hard-working President Denny went on to apply the Jacksonian spoils system to tennis by appointing two more West Coasters to key jobs." Yet none of those new officers or committee chairs were unknowns, or revolutionaries. Denny, like all his predecessors, paid homage to past presidents and administrations. The changes were gentle and slow, driven as much by steady westward expansion as they were by differences of opinions, even with the issue of amateur rules. Denny did not advocate dramatic and immediate change. French proposals for a peculiar "authorized player" category (allowing top players to ignore playing restrictions and "squeeze" tournaments for whatever they could get) prompted Denny to label those players "legalized 'tennis bums.'" Such changes were not the Association way. Public respect for the past always balanced the private urge for change. Consensus was more important than immediacy. Perhaps "quiet backstage politicking" is best viewed as just another description of representative democracy.[114]

Denny's "streamlining" of Association procedures prompted a gentle warning from Ned Potter, a well-respected and long-time tennis writer. Matters up for decision by the Association's annual meeting now were discussed and vetted at preliminary meetings. By the time they reached the annual meeting, controversies had been resolved. Those who could not attend those earlier meetings could only know "the facts which are public property." Secrecy had arrived.[115]

Still, Denny was a breath of fresher air. When he left the presidency in 1960, he wrote a farewell that depicted the national Association as a populist organization that was not made up of "stuffed shirts" but one that cared deeply about tennis at the local level. Strikingly, he dismissed the claim that private clubs were the primary focus of play. James Dwight must have spun gently in his grave.[116]

The money problems did not disappear with individual membership. By 1961 the Association was asking (pleading) for contributions to help pay for Davis Cup travel expenses abroad and for the national junior tennis development program. Hardly an effective fund-raising effort.[117] Eventually, the solution would be open tennis—but there were hurdles to jump before that could come about.

The USLTA was adamant about having its own national (amateur) championship even if the Association chose also to have a similar (national) open tournament. One fear was the professionals would take so much money out of the proceeds that Association finances would be threatened. They quoted Wimbledon officials similarly expressing objections to loss of control over their own event. Yet, Association leaders and others agreed that the American public was solidly in favor of open tennis. Proposals for special reimbursement rules (i.e., pay) for top or "authorized" players were rejected by the ILTF. The real issue was not open tennis, but "authorized players," one officer argued. "Unless we are put in trading position [i.e., pay the players], we are going to lose them [to the professional tour]. We just can't take that risk." USLTA representatives at Federation meetings concluded that the four major tennis nations—the United States, Britain, France, and Australia—could not agree on how to deal with the "shamateurism" problem. Stronger enforcement would not work. Simply put, the Europeans, and American promoters and clubs, wanted to pay the players—a dilemma that would perplex college sports in America into the twenty-first century.[118]

Association officials (privately) and members (publicly) condemned the professional tour in general and Jack Kramer in specific for creating the dilemma. One angry devotee of amateur tennis summed up the frustration of others like him in a letter to *World Tennis*: "The President of the USLTA, sitting precariously on the fence between the honorable amateur game and the not-so-honorable pro game, should carefully weigh the words of the great Winston Churchill who said: 'I did not become Prime Minister of Great Britain to preside over the dissolution of the British Empire.'"[*sic*][119] Julian Myrick, apparently eschewing his 1928 prediction that an open championship was inevitable, condemned Kramer as a "vulture" hovering "to grab the young" without considering "the good of the game." One member, who claimed to have been a "good friend of Jack Kramer's ever since we were kids," accused Kramer "of . . . trying to rape us." But the real villain was the unenforced and unenforceable amateur rules, accentuated by the Association's understandable passion for bringing the Davis and Wightman Cups back home, and for getting the names of Americans inscribed on Grand Slam trophies. Being competitive had a price.

Perhaps the last gasp of support for amateurism in tennis began in 1962 when the Association president, George Barnes (a member of Turville's open study committee), called for ILTF nations to support preservation of "amateur traditions" but then admitted that the Federation had neither the resources nor the will to enforce its own amateur regulations. Proposals that any mention of "amateurs" be changed to simply "players" would, wrote Barnes, prompt creation of a "Players' union" (obviously a scary thought). To prevent that, he called for retaining the amateur and professional "classes" of players, hardly a solution to the "double standard" he admitted existed. Unless the amateur-open conflict was resolved, he warned, the major nations might well break away from the international federation. As he had argued two years earlier, the root cause was national federations that had "forsaken amateurism for financial considerations and national prestige." He wrote of "greedy top players" who could not be persuaded "that it isn't legal or moral" to "cheat" on expenses and under-the-table pay. As he repeatedly warned during his presidency, Association revenues from its two cash cows, Davis Cup and the nationals, were threatened because top players were turning pro before they could gain name recognition as amateurs. It was principle (amateurism) versus spectators (revenue and popularizing the game). The USLTA remained firm that "national self-determination" for all members of the ILTF should prevail "in the matter of any form of open competition." The Association again decided to ask the international federation to allow an experiment with open tournaments. Once again, the Federation refused. Changing Federation policy required a two-thirds vote, a high hurdle in the face of some purists, some of whom wanted to maintain and expand ILTF authority and some of whom believed the current situation benefitted their own country's situation. Change seemed inevitable, but everyone was marking time.[120]

The Federation's refusal either to enforce or change its rules brought the argument among Americans to a head. At the 1963 annual meeting, the Association considered resolutions declaring opposition to "the principle of Open Tennis" and instructing its delegates to the ILTF to oppose any Federation actions or proposals in furtherance of open tennis. The resolutions came from the delegates assembly in a unanimous vote, and reflected strong, even vociferous, support for demanding that the ILTF enforce its amateur rules. The sections believed that enforcement was the appropriate American response to "shamateurism." During an unusually lengthy discussion, younger speakers, like President Ed Turville and the Southern California delegate Robert Kelleher, seemed to favor open tennis, though that was not the direct subject of the vote. Kelleher argued that the pros did bring things to the game, whereas older delegates accused touring pros of just taking from the game. The resolution passed, 49,856 to 36,481. The Association was still marking time.[121]

Allison Danzig, the dominant reportorial voice in tennis since the passing of S. W. Merrihew, had received the inaugural media award from the Association. The decision had been a slam-dunk, with speaker after speaker vying to heap the highest praise. He sat on the special committee chaired by Turville charged with examining the pros and cons of open tournaments, a committee that recommended giving open tournaments a try. But the 1963 resolutions committing the USLTA to firm opposition to open tennis brought on a remarkably angry condemnation from Danzig. He claimed that "a cabal of politically ambitious sectional representatives, most of them from the East," had voted against both international self-determination (letting each nation decide for itself) and an open tennis experiment, all in the hope of putting themselves in office. A cabal? Perhaps, although Danzig himself admitted that most of the sections were legitimately worried that open tennis could jeopardize amateur tennis in the sections. Granted, the Association had long supported home rule on the issue of one or two open tournaments, but by the 1960s that was no longer the debate.[122]

Danzig's comments had little immediate effect, as the mid 1960s found the Association in a holding pattern on the issue of open tennis and the ILTF. In 1964 Turville tried to drum up support for a British proposal that the Federation permit the Wimbledon championships to be an open tournament on an experimental basis, but the Association felt bound by the 1963 resolutions. For a while it seemed as if the only pressure for addressing the near universal ignoring of amateur rules on expense money was the denial by the International Olympic Committee (IOC) to allow tennis into the Olympic games because of what IOC leader Avery Brundage labeled "shamateurism" in tennis. Efforts to revamp and clarify the rules were piecemeal attempts to bring order out of chaos, even if they tried to move gently toward liberalization.[123]

By this time, the Association's presidential politics were viewed by some in the news media in terms of a stark division between "'Open and

No-open' groups." The election in 1965 of Martin Tressel, "the real-leader of the power-hungry group" that opposed open tennis, could have been amateurism's last stand, but by then the die was cast.[124]

As soon as Robert Kelleher became president in February 1967, he faced a proposal from the delegates assembly that would have eliminated his authority to appoint half the members of the administrative committee—the key operating committee since the executive committee met only twice a year. The records fail to indicate whether or not this was related to Kelleher's stand on open tennis. The supporters of the change appealed to democracy and argued that the committee was too large and unwieldy. Kelleher refused to express his position, though he did state that he interpreted the proposal as intended to limit the power of the president. Clearly knowing he had the votes, he moved the discussion along expeditiously.[125] The time had come to stop marking time and move ahead.

6

OPEN TENNIS

1968–1990

> "The USLTA has gone as far as it can as a basically volunteer organization."
> LONG-RANGE FINANCIAL PLANNING COMMITTEE, January 15, 1969

During the U.S. nationals (not yet the U.S. Open) at Forest Hills in September 1967, a new pro tour that would become World Championship Tennis (WCT) signed contracts with a number of then top-ranked amateur players—particularly John Newcombe, Tony Roche, and Cliff Drysdale. As Newcombe later told the story, when Roche asked him if he'd "like to make a million dollars," Newk thought "it sounded pretty good," especially since he "was clearing [only] about $15,000 a year as the No. 1 amateur in the world." He signed for a bit less than a million—$55,000—but that was nearly four times more money than his annual amateur "earnings."

There had been earlier indications of the impact of the professional tours on the revenue stream enjoyed by the British and American lawn tennis associations. In the United States, Jack Kramer's circuit had an effect on attendance at the U.S. nationals at Forest Hills since the top players could not play—they were pros. The same for Davis Cup, long the Association's bellwether for income. Money was not everything, but it mattered.

Those signings likely pushed the chairman of the All England Club, Herman David, during a meeting of the British lawn tennis association in October 1967, and his committee (who essentially comprised the board of the British national association), to step up their long-standing efforts to hold an open Wimbledon. Then, on December 14, David and the association threw down the gauntlet, declaring that beginning with the British Hard Court Championships in April 1968, sanctioned tennis tournaments held in Great Britain would be open to all without distinguishing between professionals and amateurs. The International Lawn Tennis Federation threatened expulsion, but that rang hollow in the land where lawn tennis had begun and that hosted the game's most prestigious tournament. As Wimbledon went, so went the tennis world, at least in 1968.[1]

Much then fell into place. When the ILTF met (in Paris, of course) in a "hastily reconvened" meeting of March–April 1968, the Americans, led Robert Kelleher, who had been just reelected to a second one-year term as USLTA president, stood shoulder to shoulder with the British representative, Derek Hardwick, offering some comfortable compromises designed to give the Europeans (and some Americans) time to adjust. The French, always more interested in running the ILTF than in preserving amateur standards, conducted the first French Open a few weeks before the Wimbledon tournament that began on June 24.[2] The Open Era had begun.

USLTA leadership had recognized the pressure building on the ILTF. Early in 1967, the British and the Australians had each proposed that, on a two-year trial basis, the Federation permit open tournaments; that is, events that allowed amateurs and professionals to compete, that offered prize money for professionals, that allowed amateurs to keep that status. The details of each proposal differed a bit, but the intent was clear—get open tennis on the ILTF's formal agenda. The 1963 resolution by the USLTA declaring opposition to open tennis was repealed at a special meeting of the Association in June 1967, so as to give their representatives (Kelleher, Denny, and Baker) the leeway to negotiate at the upcoming ILTF meeting about self-determination and autonomy for Federation members on holding open tournaments. Nothing came of those negotiations.[3]

Despite the flaunting of ILTF amateur rules by almost all national federations, at the Federation meeting in summer 1967 the United States had not supported an earlier British proposal for eliminating the distinction between pros and amateurs, largely because a number of executive-committee members, led by Dick Sorlien, chair of the amateur rules committee, opposed mixing professionals with amateurs. That September, Sorlien made an anguished appeal for ending the hypocrisy that existed. The specific matter was enactment and enforcement of a rule prohibiting players from accepting "cash payments in significant amounts" from sporting-goods companies to endorse and play with their rackets. But Sorlien's plaint ran the gamut. Like many in the Association, he staunchly supported retaining a clear distinction between amateurs and professionals, but he challenged the Association, saying, "In the critical area of good citizenship and character; as judged at the highest tournament level [i.e., enforcement of amateur rules], it [the Association] is doing a totally inadequate job, and the consequences of vacillation and indecision grow more serious every day."[4]

Royalties for an Amateur Association

At the September 1967 executive committee meeting, a lengthy discussion ensued about getting "royalties" from the manufacturers for the Association's officially approving tennis balls that met its standards. The players who used the balls got nothing, of course. When one executive-committee member expressed concern about the commercial sound of the word "endorsement," Kelleher quickly retorted: "The use of a ball in our National Championships is an endorsement, just like Jack's [Kramer] name on a Wilson racket, for example. This is regarded as true by the manufacturers and they have, in the past, paid us for that very advantage that is involved there, and hence the thought was that we should, in effect, continue the practice that has existed in the past and that is, require payment for the endorsement of the ball, and one of the endorsements that we give is to use it in our National Championships." Kelleher could not have missed the disconnect of the "governing body" of amateur tennis getting royalties, while top players could not without losing amateur status. Perhaps he knew his Board wasn't quite ready for change; perhaps he was trying to get them to recognize the hypocrisy–although a similar disconnect has continued in American intercollegiate sports up to this writing.

Then, just a month before the December bombshell—the British declaration of open tennis in their tournaments—Kelleher reported requests from England, Sweden, and France for the American view on the proposal for an open Wimbledon. By then, Kelleher had the votes on his executive committee. Sorlien's memorandum was the agenda, but with no recorded discussion, in a single tightly worded resolution, the Association lurched from a romanticized past into the practical present. The future would come quickly:

> [Moved] "That this committee request the insertion in the Call [of the agenda of the annual meeting of the USLTA] in appropriate language, with the assistance of the Chairman of the Constitution and Rules Committee, a proposal that the Constitution and By-laws of the USLTA be changed so as to embody—
>
> 1. The abolition of distinction of players between amateur and professional.
>
> 2. That provision be made for the inclusion of the administration of professional tennis, within our organization.[5]

> 3. That consideration and decision be given to the granting of permission to allow our players to participate in an open Wimbledon.

That was quickly followed by a vote to request a special meeting of the ILTF, with the USLTA represented by Kelleher and two former presidents, Victor Denny and Lawrence Baker—who had reservations about open tennis. Kelleher later said that Baker told him that open tennis "would be like opening the temple to the money-changers." When Kelleher observed that such was already the case, Baker just replied, "Oh, it isn't a perfect world." Kelleher later commented, "I thought it was inevitable that tennis would have to go professional, and to tell the truth I'd do it all over again if I had to."[6]

By the time for the eighty-seventh annual meeting of the USLTA on February 3, 1968, at the Hotel del Coronado in California, across the harbor from San Diego, Herman David and Britain's lawn tennis association had issued their non-negotiable demand for open tennis.

The annual meeting was tricky business. In an interview for *Sports Illustrated*, Kelleher apparently criticized East Coast traditionalists as "old goats who made crooks out of little kids by making them take money under the table instead of paying prize money." The East Coast label was inaccurate but effective propaganda, since many who supported open tennis were from the Northeast. The "little kids" phrase was over the top since young people under eighteen were not involved. More important, Kelleher needed the support of every "old goat" he could muster. Learning that the issue of *Sports Illustrated* would hit newsstands just as the annual meeting began, staff members managed to buy the copies being sold near the hotel.[7]

Here Comes the Judge—Robert J. Kelleher

Robert Kelleher was a nationally ranked doubles player, referee, and Davis Cup player and captain. He was appointed a federal district judge in 1970, making national news in 1977 as the trial judge in the case of the Falcon and the Snowman—two young men convicted of supplying classified information to the Soviet Union. He was a great bear of a man, who popped up like a Biblical prophet at crucial (and not so crucial) moments in the Association's history.

It was as president (1967–68) that his impact on the Association was the greatest. Kelleher was the effective agent, the facilitator, of open tennis in 1968. The Brits called the bluff of defenders of faux amateurism by putting Wimbledon on the line as an open tournament. But that could have been a pyrrhic victory except for Kelleher's construction of a practical settlement. Whatever the chaos, he sent open tennis in a rational direction, massaging the French, calming the British, proposing temporary agreements. During an executive-committee meeting six years later, with the turmoil created by open tennis still swirling, the Davis Cup committee chair admitted he had infuriated Jimmy Connors by sarcastically referring to "The Little White Charger" after Connors finally agreed to play a Davis Cup match. Disdaining the microphone, the judge bellowed that "something the USLTA had better recognize is that we are all a bunch of brass hats." After that attention getter, Kelleher pointed out that there were "only three real tennis players in this room [Gene Scott, Dennis Ralston, and Jack Kramer]." As for Davis Cup and "high-level competition," he warned that letting agents and tour promoters ("alphabetical things") control that competition would kill it. The solution? Put it "in the hands . . . of tennis players." It was a brilliant if bombastic performance, though it was far too late for the Association to take control of professional tennis.

In the 1990s, Davis Cup obsession overcame the good judgment of two former presidents who managed persuade the USTA to change the records and list them, rather than Dennis Ralston, as having been Davis Cup captains at various ties during 1972, a winning year. Kelleher responded furiously. He "seriously considered resigning from the bench" to take the case. The record was re-adjusted and Ralston got an out of court settlement from the Association of $65,000. Kelleher was frequently right, but never in doubt.[8]

The mayor of San Diego began the proceedings with a long, flowery welcome. Routine business went on as usual—credentials for delegates; a membership-enrollment report; the treasurer's report (for 1967, the Association reported cash and investments of $170,000, $4292,000 income, $278,000 expenses, and a fund balance of $4,150,000); a contract extension for the official magazine; a report from "the boss of women's tennis" (a woman, Donna Fales); Davis Cup; international play (casual amateurs); and the national championships. Then came the formality of accepting the nominating committee recommendations (including the carefully planned reelection of Kelleher to another term), and on and on. Finally, the rubber hit the road.[9]

After an explanation from Kelleher of how a call item got to the floor for a vote, the annual meeting voted *against* eliminating the distinction between amateurs and professionals, voted for trying to bring the professionals into the Association, and with minor amendments, voted in favor of allowing American players to play an open Wimbledon without jeopardizing their amateur status. The vote against no differentiation between pros and amateurs might seem a defeat for the Kelleher cohort, but they understood and, to some degree, agreed on the need to differentiate between amateurs and professionals. Not only had the delegates assembly voted that way, but there were practical reasons as well. The vote in favor of letting all Americans play Wimbledon was clearly a vote in favor of open tennis. They then agreed to adjourn but not conclude the meeting and to reconvene two months later to consider what would have, by then, transpired at the ILTF meeting. In Alastair Martin's oft-misquoted words: "The tennis community holds its breath and hopes."[10]

Given what was to follow in Paris, perhaps the most important decision was Kelleher's reelection at that February meeting. With Britain adamant, the Aussies agreeing, the French compliant, and the United States on board, the war was over. But there were some battles to be fought to determine the terms of the armistice.

The 1968 annual meeting reconvened (easier than calling a special meeting) in Dallas, Texas, on April 6 at 9:00 a.m. The stated purpose was to receive reports about the ILTF discussions about open tennis, and to react as necessary.

Kelleher's opening summary was to the point. The overall agreement reached at the Federation meeting gave the Americans nearly everything they asked for:

1. Keep amateurism as part of Federation rules, including recognized amateur championships.
2. Self-determination for national associations to determine the status of players except for relations with professionals, which requires establishment of a common ILTF policy; however, professionals could compete in nationally sanctioned tournaments with other than professionals only if that tournament had been declared open to all.
3. Creation of a "strictly limited" number of open tournaments approved by the ILTF.

In addition, a new rule defined an amateur and established a new amateur category inside national associations, that of a "registered" player "who, (having reached the age of eighteen), is authorized to derive material profit from the Game, whilst not making tennis his profession." National federations had the option of adopting either or both statuses, or of eliminating any distinctions (as the British proposed) except to prohibit those under eighteen from playing for "material profit." The obvious purpose of that tortured definition was to allow professionals to play in Davis Cup competition. Professionals who played for profit in events not sanctioned by their national association (the professional tours) could not play in sanctioned events unless they were approved opens. Teaching pros were considered pros unless their national association permitted them to remain amateurs.

A justifiably satisfied Kelleher concluded: "So, to summarize, we have the right to run our own show. We also have the right to institute, if we see fit to do so, open tennis in the United States with our National Championships to be opened if we so decide."[11]

The Alastair Martin show followed. Kelleher whimsically introduced Martin "as the gentleman from Ecuador." The actual delegate from that country, having "had his fill of flying by the time he reached Paris," had given his credentials to Martin. Whether bad weather or the lights of Paris were the cause, the American became "the gentleman from Ecuador."

The Alastair Martin Show

According to one reporter, Alastair Martin got into the progression for USLTA president as a "compromise" candidate from the Eastern Section, following "another petty, and all too familiar, personality power struggle in the U.S.L.T.A."

Martin's wry sense of humor shows through even in the dry dusty pages of Association minutes. After he had succeeded Kelleher as president, he opened the February 1970 executive-committee meeting with this sally:

> I thought that it would be wiser, rather than to make a serious Introductory Remarks at this meeting, to describe a letter I wrote to my daughter very late yesterday evening.
>
> It went something like this:

. . . Arrived here Friday to find my Ranking Coordinator had resigned.
. . . Monday, East out of control.
. . . Tuesday, West out of control.
. . . Yesterday, officers out of control.

... Today, promoters out of control; players out of control; I.T.P.A. and I.L.T.F. out of control; committees out of control; Jimmy Van Alen out of control.

... Tomorrow, plan on moving to Old Tucson until the damned thing blows over!!

Thank you.
May we now have the Secretary's Report?[12]

On another occasion, when Kelleher worried about raising enough prize money for the first U.S. Open, Martin said he would put up the money if need be. And yes, he was the president who, when asked what he did, responded "I guess I'm a beneficiary."

Martin's summary of the background to the ILTF meeting, combined with some other sources, offers an unusual insight into the give and take at international meetings. After the British "bombshell" (Martin's word) of December 1967, the ILTF Committee of Management met and "took a very dim view" of the British declaration. The Swedes and the Brits wanted a special meeting of the ILTF on the matter of open tennis, and the USLTA agreed. They persuaded enough other members, and a special meeting was scheduled.

Then, Martin continued, Kelleher had cabled other Federation nations (it is unclear which ones or perhaps all) after the first part of the 1968 USLTA annual meeting, explaining the U.S. position on open tennis. Martin and Kelleher then headed for Paris. (See gallery, image 18.) Almost as soon as Kelleher arrived, he met for breakfast with Jean Borotra, who "ran tennis in France" and who headed the ILTF Committee on Amateurism.[13] Borotra seemed resigned to open tennis, but held out for a "registered player" category—a hybrid between amateur and full-time professional that allowed national federations to require playing Davis Cup matches. Kelleher offered a deal, open tennis for "registered" players—also known as "authorized" or "designated" players. The Frenchman agreed and, lo and behold, open tennis was approved unanimously at the ILTF meeting—forty years after Julian Myrick's 1928 prediction: "There is your amateur championship and your professional championship, and eventually, as that develops, you will have your open championship." The British groused that "the authorized player is the quintessence of hypocrisy," for players would continue to receive "money under the table." They were right. The ILTF wanted to allow "authorized" players to play Davis Cup while other professionals could not. As one sportswriter observed, "the authorized player was an anachronism at birth and died after a short and useless life a couple of years later."[14]

With pretty much everyone, including the smaller nations (thanks presumably to the French) on the same page, the proposals went through the Federation annual meeting unanimously, despite concern when a flustered Soviet delegate who was expected to vote against, arrived late—and said nothing.[15]

Martin, somewhat contradictorily, pointed out that only the Americans seemed aware that the ILTF had no jurisdiction over the Davis Cup and that the Australian delegate had commented that the Federation was out of order even to make recommendations about that competition. Martin ended his report noting "they did have a very fine lunch, thanks to the French delegation."[16] Some things never change.

With international open tennis explained, the USLTA annual meeting turned to the details. There were lots of questions; some were answered, many not. Some had to be dealt with immediately, the most important being which and how many U.S. tournaments would be designated "open." Other questions required study and time to shake down. This all had little immediate effect on everyday tennis in America. What quickly became the U.S. Open was not yet an iconic event.

Kelleher then moved to proposed Association bylaws already prepared by the constitution and rules committee—that the U.S. championships would be open was a given. It took a while to get to the pressing question; where would the U.S. National Championships be held? The traditional site of the national doubles championship, the Longwood Cricket Club, rumored to be interested in gaining the national championships, said it wanted to keep that doubles tournament as an amateur event. But that was just a lead-in to an impassioned plea from Edward Hickey, a vice president of the bank that had sponsored the National Professional Championship—at Longwood—for some three years. Hickey offered to take that professional championship (and the time slot) and make it the U.S. Open. A fascinating offer, even if the international schedule for the Slams made it an unlikely alternative.[17] As with most unsettled matters, it was referred to the president for further study.

Questions and discussion about revision to the Association's amateur rules quickly descended into a debate evocative of medieval monks arguing endlessly about picayune theological points, legalistic to the point of becoming incomprehensible. Some examples typical of the new rules: amateurs could make endorsement agreements with manufacturers and there was concern about the situation of teaching pros and some regrets that the Association had not been able to incorporate them into the USLTA. Although the British wanted to eliminate all distinctions, they had agreed to allow national organizations to determine their own rules for national play, allowing the USLTA to separate teaching and touring pros. Kelleher noted that in Britain, teaching pros were members of and certified by the lawn tennis association there.[18] When "the Spy," Bill Clothier, asked about keeping the twenty-eight-dollar-a-day limit on allowances for amateurs, the response came (spelled out) D-E-A-D. One delegate wisely recommended that the Association caution amateurs to keep good records since the IRS would expect to receive taxes for any excess of payments over expenses.

The rules discussions were arcane; those about money were to the point. A delegate questioned the new rule requiring a sanction fee be paid to the ILTF of £250 to hold an open tournament and £500 (some $1250) for an open championship. Kelleher responded first by pointing out that, in the past, international tennis had suffered because the ILTF had been an "ineffective and indeed almost non-operative" organization, implying that it needed the revenue to become effective. Then he assured the delegates the USLTA was responsible for that fee. The discussion quickly revealed that the Federation's desire to limit the number of open tournaments was a dream. Delegates at the USLTA meeting quickly spoke of their sectional championships and worried that they would be priced out of the market. That the ILTF was ready to immediately sanction the U.S. nationals and three other tournaments was not enough. As one delegate put it: "I want to say right now, as far as Southern California is concerned, we want to be sure that we have an open Championship this year, and I'd like to make an application as soon as possible." Kelleher continued the rhetoric of "the principle and concept of strictly limited tournaments," but added presciently, "at least for the present."

The ILTF and Amateur Rules

Why did tennis federations from nations with a relatively small number of tennis players fail to support and enforce a strict interpretation of the ILTF's amateur rules? Why did the ILTF fail to discipline those federations?

Davis Cup matches, particularly home "ties" (meaning a knockout round—the language of tennis is nothing if not arcane), generated most of the revenue small federations needed to survive (and pay expenses for bureaucrats—"tenniscrats"—to travel to ITLF meetings). Those national federations could compete in the major international competition, Davis Cup, with just two very good (if tireless) players, each playing two singles and one doubles match in three days. But for those "very good" players to compete, they had to play in various tournaments around the tennis world so as to be competitive. That cost money that small federations did not have, and that money came from various forms of under-the-table payments—and had come that way for some two decades. To quote the acid-tongued Richard Evans: "amongst the various national federations . . . there was a heavy bias in favour of those who were in love with the word 'amateur,' afraid of the word 'professional' and desperately anxious about what Open Tennis would do to the perks and the stature that came with their honorary jobs."

The ITLF's leaders maintained the support of the majority of the smaller federations by evading and avoiding their own amateur rules. One example: just after the ILTF president, Giorgio de Stefani, an ambidextrous Davis Cup player for Italy thirty years earlier, threatened to exclude the British from international competition for declaring "open" tennis, a London newspaper reported that the Italian Davis Cup star, Nikki Pietrangeli, had earlier been persuaded "a couple of times" by de Stefani (also president of the Italian Tennis Federation) to reject offers from Jack Kramer's pro tour. "'I'm not prepared to say how much, but they paid me money,' said Nikki." Whatever de Stefani's ambidexterity, it made the president of the ILTF "simply look silly."[19]

Late in the afternoon, deep concern emerged about open tennis stimulating the establishment of some sort of professional tennis or professional players organization; the dreaded "union" foreseen in 1962 by George Barnes. John Sisson of Southern California warned that the USLTA had to make concessions and adopt a policy of fifty-fifty with the professionals or they could face a professional championship "in direct conflict" with "some Open Tennis Championship"—the fate of the U.S. nationals and the U.S. Open was the real concern. The matter was referred to the president but would soon come up again. Eventually, such a challenge would come from the professionals in 1985.[20]

One of the last items was the "registered player" category. Should the USLTA adopt it? As Kelleher pointed out, they had gained "self-determination" without jeopardizing their international status, so they could refuse to allow "authorized players" to compete as such. No one referred to the deal between Kelleher and Borotra, though there were hints. Although a motion to reject the "registered" player category was barely tabled, the new Association amateur rules did not call for such a category, and those rules were later adopted, leaving the USLTA with but two categories, amateurs and players. The ILTF would flail around for a few years with its four categories, but eventually changed the rules of tennis to follow the American model. Kelleher was on the mark when he proudly proclaimed, we got everything we wanted.

Other than a comment that the U.S. Olympic Committee under Avery Brundage had taken an extreme antiprofessional position and seemed quite "unfriendly" toward the USLTA, that was it for what was a momentous annual meeting.[21]

Despite the USLTA's complex and convoluted amateur rules and its commitment to enforce those regulations as of the late 1960s, the Association was equally complicit (though a bit less blatant) in the collapse of the international amateur regulatory structure. After all, the USLTA wanted to win the Davis Cup and be competitive internationally just as much as any other federation.

After voting expenses for the unbudgeted and unexpected trip to Dallas for themselves and other official attendees be paid by the Association, the delegates finally concluded what likely was the Association's longest, and certainly longest-traveled, annual meeting. They had decided; the revolution had begun.

The administrative committee met immediately afterwards but focused on routine matters except to eliminate the standing order that had prohibited amateurs from staying in Europe after the Wimbledon tournament, a rule designed to ensure they were not making a career out of playing tennis.[22] It was the kind of rule that Brundage insisted on for Olympic amateurs.

It is nearly impossible to document the details of meetings and decisions adjusting to the new ILTF rules, and little need to do so. Four (or five) categories of pros, sort of pros, pros by a different name, and part-time pros were all created, defined, and re-defined. Top amateurs worried that they would be left "out in the cold." But within about a year, a degree of sanity returned and reasonably straightforward definitions and rules emerged. Whatever the widespread confusion over interpreting the new rules, which were ambiguous at best, suffice to say that by the June 1968 meeting of the administrative committee, Martin could give a report on the activities of something called the U.S. Open Committee—a committee that included the names of Jack Kramer (the promoter the Association loved to hate) and Arthur Ashe (not only black, but a highly ranked player about to turn pro after earning twenty-eight dollars a day for expenses as an amateur at the U.S. Open).

Whether or not Davis Cup should be an open competition turned out to be a short but emotional debate for the Association. Although the big four of Davis Cup—the British, the French, the Australians, and the Americans supported, in principle, an open Davis Cup, the developing war between "contract pros" and "independent pros," along with the desire of smaller nations to maintain control over their players, prompted the Davis Cup nations to continue with a "silly double standard" that allowed national associations to permit pros they controlled to play as "registered" players. The USLTA itself, torn between reality and the desire to keep costs down, finally caved in when the Davis Cup captain, Donald Dell, and the team, refused to play Davis Cup matches (ties) without being paid prize money. In February 1969 the Association created the "player" category, a subterfuge to allow professionals and amateurs to compete in events like Davis Cup. There were some recalcitrants. Baker argued that the Association should vote against allowing "registered" players competing in Davis Cup. Martin disagreed since the ILTF had intended such players to participate.[23] "Pete" Davis (Dwight's son) read a prepared statement from the family that said they were "open-minded" about an open Davis Cup but wanted reassurances that the purpose of the Cup would be upheld and that the competition not be made "subservient" to the "individual benefits" of the players.[24]

At the same time, Arthur Ashe, America's top amateur and winner of the inaugural U.S. Open in 1968, was threatening not to play Davis Cup as a protest against South Africa's apartheid (extreme segregation) policies. It was a temporary distraction for the USLTA that would soon develop into a full-fledged war. In some ways, the story is more about the Association's obsession with the Davis Cup competition and the growing leverage of top players than it is about racism in South Africa or anywhere else.

International pressure on South Africa had spread to the sports world by 1968. There were boisterous protests throughout western Europe at soccer (football) and other events. Some non-white athletes had boycotted the 1968 Olympics. Others, most famously two Americans, Tommy Smith and John Carlos, who won Olympic medals in track, gave a black glove, closed-fist, Black Power–style salute during the playing of the U.S. national anthem. Other symbols of support from athletes against racism were rampant. It was dramatic demonstration that the Olympic claim to be nonpolitical was not possible—although a number of USLTA leaders would continue to insist on taking the politics out of international tennis.

The horror of Munich in 1972 when terrorists killed eleven Israeli athletes and the ineffectiveness of American boycotts of the Olympics in 1936 (not implemented) and 1980 and the 2014 winter Olympics in Sochi would all demonstrate that to think politics and sports could be compartmentalized was just silly. Perhaps the least edifying argument came in the immediate aftermath of the downing of a civilian passenger plane over Ukraine in 2014. Alleged Russian involvement in the shooting prompted public calls for Fédération Internationale de Football Association (FIFA) to review the decision to give the 2018 World Cup (soccer) games to Russia. FIFA officials responded that "isolation or confrontation are not the most effective ways to solve problems." Rather the event "can be a powerful catalyst for constructive dialogue between people and governments." So a positive result is not politicization? To be fair, a Russian official was a bit more candid; we're hosting the games "for footballers, for the fans." Prestige was assumed.[25]

But Bob Kelleher was not one to ignore the reality of discrimination. According to Ashe, in 1967 when it appeared that the United States would meet South Africa in Davis Cup semifinals, Kelleher had told him, "let's do something that's never been done in the history of Davis Cup competition." Since the United States had the choice of venue, he wanted to insist on playing in South Africa to "go down there and beat the crap out of them. Let South Africa see a black person win in their own backyard." The scenario failed to play out when South Africa was upset in the quarterfinals by Spain.[26]

Not long afterwards, Ashe applied to play in the 1970 South African Open Championships. As far as the tournament committee was concerned, it was open to all whose tennis record qualified them. But the South Africa government determined otherwise. Ashe's visa request was denied despite being endorsed by Kelleher, who was by then former president of the USLTA. The U.S. State Department expressed "deep regret" at the decision, and the worldwide media offered stronger language. As it turned out, it was another example of the power of sports and elite athletes.[27]

In January, Alastair Martin, in a letter to the South African consulate in New York, condemned the visa refusal as based solely on race. By then political pressure had built up in the United States and throughout the world. A subcommittee of the U.S. House of Representatives heard testimony from Ashe and others, including the general counsel of the USLTA, George Gowen. They spoke in support of action against the government of South Africa but opposed denying visas for individual South Africans who wished to play in tournaments held in the United States. "We do not subscribe to the theory that two wrongs make a right," stated Gowen.

"We believe that by encouraging tournaments open to all the world's finest athletes, regardless of race, creed or political persuasion, we also, in some small way promote world peace and brotherhood." Some athletes complained that Ashe was "politicizing" the game, but the two top South African players (both white, of course) agreed that South Africa should be excluded from Davis cup competition.[28]

A few Association leaders also privately spoke disparagingly of politicizing tennis—even though the South African government had already done that. In early 1970 South Africa's apartheid policies finally got the USLTA's official attention on what Martin labeled "a slight problem." After a good deal of on-the-one-hand, on-the-other talk, the executive committee agreed that, even though the ILTF continued to wobble, not playing Davis Cup was a done deal.

Yet some Association leaders insisted, indirectly, that the game was more important than the social principle. The day after the Davis Cup nations banned South Africa from the competition (March 24, 1970), Vice President Robert Colwell made the news by denying that Ashe's case had influenced the decision to ban South Africa. Donald Dell, immediate former Davis Cup captain, clearly puzzled, settled for an uncharacteristically brief statement: "I wonder why he would deny that?" Later in the day, Colwell explained that it was not the failure to issue a visa but the danger that so many other nations would withdraw and ruin the competition that determined the U.S. position. That despite Martin's and the Association's public statements that the visa denial was a "clear case" of racial discrimination. It is hard to say what prompted Colwell's comments, perhaps sensitivities within the United States or the USLTA regarding race relations. It may well have been a reflex action to return to the long-standing Association position—it's the game that matters. In any case, the Association remained reactive not proactive on racial discrimination. A few years later when the Davis Cup nations threatened to expel South Africa because of apartheid, USTLA president Stan Malless warned that the United States would withdraw from the competition to protest the expulsion of any nation just for its politics. The vote to exclude the South Africans lost, 24–22. Observers believed the U.S. position prompted a number of delegates to go against voting out the defending Davis Cup champions. Throughout the early and mid seventies, the Association stuck to it guns—supporting suspensions against nations that withdrew from a Davis Cup competition because they would have to play South Africa.[29]

To follow the story to its conclusion, South Africa was reinstated in 1974, and won the Davis Cup by default in 1975 when India refused to travel to South Africa for the finals. In 1977 Slew Hester, then deeply involved with the Flushing Meadows, National Tennis Center project, announced that the United States would play a Davis Cup match against South Africa (sandwiched into the "Americas" group) at Newport Beach, California, whether or not the African nations approved. The next year, with a Davis Cup tie between South Africa and the United States scheduled to be played at Vanderbilt University in Tennessee, one Peter Lamb, a "colored" (mixed race) South African student on the tennis team at Vanderbilt was selected for the South Africa team in what was clearly a token gesture. There were loud but nonviolent protests. A spokesperson for the university defended the decision by citing the school's "Open Forum Policy," a "well-established policy allowing any group to assemble and speak on campus." In an argument that would have puzzled a Supreme Court justice, the university argued that the tennis match had "symbolic content," thus rising to the level free speech—an unbreakable principle of the university. The USTA relieved Vanderbilt of its responsibility to pay a $50,000 guarantee, but the match was played despite vigorous nonviolent protests. As more nations threatened to back out of Davis and Federation Cup competition so as to avoid the "risk" of having to play South Africa, in 1978 the ITF began officially "investigating" South Africa and apartheid, a bit belatedly. Canada, Mexico, Venezuela, and Caribbean Commonwealth (British Commonwealth nations) all withdrew, while the Soviet Union had already been banned by the ILTF for refusing to play South Africa.[30]

During the 1970s the USTA routinely threatened not to enter the Davis Cup draw. That never happened, although Association pushed hard to punish nations that had entered the draw for dropping out for "non-tennis" reasons. Association leaders, vocally uncomfortable with the propaganda benefits gained by the Soviet Union and its satellites by boycotting Davis Cup ties against South Africa and Rhodesia, or by refusing to play Chile because of its governing junta, took the high ground, such as it was; the competition should not be affected by irrelevant social and political disputes. Fine, said some, tennis is not an instrument of reform. Absurd, responded others, injustice requires commitment. Later arguments that Davis Cup was "a political football" have had to stretch a bit to illustrate such claims, with the exception of the South African imbroglio. For the world, what tennis did was relatively unimportant; for the tennis world, it seemed defining. Although the USTA doggedly stuck to its "principle" that the game came first, worldwide tennis was somewhat more favorably reviewed on its handling of South African apartheid.[31]

In the decade that followed, tennis continued to shy away from full participation in the anti-apartheid movement that most international sports had embraced—almost always at the insistence of their athletes. As the pressure in South Africa against apartheid grew in the late 1980s, the South African government declared a state of emergency allowing extralegal measures, which only stepped up the brutal scenes of death and destruction. Nonetheless, in 1988, the ITF evaded a formal boycott of South African tennis by stating it would not "require" players to compete there—yet leaving a Grand Prix tournament in South Africa in place. It was the same "freedom of choice" argument that the USTA had made regarding racism in its sections. A few months later the Grand Prix schedule was changed.[32]

The strongest pressure on USTA and ITF behavior came from their own strong desire to remain a permanent part of the Olympic games, finally prompting both organizations to support expelling South Africa from the International Tennis Federation.[33] The USTA warned American players that participation in the Olympics plus Davis and Federation Cup matches could be denied to those participating in tennis events in South Africa. A press release stated that "The USTA does not support apartheid or discrimination, a stance expressed over a decade ago." But the Association would not deny entry into the U.S. Open for tennis-qualified individuals legally in the United States, asserting that "would be counter to the rules of international tennis . . . and counter to the concepts of individual rights." Sports should not serve political causes—the same argument used by Holcombe Ward forty years earlier when he rejected the appeal of Richard Cohen, a black man, to be allowed to enter the nationals. Finally, in 1989, the ITF decided not to sanction any tournaments held in South Africa.[34]

Still, the Association was trying. When, in 1988 "prominent members of the USTA" played in a tournament in South Africa set up by the International Lawn Tennis Club of the United States, the Association board sent a letter to the club's president pointing out that USTA opposition to apartheid included "forbidding employees or officers of the Association to participate in such events in South Africa." Significantly, the board went on to discuss complaints of racism from a well-known African American journalist, Doug Smith, and accusations of racial bias in junior programs.[35]

But social issues were not what prompted Alastair Martin's tongue-in-cheek letter to his daughter complaining that everything was "out of control." It was all too accurate. Even as the advent of open tennis, major rule changes, and the South African mess all swirled around, the Association faced reorganization proposals generated by a special committee set up by Kelleher just before Martin succeeded him.

A good part of the push for reform came from obvious signs that the Open Era would make tennis more popular, forcing the Association to adjust to its new status as an organization for amateurs that was, at the same time, a revenue-producing business. A harbinger of such changes appeared when one Ed Mooney of the Licensing Corporation of America spoke to the executive committee in February 1969. His corporation had been hired to develop apparel and other products endorsed by the USLTA. Mooney was "bullish" about the results and the opportunities for revenue, "a million dollars . . . every year.

But, he said, manufacturers had some serious complaints. Potential licensees frequently asked, "the USLTA, what are you talking about? They never heard of this alphabet soup." More substantive was that various Association teams, like Davis Cup and international cup teams, were not wearing the products of USLTA-licensed manufacturers, prompting one major clothing business to pull out of the program.

Executive-committee members insisted that in the absence of a contractual agreement amateurs should not be required to wear or use the products of licensees. But the vigorous debate ended when soon to be first vice president Robert Colwell commented, "we have a very strong moral obligation to do everything we can to cooperate with this kind of a financial program. . . . The new [executive] committee will work on it." In other words, money talks. A small name change—elimination of the L(awn) in USLTA—would make the alphabet soup a bit more digestible, but reorganization would be a greater challenge.[36]

Reorganization meant more than just product licensing and marketing. It meant streamlining, or at least modernizing, a governance and administrative system that had developed nearly a hundred years earlier, evolving geographically, but not structurally.

A routine criticism of the Association was (and is) that it was too presidential; the focus for each president's term ("reign" was the word used by critics) was set by that person's personal agenda, replete with catchy slogans and, more recently, PowerPoint presentations. Rather than continuing down paths already blazed, new presidents seemed to insist on brave new directions. Yet, at the same time, critics condemned the Association for its conservatism, its caution, its unwillingness to change. The long history of the US(NL)TA suggests that all the critics were (are) both right and wrong. Most presidents preferred an "evolutionary" approach, offering old wine in new bottles. But a few took chances and pushed the Association to move significantly.

The presidency of Judge Robert Kelleher had a palpable impact on the short- and long-term makeup of the Association and on American tennis. The acceptance of open tennis, which Kelleher worked hard to make happen, is his best-known achievement. But a perceptive report, prepared by a special presidential committee he appointed (Long Range Financial Planning Committee or LRP), recommended changes that could fundamentally restructure the Association and its role in American tennis. That study began in September 1968, when a discussion arose about how to determine the "distribution" to the sections, an important question given projections of increased revenue because of open tennis. Kelleher tasked the committee with examining the long-range financial plan, adding sagaciously, the words "and administrative structure." The committee, surely guided by private conversations with Kelleher and other Association leaders, took the ball and ran with it.

In January 1969 Kelleher, not given to hyperbole, described the result as "a monumental work. . . . not equaled by any similar report," so extensive and far-reaching that "it would be *untraditional* to act upon it at . . . an Executive Committee meeting." His successor, Alastair Martin, said that he viewed that as a green light for his administration to start tackling the problem. The executive committee agreed and unanimously recommended that "many" of the report's "broad aspects" be studied and implemented "at an early date."[37]

Decades later, a past president read the old report and reacted, "wow! This should be and have been required reading for every Board Member, Staff Member and Sectional leadership. . . . It definitely set the path."[38] But did it?

The twenty-six-page LRP report (plus exhibits) began with four questions, each with a succinct and dramatic short answer:

(1) Who should the USLTA be?
(2) What should the USLTA do?
(3) Who should manage the USLTA?
(4) How should the USLTA be financed?"

Who should the Association be? It should administer all tennis in the United States; that embraces amateurs, playing professionals, and teaching professionals.

What should it do? It should run major, "big-time" events that promote the game and generate the funds needed for the USLTA to broaden its scope. That should include allowing Association members to play for prize money and to "allow all players to compete in traditional tennis environments" (an overly cautious call for self-determination and for open tennis, including Davis Cup).

Who should manage the Association? "A staff of competent professional managers, while the elected USLTA Executive Committee should serve in an advisory capacity," like a corporate board of directors, plus an executive secretary. In the words of the report, "The USLTA has gone as far as it can as a basically volunteer organization."

Association financing? Revenues should jump to $1,400,000 by 1972, the report projected, with a surplus of $400,000, which could be spent to expand the game (the de rigueur refrain). This was no pipedream; the Association's income in 1968 was $368,000 while expenses came to $280,000.[39]

The financial outlook, predicated on promoting "big-time" tournaments, especially growing revenues from the U.S. Open, was exciting. The notion of administering "all tennis in the United States" was a heady potion, although as things turned out, it was already too late to bring the touring professionals into the USLTA family.

But turning over management of the Association to a bunch of "professional managers?" That was radical for a hard-working, climb-the-ladder group of national volunteers who assumed that "perks," power, and promotion was their due. Such volunteers had long been the hallmark of the Association, but by the 1970s they had become indispensable to its expanding operations. In a wonderful way, they combined execution and policymaking in all that they did. For most of those local, sectional, and national volunteers, just getting the job done (sitting on committees, officiating, organizing tournaments, setting up junior programs, doing publicity—the list is endless) was reward enough.[40] But the USLTA top leadership, which had begun with great champions a century earlier, had become dominated by businessmen, albeit men who loved the game. Success (however defined) was what they had spent a lifetime seeking and achieving. The Association had slowly moved forward, but now a committee of those same businessmen, advocated a dramatic governance change. In the words of Alastair Martin: "We're moving into tennis as big business."[41]

This was not the first call for a reorganization of the Association. Back in 1962 the incoming president, George Barnes, suggested that the USLTA needed to look at itself. He then referred to a report from the Research and Planning Committee titled "A Hope and a Prophecy—the USLTA in 1972, a Preliminary Ten-Year Plan." It discussed finances and proposed a reorganization of the Association. But its time had not yet come.[42]

Not so for the 1969 "Long Range Financial Planning" report, which was mostly long-range and only tangentially about finance. The report generated discussion and enough support to warrant the ultimate stamp of approval—getting a consultant's report. Not surprisingly (knowing who paid the bill—actually, Alastair Martin paid part of it) that a report from McKinsey and Company (the first of many over the next three decades), delivered in September 1969, echoed and built on the recommendations of the January 1969 LRP report. After the usual persiflage based on interviews with all of seventy-five people, it followed the script laid out nine months earlier.[43]

Taken together, the two reports offered a strikingly accurate picture of the Association and the challenges it faced:

(1) Membership growth was lagging, requiring "vigorous, positive action," an early version of the "grow the game" mission. But, in a reference to open tennis and the pro game, the Association was in the midst of a "tidal wave" of change, and more coming. If the USLTA could not agree on handling the changes, they had the "explosive" power to "tear this organized game of tennis apart." Hence "decisive leadership" from the USLTA was necessary.[44] (Little did they know how prescient that remark was. The "tidal wave" of popularity came in the '70s and '80s, before the Association was strategically or psychologically prepared.);
(2) policy-making mechanisms were not geared to the rapid pace of change;
(3) the Association had insufficient staff "to provide day-to-day direction and assistance to national and local activities";
(4) it acknowledged the indispensable role of the volunteers ("if you ever do anything to undercut the loyalty . . . of its volunteer base, you will find it will collapse"), yet the consultants' report concluded that "the (volunteer) committee structure has become cumbersome, sluggish, and inadequately controlled."[45]

The consultants called establishment of an executive-secretary position a step in the right direction but warned that the policy-making structure needed beefing up by making the executive secretary the executive director with the staff needed to manage day-to-day operations. More strikingly, they recommended creation of a full-time, salaried, executive vice president "responsible for working directly with the President and other officers in shaping the direction of the association." As the consultant told the executive committee: "Don't kid yourself that you can have a volunteer president who is going to work at this with one hand. Uh-uh, this is a full time job from now on." That executive vice president should have the stature to lead nationally and internationally, to "maintain the allegiance" of top players, and to manage an organization as large and complex as "the USLTA is destined to become." It was not the first call for a tennis "Czar." Three former presidents had earlier supported creation of an executive vice president–type job. *World Tennis*, for example, had repeatedly recommended a "powerful Director of Tennis." But it took the two Association-sponsored reports to get the attention of the leadership.[46]

Before 1916, the Association apparently had no employees of any kind and no central office. Its work was performed by the officers out of their homes or businesses. The field secretary position, created in 1916, was for someone who, with a couple of stenographers, would answer requests for information on such topics as tennis court construction, disseminate reports to committees, and generally assist the president. As the Association grew, so did the amount of work, prompting a title change in 1923 to executive secretary. But neither post had a decision-making role.[47]

Hiring a prestigious professional to head up the Association had come up seriously in 1967, when the new president Robert Kelleher pushed for a big name to be the Association's executive director. His initial suggestion was former Oklahoma University football coach, Bud Wilkinson. But when Wilkinson explained he could only work half time and would need an assistant to handle the administrative work, the Association looked elsewhere. Apparently unable to persuade a well-known figure to take the job, they arranged for the retirement of longtime executive secretary Edwin Baker and settled on Robert Malaga who, in March of 1967, had become an "Executive Assistant" to the president and the executive committee. Kelleher had hoped Jack Kramer could become "high commissioner" of tennis, but Kramer had rubbed too many people the wrong way.[48]

Two years later, when the two long-range reports came before the executive committee, the recommendation for hiring an executive director received solid support. President Martin, acting a bit surprised, commented: "I certainly appreciate your approving all of these . . . revolutionary decisions. . . . which are far more revolutionary than I think any of us really envisages"—that despite his statement to the Association leadership that "We cannot hope to exert effective tennis leadership if we cannot put our own house in order. The central office of the USLTA must be modernized."[49]

Perhaps they were too revolutionary for Martin and the leadership as well. Just before the 1970 annual meeting in Tucson, Arizona, he gave a candid explanation of his decision not to hire a "tennis Czar" despite a strong recommendation to fill the proposed executive vice president (CEO) slot. Even as a candidate was being offered the job (which he subsequently turned down), Martin and "several others" on the special committee had second thoughts. He gave a laundry list of problems along with a roster of promised initiatives. The problems were serious, starting with the establishment of open tennis and the Association's relationship with "star players" as well as the professional tennis world of competing pro tour groups. Then there were the disputes with South Africa over apartheid and Arthur Ashe's application to play the South African Championships, disagreements over ILTF rules and categories of players, on down to revising the USLTA constitution and bylaws, and "ball rotation." From the sublime to the ridiculous.

Martin declared that "the tennis world was in turmoil," an accurate assessment, and concluded, "In general . . . the progress we were making . . . would be slowed, rather than improved, by the introduction of a highly paid, highly publicized personality into the U.S.L.T.A. organization." Martin's hint that he was not opposed to a czar but that 1970 was not quite the right time, may have been genuine, but that "highly paid, highly publicized personality" also posed a threat to traditional volunteer leadership.[50] There was a gentle push-back from those on the search committee, but the czar proposal died. So Bob Malaga moved into the executive director slot. He was an efficient, effective administrative assistant, but his authority was simply a subset of the president's wishes.

The Open Era and the fast-growing U.S. Open Championships with its steadily increasing revenues created an even greater need for professional staff and for a director with a large scope of authority and responsibility. The 1970–71 revised constitution and bylaws specified that there be an executive director, but when Malaga departed in 1972, the Association went quietly back to the executive-secretary position—with the title's implied limitations. The volunteers at the top remained in full control.

The Association's dilemma was neatly captured by Lamar Hunt, the financier of World Championship Tennis, one of the competing pro circuits: "As for [Jack] Kramer's suggestion that there be a tennis commissioner . . . Pete Rozelle is in charge of pro football, not college football as well."[51] The USLTA and the ILTF could control amateur tennis, but professional tennis was beyond their authority. Alastair Martin challenged that by traveling repeatedly to Europe and around the United States trying to convince professionals to accept some kind of outside leadership. But to no avail.

As the crucial USLTA executive-committee meeting in September 1969 wound down, it heard about another "revolutionary" change. Since the founding of the Association, no single issue had garnered more annual-meeting time and generated more turmoil and tension than the annual battle over rankings. Based on endless and incomplete reports, collated by hand, accompanied by all-too-subjective analysis, the rankings (which had to be approved by the annual meeting) were all too arbitrary for the players and their supporters. This was what the early leaders of the Association had really cared about. But at that 1969 meeting, a ranking committee reported testing a computer program that would calculate rankings—for the men's singles that would have data for 1,200 players. The goal was to fund and use the program for 1970 rankings. The future had arrived quietly on cat's paws. Then, two years later, an equally consequential revolution appeared! Yellow tennis balls were approved (tentatively) by the executive committee.[52] Just try to find a can of white tennis balls today. So which was more important, yellow tennis balls, computerized rankings, or the relatively minor adjustments the Association made in governance in the early seventies?

Perhaps the most important change was the "professionalization" of tennis officiating. For over a century, tennis officials had been drawn from the club or facility hosting a tournament. But as players began to make a living from the game, the stakes got higher. Elderly gentlemen, whose main reward for spending a hot afternoon calling lines was a few drinks at the bar (sometimes between matches), no longer seemed adequate, whatever their good intentions. The path to today's worldwide coterie of experienced, well-trained women and men, all following ITF and (in the United States) USTA regulations, was long and often painful. Perhaps the most recognizable step in that direction came in a report to the Association's executive committee in February 1969 from Michael Dunne, chair of the Umpires Committee. Much of his presentation related to specific rules, but proposals for an "eye test or eyesight requirement" presaged positive change. A proposal for an umpire emeritus status indicated a sensitivity to club members; Dunne's complaint that proposals for shortening the deuce set problem (presumably Jimmy Van Alen's tie break)—i.e., the requirement of having to win a set by a margin of at least two games—had never been referred to those who might know best, the umpires committee, made too much sense to be ignored.[53]

1. Apollo, history's first tennis player? Giovanni Battista Tiepolo, *The Death of Hyacinth*, 1752–53, Museo Thyssen-Bornemisza, Madrid. Credit: Museo Thyssen-Bornemisza/Scala/Art Resource, New York.

2. (*right*) Walter Clopton Wingfield in full regalia. Wingfield wrote the first set of rules for the game he christened "lawn tennis." Credit: George E. Alexander, *Wingfield: Edwardian Gentleman*, with the permission of Peter E. Randall Publisher.

3. (*below*) As Wingfield wrote: "The ground need not even be turf, the only condition is, it must be level." The proof of the pudding is in the "playing." Credit: Courtesy of the Russian Tennis Federation.

4. (*top*) Playing Wingfield's game: saggy nets, vests, and without sneakers at J. P. Morgan's Dover House, Putney, London, England, 1876, five years before the birth of the USTA. Credit: USTA Archive.

5. (*bottom*) Men and women (lots of women) playing indoor tennis in New York City as the USTA was being organized. Credit: *Harper's Weekly*, December 10, 1881/USTA Archive.

6. (*opposite*) James "Jim" Dwight—the "dapper little cuss." The true founding father of the USTA, of which he served as president for twenty-one years. Credit: USTA Archive.

7. (*above*) Dwight Davis, donor of the Davis Cup, political player in the nation's capital (before the Beltway) and possessor of a fine backhand. Credit: USTA Archive.

Ethel gives sick Yagenka a bottle of medicine

Leo chases a squirrel which fortunately he can't catch

A nice policeman feeding a squirrel with bread; I fed two with bread this afternoon.

Father plays tennis with Mr. Cooley.
[Father's shape & spectacles are reproduced with photographic fidelity; also notice Mr. Cooley's smile]

8. The only image of President Teddy Roosevelt playing tennis—a sketch in a letter to his daughter, Ethel, dated June 23, 1904. Credit: Theodore Roosevelt "picture letter" to Ethel Roosevelt (his daughter), Theodore Roosevelt Collection. Houghton Library, Harvard University, MS Am 1454.48 (29).

9. S. W. "Pops" Merrihew (*left*) talking to another tennis enthusiast in Miami, 1944. Merrihew remains the dean of tennis reporters. He edited and published *American Lawn Tennis* magazine for some forty years (1907–1947). Courtesy of the International Tennis Hall of Fame, Newport, Rhode Island.

10. "Big Bill" Tilden doing what he did best. Credit: USTA Archive.

11. Suzanne Lenglen (*right*) and British champion Kitty Godfree at a garden party in Regents Park, London, July 5, 1932. The French champion was both a court and a media star. In the words of one tennis writer, "Lenglen drank, swore and had lovers by the score—and played tennis incomparably, losing once in seven years." Credit: Graphic Photo Union/USTA Archive.

MEMBERSHIP TERRITORY OF THE U. S. L. T. A.

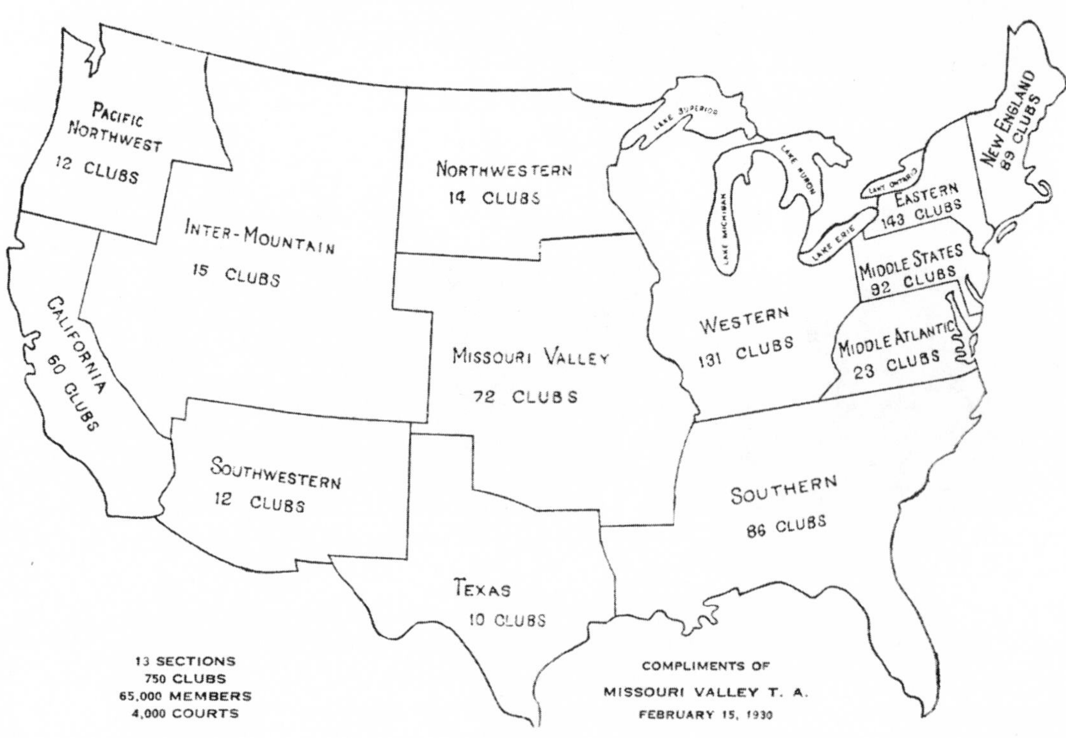

13 SECTIONS
750 CLUBS
65,000 MEMBERS
4,000 COURTS

COMPLIMENTS OF
MISSOURI VALLEY T. A.
FEBRUARY 15, 1930

12. (*opposite top*) U.S. president Calvin Coolidge (*left*) making the 1924 Davis Cup draw with Dwight Davis. Credit: *American Lawn Tennis*/USTA Archive.

13. (*opposite bottom*) The thirteen USTA sections as of 1930, curiously labeled the "Membership Territory." Credit: USTA Archive.

14. (*above*) Alice Marble (ca. 1933). She stood up to Julian Myrick in the 1930s, successfully played as a pro in the forties, and publicly defended Althea Gibson's right to play in the U.S. Open in 1950. Credit: USTA Archive.

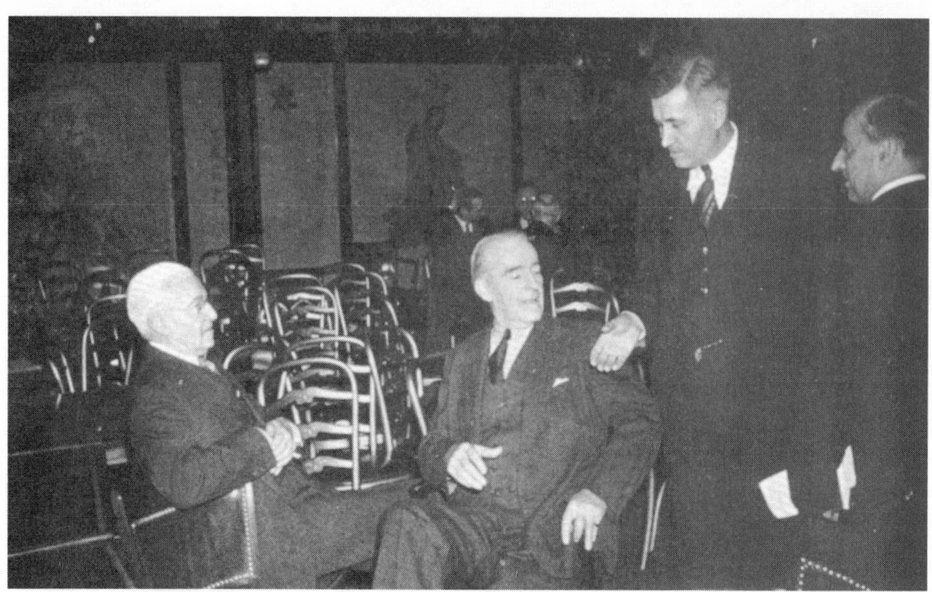

15. (*top*) The aging leadership 1941 (*left to right*): Julian "Mike" Myrick (age sixty-one), Holcombe Ward (sixty-three), and Lawrence Baker (the youngster, at fifty-one). Credit: USTA Archive.

16. (*bottom*) In 1944 Tilden arranged a series of matches to entertain members of the armed forces stationed in southern California. As part of the show, Tilden (*left*, as Wilhelmina Shovelshot) and Walter Wesbrook (aka Sophia Smearone), both dressed in drag, played a "ladies single" match and then teamed up against Gloria Butler (*left*) and Gertrude (later "Gorgeous Gussie") Moran. Credit: *American Lawn Tennis*.

17. "Unfunny 'Comic' Books Win Friends for Tennis," 1956. Connecting with youngsters was the goal. Credit: USTA, courtesy of Warren F. Kimball.

18. Alistair and Edith Martin, and Bob "the Judge" Kelleher (*right*) before heading for Paris to save open tennis, March 1968. Credit: USTA Archive.

19. The Original Nine in 1973 (*clockwise from bottom right*): Gladys Heldman (sitting in for Julie Heldman), Rosie Casals, Kerry Reid, Judy Tegart Dalton, Valerie Ziegenfuss, Billie Jean King, Nancy Richey, "Peaches" Bartkowicz, and Kristy Pigeon. Courtesy of the International Tennis Hall of Fame, Newport, Rhode Island.

20. Althea Gibson—too talented to bypass, ignore, or discriminate against. Wimbledon semifinals, July 4, 1957. Credit: Associated Press.

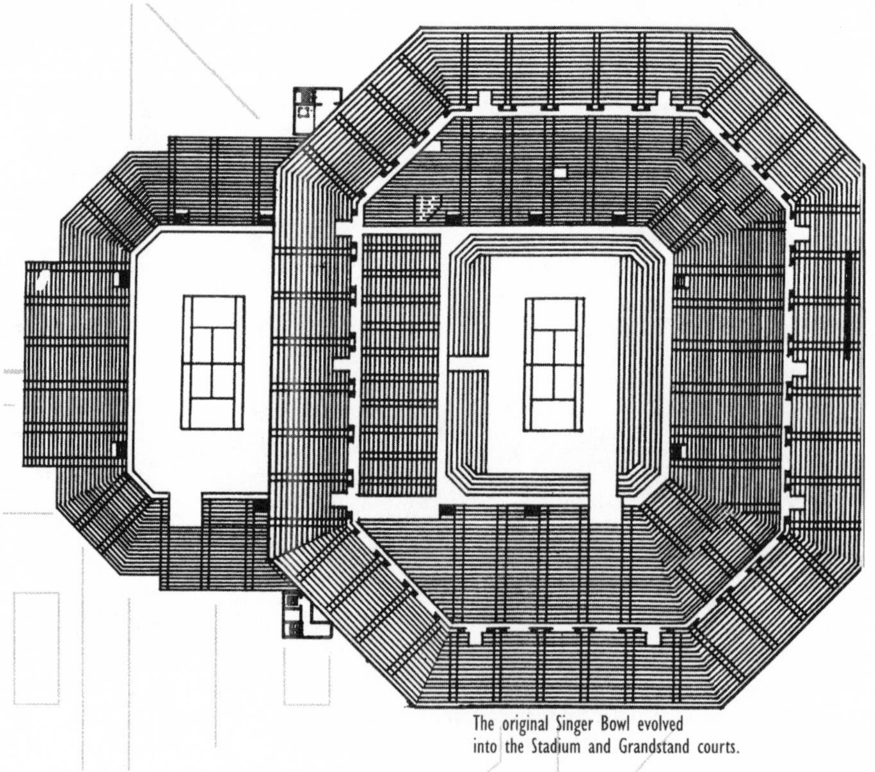

The original Singer Bowl evolved
into the Stadium and Grandstand courts.

21. (*opposite top*) The Singer Bowl in Flushing Meadow–Corona Park, Queens, New York. Built by the Singer Corporation and donated to the 1964–65 World's Fair, it became a venue for sports events and concerts before falling into disuse. In 1977 the New York City Parks Department signed a lease with the USTA to allow the stadium (renamed Louis Armstrong Stadium in 1973) and surrounding land to become the USTA–Billie Jean King National Tennis Center and site for the U.S. Open. Credit: Brian Beglane (USTA staff); New York City Parks Photo Archive.

22. (*opposite bottom*) Bowl on a bowl: the new Louis Armstrong Stadium, 1978. Credit: Drawing by Kenneth Specter, from *Tennis Week*, courtesy Matthew Specter.

23. (*above*) Breaking ground for the stadium at Flushing Meadows, October 6, 1977 (*left to right*): New York City parks commissioner Joseph Davidson, Queens Borough president Michael Manes, Lucille Armstrong, Slew Hester, and a very bored Alan King. Slew Hester, like Winston Churchill, seems undressed without a cigar. Credit: USTA Archive.

24. (*above*) An artistic rendering of Arthur Ashe Stadium, 1995. Compared to Louis Armstrong Stadium and the grandstand (*top left*), the expansion of the U.S. Open site is striking. Credit: USTA Archive.

25. (*opposite*) The seventeen USTA sections since 1983. Credit: USTA Archive.

USTA SECTION OFFICES

1	USTA New England	(508) 366-3450
2	USTA Eastern	(914) 697-2300
3	USTA Middle States	(610) 935-5000
4	USTA Mid-Atlantic	(703) 556-6120
5	USTA Southern	(770) 368-8200
6	USTA Florida	(386) 671-8949
7	USTA Caribbean	(787) 726-8782
8	USTA Midwest	(317) 577-5130
9	USTA Northern	(952) 887-5001
10	USTA Missouri Valley	(913) 322-4800
11	USTA Texas	(512) 443-1334
12	USTA Southwest	(480) 289-2351
13	USTA Intermountain	(303) 695-4117
14	USTA Pacific Northwest	(503) 520-1877
15	USTA Northern California	(510) 748-7373
16	USTA Southern California	(310) 208-3838
17	USTA Hawaii Pacific	(808) 585-9503

Note: For precise geographic section boundaries, see section summaries and pages 87-89 of the USTA Bylaws.

26. The indomitable Martha Summerhayes, who watched, and surely played lawn tennis in Camp Apache in October 1874, seven years before the USTA was established. It took over a century before women would be named as association president. From *Vanished Arizona* by Martha Summerhayes (University of Nebraska Press, 1979).

27. (*clockwise*) Women presidents of the USTA came more than 125 years after Martha Summerhayes: Judy Levering (1999–2000), Jane Brown Grimes (2007–8), Lucy Garvin (2009–10), and Katrina Adams (2015–18). Credit: USTA Archive.

28. The "Golden Goose." U.S. Open, September 2016, at Arthur Ashe Stadium—with a roof. Credit: Rhea Nall/USTA.

The next major step would not come for nearly two decades. Apparently prompted by the on-going rude and disruptive on-court behavior of a number of top professionals, a proposal came in 1986 to create a professional umpires committee. The concept was to develop consistent training standards, providing a structure for umpires to move through "as individual skills increased." In time, the ITF would take over professional officiating for ITF-sanctioned events. The effects of such standards would soon filter down to the local levels. The need for professional officiating standards for professional tournaments was obvious and compelling. The stakes were increasingly higher. Whether or not the increased cost (professional means paid) for local tournaments was worthwhile is a different issue.[54]

The 1969 McKinsey report had recommended an evaluation of the advantages and disadvantages of incorporation. While Martin shied away from the most radical change—establishment of a tennis czar, or in more businesslike terms, a chief executive officer, with authority over day-to-day operations—in 1970 he instructed the relatively new USTA general counsel, George Gowen, to rewrite the USTA constitution and bylaws as a step toward incorporation. Martin added an instruction not to touch the nominating committee, an injunction repeated in 1985 when the board of directors replaced the management committee—a most revealing exception that testified to the politics of change.

That was a reform rejected that related to the crucial and determinative nominating committee. The oft-offered argument began with proposals that the nominating committee should be expanded so as to allow more sections to be represented. On cue, popular as opposed to representative democracy popped up. The southern region (composed of the Southern and Florida Sections) had more players than any of the other three regions, so it was underrepresented. Popular democracy was represented (to play with words), though imprecisely, by the dues structure since clubs paid dues in accordance with groups of gross numbers and eventually the total number of members. But other governance bodies—the executive committee, the administrative committee, the nominating committee—bore only vague resemblance to the number of members. Perhaps the most important aspect of all that is to note the number of "governance bodies." With sixteen sections, seventeen once Puerto Rico joined the list in 1983, representation for each section on every governance body became unwieldy, hence the decline of the executive committee as an effective governing tool. But representation strictly by membership numbers exposed smaller sections to the "tyranny of the majority." The Association would continue to tweak the rules for membership on the nominating committee, each tweak coming after extensive study and debate, but the division of powers that developed, largely as a reaction to challenges rather than a careful logical plan, brings to mind the Great Compromise of 1787 when the U.S. Constitutional Convention created the House of Representatives and the Senate. That awkward and often deadlocked structure may have been necessary to the nation's unity; perhaps the same is true for the Association. Little surprise then that leadership approval for constitutional and bylaw changes in the early 1970s and again in 1985–86 was accompanied by the injunction not to change the procedures for selecting the nominating committee's membership. A handful of volunteers remained able to materially, if indirectly, determine the direction of policy by selecting leaders who shared the committee's preferences.[55]

Over the next few years a series of constitutional and bylaw changes moved the Association into compliance with the New York State not-for-profit law and toward creation of a management structure that paralleled, without replicating, that of most business corporations. Obvious constitutional "reforms" easily passed muster. The executive committee was enlarged a bit, adding a female and a male player, and limited to two meetings per year, and the administrative committee was abolished, replaced by a management committee composed of the nine officers of the Association. It was a change without a difference. Whatever the LRP and McKinsey reports had recommended, the same structure under different names was not it. Failure to create a czar or commissioner of tennis, or a CEO of the Association, did not mean rejection of organizational reform, but the changes that came were, however sensible, hardly revolutionary.[56]

On October 16, 1973, the Association received its charter of incorporation from the State of New York. In "reforming" the constitution, the word "amateur" in the description of the USLTA's purpose (section 2 of the constitution) generated one of those angels-on-the-head-of-a-pin debates to which the Association seemed addicted. One speaker called the USLTA hypocritical for not recognizing that, with open tennis, it was involved with professionals as well. But it wasn't angels the executive committee was worried about, it was the Internal Revenue Service. The IRS, always with an eye on increasing revenue, had made changes in the federal tax code, and Association lawyers were keen to avoid attracting attention that could threaten its tax status, a sensitive issue with the advent of open tennis and the success of the U.S. Open. All was settled amicably, with the lawyers satisfied. But the argument offered another small glimpse of the direction the Association was taking.[57]

Noodling with the constitution continued after incorporation. In 1975–76 the Association eliminated a change in the membership rules that disallowed club membership status for commercial clubs. The bylaw change was tied to a requirement that all member clubs have a "constitutional structure through which the individual members have a voice in the Club's tennis affairs and have a controlling voice in the selection of its delegate or delegates to its District or Sectional Association." There was an undercurrent of concern that commercial clubs might be able to take over control of a section for reasons of financial gain, not the good of the game. That vestigial remain of the arguments for "pure" amateurism quieted as the Association adopted voting-strength rules that, when combined with a "constitutional structure," ensured that dollars for dues determined voting strength and, later on, that the number of individual members composed the dominant factor in sectional voting strength. Nevertheless, as the general counsel told the 1977 annual meeting, "the voting strength of the USTA and the manner in which the votes are determined have been changed from time to time and the sections have sometimes been late in catching up with those changes."[58]

Another hint of things to come was a proposal in 1970–71 from one Jack Turpin, a Dallas businessman, to bring the USTA headquarters to Dallas. George Gowen added up the numbers and suggested that it could cost "close to" the same as the New York City office since they could not count on the voluntary contributions from folks in Texas that Turpin said would financially support the move. The officers agreed that the New York quarters were "horrible," yet they were dubious about Dallas. Apparently, the settling argument was concern about getting out of their lease since the rental market had become weak. But the dramatic collapse of enthusiasm in just five months suggests that a shift from New York City to Texas was too uncomfortable, and perhaps too far from the site of the U.S. Open championships, though no mention of that made it into the various minutes.[59]

"We are doing the best we can and we are competing with a very fast-changing world, with a very slow-changing organization," one Association president had commented in 1972, to empathetic laughter. Everyone understood.[60]

There is something ineffably sad about people like Alastair Martin (and many others), lovers of the game, not motivated by perks, who worked endlessly to preserve the Association and the game of tennis they had grown up with. But their arena had changed. In their gentle self-confidence, they failed to see what older generations almost always fail to see. It was a new ball game. The lesson was clear—adjust to the new world that can be, rather than defend the world that used to be. Principles matter, but only if everyone agrees they are principles.

In reality, by 1970 an overall tennis czar was impossible for the USLTA. That boat had left the dock. In February of that year, the *New York Times* warned that "another war seemed imminent in American tennis" after WCT and the National Tennis League turned down the Association's proposals for joint cooperation, particularly regarding open tournaments.[61]

With the arrival of open tennis, professional players, whatever their love of the game, were focused on one thing—the right to control their tennis lives. That included, but was much more than, making as much money as they could. They wanted input into scheduling; they wanted to escape the cloying control of national federations, which all too often benefitted "tenniscrats" rather than the game and the players; they wanted protection against what seemed arbitrary decisions by national federations and the ILTF about eligibility for Davis Cup, Grand Slam tournaments, the right to use the tie-break system, and so on. The pressure was inchoate, but very real. While the 1972 U.S. Open was underway, a number of male players met to talk about creating a players organization—something Association leaders both expected and feared—a union or guild. Alastair Martin's peregrinations around Europe had been aimed at making the USLTA (and the Slams) that organization, but distrust of the United States plus ILTF dependency on the small federations throughout Europe made it impossible. So despite the best efforts of USLTA leaders, the inevitable happened. In September 1972 the Association of Tennis Professionals (for men), the ATP, was formed. As Richard Evans colorfully put it, once "the ATP was formed, the cliché became reality. The game would never be the same again."[62]

It came upon a scene already in disorder. Open tennis brought a new off-court contest to the game—contract competition. The professional tours that had been organized by various promoters (including Jack Kramer) suddenly had a far larger coterie of players to bid for. For the men, early in the 1970s it boiled down to the WCT tour, Bill Riordan's Independent Players circuit, and the Grand Prix circuit—proposed by Kramer and adopted by the ILTF (and eventually by the ATP). Additionally, there were local circuits like the European Spring Circuit and an indoor circuit in the United States. Schedules conflicted; the Slams tournaments (U.S., British, French, and Australian Opens) were threatened by the fierce bidding for the top players; the ILTF rules and regulations were ignored and suspensions handed out. It was a mess!

For the women, there were no truly international circuits, nor an effective players association, so initially, their battle was largely within the United States where promoter and *World Tennis* publisher and editor, Gladys Heldman, challenged USLTA control over sanction fees and scheduling—and gender politics as well.[63] It would not be long before they too got caught up in the ILTF's war with the World Championship Tennis circuit.

Heldman's challenge to the USLTA's control had begun with a campaign for women professionals' earnings to "equal" what the men got—or at least a reasonable facsimile thereof. It ended with the circuit she created by essentially taking over the USLTA's women's tour. Women pros had earned much less from the outset as promoters claimed that women's tennis didn't draw big crowds. When in 1970 Jack Kramer set up a tournament with a supposed twelve-to-one prize-money ratio for men and women, some women players called for a boycott. In one observer's words, "the prize money circuit run by Jack Kramer neither included nor tolerated a competing women's event . . . about the same time as his." When Heldman instead organized a women's invitational in Houston, the Association refused to sanction the tournament and threatened to suspend those who played.[64] Heldman then signed nine top women ("the original nine") to one dollar–one week personal contracts, replete with a wonderful staged photo of her and the players waving dollar bills. (See gallery, image 19.) With the banning of television cigarette ads in January 1971, the Philip Morris corporation was eager to find a marketing opportunity for its Virginia Slims cigarette brand. Women's tennis was an ideal connection that linked smoking "to women's freedom, emancipation, and empowerment," in the U.S. Surgeon General's words (albeit thirty years later).[65]

Heldman, supported by Joe Cullman of Phillip Morris, seized that opportunity, giving her the money she needed to create the Virginia Slims circuit. By the end of 1971, the tour had signed forty players. With talk of antitrust violations already being bruited about, the Slims tournaments received sanctions and peace broke out—although not without rancor.[66] The USLTA solution focused on getting a sanction fee of 6 percent (with apologies to Sherlock Holmes) of the prize money, not on promoting women's tennis. Heldman became director of women's professional tennis for the Association, a volunteer post.[67]

For a brief moment, all the top women could enter Slims tournaments without fear of conflicts with the ILTF or their national federations (i.e., the USLTA). But not for long. Midway through the year, Heldman resigned her USLTA job and then announced a Slims tour for 1973 that she would operate without a USLTA sanction.[68] As with the WCT and the men's game, "peace" proved fleeting.

"Five Sets on Clay with No Tiebreaks"—Gladys Heldman

A box on Gladys Heldman in a history of the United States Tennis Association? The woman USTA leaders loved to hate? Absolutely. The simple equation is that the U.S. Open funds the Association; professional tennis is the essence of the competition; the women's draw at the U.S. Open is a key element in the tournament's success; and, at the beginning of the Open Era, Heldman forced the USTA to confront the inequities faced by women tennis professionals. In the words of Billie Jean King: "Not one woman professional player would have the life they have today without her." In 1953 Heldman founded *World Tennis*, which eventually became the best tennis magazine since Merrihew's *American Lawn Tennis*. She used it not only to promote the game but to prod the Association into facing up to the dramatic changes that began in the late 1950s, culminating with the establishment of open tennis in 1968. She was difficult, as USLTA leaders constantly complained. Even a federal district judge seems to have agreed. She clearly did not trust the USLTA (and vice-versa) but was trapped by the Association's legitimate role as what came to be called the "governing body" of tennis in the United States. She lost that legal fight, but in the end, the Association compromised, and in 1973, women got equal prize money at the U.S. Open.

The ATP, far more chauvinistic than the USLTA, had ignored the women. But Gladys Heldman would not be ignored; she held everyone's feet to the fire. "If she didn't get her way, she was prepared to go five sets on clay with no tiebreaks," said former *World Tennis* editor Neil Amdur.

Wonderfully, in July 1979, six years after Heldman left the arena of tennis politics, *World Tennis* became the official USTA membership magazine. By 2012 tournament purses on the women's tour came to $96 million.[69]

An ILTF threat in 1972 to ban women contract pros (who apparently called their organization the Women's International Tennis Federation, though it was essentially the Slims tour) from Wimbledon and other international tournaments forced the women to focus. Moreover, the USLTA was setting up a circuit with Chris Evert. Evert, then only seventeen years old, was at the beginning of her career and in an impossible position. She rejected Heldman's offers to sign with the Slims for 1973, kept her mouth shut, and kept winning—leaving the politics to the women professionals, Heldman, and the media. One journalist labeled her a "scab" (strikebreaker) but that peeled off once the Association and the women came to terms. Evert had good company. Two other talented women, Evonne Goolagong and Virginia Wade, did not join the Slims tour.

In January 1973 Heldman and Billie Jean King filed a joint suit against the USLTA—a suit the Association's general counsel characterized as having "perhaps the greatest degree of complexity of any matter" he had worked on for the Association.[70] Illegal restraint of trade under U.S. antitrust statutes (specifically the Sherman Act) was the issue. United Press International reported that Billie Jean King charged that the "Association threatened to bar her for life if she played in non-sanctioned tournaments." When a federal district court denied the Heldman-King suit for an injunction against the USLTA, a negotiated settlement (rather than an appeal) followed. The Association was willing to compromise because of the likelihood of very extended and thus expensive litigation, because they were unlikely to get damages from Heldman, and because a protracted argument would not give the public what it wanted—"an intelligent, unified women's circuit."

A greater complication was the intense personal dislike for Heldman on the part of the Association leadership. It was more than just palpable, it was stated unequivocally, even by such measured thinkers as the Association's general counsel, George Gowen, who identified three goals for USLTA in the negotiations: first, women's tournaments be sanctioned; second, the women agree to accept USLTA or other national association rules; third, elimination of Heldman from any major role in women's circuits—something President Walter Elcock also insisted upon.[71]

The advent of open tennis had brought to a boil long-standing disagreements between the ILTF and the Association. The background to those disagreements went back to the Federation's start in 1913. Within a few months the Americans had refused to join, complaining that the new "international" organization not only wanted to designate Wimbledon the "world" championships, but gave Great Britain six votes, more than any other nation.[72] The Association had reluctantly joined a decade later, partly because "world" championships designation was dropped, and partly out of fear that the ILTF would try to take control of the Davis Cup competition leaving the USLTA on the outside looking in. American concern about the Federation's voting structure remains to this day, despite its claims that U.S. membership made the organization "truly international." The ILTF long seemed to Americans a foreign organization, disconnected from U.S. concerns. For tennis players (and most administrators), the original purpose of the Association—standardized rules—remained central. The whole world should play lawn tennis for fun.

The arrival of open tennis in 1968 (some forty years after it had first been proposed) changed the landscape. Various professional tours and circuits appeared and disappeared as promoters tried to turn open tennis into profits, and players tried to make a living—and then some. The Federation, with its own "tenniscrats" and dependence on the votes of national federations (mostly European to start with), all too frequently found itself in conflict with the Americans. But it was more than just allowing open tennis. Professionals had problems gaining access to enough prize money to make a good living. What was needed was business acumen, which is where World Championship Tennis came in.

Lamar Hunt made tennis more than just a sport, he made it a business. With what turned out to be exquisite timing, he set up the WCT in 1968 as quite different from a tennis organization that owned a few tournaments or simply promoted a tour or even individual events. The rules and organization and development of the game were not his concern. The profit (and loss) was. Without apparent intent—this came before the Heldman-King suit against the USLTA—Hunt gathered around the WCT the cloak of the veto power of the United States. Then, as of 1972 Bill Riordan's antitrust lawsuit made clear that tennis organizations could not restrict the rights of professionals to make a living in the United States. Given U.S. antitrust statutes, that guaranteed that, in the United States, management (the WCT) and labor (the players) were separate. Attempts by any tennis organization to control both players and "the business," would constitute a monopoly and open the way for legal action. The veto came because no international tennis structure could function without the United States (and the USLTA).

At various junctures, the ILTF, the USLTA, and the players, all hoped to become the controlling factor for international professional tennis. But those efforts came either too early, or too late. A number of tennis historians depict creation of the Open Era as a series of attacks on the ILTF's authority. Their arguments are persuasive but, given the Federation's relative weakness to begin with, not the full story. Self-determination for national federations had its ugly side, where greed and privilege motivated actions, but it had its less sordid aspect. For the USLTA, it meant that U.S. government statutes regarding antitrust and restraint of trade were indirectly (and conveniently for the Association) imposed on the ILTF. The authority of the Federation came from the national federations. Yet, indirectly, the ILTF itself was increasingly dependent upon the professional players since the best players were signing with various pro tours. The root of it all was that tennis was becoming a business.[73]

The early seventies saw increased tension between the ILTF and the WCT, primarily over scheduling conflicts and demands that the ITLF's Grand Prix pay travel and other expenses for WCT contracted professionals playing that circuit. A fragile "peace" collapsed when the Federation banned contract professionals from all its sanctioned tournaments and connected facilities. Gladys Heldman's monthly "Around the World" column in *World Tennis* was a bombastic, sometimes exaggerated, treasure trove of short paragraphs describing the silliness of the ILTF ban on clubs that held WCT events. The most absurd of all (a high hurdle in this situation) was when some local tennis associations had to petition the USLTA to protect tennis officials and ball boys (all then volunteers) at WCT events from being banned for life from ILTF events. Ball boys! The USLTA president flew to London and pressured the Federation to drop its ban—which it did, though there was much more at stake than ballboys. After WCT contract players were banned from ILTF-sanctioned tournaments, the WSTC (Forest Hills) proposed holding a professional tournament in lieu of the 1972 U.S. Open. When the club procrastinated on signing a contract for the U.S. Open, Walter Elcock and the Association played hardball and made it clear they would move the U.S. Open to another site if necessary.[74]

The arguments persisted. While scheduling conflicts often constituted the immediate cause of conflict, USLTA reluctance to cooperate and its insistence on "self-determination" posed an insurmountable challenge for the Federation. In 1972 the powers that be proposed dividing up the 1973 tennis schedule in a way that would give the WCT exclusivity for the first four months of each year and the ILTF (Grand Prix) exclusivity for the following eight months. During the WCT-owned four months, no tournament with more than twenty thousand dollars prize money would be sanctioned, which conflicted with Riordan's indoor circuit (Independent Professionals Association—IPA).[75] That WCT-ILTF peace agreement was approved by the Federation in July 1972 to begin in 1973. The USTLA went along with it, with only Slew Hester, then second vice president, voting against. He believed the deal would violate United States antitrust legislation and refused to sign off on the plan. According to tennis writer Neil Amdur, that vote resulted in Hester being "dumped" as vice presidential nominee. Fortunately for the Association, Hester's absence from the USTA slate of officers was as brief as the existence of the "peace treaty." The latter fell apart when Riordan (who owned Jimmy Connors's contract), filed an antitrust suit against both the USTA and the WCT. Hester's year-long exile found him back as second vice president and back in the implied "succession" to move on up the ladder.[76]

A short meditation on the role of individuals in history. Whatever the machinations that bounced Slew Hester out and then brought him back, without his driving force one wonders what the USTA and its stellar event and site, the U.S. Open in Flushing Meadows, would look like today.

Bill Riordan fought back. Not only the promoter of a professional circuit of tournaments, but the delegate from the Mid-Atlantic Section, he challenged the Association's acceptance of the ILTF regulation giving the Federation authority over sanctions for tournaments offering prize money over five thousand pounds—essentially control over professional tennis. Riordan managed to round up enough sectional support to call for a special meeting of the Association membership to take up the matter.[77] It was a long, tendentious meeting during which the delegates agreed that interfering with the WCT or any other tour (no mention of Riordan's IPA circuit) would be in restraint of trade and illegal in the United States. But amid the discussion came a pointed argument. Did the language of Riordan's resolution, that the Association "rejects the decision of the ILTF," constitute (by implication) a USLTA resignation from the Federation? As "a voice" put it: "I would say we have to abide by that rule until the ILTF changes the rule; otherwise we, in effect, are seceding." Led by Malless and Elcock, the opposition to Riordan's proposal won out, and the resolution failed, gaining 89,997 votes while needing roughly 97,000. The tone of the discussion suggests that the delegates all understood the implications of the vote, since advance notice of the special meeting gave the sections time to make a considered decision. The special meeting settled for a weaker motion that the USLTA's representatives would "do all possible to amend" the ILTF regulation to apply only for tournaments with over fifty thousand dollars prize money. That regulation became moot in the wake of more legal actions and U.S. antitrust law. The long-lasting result was resentment towards the Federation for interfering with the USLTA's "self-determination."[78]

The convoluted twists and turns went on for some five years. Restraint of trade is a three-edged sword. The government (theoretically) wants to ensure that a free market operates. The promoters want to use the free market (i.e., appearance money and such) to enhance their profits. The players want the free market to let them sell their talents to the highest bidder. Eventually, all agreed that law and order (i.e., scheduling agreements, etc.) was better than an unregulated "free" market.

In 1974 World Team Tennis (WTT) (led by Billie Jean King and her husband, Larry King, with innovative scoring and such) created controversial scheduling issues. The ILTF had sanctioned WTT for a while, but protests from Germany, France, Italy, and Sweden came when WTT events conflicted with both the French and the Italian Open. Two of tennis's popular players, Evonne Goolagong and Jimmy Connors, were banned from the French and Italian Opens, not by the ILTF but by the national federations, for playing in WTT events. The ATP eager to protect its new Grand Prix circuit, initially supported the ban but changed its position after the Federation and the USLTA sanctioned the WTT events.[79]

By that time ennui had set in. Victory seemed less important than compromises that would let everyone get back to playing tennis and making money and controlling their own lives. The USLTA wanted the top women to play its open; the top women wanted the same thing. When the Association essentially agreed to absorb the Slims tour into the USLTA women's circuit (Chris Evert and all), the rest was easy. The Slims tournaments received retroactive sanctions, the women agreed not to sign new contracts with Heldman and in 1974 to play in the Association's women's circuit. The USLTA would get forty thousand dollars in lieu of sanction fees. The Association would get rid of Heldman, but not for another year, since so many of the players had personal contracts with her. She directed the USLTA circuit in 1974, then moved on.[80]

A coda to the era of lawsuits. In May 1976 Bill Riordan sued for 15 percent of Jimmy Connors's earnings since March 1972, claiming he had been Jimmy's "exclusive personal manager." "I've got to give him credit for being consistent," wisecracked Connors.[81]

After a number of similar lawsuits by players, promoters, and agents, the Association accepted the fact that it could not prevent players from joining this or that tennis circuit or tour. As Gowen lucidly explained to the 1975 annual meeting, "neither this organization *nor any other* [i.e., the ILTF] . . . has the legal right to threaten the livelihood of any player. . . . If you don't believe it from me, you're going to hear it from the Justice Department." Moreover, such attempts would almost certainly attract the attention of the Internal Revenue Service. Bad idea![82]

When in 1974, the time came to renegotiate the U.S. Open contract with the West Side Club, the Association insisted that it be open to all qualified players without regard for any "professional affiliation or organizational allegiance." In other words, the Forest Hills club could not reject entries because of ILTF threats to refuse international sanctions for clubs that allowed WTT or WCT contracted players to play their tournaments. The Association had quickly found antitrust laws a valuable asset for limiting Federation efforts to expand its control. In February 1974 Stan Malless gave the executive committee a lengthy explanation of ILTF attempts to ban all players who were under contract with World Team Tennis and/or World Championship Tennis. The Americans made it clear to the Federation that they could not and would not be able to accept or enforce that rule. Jack Kramer, after attending a meeting of the ILTF, described the explanation of U.S. restraint-of-trade (antitrust) laws given by Malless, as "a professor's job." The Federation reluctantly dropped such rulings for tournaments played in the United States, which eventually gutted the rule.

It cannot be mere coincidence that a letter of April 20, 1975, from the IRS reaffirming the Association's tax-exempt status turns up in the files next to a letter dated three days later from the USTA's general counsel to a U.S. Justice Department official who had raised the question of antitrust and restraint-of trade-violations. Gowen took the official back to the 1973 decision that upheld the USLTA in the case filed by Gladys Heldman and Billie Jean King. This was serious business.[83]

The Association's position on restraint-of-trade matters was memorialized for both the ILTF and the Justice Department in 1976 with the adoption of this amendment to the USTA constitution:

> The Association is an independent tennis organization and, as such, cannot take any action at the request of any international tennis body which is inconsistent with the provisions of this Certificate of Incorporation or any By-Laws or Standing Orders issued hereunder.

That provision still existed, with minor wording changes, in the 2015 USTA constitution.[84]

A rant by Slew Hester, later the USTA president who would move the U.S. Open to Flushing Meadows, illustrated the ethnocentric attitude of both Americans and Europeans. On the voting structure in the ILTF, which gave greater representation to smaller nations with few players or tournaments, Hester observed, "I think it is good from the standpoint of democracy and it doesn't hurt us any because we don't have many votes and certainly they don't like us. The only thing we got passed was Walter." (The election of Elcock as ILTF president.) The Federation nations blamed the United States for most of the problems with international tennis and pushed back saying "with all of your money you are not going to take over tennis." One delegate even proposed ejecting the United States from the Federation. Yet in the end Hester concluded that the Association needed the Federation, admitting that "we need to be diplomatic." But it may have been diplomacy be damned. During Hester's term as president he refused to serve on the ILTF committee of management so as to concentrate on the USTA and the U.S. Open.

Even the international federation acknowledged the tensions between that body and the USTA. Elcock's successor as ILTF president, Derek Hardwick, candidly told the Association's executive committee that one of his major missions was to "create greater liaison and cooperation" between the USTA and the Federation, something that had been lacking for the past eighteen years.[85] An ILTF timeline (see "The ILTF Wars" box), excerpted (with edits) from the Federation web page, illustrates its and the USTA's frustrations and maneuvers during the seven years following the inauguration of open tennis. It was, by any standard, a chaotic nightmare. But by 1975 some semblance of order existed. The Federation had been forced to back off on control, giving a seat at the table for both women and men professionals. It could not discipline the Americans thanks to the antitrust laws. The USTA could happily hide behind that fence, yet it had to work with the Federation and the professional circuits since the game itself was international. Little did Dwight Davis imagine just what international cooperation would entail.[86]

The ILTF Wars

1968—After ten years of division and struggle, an emergency meeting of the ILTF agreed in principle to open tennis. A breakaway tennis circuit, the WCT began in opposition to the official ILTF circuit.

1971—The ILTF decreed that no player contracted to the WCT could play in any event authorized by a national association. This meant that John Newcombe could not defend his Wimbledon title that year. In March 1972, the WCT and ILTF finally joined forces to promote a unified circuit for the benefit of all players.

1971—The Virginia Slims Tour was organized, providing a women-only circuit. This also caused confrontation between the tour, the national associations, and the ILTF. In 1973 after much discussion, peace was declared and the Virginia Slims Tour was ratified.

1973—Because of the nine-month suspension of Yugoslavian Nikki Pilic over his non-appearance for his country's Davis Cup match, the ATP announced that their members would boycott Wimbledon. Eighty players withdrew from the 1973 Wimbledon Championships.

1973—The Grand Prix Committee was formed, which became the Men's International Professional Tennis Council in 1975, providing a governing body for men's professional tennis. This organization consisted of the ILTF, the players, and the tournaments (presumably the Grand Slam events).

1975—The Women's International Professional Tennis Council was shared between the ILTF and the Women's Tennis Association. The purpose of the council was to promote, control, and govern the organization and development of the women's professional circuit throughout the world (implying that control and governance had not been present previously).[87]

Equal prize money for women came, surprisingly, through the USLTA. The relevant minutes contain no mention of the decision to offer equal prize money for women and men at the 1973 U.S. Open. If there was opposition, it was expressed privately. One observer commented that "Billy Talbert was chair of the U.S. Open and was instrumental in the equal prize money decision. Some decisions were made without specific approval of the USTA governance structure. Talbert was interested in sponsorship and was open to equal prize money and no objections were heard." Fittingly, the move was expedited (or rather marketed) by a corporate donation: "Stepping in to rectify a situation that Mrs. Billie Jean King once said 'stinks,'" wrote a *New York Times* reporter, "Ban deodorant announced yesterday it would donate $55,000 in prize money to make the women's purse at the 1973 United States Open tennis championships equal to the man's [*sic*]." Joe Cullman, the Phillip Morris executive who had put up the money for Gladys Heldman's Virginia Slims circuit, apparently arranged additional sponsorship. Heldman had long advocated equal prize money in the pages of her magazine, *World Tennis*. There was no apparent connection between King withdrawing from the lawsuit and the USLTA adopting one of her (and Heldman's) favored requests, but perhaps it was like chicken soup—might have helped, couldn't have hurt.[88] No one then would have thought to predict that some forty years later, the *Wall Street Journal*, hardly a publication at the forefront of social change, would devote two full pages, with color photography, to a story titled "The New Faces of Women's Tennis."

Yes, "you've come a long way, baby."[89]

Equal prize money put the Association in the forefront of dealing fairly with women players. The other Grand Slam events were slow to close the prize gap. The Aussies went on and then off and then on again in 1984, 1995, and 2001. The French came aboard in 2006 for the singles champions. The Brits held out for one more year, awarding equal prize money in 2007 with ill grace, thirty-four years after the Americans broke the glass ceiling. Begrudgingly, Tim Phillips, the head of the All England Club, announced that,

> As in every other year, the Committee has again analyzed all the relevant information and then made a judgment. This year, taking into account both the overall progression and the fact that broader social factors are also relevant to the decision, they have decided that the time is right to bring this subject to a logical conclusion and eliminate the difference.[90]

What wonderful persiflage. Intentionally or not, the equal-prize-money decision gave the Association leverage in dealing with the professionals who were indispensable to the financial success of the U.S. Open.

That same year, 1973, the ATP quickly validated its existence when it called for a boycott of the Wimbledon championships. The spark that started that fire came when a Yugoslav Davis Cup player, Nikki Pilic, who was under contract with Lamar Hunt's WCT, refused orders from the Yugoslavian federation to play in a Davis Cup match because he had qualified to play in the WCT doubles championship, scheduled at the same time. The Yugoslavs appealed to the ILTF, which told all national federations to bar Pilic from their tournaments. When he applied for entry into the 1973 Wimbledon championships, the application was rejected. The brand new ATP took up Pilic's defense, not because of Pilic but because (to paraphrase Jack Kramer) the ATP leaders understood that the ILTF and the British federation opposed the ATP's demand that national federations should not control independent/contract pros.

Britain's Allan Heyman, as president of the ILTF, had apparently assured the USLTA president, Walter Elcock, that "the players would never boycott Wimbledon." The consensus was that the players wanted the prestige and needed the prize money more than the other way round. But the ATP boycott happened. Only a handful of independent professionals entered. The mystique of Wimbledon's irresistible appeal took a body blow, and all the Slams (France, Australia, Britain, the United States) took the lesson to heart. One cannot have a true Grand Slam without the best players. It had taken tennis nearly a century to learn that and to establish open tennis. It took the Grand Slams one bad experience to move, a bit reluctantly, in a different direction and to look for ways to work with the professionals.[91]

In February 1974 Elcock was elected to a second one-year term as president of the USLTA, but resigned six months later to take over as president of the ILTF—in the middle of the WTT-ILTF feud. Elcock had somehow convinced the ILTF countries (e.g., the Europeans) that he was empathetic or even in agreement with their desire to maintain national federation control over professionals. He tried to persuade the USLTA leadership that the Association president ought to be recommended, not prohibited as was proposed, as the American delegate on the ILTF management committee (and, therefore, eligible to be its president). A goodly number of Association leaders expressed concern that Federation proposals could differ from Association policies, creating a conflict of interest. Elcock argued that the interests of the Association and the Federation were one in the same, but to no avail. The long debate ended with neither a prohibition nor an endorsement. Elcock later disingenuously claimed, "I really hated to resign when I did as President of the USLTA. But really thought it was the best thing to do because of the conflict of interest." Between February and July 1974, something or someone prompted Elcock to resign as USLTA president in order to accept the post of ILTF president. Selection to the ILTF management committee was and is, much coveted. Both the power and the "perks" are seductive. But it was also an opportunity to do good things for international tennis. For the USLTA, Elcock's job was to "hold the ILTF at bay," lest it complicate the situation by trying to discipline players or prevent a settlement of the Heldman-King suit.

Whatever the reasons, after Elcock resigned as USLTA president it seemed as if he would be the "last American president of the ITF." Forty years later, in September 2015, the ITF elected David Haggerty (USTA president 2013–14) to a four-year term as its president. That was a quite different post by then, having become in 1991 a full-time paid position rather than one filled by a part-time volunteer.[92]

Amidst the chaos created by open tennis came a true circus, promoted as the "Battle of the Sexes"—the Billie Jean King–Bobby Riggs exhibition (sanctioned by the USLTA!). It proved a marketing success. Over thirty thousand attended at the Astrodome in Houston in September 1973. Fifty-five-year-old Riggs had previously defeated the great Australian champion, Margaret Court, 6–2, 6–1. Billie Jean (twenty-nine-years-old) clobbered Riggs, 6–4, 6–3, 6–3. Who cared? Americans did, that's who. Whatever the match meant for gender equality (a question best left to sociologists), the "ballyhooed extravaganza" (in Bud Collins's extravagant phrasing) did wonders for the bank accounts of the players and promoter and demonstrated to the American public that tennis was not the boring, staid sport of earlier generations.[93] Changing that image (something the Association had little to do with) was likely the key to the tennis "boom" of the 1970s.

Somewhere along the line, the Association's budget for public relations nearly doubled, going from twenty-six thousand dollars to fifty thousand. Little wonder.

The Association had only a little to do with the changing image of tennis, though it tried. The "lawn" in "lawn tennis," with its elitist connection to private clubs, particularly in the Northeast, needed to go. Unlike the discussion in 1920 about dropping "National" from the Association's name, "mowing the lawn" came without serious argument or objection—though it had been suggested a number of times in the past. The Middle States delegate, Dick Botsch, pointed out at the 1975 annual meeting that half of the sections did not have "lawn" in their name. More important, the Association represented only an "embarrassing one quarter of one percent of all the tennis players in this country," a reference to the dramatic growth the game was experiencing in the 1970s. Botsch reminded the delegates that, oddly, the word "lawn" defined the specifics of the rules, not the surface, then argued that the name change would improve the Association's image, which had been inherited from its origins at "exclusive eastern country clubs." That would make membership more attractive to new players. On March 28, 1975, the official name of the Association changed to the United States Tennis Association—the USTA. The international federation followed the American lead two years later, becoming the International Tennis Federation—the ITF.[94]

But the key happening of the 1970s was the amazing tennis boom. Assuming that USTA membership numbers at least suggest the outline of that expansion, Association growth averaged a remarkable 13 percent a year for eleven years, from 1972 to 1983. Total membership nearly quadrupled, going from roughly 62,000 to 223,500. The guesstimates for the number of people playing recreational tennis throughout the country were vastly greater.[95] Why did that happen?

Some speculation. It was an era of great social change. Women had played lawn tennis from its inception. Black Americans played as well. Although both women and blacks were discriminated against (in quite different ways), their increased presence in the tennis world certainly helped. But the most powerful change was the advent of open tennis. What seems to have leveled the playing field, so to speak, was the development of an enlarged coterie of professional players. The professional tours had begun in the late 1920s, but only a handful of players participated. Still, the popularity in that early era of someone like Suzanne Lenglen demonstrated that there was appeal for tennis as a spectator sport. The tennis boom of the 1970s did not just pop up like a dandelion in the spring, it grew from a number of beginnings.

Timing was a factor. Women's liberation and the civil rights movement played a part in the boom, but so also did American prosperity. The high standard of living provided an essential for tennis growth—leisure time. It also made possible construction of more public tennis facilities since municipalities had more tax money to spend. Public awareness and interest was sparked by television, which grew relentlessly, and was reinforced by news coverage as colorful public arguments arose over the growing pains of professional tennis, different circuits, conflicting schedules, struggles for control of the pro game, lawsuits that were usually about restraint of trade when the USTA or the ITF tried to discipline players and promoters, and so on. But the colorful superstars—Chris Evert, Jimmy Connors, Evonne Goolagong, Arthur Ashe, Bjorn Borg, Ilie Năstase, et al., seem to have been the glue that pulled everything together. Certainly their faces dominated the social media of that day (magazines, for the most part). In the words of Jimmy Connors, with open tennis, "to survive, tennis had to drag itself out of its comfortable little corner. It needed a facelift. The guys of my generation provided it. Suddenly there we were, a group of rebellious bandits, shooting from the hip. . . . The new breed of fan . . . suddenly had something they could relate to."[96]

The seventies boom (actually 1972–83) was not the first time that tennis had experienced such growth. Back in 1914 club membership jumped over 50 percent without any organized effort by the Association (pretty much as in the 1970s). Eighty new clubs joined, bringing in an estimated fifteen thousand tennis players and over one thousand courts. But growth comparisons between 1914 and the 1970s–80s are apples and oranges, since the Association admittedly had "no statistics as to the average membership of each club." Certainly the pool of potential tennis players had grown—in the sixty years since 1914, the U.S. population more than doubled, from roughly 99 million to 214 million.[97] But whatever the numbers, however impressive the growth spurts in 1914 (and other times), USTA growth of nearly 400 percent in the seventies boom is astounding.

Again, why did that happen? Clearly an array of new, recycled. or renamed tennis programs took advantage of the boom, with the USTA Leagues far and away the most successful. The noticeable growth of indoor playing facilities let growth happen. But why the sense of excitement about the game? The USTA has spent significant resources—human and monetary—trying to replicate that phenomenon. The Association's archive is loaded with various studies and proposals for increasing membership and/or simply increasing the number of people playing tennis in America. Marketing experts have proposed all the usual "come-ons" and loss leaders. But to no avail. The 1997 plan for growth proposed a panoply of actions to "grow the game," but nowhere are there the historical analyses that might explain why the seventies boom happened.[98]

Even as this is written, the Association is embarked on yet another study. A Membership Innovation Study Group is "identifying guiding principles for testing, and establishing a process that allows for socializing the testing concepts down to the lowest grassroots level." That, after "amendments to the USTA Bylaws and USTA Regulations were made at the Annual meeting to provide an ongoing stable membership-related funding base. The changes assist in preventing further erosion of membership-driven association metrics including: Sectional Association allocation, voting strength, and quotas while the association studies and tests additional membership models/offerings to potentially add to the existing membership business model."[99] Again, amid the jargon, historical analysis is missing.

What is clear, is that the USTA's major contribution to the boom came from its nationwide network of volunteers—a network that itself benefitted from the growth spurt. There were tennis enthusiasts in nearly every nook and cranny of America, eager to help others learn and play the game that they loved. That decentralized volunteer cadre drove the USTA rather than the other way round. Perhaps the best example is the USTA League program—the most successful program in the over 130 year history of the Association. Despite initial skepticism and very little support from USTA headquarters, local volunteers, with guidance from the USTA's Education and Research Office, persisted. Using a tennis-rating system developed by Spike Gonzales and Alan Schwartz that grouped players of compatible skills (handicaps such as those in golf did not work in tennis), league pilot programs in four sections (Southern, Western, Mid-Atlantic, and Middle States) had enjoyed remarkable success during the late 1970s. As even the official magazine pointed out in 1980, "somewhat belatedly" the USTA had recognized the potential in organized league play. The program eventually had over a half million players annually. From 1958 the first year of individual membership, the numbers for juniors exceeded those for adults. Between 1978 and 1980, they ran roughly even. Then, in 1981 adult memberships went ahead of juniors by 10,000. That gap steadily increased through 1992, when there were 291,000 adults to 165,000 juniors.[100] Since regular tournament play does not account for the growth of adult league membership, it must have been league play.

The obvious effect of the league program prompted a budget projection for the USTA Leagues in 1984 that came to $500,000 after being budgeted for just $30,000 in 1980, a huge percentage and dollar increase. But that was less impressive than the increased revenue from individual membership dues that was projected at $1,731,510 after being only $175,737 in 1975. Spending would go up by $470,000. Revenue would jump just short of $1,000,000—a two-to-one ratio. Not bad.[101]The USTA League program illustrated that the association had come to depend heavily on its vast cohort of volunteers, not just at the national level, but from bottom to top.

As the USTA grew, so did its pilgrimages. Initially there was only one, the annual meeting during the first quarter of the year. That meeting was important and colorful from the start. After all, it was the Association's final authority. The political circus of 1911–12 (chapter 2) and the description by Merrihew and *ALT* writers of the special chartered train from New York to the 1930 annual meeting in St. Louis are just two examples (chapter 4). In the early years, the number of attendees increased to perhaps a couple of hundred, many of whom were delegates representing their clubs. But as lawn tennis grew, so did the number of clubs and, therefore, the number of delegates at the meeting. Equally important, the number of volunteers on national committees grew, particularly after the Second World War.[102]

Annual meetings had very occasionally been held outside New York City, but in 1958 a pattern began of going to resorts in warmer places. Perhaps the meeting in 1957 in Chicago's Edgewater Beach Hotel—in frigid January (the average daily low that month was 11°F.)—influenced that southward decision, although one Chicagoan grinned and quipped "Forget the weather. The Edgewater Beach fit the mold of elegance." But the decision reflected other pressures. In what was perhaps a precursor of the tennis boom of the 1970s, USTA volunteers had come to play an increasingly active role. The annual meeting became an opportunity for those dedicated volunteers to interact and to influence the development of policies. In the words of one longtime volunteer: "It clearly was a gathering of the USTA family from across the country. It was a celebration of volunteers as the backbone of the USTA."[103] Association leaders had long enjoyed the convenience and comfort of meeting at the best hotels in New York City, but if "national" volunteers were to be involved, venues more appealing to families and more conducive to playing tennis made sense. Deeper volunteer involvement, more revenue from the U.S. Open, and more accessible air travel prompted (impelled?) the association to pick up the cost of travel and accommodations for national and section leadership groups, not just official delegates, creating a powerful "perk" for volunteers.

So too for the "semi-annual" meeting as the second pilgrimage came to be called. That gathering developed sometime in the 1960s without a master plan or formal wiring diagram. Not until 2004 was it mandated by the Association's bylaws.[104] The executive committee (later the management committee and then the board of directors) had for scores of years routinely met in September during the Association's national championships at Forest Hills.

After the Second World War, as the USLTA slowly began to grow in size and revenues, as volunteer participation increased, as the national championships, and then in 1968 as the U.S. Open championships pulled more volunteers to New York City in September, members of the executive committee (many of whom were committee chairs) began to hold meetings of their committees. From there on it kept expanding. Along the way, the Association started paying for travel and accommodations for committee chairs in addition to the executive committee. The U.S. Open plus the excitement of New York City not only attracted USTA volunteers, but made for efficient (shorter) meetings as people got anxious to get to the matches. The pace at the annual meeting was a bit less frantic, but with the venues invariably (since 1958) at resorts in warm places, the volunteers remained eager to combine tennis meetings with playing the game, often bringing their families for a vacation.[105]

Each was an opportunity to be in contact with policy decisions; each was an occasion for volunteers to connect with each other. "Same Time Next Year" was and is a powerful bond.

Amid the chaos of open tennis, the South African mess, and reports recommending major changes in governance and operations, there came a small bright light. In 1971 Eve Kraft and John Conroy convinced the powers that be to create an educational advisory committee. The Association's not-for-profit tax status had prompted creation of a Tennis Education Foundation in 1951, but it had not been active except to take tax-exempt donations.[106] Kraft and Conroy called education both tax protection and an asset, but the proposal also fit in neatly with the reforms suggested in the 1969 LRP and McKinsey reports. The education advisory committee soon became the Education and Research Office (E&R), located in Princeton, New Jersey, where Kraft and Conroy lived. They recruited a motivated, imaginative, talented staff (including Henry Talbert, the first black American to hold a salaried staff job with the USTA), which came up with a multitude of ideas on how to expand public participation in tennis—programs for schools and recreational tennis, community tennis development tools, a tennis-film lending library and publications department, and tennis-teacher clinics—and was the first USTA unit to work formally on player development.[107] Perhaps the best known of its ideas was the National Tennis Rating Program, which enabled the USTA League program by establishing broad competitive groupings based on both skill and age—tennis's answer to golf's handicap system. In Tom Norris's assessment: "Growing the game had become central to the mission of the USTA." The "R" in E&R would morph into "Recreation" and later "Resource," but the office was one of the few Association initiatives that helped create the dramatic growth of tennis in the United States during the 1980s. Its autonomy would end in 1989 as the Association sought to centralize control of various staff activities.[108]

"Community" became a key descriptive adjective for the USTA sometime in the 1970s. Tennis had long been an activity in large and small communities all around the country, increasingly so as the game spread out from private clubs. But "community tennis" carried with it the inference of organization. E&R was at the forefront of community tennis, convinced that organized community involvement was the key to increasing public participation. The Association had often talked about broader participation but had remained focused on its birthright—competitive lawn-tennis play. Today's "little tennis," with Nerf balls and short courts, would have confused and disturbed the Association's fathers (no mothers for over a century, which may have been part of the problem), with their intense focus on consistent rules and standards. "Grassroots" became a mantra for the Association, one that various elements within the organization tried to expropriate. If a program, an initiative, an expenditure claimed it was good for the grassroots, it took on an aura of goodness and virtue. Eventually in the late 1990s, reality set in and the Association set up two business divisions, professional tennis and community (grassroots) tennis. But of course the job of the former (which focused on the U.S. Open) was to provide money for the latter.[109]

"Governing body" is a powerful phrase. It suggests a degree of authority, control, and prestige that any amateur (or professional) sports organization would seek. Yet, while the Association had for most of its existence assigned to itself that designation, there is no evidence of formal recognition of that status before the Amateur Sports Act of 1978. Still, how you act can be what you are. Merrihew routinely referred to the "governing body" in *American Lawn Tennis*, as did USLTA officials. Holcombe Ward claimed that the U.S. Board of Tax Appeals, in its 1943 decision on Association tax liability, "recognized the USLTA as an amateur sports governing body," although the actual words seem not to be found in the lengthy decision.[110] One might have argued that recognition of the Association as the ILTF's "national federation" for tennis in the United States amounted to the USLTA being the governing body, but why argue? No one in America challenged, or accepted, a designation that came from an international organization.

Presidents: United States and USTA (cont.)

During the Second World War, stories and photos twice appeared in *American Lawn Tennis* about U.S. vice president Henry A. Wallace playing tennis. President Franklin Roosevelt, crippled by polio, appeared in a photo with Mary Browne, the three times U.S. singles champion, pinning a Red Cross button on FDR's lapel.

In March 1947 Harry Truman did the honors for the Davis Cup draw, remarking that, although he did not play tennis, his wife did when she was in high school. An editorial in *American Lawn Tennis* dreamed about the future: "Already we can see the flags of many nations flying above the jam-packed Forest Hills stadium and we can hear a voice from the amplifiers atop the bulging marquee saying, 'Ladies and Gentlemen: The President of the United States!'"

Dwight Eisenhower, John Kennedy, Lyndon Johnson, and Gerald Ford seem to have escaped any public connection with tennis or the USTA, although in 1959 Vice President Richard Nixon sent a letter supporting National Play Tennis Week. Ronald Reagan sent a congratulatory message on the USTA's one-hundredth birthday.

Jimmy Carter played tennis, allegedly exercised personal control of the White House tennis court, and as former president attended a U.S. Open match in September 2000 (Pete Sampras versus Marat Safin). George H. Bush was a regular tennis player, although his unhappy upset stomach during a state dinner in Japan, blamed on his playing a rigorous tennis match that day, may not have been the publicity the USTA hoped for. As president, George W. Bush's closest brush with tennis seems to have been a tennis ball bounced off his limousine during the inaugural parade in 2001. Eight years later, tennis enthusiasts winced when Barack Obama had basketball lines painted and removable hoops installed, but the tennis court remained playable.

Why does this matter beyond public relations? In large part because the Association had long sought designation as the "governing body" of lawn tennis in the United States. What better way to appear like the governing body than to rub shoulders with the president of the United

States? Instant cachet. The USTA acted as such, and its leaders referred to it that way. Formal designation by the U.S. government finally came with the Amateur Sports Act of 1978, which recognized national governing bodies for international sports competitions (Olympics, Pan American Games, et al.).

The bottom line: In September 2000, Bill Clinton became the first and, as of 2016, the only sitting president to attend the U.S. National/Open Championships. But I don't recall the public address announcer saying, "Ladies and Gentlemen: The President of the United States!"[111]

The Amateur Sports Act of 1978 changed all that. For decades the Amateur Athletic Union (AAU) and the National Collegiate Athletic Association (NCAA) had quarreled over which body had authority over amateur athletes and the events in which those athletes participated. Both organizations assumed they knew what was best for both a specific sport and for the athletes who competed. Public and media pressure eventually prompted Congress to decide it knew what was best.

The Olympic games had included lawn tennis from 1896 through 1924. After those games, the ILTF, under pressure from the United States and Great Britain, warned that participation by Federation members "was virtually impossible" unless the International Olympic Committee allowed the ILTF greater involvement in governance and technical matters (i.e., rules); agreed not to call Olympic tennis competitions "world championships"; and adopted a definition of an amateur "as it concerns tennis." This at a time when the Association was beginning to insist on "self-determination" for members of the ILTF and disingenuously suggesting that national federations could hold open tournaments for fun and profit.[112] Over sixty years later, in 1988, tennis returned as an Olympic sport, but by then the USTA was already designated as the governing body of tennis in the United States via the 1978 Amateur Sports Act.

Although the Association, still smarting over the longstanding friction with the Olympics, asked Congress not to include tennis in the legislation, the Amateur Sports Act authorized the United States Olympic Committee to designate the "governing body" in America of sports that competed in recognized international events. The USTA . . . But why rewrite the words of George Gowen, the USTA's key player in all that went on?

> Prior to the Amateur Sports Act of 1978 no sports bodies were officially recognized by Congress as the governing body of a sport. For

> years prior, the AAU and the NCAA had conflicting rules as to the sports they claimed to govern. Even Douglas MacArthur was drafted to settle those disputes—to no avail. After the 1972 Games, the disputes between these two organizations, to the injury of athletes, received such attention that in 1975 President Gerald Ford named a commission to study and resolve. In 1977 the commission issued its final report and recommendations. The commission's recommendation was to clip the powers of the NCAA and the AAU, and to create an overall governing organization (U.S. Olympic Committee) which in turn would recognize governing bodies for each sport included in the program of the Olympic or the Pan American games. Tennis was caught in the net because it was included in the program of the Pan Am Games. The USTA lobbied against the inclusion of tennis, but other Pan Am sports had no objections. In 1978 the Act was passed. A couple of years later the USTA signed up and was officially recognized as the National Governing Body for tennis.[113]

The Association's complicated relationship with the ITF and its member nations, inevitably involved the Davis Cup matches. Davis Cup began in 1900 as an Anglo-American challenge but steadily evolved into a broad international competition. From the beginning of the Federation in 1913, the Association had regularly rejected giving the International Federation control of Davis Cup. But the United States was hamstrung since the competition was an international event. The United States owned the actual cup, and Davis Cup nations made the competition rules, but the ILTF determined the rules of tennis and that included defining an amateur. A two-thirds vote of the (mostly European) Davis Cup nations could move control to the Federation. Still, in 1930 when the ILTF proposed that it manage the competition, the Association refused.[114] But as the number of Davis Cup nations grew, so did pressure to give management control to the Federation. By the end of the century, over one hundred nations entered teams in the annual event. Open tennis shifted the balance as more and more nations became able to put together competitive, even winning Davis Cup teams. The ever-expanding list of Davis Cup nations ostensibly managed the event until most or all agreed in 1978 to let the ITF handle arrangements. With disarming casualness, ITF president Philippe Chartrier told the USTA executive committee: "By the way, the ITF is back in control of the Davis Cup. It may sound technical to you, but I thought it was important that the Davis Cup would be directly managed by the ITF, which is our biggest event."[115] "By the way"? "Back in control"? Whether or not USTA officers had any inkling of what Chartrier would say, no one made a comment or raised a question, at least none that made the minutes.

Davis Cup—Championship Patterns

An ITF history attributes the U.S.-Australian "virtual monopoly" to the Cup's initial concept as a "challenge"; that is, the Cup holder (the previous winner) would be challenged by whichever team managed to win all its matches (ties) leading up to the challenge round (calling six French and nine UK championships "brief intermissions"). The challenge round was eliminated in 1971 so that all in the competition had to play through the draw. Yet from 1960 through 1971, "new" nations broke that choke hold nine times. While the Big Four (Australia, Great Britain, France, United States) remained competitive, the "monopoly" was broken. Why?

The reasons seem obvious—talent, interest, and commitment. By the 1960s tennis had gained internationally in popularity due in part to the efforts of the ILTF. Italy, Mexico, Spain, Romania, and West Germany all made it, undefeated, to the final round. Talent, interest, and commitment paid off.

Then, in 1975 the floodgates opened. (Skipping 1974 when South Africa won almost by default during the apartheid controversy.) What accounts for so many "new" nations challenging and winning the Cup? Non-Big Four nations winning twenty-seven times between 1975 and 2015. The likely candidate is open tennis. The smaller nations, which had opposed open tennis, now benefitted. Whatever the reasons from nation to nation, the coincidence of open tennis with increased skill levels in countries other than the Big Four is connected. Put another way, when the pot at the end of the rainbow is more than a medal and a pat on the back, a nation's best athletes get interested—and so do sponsors, organizers, and governments.[116]

The basic rules for the competition were still set by the participating countries. But management of an event bestows a kind of ownership—even though the United States "owned" the cup, even though the United States "owned" the trademark for the competition, essential if mundane issues like sponsorship intervened. Sure enough, in 1981–82 a dispute arose between the ITF and the USTA over those Davis Cup proprietary rights. After the Federation voted to have "all rights and properties" for the Davis Cup competition "vested" in the ITF, the Association protested. In the words of its general counsel: "The [Davis Cup] nations' surrender of some of their traditional independence [in 1978] was nothing compared to what was about to be asked of them in the summer of '81." (A comment written in 1982 that indicates some Association leaders were aware and critical of the 1978 decision.) Eventually agreement was reached allowing the USTA to exercise proprietary rights (i.e., trademark rights) within the United States, but clearly the business side of Davis Cup was "owned" by the Federation. Almost two decades later when Association leaders looked to gain back the Davis Cup trademark, their general counsel warned it would be too difficult and expensive. Pointedly, the initial reason given was that the U.S. delegate to the 1981 ITF meeting that voted to assume all Davis Cup "rights and properties" cast his ballot in favor of the motion. As in 1978 (if the American delegate voted), whether or not that delegate fully understood the significance of the decision is unclear. What is clear is that neither decision was discussed at any of the Association's management or executive committee meetings held in 1977–78 or 1981–82.[117]

Domestic challenges likewise concerned the Association. It could not have become the $300 million corporation it is today were it not for the Internal Revenue Service decision to designate sponsor payments to the Mobil Cotton Bowl as "acknowledgments" rather than "advertising." Acknowledging a contribution is a thank you; the purpose of advertising is to increase revenue for the advertiser. The IRS went for the high visibility target, one it had identified back in 1977—college bowl games, specifically the Cotton Bowl in Dallas, Texas. A politically foolish tactic. As one lawyer put it: "with three Texans on the House Ways and Means Committee," the Cotton Bowl "could never be taxed." The IRS effort failed in 1977, and again in 1992. Without debating the wisdom of the tax code, the IRS had a compelling argument, but chose a near-invulnerable target. Television revenues had made college bowl games an obvious and valuable subject. Fortunately for the USTA, the IRS foolishly (arrogantly?) chose to go after a not-for-profit event that had higher visibility, at that time, than the U.S. Open. The Association had few if any friends in Congress; the Cotton Bowl and other college bowls had many and powerful ones. Politics trumps logic and law, and the outcome was inevitable.

When in 1978 the USTA built the National Tennis Center (NTC) in Flushing Meadows, the IRS challenged the 1943 tax agreement that included the West Side Tennis Club. With a U.S. Open facility in a public park, and revenues still relatively low (at least compared to 2015), the IRS, aware of the collapse of the Cotton Bowl audit, settled. The USTA went from a (c)

(4) not-for-profit organization to a (c)(6) professional league (income-tax exempt), while the USTA National Tennis Center, as a public "charity," remained (c)(3)(fully exempt). Open television and most other proceeds were tax exempt. There USTA tax liability has rested, cautiously, ever since.[118] (I apologize to you, the readers, for boring you with such esoteric tax code information. But I did think it appropriate to remind all that not only the USTA could get deeply, once again, into how many angels can dance on the head of a pin.[119])

There was a lot going on for the Association in the late seventies and eighties. The tennis boom was part of it, as was another McKinsey report on governance and management—both formative for the Association. Similarly the Amateur Sports Act forced the Association to change its policies and seek to have the Olympics include tennis. Less formative but highly publicized was the flail over transsexual Renée Richards's application to play in women's matches.[120]

But the elephant in the room was, without question, construction of the National Tennis Center in Flushing Meadows and moving the U.S. Open out of Forest Hills to the new stadium.

The long and prickly relationship between the Association and the West Side Tennis Club in Forest Hills focused on two anchor points: the U.S. National Championships/U.S. Open, and, in the mantra of real estate agents—location, location, location. Shorthand for the national championships was "Forest Hills," imitating "Wimbledon" as a synonym for the British national championships. With the USTA, the tournament, and the club all in New York City, West Side members became more involved and influential within the USTA than their numbers warranted—in today's idiom, they were "inside the beltway." Three Association presidents had been president of the club; others had been members; many of the Association's officers and executive-committee members routinely came from the Forest Hills club. The USLTA had capitalized construction of a permanent stadium there in the 1920s. The club found it difficult to pay for its share of those construction costs, particularly during the Great Depression. In 1940 hassles over those debts prompted resentment within the executive committee and suggestions that the Association might wish to move the nationals to a different location. The rift between two organizations was widened by IRS decisions in the thirties and forties that were unfavorable to the WSTC and favorable to the USLTA.[121]

Nor was Slew Hester the first Association president to call for moving the U.S. Open out of Forest Hills. In 1972 the club's insistent demands for money aggravated president Bob Colwell to the point of asking for authority to look elsewhere unless they could reach an agreement. The squall blew over, but it was another mark against the Forest Hills club, one that surely remained in the memory of Second Vice President Slew Hester when, five years later, as USTA president, he abruptly ended contract discussions with the club and took his fateful plane ride over Flushing Meadows.[122]

But by the late 1970s, there were bigger issues. The WSTC was private and elitist. So was the USTA, but it was changing and concerned about its public image. The club's exclusiveness stood in opposition to the USTA's slow but steady move toward diversity and public participation in the game. Forest Hills members insisted on getting Association support for clubhouse improvements, and a much larger share of tournament revenues. Association leaders, including some connected with the Forest Hills club, expressed discomfort with its demands. The trigger for confrontation was the dilapidated condition of the club's facilities and amenities. "Almost insultingly shabby," wrote one reporter. Billie Jean King in 1974 described the club as "rinky-dink" with "bad" grass courts and the dressing rooms "a mess. And those pompous U.S.L.T.A. officials were prancing around everywhere."

The stands were rickety, with aisles and walkways too narrow; parking was an unpleasant challenge with fans forced to cruise around Forest Hills looking for residents hustling to "rent" their driveways; locker rooms for the players were grossly inadequate, which, combined with the haughty attitude of club members, prompted the ATP to complain that a poll of 215 men players found the U.S. Open at Forest Hills "the least favorite" men's tournament. Players were not allowed to use the clubhouse, only the cramped locker rooms.

But most of all, the lack of enough stadium seats precluded the future that Hester & Co. imagined. They recognized that expansion of the stadium would provide resources for the growth of the USTA and the game of tennis. Expansion was possible in Forest Hills but required a capital investment well beyond the six hundred thousand dollars the Association had in the bank and would not solve issues of parking and transportation.[123]

But whatever the long-term imagining of USTA leaders, the niggardly, self-indulgent greed of the membership of the West Side Tennis Club broke the camel's back. The club insisted on improvements to the clubhouse, benefitting primarily members, despite the fact that members paid strikingly low club dues made possible by U.S. Open revenues. There was a good deal of weeping and gnashing of teeth by those with a romanticized image of Forest Hills, with grass courts (clay as of 1975), lovely faux-Tudor buildings, walls covered with ivy, and a visual gentility that harkened back to bygone days. But as dozens of news articles pointed out, those days were gone.

The contract for the U.S. Open was up for renewal after the 1977 tournament, and the break came quickly. The fact that Hester did not have the ties that his predecessors had with Forest Hills made it a different ball game. Negotiations between the club and the USTA stalled in October 1976 and collapsed in January 1977. In July 1977 after news of a deal with New York City had been reported, a public argument between Hester and the president of the WSTC, Lindley Hoffman, broke out. Hoffman claimed the USTA had refused to negotiate, arguing that a seven-hundred-thousand-dollars-per-year figure was "never a demand." Hester retorted they thought it was and besides, he had heard club members state the club would be better off without the tournament. As the back and forth became angry, the USTA public-relations director (Ed Fabricus) ended the press conference. The ugly incident where a WSTC board member made disparaging remarks about the ethnic makeup of the community near Flushing Meadows—95 percent "Negro" he claimed—illustrated the bitter reactions of club leadership.[124]

No one in the history of the USTA deserves a "box" more than Slew Hester. But it is nearly impossible to capture both the man and what he did for the USTA in a small box. Hester has long been depicted by tennis writers, all too often in smarmy fashion, as some sort of lucky gambler who made his money as an "oil [always spelled by the writers as 'awl' to suggest his drawl—of course most native New Yorkers pronounced the word 'erl'] wildcatter." The image was of someone wandering around Texas and the Gulf Coast, randomly sticking a drill in the ground and hoping to get lucky. In fact, a "wildcatter" was simply an independent speculator in oil futures, whose success rested on shrewd assessments (much more scientific than a dousing rod) of where new sources of oil might be, combined with the ability to persuade others to put up the money. Hester honestly described himself as a "con man." If New Yorkers—union leaders, politicians, or reporters—underestimated him it was at their peril, and the impression that he lacked sophistication did not last for long.

But better to hear (read) about the process in Slew Hester's inimitable style—albeit perhaps made a bit more colorful by his famously heavy drawl, which likely left the stenographer's head spinning.

In September 1977 Hester delivered to the executive committee an extraordinary chronicle—a saga—describing in colorful, idiomatic language just how the United States Tennis Association had gotten to the point of no return (though he never said just that). His lengthy summary and the brief discussion, altogether taking fifty-six pages of the minutes, were both informative and delightful. Intentional southern "corn pone" at times, insightful analysis routinely, selective but honest history all the time.[125]

The tone was occasionally defensive following an angry letter from Judge Kelleher complaining that he was "appalled" that the executive committee had been ignored in the process of signing a contract with the City of New York that changed the venue for the U.S. Open and incurred a five-million-dollar debt. It was all "ultra vires" (beyond the authority), he argued, "unless the Executive Committee is to be deemed a meaningless body"—which was, by then, precisely the case. Although Gowen took the blame, after a lengthy legal explanation about the authority of the management committee, he courteously but firmly dismissed Kelleher's complaint: "The contract arrangements for the site of the U.S. Open would appear to be a management function."[126] Hester, just installed as USTA president, had purposefully evaded the executive committee. At the February annual meeting in 1977 in LaCosta, California, the management committee met before the executive committee. Hester reviewed the talks with the WSTC. Then, after "much discussion" the management committee authorized the president to "explore certain avenues" (Hester's words), to spend up to ten thousand dollars in doing so, and to present "any new proposals" to the executive committee. None of this came before the executive committee when it later met a couple of days later.[127] Why? As Hester put it in his September briefing to the executive committee: "We had been told by the mayor if it leaked, we were dead. . . . So that is the reason I did not make the full disclosure at LaCosta."[128]

Hester's tour de force began with a refutation of West Side's public claims that the Association had not negotiated in good faith. In October 1976 the USTA had in fact offered a six-year extension of the contract for the U.S. Open with revisions that could mean $150,000 to $200,000 additional for the club. Moreover, a clause called for the WSTC to get 25 percent of all revenue over $500,000, a number that was sure to be exceeded. But the club, said Hester, offered a set of plans ("they say they don't exist but I have a copy") to build eight indoor courts with eight more "on top in a double-tiered thing," at a cost of $4.8 million they wanted to charge to the U.S. Open. "And we all said you've got to be kidding." Despite Hester's best efforts, West Side leaders were always unavailable: "Elk went to Bermuda, Lindley went to Florida, and I don't know where Dick went, probably back in the wood-work."[129]

When they did hold a luncheon meeting in late January 1977, the club had revised its wish list. When Hester found that too complicated and asked for an alternative, they said "$700,000 a year minimum," for ten years. Hester, incredulous, responded "Gee, you have got to be kidding." "Suppose we refuse it," he asked. "If you refuse this, the West Side Club would be better off without the U.S. Open." Hester asked again, and was told, "If you don't give us $700,000 a year, our members do not want the U.S. Open." "Pay the check," Hester told Mike Burns (USTA executive secretary). As the club negotiators followed them out they said they wanted to continue the discussions, but Hester retorted we negotiated twice and came up with the same $700,000 a year. "We have no place to negotiate." "And we all disintegrated."

Hester obviously had developed a plan well before he met with WSTC negotiators in late January. In late December, when flying into LaGuardia airport, located in Queens right next to Flushing Meadows-Corona Park, he noticed the decrepit remains of the Singer Bowl, built for the 1964–65 World's Fair and renamed Louis Armstrong Stadium (honoring "Satchmo" who lived in Corona, Queens, for the last three decades of his life). (See gallery, image 21.) The park had been developed from what F. Scott Fitzgerald in *The Great Gatsby* called "a valley of ashes," and the stadium seemed intent on returning to that former existence.[130]

Hester then went to New Orleans where he played some tennis with Moon Landrieu, the city's mayor. Hester knew that Landrieu, as president of the U.S. Conference of Mayors, had gotten credit for helping to persuade the U.S. Congress to provide federal loans to prevent New York City from declaring bankruptcy, after President Gerald Ford rejected any bailout, prompting the classic *New York Daily News* headline "Ford to City: Drop Dead." Abe Beame had been mayor of the city then, and still was—and Slew Hester wanted to talk to him, right away.

Hester already had a concept by the time he talked to Moon Landrieu on a Sunday. Landrieu said he didn't want to give the U.S. Open to New York: "Take 40 acres in City Park; build it in New Orleans." Hester knew the tournament belonged in New York City, Landrieu called him "stupid," and the next day came a call from Mayor Beame's office followed by a call from Lew Rudin,[131] described by Hester as "the most powerful man in New York. "If want to get a waterline changed or transformer moved, you call Lewis and two hours later Consolidated Edison [the huge city power company] is giving you the approval." Two days later, on a Wednesday, Hester met in New York with the city parks commissioner and in a few hours worked out an agreement in principle.

The city's goal was straightforward—get the USTA to rehabilitate a portion of a 1,200 acre public park, not only at no cost to the city, but with some payments (though far less than seven hundred thousand dollars a year). When Mayor Beame asked about the "Singer bowl," the parks commissioner responded: "We've been trying to give it away for five years." One USTA observer later commented: "They were throwing permits at us. We could have built anything we wanted to there."[132]

But principle had to be translated into plans, and to get the stadium built in time for the 1978 U.S. Open, the city needed a "plot" (site) plan on Mayor Beame's desk by 11:00 a.m. on Friday—just two days later. Once again, Lew Rudin to the rescue. He supplied the names of four architects, and according to Hester, the first one to answer, after working hours, was David Specter. "We met him at 6 o'clock (p.m.) . . . and on Friday morning delivered to the Park Commissioner and the Mayor. . . . That is how quick we were." The result was a "letter of intent" from the USTA requesting permission to use the Flushing Meadows site.[133]

Bids for a permit to use the Louis Armstrong Stadium had apparently gone out in the autumn of 1976 and were due to close on April 4, 1977. That gave the USTA only two months to put together architectural and legal plans in enough detail to make a formal bid. Only one other bid appeared, "but the tennis proposal was much more extensive," according the Parks Department, and the USTA won the right to negotiate.[134] Talks with the city went on until late May, when the city granted the permit. New York City was promised a rehabbed Armstrong Stadium, a public tennis center open ten months a year, a guarantee of at least $125,000 a year from court fees, and a commitment from the USTA to spend at least five million dollars on its new tennis center. Hester summed up the terms with wonderful succinctness: "Generally speaking of it, some 16 pages, this is what it says: we have 16½ acres of Corona Park, Flushing Meadows and the Louis Armstrong stadium. If they hadn't given us the Louis Armstrong stadium, we would have been half a million and six months better off. But they wanted us to take it and rehabilitate it. So we have it."

But what did they have? They had a dilapidated stadium: "Cosmetically, the estimate was . . . $200,000 to clean up. I think it would cost that much to get rid of the pigeons." Hester extolled the old beautiful trees they were not allowed to cut. They added "a gracious touch, like an old Southern plantation," he told reporters, talked about corporate tents and boxes, twenty-six lighted outdoor courts, concessions, expanded parking at Shea Stadium right next door, vastly increased seating, and ever-expanding revenues. Good thing, since Hester also reported that "fast-track" building would raise costs—costs which continued to mount until they doubled the original estimate of six million dollars.[135]

But Slew Hester's speech came in September 1977, just a month before ground was broken for what would become the National Tennis Center. (See gallery, image 23.) Twenty years later it would take four years to complete Arthur Ashe Stadium. Hester built his "Taaj Mahaal" in less than one.[136]

The dilapidated stadium was a challenge—too wide to provide good viewing of tennis. Knock it down and rebuild? Slice it in half? David Specter, the architect who answered his phone, and obviously someone with a spatial imagination, envisioned a new octagonal bowl placed over the side of the oval-shaped Armstrong stadium. It was a brilliant insight that allowed a brand new stadium to be built, while retaining the advantage of an existing structure (albeit one that needed help). The "grandstand," familiar to U.S. Open fans was the result. (See gallery, image 22.)

The West Side Tennis Club twice more tried to reopen negotiations, and publicly complained that the USTA had treated them unfairly, but Hester was having none of it. His now realizable dream was far better and bigger than anything Forest Hills could offer.[137]

The final year of the U.S. Open at Forest Hills was bizarre. To gain a sense of the crazy, confused, chaotic atmosphere in 1977 at the tournament, all within the context of a crazy, confused, chaotic summer in New York City, there is no more evocative, insightful read than Michael Steinberger's "Queens Was Burning Too: The Chaotic Spectacle of the 1977 U.S. Open":

> Soon after the match started, a commotion in the stands halted play. A spectator had been shot in the leg; the bullet, the police later surmised, was fired from a nearby apartment building. At the time, New York was still reeling from the citywide blackout in July and the looting that followed. It had been terrorized for much of the summer by the Son of Sam, and now a scene straight out of *Black Sunday*, a film about a planned attack at the Super Bowl released earlier that year, seemed to be unfolding at the Open. . . .
>
> Those two weeks in Forest Hills included a transgender controversy, mutinous fans, appalling breaches of etiquette and a jerry-built racket strung with Venetian-blind cord that threatened to upend the whole event. . . . and a near riot in the stadium when officials tried to switch an afternoon match to the evening session."[138] [True! I know. I was there yelling, "Hell no, we won't go."]

Calm was restored by the time the 1978 U.S. Open was held at the new National Tennis Center, beginning on August 28. It was a huge success, getting rave reviews in the press. In the words of David Specter, it "was raw around the edges and the special paint on the asphalt pavement hadn't quite dried, but over 400,000 people came."[139] The stories about Slew Hester are legion. He gave beer parties for workers on the site. He insisted on putting out an ivy plant as a gentle dig to folks who mourned the loss of the ivy-draped Forrest Hills stadium. His close assistants—Mike Burns, George Gowen, Don Conway—all pulled their weight. But it was Slew's house.[140] George Gowen deftly described the risks and the results:

> When we lifted the Open from Forest Hills we did so to gain undisputed ownership and control. We gambled every cent we had and even what we could expect from the future.
>
> It was only four miles from West Side Tennis Club, but the distance travelled by the USTA in eighteen months could not be measured in miles.[141]

Constitutional change in the early 1970s may have been stillborn; finding a new location for the U.S. Open propelled the USTA into a new era. But constitutional changes in the mid 1980s were expected as the Association moved to adopt what it saw as the generally accepted business model. Just the time for a consultant's report.

After praising the USTA for being "up to the challenge" raised in McKinsey's 1969 report, their new (1985) report once again found that the Association had arrived at "another critical juncture." An immediate restructuring of management, and greater reliance on professional managers (staff) were imperative. Those were, or course, the same recommendations made in 1969, ones that were a bit too uncomfortable, too "revolutionary" back then.

The 1985 McKinsey report made a very specific recommendation about the role of the about-to-be established board of directors. "The affairs of the Association shall be *managed* by the Management Committee," read the existing constitution, whereas the report recommended "The affairs of the Association shall be *directed* by a Board of Directors," language that appeared in the 1986 constitution: "managed" to "directed." One changed word portended significant change. That potential change was further defined and strengthened by the recommendation that the "position of President of the Association be transformed into the Chairman of the Board . . . [and] Chief Executive Officer," while defining the executive director "as Chief Operating Officer and President of the USTA." The consultants must have been warned that shifting the title of president would meet with opposition, for the report suggested allowing time, "roughly one year," for the term president to lose "its current symbolism" by dropping *public* use of the title "President," instead referring only to the chief executive officer (later adding chairman of the board) and the chief operating officer (later president, executive director).

Reflecting the consultants' worry that "without reassigning the presidential title . . . the Chairman and the USTA's other top officers will *continue* to become mired down in day-to-day operating decisions," the report assigned the executive director, chief operating officer, president "full responsibility for day-to-day managing, planning, organizing, and controlling of all the affairs and activities of the Association, within Board directives and totally accountable to the Board for results." One executive director had tried to exercise that kind of authority, apparently thinking it went with the title, and was fired.[142]

It proposed, in vague terms, turning the executive committee, since it operated out of the decision-making mainstream, into the "lead committee of the Board of Directors." The report expressed concern about poor communications between the sections and the USTA, proposing establishment of a reporting relationship that did not interfere with the "tradition of intense negotiation" with each other and with the USTA. How that squared with the report's call for the sections to maintain their "autonomy" remained unexplained. Centralization and accountability seemed at the core of relations with the sections. There was no mention of the delegates assembly, which offered the sections a potential avenue for influencing policy as a group but which, as a standing committee, was a casualty of the constitution-bylaws changes in 1970–71. Moreover, the report did not understand the governance-management dynamic created by USTA committees. As one executive director (Don Conway) lamented, managing volunteer committees proved impossible since they insisted on reporting directly to the president who had appointed them. There were three silos, he observed—staff, U.S. Open, and volunteers—again not detected by the McKinsey report.[143]

The management committee took up the McKinsey report, which had been distributed in advance of its October 1985 meeting. Once the consultants reviewed the report, "an informative discussion and question and answer session followed." They and USTA staff members then left the room and, "following lengthy discussion, the Committee unanimously concluded."—a list of seven conclusions followed. Nothing else. Not a word in the minutes about or from the "informative" and "lengthy" discussions. The seven conclusions kept governance and management of the Association just where it had been, with the exception of a few name changes. The nominating committee (which the report writers surely knew could not be changed) and the executive committee expressly remained the same. Officer positions likewise. The president remained the chief executive officer, adding chairman of the board of directors, which, itself, replaced the management committee with simply a change of name. The *only* substantive change was that the executive director would "manage" the Association's affairs while the board of directors would "direct" the Association's affairs. That for a report which, along with the executive-director job search that would follow, cost over one-quarter million dollars.[144] The volunteers remained firmly in charge.

Internal, organizational reform was the main thrust of the 1985 McKinsey report, so there is a good deal of revealing history in examining the nature of the executive-director position. The Association's volunteer leadership had great difficulty deciding in the 1970s and 80s whether or not there should be an executive director with authority to carry out the policies they adopted.

What's in a name? For roses, nothing. But for a business–corporate management structure, titles and what they imply are serious business. An executive secretary posed no challenge to personal, volunteer leadership, but in business parlance an executive director took the top leadership out of the trenches and assumed that volunteer boards and committees were involved with policy-based governance, not day-to-day details. The provision in the 1970–71 revised constitution requiring an executive director was unambiguous ("The Association shall have an Executive Director who shall be the chief administrative officer"), while the formal title of executive secretary was removed from the bylaws. Yet the USTA quickly returned to having an executive secretary, going without an executive director until 1980, when Rick O'Shea was hired, with a handshake "contract," at an annual salary of seventy-five thousand dollars. He lasted less than a year. His decisions on compensation and promotions, made without getting approval, upset the management committee, which was accustomed to close, personal relationships with upper level staff. He was, obviously, asked for his resignation and complied. When O'Shea sued for four months' pay (twenty-five thousand dollars) claiming he had an oral agreement for a year's salary, the USTA filed a countersuit asserting that he had acted without authority causing "substantial damages." That unhappy experience may well have affected the USTA's take on just what authority the executive director ought to have. Certainly it prompted the Association to go to a monthly salary without a written contract for O'Shea's successor.[145]

The Elusive Executive Director

Arguments over the role of the executive director focused on whether or not the president should have day-to-day management authority or should the volunteer leadership be restricted to policy-based governance. Hence:

circa March 1967: Kelleher proposes an executive director-"high commissioner" (search fails).
1969: LRP and McKinsey reports recommend an executive director; ExCom agrees.
late 1969–February 1970: candidate identified, selection postponed.
1969–72: executive director in title only (Malaga).
1970–71: revised constitution states "The Association *shall* have an Executive Director" (emphasis added).
May 1980: an executive director is hired and fired seven months later (O'Shea).
December 1980–May 1981: interim (acting) executive director (Burns).
May 1981: executive director position "reduced" to chief administrative officer and hire made (Conway).
1983: title changed back to executive director-chief administrative officer (Conway).
1985: consultants (McKinsey) recommend giving executive director the title of president, with the volunteer chairman of the board as CEO.
January 15, 1986: special meeting created a board of directors that "directs" Association affairs, a chairman of the board as chief executive officer and president; and an executive director as "the chief operating officer responsible for executing Board decisions and day-to-day operational programs, policies and procedures." (See appendix 5 for a full list of the senior staff persons.)

Thereafter, no written changes, although:

1999–2000: during discussions about "state alignment," designating the executive director as chief executive officer came up but disappeared along with "state alignment" and the resignation of the then executive director.

In 2003-4, the board of directors, with the president's support, voted that in the event of a deadlock between the executive director-chief operating officer and the president on a major issue, a board vote would resolve the matter. (A board procedure not codified in the bylaws.)[146]

Donald Conway, a well-qualified certified public accountant, was hired as chief administrative officer and remained in that restricted role despite being called executive director after 1983. Conway's connection with the Association is, in itself, a story. During a golf game between the chairman of the board of the New York Mets baseball club and Billy Talbert, tournament director of the U.S. Open, Talbert mentioned that Madison Square Garden (in New York City), which sold tickets for the U.S. Open, seemed to be charging too much for the service. The Mets board chairman told his controller, Don Conway, to send the USTA a proposal for the Mets' ticket office to handle U.S. Open ticket sales, a proposal the Association accepted. When the USTA moved the U.S. Open to its new stadium at Flushing Meadows (next door to the Mets), it again worked out an agreement with Conway and the Mets to have responsibility for planning, staffing, and running stadium operations for that initial U.S. Open at the National Tennis Center—negotiating contracts with four unions; staffing for the event; coordination of food concessions; crowd control procedures; establishing grounds and court maintenance procedures; contracting for outside services; establishing first aid stations; tournament credentials; liaison with government authorities concerning bomb-threat procedures; and, of course, tournament ticket sales. With the USTA and Slew Hester focused on construction, and the tournament about to begin, such stadium operations became critical. Conway recalled Hester saying just before the tournament started that, for the next two weeks, his reputation as USTA president was in Conway's hands. It was, for Conway, "the challenge of a lifetime."

Following the inaugural U.S. Open at Flushing Meadows, the USTA hired a team to handle stadium operations for the 1979 tournament. Yet, a few days after the tournament began, the Association asked Conway, who had left the Mets in the interim, to take over tournament operations, and he accepted. Sometime early in 1981, when the USTA began its search for a replacement for Rick O'Shea, Conway applied for the position, re-labeled "chief administrative officer"—an intentional downgrading of authority. For the next five years, the Association had a senior staff person who got the job done without running into problems with the president or the board of directors. No hint of criticism, or explanation, appeared in the management committee or board minutes when the Association began searching for an executive director in 1985.

Nor did Conway get a warning. When the USTA public-relations director showed him a report in a New Orleans newspaper—the home city of the Association president—about the search for an executive director, Conway quietly resigned. And so the USTA parted company with the man who successfully directed stadium operations for the initial U.S. Open at the National Tennis Center, the man who was called in to take over those operations for the following U.S. Open, the man who earned the executive director title halfway through his five-year tenure.[147]

There was some pushback. One sectional executive director circulated a letter to the full committee arguing that Conway, who had already resigned, should be retained and that the executive director's position ought to be "strengthened."[148] But the strongest dissent came during the special meeting of the executive committee, which had been called to vote on the watered-down proposals generated by the 1985 McKinsey report—essentially changes in nomenclature. Discussions at that special meeting revealed what the anodyne minutes from the October management committee meeting had hidden.

The chair of the Association's constitution and rules committee (Forrest Hainline) moderated the debate, often displaying discomfort and impatience. Clearly on a mission, he worked hard to aim the discussion in the direction preferred by the president and the board. It was not all about the McKinsey report, he stated, but about the "call"—the specific amendments proposed. But it really *was* about the McKinsey report and its recommendation that the executive director should have the title of president, with its implied authority. Those opposed argued that, in the words of President Gregson, "They treated us too much like a business. The strength of this association is in its volunteers." That said just after he spoke proudly of a "$35 million operation under the supervision of the board of directors"—a dollar figure made possible by the U.S. Open.

Hainline pointed out the obvious, that the changes offered by the board were essentially an update of the status quo—in his words: "In effect, the proposed amendments simply describe the past operations." David Markin, who was about to become volunteer in chief, took an either/or approach, vociferously arguing that the Association was run by volunteers: "it was the feeling of many of us that the connotation that a *hired gun* is the president of the association just wasn't all that good in terms of what we truly are. We are basically a voluntary organization. We are directed by volunteers. All volunteers are on the board of directors, management committee."

"Volunteers" is a wonderful word. It connotes a populist, democratic political structure that empowers all—equally. But no one questioned the assumption.

Former president Ed Turville took things in a somewhat different direction, alleging interference by board members in the work of the professional staff: the report "is saying, our staff reports to the chief operating officer and no one else. It is not just telling the staff that. It is also telling all of us that. Quit going in there and telling underlings what they are supposed to do. Some of you may not like that, but that is what it says." A major argument over clarifying the relationship of the board to the president seemed aimed primarily at ensuring that members of the board could not bypass or ignore the president and the full board, particularly in dealings with the executive director.

As for the McKinsey report's recommendation for the executive committee, Hainline stated (accurately) that it "has not been involved in policy making," which aroused concerns. Eventually, Markin and Hester got to the point, insisting that the committee provided a much-needed "buffer" that protected the Association from being strong armed by three or four large sections. In the executive committee, they pointed out, every section was represented, but (without mentioning the makeup of the U.S. Senate) everyone had an equal say and vote. So much for volunteer populism.[149]

But the decision was in. The bylaws adopted at a special meeting of the executive committee and the membership in January 1986 stated firmly that the chairman of the board remained both president and chief executive officer and that an executive director "shall, subject to the direction of the board of directors and fully accountable to it, *manage* the day-to-day operational programs, policies and procedures of the association." A summary of those bylaws published in the 1986 *Yearbook* had it a bit different: "the Executive Director becomes the chief operating officer responsible for executing Board decisions and day-to-day operational programs, policies and procedures." The word "manage" failed to survive editing—an omen of things to come.[150]

The McKinsey report prompted the USTA to pass over Conway and look for an executive director with the public credentials and experience appropriate to a high-visibility position. The search committee described the job in the terms proposed by the McKinsey report. In May 1986 the board agreed to an open-ended contract with John T. Fogarty, a long-time top executive with First National City Bank, to be executive director-chief operating officer with a reported annual salary of over two hundred thousand dollars. Fogarty got involved with the Education & Research department, and the Tennis Industry Council, and once said that serving the USTA was "a delight." Yet, in just two years (in July 1988), he and the USTA went their separate ways. There is no written explanation of why he left, but one can guess. Despite the support of outgoing president Randy Gregson for the McKinsey recommendations, Gregson's successors—first Gordon Jorgensen then David Markin—clearly opposed making the executive director the "president" of the USTA. That opposition was, obviously, more than just a matter of titles. In the words of one observer, when Fogarty was hired, "he actually believed he was going to run the show—then he ran into David [Markin]."[151]

Governance aside, the 1985 McKinsey report offered a number of useful observations and recommendations, starting with the crucial importance to the Association's mission of the U.S. Open—"the crown jewel in the international Grand Slam crown." Public relations, particularly with regard to television and newspaper coverage, were key. Relations with the City of New York, which accommodated both the U.S. Open site at Flushing Meadows and serviced roads and public transportation to the tournament, were equally so. Even more so were the revenues from the tournament. In the words of the report: "The Association must be continually on guard that its financial policies and objectives for the event are continuously optimizing public interest." The report focused on the U.S. Open with impressive statistics:

Attendance: 1970—123,000 1985—409,000

Television: 1970—3 hours 1985—81 hours

Revenue numbers were not provided, and profit was, of course, the forbidden word for a not-for-profit corporation, but the inference was clear. The U.S. Open was the engine of growth. "Optimizing public interest" would later be captured by insistence on creating a "buzz" around the tournament. Entertainment was, after all, the essential fuel (just as Jimmy Connors understood). Unmentioned but crucial was the television contract with the Columbia Broadcast System (CBS). That began in 1968, and two years later a five-year contract called for one hundred thousand dollars a year to the Association's coffers.

The long-term financial gains for the USTA were enormous. The relationship with CBS lasted for forty-six years, increasing regularly until, in

2014, when the contract expired, the USTA was reportedly receiving $30 million per year, with escalation provisions. The new arrangement with ESPN reportedly brings an annual payment of $75 million to the Association. Davis Cup, once the Association's cash cow, did not lend itself to the scheduling demands of television or to the interest spans of the general public. By September 1969, there was no television contract for Davis Cup and no expectation of substantial revenue. Eventually, Davis Cup matches would become part of overall packages with various television sports channels.[152]

That "entertainment" modality may have prompted the McKinsey consultants to point out that, according to David Caulkins (the Association's compensation consultant), the USTA staff was underpaid for what they were doing, "many to a significant degree." That would change.[153]

Amusing, and revealing, is the report's conclusion: "In fact, the National Championships, which evolved into the Open, were initiated in 1881 as the final round of amateur play in the newly-founded Association's tournament network." The implication of structure and control—a "network"—key goals in every McKinsey report, brings a chuckle. James Dwight may have dreamed back in 1881 of organizational success, even structure and control, but the reality was that back then Association founders were scrambling for existence.[154]

The report did not generate major changes, but a series of small changes can become fundamental. The U.S. Open became the eight-hundred-pound gorilla—though a productive not a destructive one. Once the USTA got out from under the early indebtedness required to build the National Tennis Center at Flushing Meadows, a huge world of spending opportunities appeared. The 1985 McKinsey report had warned that the public perception of the U.S. Open had to be carefully cultivated, and the Association heeded that advice. The sections all had ideas about how to get more people playing tennis, and to satisfy those who were playing; player development advocates dreamed about having facilities where they could bring in the best young players and train them to be the best in the world; the Association could gain more members by better marketing; an expanded national staff along with higher staff salaries, initially boosted by the Caulkins study, seemed the best way to expand game and the Association; board expenses grew steadily as international tennis seemed to demand that the USTA be represented at each and every meeting. No project was too small to seek funding. Ironically, the Association's most successful program, the USTA Leagues, operated on a minimalist budget—but even that kept expanding. Let the good times roll, Slew Hester would have drawled.

Controversial as governance was, those who defended volunteer leadership had a point. Whether by design, imaginative leadership, or just plain good luck, the USTA was financially secure, politically stable, and growing steadily. Nevertheless, the 1990s would bring renewed challenges to the volunteer-staff dynamic. Old arguments would continue, heightened by the ever-increasing revenue stream from the U.S. Open. But an increasingly active ingredient in the mix would be a growing concern on the part of the sections about centralization of governance and staff management.

7

WHO DECIDES?

1990–2002

> "Working as an employee for the USTA was the worst professional experience of my career."
> ANONYMOUS STAFF

In 1989, a consultant's report on involving minorities in tennis captured the essence of the Association's quaint and cumbersome governance procedures:

> The structure of the USTA is one of a kind: a volunteer Board of Directors, 17 relatively autonomous sections and a national staff in four locations all within a 100 mile radius.
>
> No national voluntary organization, for profit corporation or sports governing body has a similar structure.[1]

For the next decade the Association would struggle with reforming that structure in order to deliver programs more effectively to the general public—in order to reverse a troubling slow-down in membership growth and, briefly, even gross membership numbers; in order to identify and develop "world-class" players the way the Swedes and West Germans seemingly had done with athletes like Mats Wilander, Stefan Edberg, Steffi Graf, and Boris Becker; and in order to protect and enhance the U.S. Open.

The Association's unwritten business model had changed with the adoption of open tennis in 1968 and the subsequent rapid growth of profits from the U.S. Open Championships. But the business governance structure remained what had essentially been created in the early 1920s. The 1990s would see real changes, eventually culminating with creation of two major business units, professional tennis and community tennis, each headed by a chief executive who reported to the executive director. But it took some time to get there.

Governance was not the only challenge for the Association. Its basic source of revenue, the U.S. Open, garnered constant attention. Louis Armstrong Stadium and its attachment, the Grandstand, both of which had been renovated in great haste for the 1978 U.S. Open, needed upgrading, and expanding revenue would require expanding seating. The stadium held eighteen thousand and the grandstand another six thousand; not enough to satisfy growing demand for tickets. There were no luxury boxes—that wonderful moneymaker bequeathed to sports since 1965 by the Houston Astrodome. The facility needed more tennis courts, food concessions could not handle demand, merchandising spaces were too small, player amenities were inadequate, there were nowhere near enough bathrooms, and on went the list. Clearly, the U.S. Open would benefit from a stadium and grounds constructed specifically to host a major tennis championship.

Almost from the very day the National Tennis Center (NTC) appeared on the skyline of Flushing Meadows, there were calls for renovations, expansion, and even a site change. In May of 1989, the board took a look at plans for a greatly improved facility. They would need twelve more acres and access from the Grand Central Parkway, but a new stadium and facility could be done. A few months later, then-president David Markin told the board he favored finding a site for the NTC outside of New York City. Aircraft noise from LaGuardia Airport (the infamous runway number 13), which angered fans and players and interrupted matches; the expiration of the lease from the city Parks Department; and inadequate parking all prompted him to push to find a site in Westchester County, adjacent to the Bronx on the north edge of the city. Markin later claimed that he outwardly favored other sites to give him negotiating leverage with New York City. He also supported building a domed stadium.[2]

Fixing the aircraft noise problem became a sine qua non for the USTA. After David Dinkins was elected mayor in 1989, he was able, through the work of Nick Garaufis, counsel to the Queens Borough president, to obtain an agreement from the Federal Aviation Administration (FAA) to stop flights over the NTC for three weeks each year, except when safety required otherwise. Thus, by 1991 with the FAA arrangement in hand and general agreement that it would incorporated in the new lease, the Association had chosen to stay in New York City.[3]

For the next seven years, the NTC expansion project preoccupied the board. And well, it should have, for it required millions of dollars that were not in the bank. Funding and borrowing threatened to mortgage the Association's future. Markin, a forceful and energetic leader, took on the project, eventually staying on through its completion despite unsuccessful attempts to move him aside. Early on, he proposed speeding up the process by letting the general contractor also act as the project quality-control supervisor—essentially the way Slew Hester had done things. But the board pulled back, set up a politically powerful committee (led by Markin's two immediate successors, already nominated), and accepted a recommendation to engage a separate firm to monitor the construction. An unusual rebuff to a former president. Nonetheless, grand undertakings like the new stadium became highly personal projects for USTA presidents. To a remarkable degree, they exercised personal control over key and more frivolous decisions. There was much ado over the placement and trappings of the president's suite and the color of the court surface, while big-picture items sailed through the board with nary a nay vote.[4]

Politics, petty and otherwise, aside, the project proved a great success. It was not as big a gamble as Hester and the board took in 1977–78, but it was still risky business. Assisted by executive director Marshall Happer, whose legal experience proved invaluable in negotiations with CBS for television rights and with New York City for a lease that included aircraft noise-abatement provisions, both the monies and the legalities were in place. Predictably, some of the sections expressed concern that the costs (estimated at between $100 and $200 million) of a new NTC and stadium would have a negative impact on the Association's ability to fund programs being run by the sections, programs that "are at the heart of its role as the Congressionally-recognized national governing body" of tennis.[5] But revenue projections and data belied that concern. By 1991 broadcast revenues for the U.S. Open alone had reached $30 million. Ticket sales, sponsorship fees, luxury boxes, and assorted revenue during the tournament (e.g., catering, pro shop sales, etc.) would add another $30 million. The financing plan was clean and ambitious:

Capital required: $150 million (it came to some $172 million)
Less sale of rights to purchase luxury suites and box seats: $64 million
Total USTA capital expenses: $86 million

Sources of USTA capital:
USTA reserves: $36 million
USTA revenue excess 1992–94: $30 million
Borrowings (bond issue or other loan): $20 million

The USTA reserve for the new project reached $100 million and the plan was to borrow another $150 million on New York City bonds. The original idea was to permit the USTA to recall the bonds after ten years with the then $25 million annual surplus being created each year.[6] The lease, due to expire in 1993, generated a mini-tempest since discussions came during the 1993 mayoral election in New York City. The droll match-up was David Dinkins, enthusiastic tennis player, and Rudy Giuliani, passionate Yankees (baseball) fan. Political affiliation mattered little; it was mano a mano. It is unlikely that tennis decided the election, although it seemed to some as class warfare. After all, tennis was, in the words of one reporter, "often perceived as a solitary sport played by the already privileged. Baseball, by contrast, is a team sport, dependent on cooperation more than personal brilliance. The red flag raised in this campaign is the red flag of class."[7]

During the campaign, Giuliani accused Dinkins of giving away the store by supporting a lease extension for the National Tennis Center that would give the USTA use of additional acreage for twenty-five years, with an option to stretch it out for a total of ninety-nine years. Giuliani expressed great concern about a clause calling for the city to be fined (by a reduction in USTA fees) if aircraft noise abatement procedures at LaGuardia Airport were not followed during U.S. Open matches. Given the enthusiastic attendance of New Yorkers at the U.S. Open, perhaps an Italian or black American finalist would have decided the election!

Giuliani won, but so did the USTA. To the new mayor's howls of outrage, Dinkins signed the lease after the election and only a few weeks before leaving office. Five years later, in 1997 Giuliani petulantly told the media he would boycott the U.S. Open and the opening dedication of Arthur Ashe Stadium because of Dinkins's deal. But the chickens came home to roost. In 2002 shortly before Giuliani left the mayor's office, he closed a deal for new stadiums for the Mets and Yankees (mainly the Yankees) that required the city to contribute $800 million in tax-exempt bonds while the State had to put up $390 million for transportation infrastructure. All the while, the USTA lease steadily pumped into the city's coffers more than the initially predicted $900,000 cash a year. Moreover, "the city has never paid fines for violations of the flight restriction provisions of the lease." As an Associated Press story put it: "Confronted with the $1 billion estimated cost of the Manhattan stadium that Yankees owner George Steinbrenner wants, the virtue of a $6.75 hamburger becomes clear: Tennis fans, not city taxpayers, are paying for their deluxe new stadium."[8]

The naming of the new stadium for Arthur Ashe, who had died in 1993, came about largely through the insistence of Judy Levering and a small coterie of supporters. In May 1995 the board "determined" that naming rights could be sold with a suggested net of $2 million dollars annually. Then in January 1997 the board unanimously decided on the name "USTA Stadium." That generated public scorn, media criticism, and petitions urging that it be named after Ashe. Just a month later, following a consultant's report and serious lobbying by Levering and others, the board unanimously voted to name it Arthur Ashe Stadium.[9] Under public pressure, the Association chose to forego the short-term revenue, and take the high road—a rarity in the age of stadia with names like Monster Park, Middelfart Stadium (honest—everyone's favorite), and Mitsubishi Forklift Stadion.[10]

The U.S. Open drove the Association in many ways. In December 1987 the entrancing dream of "player development" again popped to the surface. USTA leaders and staff were enthralled by the remarkable success of the young "B-boys"—first Bjorn Borg, then Boris Becker—who won Slams and led their nations to Davis Cup championships as teenagers. If Sweden and Germany could produce such wonderful talent so quickly, certainly the United States could replicate that feat. What could be better for the tournament than great performances by American players, right up to the ultimate—an all-American final in the women's or men's singles? One of the stream of reports generated over the next dozen years bluntly stated, "The ultimate goal is to have more American players winning major international competitions, including the U.S. Open and the Olympics." But it was complicated.[11]

Sports science had become a discipline for tennis players, thanks in good part to the efforts of Dr. Irving Glick who established the USTA's sports science program. Better physical conditioning was a no-brainer. But tennis was much more than just conditioning. The tangible mechanics of winning tennis—stroke production, form, strategy—could all be taught in a classroom and on the court. But what could not be taught were the intangibles, often summed up by words like competitiveness, courage, guts, resiliency, desire. Time and again tennis champions insisted that the only effective way to become a winner was to compete with the best players.

Compare that with a statement by the members of a board subcommittee appointed in 1987 to develop proposals to restructure the Junior Tennis Council—a volunteer body of sectional representatives that controlled junior tennis programs and competition throughout the USTA. The three subcommittee members, two soon-to-be presidents (David Markin and "Bumpy" Frazer) and one staff member (Ron Woods), "agreed that the present junior teams structure would not exist in 1988, but volunteer expertise in junior tennis will always be consulted." Translation. Junior tennis at the competitive level would remain section-focused not talent-centric.[12]

By the 1960s and '70s, college tennis was becoming the major "farm system" for young Americans hoping to become professionals. Often they were more interested in sharpening their skills than earning a degree. Others simply enjoyed the competition and hoped to get a college scholarship. Either way, young high-school stars relied on exposure in USTA national junior championships so as to be noticed by college recruiters and to compete for scholarships—and getting into "The Nationals" required a section's approval. The sections insisted that juniors come through a competitive structure that ensured that each section's top players would be "endorsed" for national championships. Sectional quotas for endorsements were fundamentally determined by the number of junior memberships in each section so that, in one sense, players all across the nation had an equal shot at getting into national championships. But strength of field within a section was not a factor.

In post–World War II America, tennis was often seen by families, who were "the" support system, as the path to a college scholarship, which was a good and proper goal but one that kept young players in their local (sectional) area rather than playing a "national" schedule of the best players (which Jack Kramer had advocated decades earlier). Those sectional endorsements became like gold. But what about sections and regions that routinely turned out larger numbers of highly talented players, creating a pool disproportionate to that section's number of endorsements? When anyone proposed any changes that might lessen the number of endorsements for a section, the reaction was negative—except from those that had large populations and warm sunny skies, and even they were reluctant to go against their fellow sections. So a populist social attitude confronted an elitist goal. National championships had to limit the size of the draws, so if for example the top 20 percent of all players were taken out of their section competition for training and national competition, accommodating some or all of those "national" players in those draws required taking away some endorsements from the sections.

The vaunted European player-development programs had no such conflict. Scholarships were almost irrelevant in societies where university-level education was essentially free. Moreover, taking time off from education to test one's skill in a sport was not disparaged as was the case in the United States. But the fundamental difference was size. Smaller European nations did not have the geographic, demographic, and climatic challenges of the United States. What seemed easy in Sweden was a political challenge for the USTA. Even so, the perspective of time suggests that the smaller nations themselves did not have a magic wand. None stayed dominant for long.

As one director of player development told the Association board, "there is no system that's going to produce world champions."[13]

USTA player-development programs deserve a separate study; unhappily, a study in frustration, except for the role it played in providing a path for effective drug testing and drug-use prevention programs. Generating world-class professional champions was only one of the goals, not *the* goal of the broad player-development concept, yet having Americans as finalists in the U.S. Open became the driving purpose. "Player Development," "High Performance," "Taking Care of Tomorrow," "Project 2000" were all names for the same dream, a dream that did not go away. "Implementation will concentrate on creating a clear, simple pathway for the development of young tennis players," promised one report. Easier said than done. As of 2001 (and 2016, as this is written), only a tiny handful of American finalists at the U.S. Open got there with significant developmental support from any USTA player-development program.[14] The USTA Secondary (Satellite) Circuit program, which began in 1978–79 may well have been the most important development opportunity for young professionals and one of the Association's most important contributions.[15]

By the end of the 1990s, community tennis-development programs, including juniors, remained separate from national player-development plans. Yet, time and again the USTA studied elite-player development; time and again the report would recognize the difficulties—identification of "excellence" required a vast bottom-to-top system of scouting that would have to be built from scratch; and getting top talent opportunities to play each other constantly meant taking them out of the junior competition system, ignoring sectional boundaries and eventually spending large amounts of money to get them together at common sites. Time and again, in one way or another, the USTA family said no—at least up through 2001. The Association could not convince Mom and Grandma that creation of a national or even regional program would help their offspring get that college scholarship—and the sections responded accordingly. (But the dream lives on. In January 2017 the USTA opened a one-hundred-court facility at Lake Nona in Orlando, Florida. To quote executive director Gordon Smith: "'It really doesn't make any sense for the national governing body to be delivering a mission from a glass box in Westchester County,' said Smith, referring to the USTA's home in White Plains, New York. 'We are going to be delivering our mission from a state-of-the-art-facility that will allow us to support and grow the game like never before.'"[16])

Player development was just one of the challenges faced by the new executive director. After just over a year with an acting executive director, in August 1989 the board authorized the president, then Markin, to offer Marshall Happer the executive-director job—with a three-year contract.[17] Happer, whose job as administrator of the Men's International Professional Tennis Council had just disappeared after the ATP won the struggle for control of the men's professional game, was a familiar face who had worked his way up the volunteer ladder before being nominated for USTA treasurer nearly a decade earlier.

Happer's written job description implied that the chief executive officer (CEO) (only once called president in the document) had authority above and before the board. Happer, as chief operating officer (COO), would implement and administer "all USTA policies established by [the] Chief Executive Officer *in concert with the Board of Directors*." "Implement . . . in concert with" made evident the business-management role of the CEO-president, with the COO (also known as executive director) reporting directly to the CEO who was also the chief volunteer (also known as president, chair of the board). Policies and objectives were "established by the Chief Executive Officer [president] and the Board of Directors," but implementation and administration went through the CEO first. Thus the CEO had to be "fully" informed, while reports to the board were to be "timely," "clear," and "concise." Plans and proposals from the COO went to the board but only after being cleared with the CEO. It was an unequivocal declaration of the CEO as the senior *management* officer—a full-time job. Moreover, in the words of one president, what the CEO could not directly manage would be managed by the "operating heads of the USTA at board level," making it impossible for the COO to be a real COO.

But it got tougher for the COO. Not only did board members deal directly with the executive director (sometimes formally, sometimes on their own), but as Happer's predecessors had complained, the job description called for policy establishment and "direction" to come not only from the board, but also from "*volunteer committees.*" Such committees could not be managed by the COO since their appointment (and authority) came directly from the chief volunteer (also known as the president; also known as the CEO). That real but unofficial alternative pathway had grown steadily wider since the 1960s; now it was declared in writing. A policy change established in a job description. So in addition to one crossover manager (the CEO, who was much more than just a supervisor), the COO (also known as executive director) had a nearly limitless number of other "bosses" whose "direction" could focus on everything from the sublime to the ridiculous, restrained only by common sense or the CEO (also known as the president—but you know that by now).[18] Two command pathways had the potential for mischief and great chaos. Imagine a committee chair with stature (i.e., political clout) who disagreed (cautiously, of course, lest one slip down a notch on the ladder) with the president's policies. The executive director gets instructed by the CEO (that's the president, remember?) while the committee chair pushes the executive director to follow a different policy. A scenario for political warfare, and a COO-executive director caught between Scylla and Charybdis (though Scylla was the heavyweight).

Nonetheless, with Happer's appointment as executive director, the position stabilized. Happer and his immediate successor, Rick Ferman, each lasted five to seven years. They would leave for differing reasons, but their departures did not indicate an overriding and deliberative agreement by the board of directors to limit the executive director's authority. In fact, the ever-increasing size (financial and membership) of the Association indirectly gave the executive director a greater *effective* reach, as did expansion of the size and salaries of USTA staff, just as the McKinsey reports had recommended . . . except for one obvious exception. The president-CEO-board chair (all one person) remained a volunteer; legally responsible to the membership, but in a way that defied effective accountability. The executive director's job came to include representing the Association at international meetings (Davis and Federation Cup, ITF, and the Olympics), yet the president led the delegations. Presidents could and did bypass the executive director and deal directly with senior staff, even though they officially worked for the COO (executive director). The 1985 McKinsey report expressed serious concern that "without reassigning the presidential title . . . the Chairman and the USTA's other top officers will *continue* to become mired down in day-to-day operating decisions." The "symbolism" of the title remained firmly in place.[19] Presidents routinely did what they wanted to do, often paying only lip service to inputs from within the Association.

Envisage a $300 million business where the board chairman-chief executive officer-president changes every two years, with each change an opportunity to launch a new, high-impact "legacy" program that has to be institutionalized in just twenty-four months, effectively establishing a two-year business-plan cycle. By the 1990s most every new USTA president presented the annual meeting with such a signature effort. Many made good sense; some achieved the stated goals. *But all were presidential initiatives, not efforts already institutionalized in the Association's strategic plan*. That pattern was behind the implied concern in all the reports provided by consultants like McKinsey and Company. One president, Les

Snyder, as he began his second year as president, gently mocked what he had done a year earlier. He suggested to the annual meeting that they "reflect on our progress and perhaps take a brief look at where we have been. No "Up With People. No acronyms." (The two-year initiatives were invariably expressed in entertainment form with slogans, preferably catchy acronyms.) In 1994 the ad hoc Governance and Planning Committee (GAP), concerned about lurching from one two-year regime to the next, as well as the politics of "climbing the volunteer ladder," recommended something similar to the 1985 McKinsey report proposals—separate the volunteer chairman of the board and the president, with the latter a full-time paid CEO and "officer" whose term was longer than the two-year terms for the board of directors. The establishment of the Association's first strategic plan in 1996 aimed at stretching things out further, but checks and balances on the president remained nominal—until the sections became concerned about centralization.[20]

Centralization of authority and power is a dynamic dilemma. Is efficiency improved by a process that, for governance issues, marginalizes all but the very top officials? At the same time, governance is a dynamic dilemma. Where would the USTA be without the vision and persistence of James Dwight? Without the courage and imagination of Slew Hester? Without Bob Kelleher? Without the personal commitment and energy of Holcombe Ward and Alastair Martin and David Markin? But also where without the acumen and dedication of various senior staff and executive directors? The growing size of the Association and its budget suggested that full-time professionals were needed, but time and again the volunteer leaders vetoed what the consultants proposed.

Happer's departure came when he butted heads with the new USTA president, Les Snyder. Snyder's initial board meeting in January 1995 was extraordinary. He bypassed Happer and set up study groups of senior staff that dealt directly with the board of directors. The executive director's only participation in the meeting concerned contracts and routine administrative details. Whatever the president's intent, the minutes show that he isolated the executive director—ironically the very person who had "concentrated" the USTA largely in one location, partly as a way to gain control over the long-standing senior staff.[21] Partway through the meeting Happer left without explanation. The minutes for board meetings thereafter show Happer giving routine reports, but otherwise unengaged.

A few months later, after Snyder requested Happer to provide copies of his job descriptions, Happer complied but included a caustic memo. He pointed out that his "actual authority" for USTA operations had been tightly limited from the outset, although that "would not necessarily be apparent from a reading of the Job Description or the USTA Bylaws." Not surprisingly, on August 3, 1995, the president told Happer that the board agreed it was time to find a "new manager." Happer immediately resigned, but stayed on until 2009 as an outside special legal counsel, negotiating and drafting major contracts related to the USTA, the U.S. Open, Federation and Davis Cup events, and sponsors.[22]

Not long after Happer's resignation, *Tennis Week* magazine devoted much of its October 19 issue to a look at what happened and why. One article, "The White Plains Incident," rode on revealing quotes from two past presidents: one from Judge Kelleher who flatly stated that "from the time Marshall Happer came in, no president ever gave him the authority to shine his own shoes on Association property." The other from David Markin: "Personally he [Happer] is a very likeable guy, but the case fell on his inability to establish rapport with both senior members of his staff and the *operating heads of the USTA at board level*" (emphasis added). Governance and operations intertwined. A second article, "Time to Reform the USTA," adopted the mantra of the McKinsey reports, calling for reversing "the powers of the president and executive director," adding that a strong professional CEO would help correct morale problems, as would a management structure that prevented "end runs" around the CEO by board members. "In an objective sense, the USTA's volunteer overseers are a nonprofessional tail wagging a professional dog."[23]

Whatever Snyder's purposes, the underlying question was whether or not the USTA could and remain a volunteer-driven organization while having an empowered professional staff. It was not who was right and who was wrong, but who was in charge? Who decides? A question that awaited the late 1990s.

Snyder seems to have recognized the dilemma. His "inverted-U" concept, however ineptly explained, illustrated the ongoing search for a balance between volunteer "ownership" through the sections, and efficient professional staff efforts at the operational level. Clearly Snyder did not believe volunteers should be restricted to policy-based governance. Rather, he told the executive committee in September 1996:

> I know this seemed like an odd concept at first, with volunteers on one side reporting to the President, while the professional staff is on the other side reporting to the Executive Director. We have had some trouble from time to time differentiating roles, the role of policy maker and overseer, and the role of implementer and deliv-

> erer have often been blurred. We have staff and we must let them implement and we have volunteers and we must structure ourselves so that the owners, the volunteers provide clear directions and policies. We quickly learned that the owners must be totally involved, also, in overseeing the operation, which is a type of quality control.

Hence the "inverted U."[24]

Starting in the 1960s, the Association had become increasingly fascinated with planning and restructuring. The 1990s brought that impulse into action, culminating with Rick Ferman, the man-with-a-plan, as executive director. Both Ferman and his predecessor, Marshall Happer, turned the USTA into a model of self-study. Ferman meticulously collected earlier materials, so his files are jammed with studies, reports, and proposals, particularly about USTA governance, although tennis programs generated their fair share. The expansion of the National Tennis Center into what eventually became Arthur Ashe Stadium and later, the USTA Billie Jean King National Tennis Center held the attention of Association leadership throughout the seven-year-planning-and-building process from 1991 to 1999, but governance and organizational concerns would not go away. There was a striking consistency in what Happer, Ferman, and their USTA "bosses" discussed and proposed.

The USTA wished to bring all the sections under the same tent. Just as James Dwight and the founding fathers sought to establish consistent rules for lawn tennis, so the Association wanted to establish consistent sectional procedures for governance and for the delivery of tennis programs. By 1976 the bylaws stated that sections could make rules and regulations so long as they would "not be inconsistent" with those of the USTA. In the 1996 bylaws, that changed requiring that sections govern "in accordance with" the USTA's governing documents and that "the governing documents of each Sectional Association shall be subject to review and approval by the Board" to ensure their consistency with those of the national Association. Any sanctions imposed by the board could be appealed to an annual or special meeting, and those sanctions were stayed until the "membership" (i.e., the annual meeting) ruled on the appeal. As of 2015, that bylaw remains the same.

One tactic for herding the sections was money. By 1981 sections were asked to report back to national on how they used an eight-thousand-dollar flat grant, earmarked for office and administrative purposes. In 1986 a committee to examine programmatic funding to sections was appointed. The committee was "charged with studying if the existing basis for distributing funds to the Sections is adequate to achieve goals, is sensitive to the variation in conditions among the Sections, and is based upon sound philosophy." Whatever that study concluded, it could well have signaled the beginning of the *great divide*—who knows best, the national Association or the sections which ostensibly represent the local folks (i.e., local tennis organizations)?[25] As of the end of the century, the Association had persuaded the sections to let a portion of the sectional grant be determined by performance-based incentive funding (PBIF). There were constant negotiations and arguments over the performance standards, and impassioned pleas for an overall larger slice of the pie, but the concept was firmly in place.

By the 1980s, the number of Association tennis programs had grown exponentially. Efficient delivery of those programs to the "grassroots" (a hackneyed but favorite leadership phrase) had to come through the sections. That required more professional staff. But where should that staff be placed? Nationally, at the sectional level, or in the community? Who would pay the costs? Who would set goals and objectives, supervise, and assess the performance of the additional staff? Prompted by a parade of reports from consultants, the USTA sought to improve its ability to expand both tennis and membership by reforming its governance and organizational structure. The sections, arguing that they were the true and effective delivery vehicle for tennis, saw less need for reform. In 1988 a report suggested that "strong district associations based on state boundaries should gradually replace the sections" and that the sections should be replaced by four to six "regional coordinating areas." That gained no traction—then. At the same time, the board pressured the sections for increased accountability, requiring that they submit "audited, accrual-based financial statements" in order to get the general-purpose grants—a requirement to be "enforced without exception."[26]

A special meeting of the membership came in November 1993 when the Georgia Tennis Association (one of nine state associations in the Southern Section) tried to purchase school memberships that would give Georgia nearly 53 percent of the voting strength within the section. If the other eight states did the same, then Southern's percentage of the USTA voting strength would jump from 19.4 percent to 32.2 percent. Indirectly the meeting related to a proposal from Georgia requesting status as a separate section—a problem growing out of the disproportionate power of Atlanta, a hot bed of tennis and league play, within the Georgia district. Georgia stayed in the Southern section, and the USTA adopted rules that prevented bulk purchasing of memberships. But there is no small irony in suppression of an attempt by a state to become a section, whatever the motives, just as talk about aligning state and sectional boundaries began to heat up.[27]

The GAP committee put on the call of the 1994 annual meeting a series of bylaw changes that hinted at increasing concern among the sections that national leadership had a tin ear—it seemed not to hear what the sections, the "owners," wanted. It is difficult to define just what the sections wanted, although the initial recommendations of the just formalized Sectional Presidents Committee offered some indications. The presidents' purpose, they wrote, was twofold—to exchange information and to communicate sectional "needs, concerns and hopes" to the USTA board. The obvious inference was that those "needs, concerns and hopes" were not recognized by the national leadership. It was a shot across the bow of the board and national staff.[28]

The GAP proposals presaged a shift in the dynamic between the sections and the national USTA, although no one seems to have sensed that at the time. The annual meeting agreed to eliminate regional vice presidents, substituting eight at-large members—no two from the same section; the nominating committee was enlarged, despite the committee's opposition, from nine to eleven members—again with a no two from the same section requirement. Both moves aimed at increasing sectional representation—a wish as old as the creation of organized sections just after the First World War. Perhaps the most powerful forewarning was overwhelming defeat of a proposal to eliminate the formal status of the Sectional Presidents Committee. The GAP proposed that the USTA executive committee act as the arbiter and balance weight between the sections and the USTA board, but nothing in the call at the 1994 annual meeting would have implemented that approach. GAP recognized the role of the sections in the governance process and assumed that the sections "owned" the Association, should they exercise that authority.

Following the partial success of its initial recommendations, the GAP committee took up proposals to adjust sectional boundaries but could not agree on specifics beyond recommending a lengthy, complex procedure for making realignment proposals. It was obviously too hot to handle. But where the rubber met the road was in a final recommendation. After pointing out that whether the sections "owned" the Association, or vice-versa, the relationship was not defined, it stated: "These recommendations will not define that relationship, but *will make clear that sections are administrative and political subdivisions of [the] USTA*."[29] Someone later commented that executive director Rick Ferman was forced to resign after "he went to war with the sections." That missed this earlier challenge from the GAP committee. In an understated coda, the committee plaintively reminded the executive committee, "we still think that the issue of sectional realignment should be maintained as a continuing issue." No one listened—then.[30]

Adding to the pressure for reform, some expressed concern that a handful of large sections (e.g., Southern, Eastern, and Western/Midwest) could control the annual meeting and hence the entire USTA, prompting a bylaw change. The second GAP report again proposed that the USTA executive committee act as the arbiter and balance weight between the sections and the USTA board, but the nothing came of that idea. Nevertheless, the concept was recognition of a growing disconnect between national and sectional. In fact, common use of the designation "national" to mean the USTA headquarters and leadership suggests that the USTA "family" was coming to view itself as a house divided.[31]

Ultimately the second set of GAP proposals had to be boiled down to three—a mere shadow of its former robust recommendations: 1. To establish concurrent voting by the Executive Committee on all issues except elections; 2. To define the relationship between USTA and the Sections; and 3. To adopt a procedure by which requests for Sectional boundary changes or new Sectional status can be reviewed "in an orderly and timely fashion by all interested parties and a decision rendered." Even just those three items did not make the "call" for the 1995 annual meeting.[32]

Realigning the boundaries of the seventeen sections had long been bruited about. They had developed organically and historically, not logically. Population, weather, and sheer physical size differentiated where and how the game could be played and grow. Hawaii-Pacific was tiny and distant; Southern, composed of nine states (even after Florida became a section), was huge. Intermountain ranged from the Canadian border to southern Nevada, much of it sparsely populated. California was divided in half—following historic habits. Texas was Texas (minus El Paso). The Northeast, the cradle of lawn tennis in the United States, made more sense; four sections of roughly equal size, each with a major metropolitan center. Much the same for the mid-western sections. Prior to open tennis and the U.S. Open, the stakes were too low to prompt serious change. One possibility came with creation in 1938 of four "regions"—North Atlantic, Southern, Central, and Pacific—but that was notional, never part of the governance structure.[33]

Sectional-state alignment. Shorthand for precisely what? A realignment of the sectional boundaries so as to make them "more equal in size and demographics?" A reestablishment of something analogous to the old "regions"? Such regional centers could help support and/or deliver USTA tennis programs and "grow the game," inferring that sections could not do that effectively? Recognition of state boundaries as historic and functional and, therefore, the best way to organize governance and delivery below the national level? Or, all of the above mixed together? Ferman's focus was on improving and localizing delivery of services, that it was not a governance matter. But others felt differently.

The Owners

Somewhere along the line, Association leaders came to view the sections as the "owners," the stockholders, to whom the USTA was responsible. That would have been incomprehensible to James Dwight and the founders, but by 1917 representatives from the West were demanding that the Association give their regions a greater role in governance or they would secede.

The sections became integral to the Association's structure in 1920, when the USNLTA formally required clubs to organize within specific geographic sections. However, integral did not automatically translate into ownership or even influence.

When a contretemps arose in the Eastern Section in the early thirties (see chapter 3), Association president Louis Carruthers firmly asserted that the authority of the sections derived from what powers the Association chose to delegate. "Ownership" as a concept remained largely undiscussed for some fifty years. But the political and, therefore, governance influence of the sections grew—sometimes quietly, sometimes noisily, but always steadily.

In the aftermath of the state-alignment battle over decentralization, the USTA League Committee attempted to discipline the Northern California Section. Mike Mee (a board officer from Northern California, 2001–2) offered a straightforward assertion: "There is no doubt who owns the USTA. The answer is patently clear in the USTA Constitutional and Bylaws. *The USTA is a subsidiary corporation which is owned lock, stock and barrel by its seventeen parent corporations* [i.e., the sections]." After all, he pointed out, the sections can amend the constitution and bylaws. Coming in the immediate aftermath of the state-alignment battle, the message was clear—the sections and decentralization had won out . . . this time around.[34]

The politics of such reforms were forbidding. However much the sections were focused on local matters and their USTA grants and funding, the thrust of any definition of state alignment required the sections to change significantly and uncomfortably. Not only would historic boundaries shift, but longstanding personal connections would be broken. Business efficiency and "growing the game" (the shorthand version of the USTA mission "to promote and develop the growth of tennis") were the reasons for such changes; certainly no one argued that the existing governance and delivery structure made sense. Similar arguments have been made since 1787 about the U. S. Senate (two votes for each state regardless of population), but to no avail. The sections believed they had been and would continue to be good stewards of lawn tennis in America. Any of the meanings of state alignment seemed to shift sectional clout away from existing large sections (Southern, Southern California, Midwest, et al.) and toward smaller and hence either more pliable sections, or ones closer to the "consumer" as Ferman presented it. No one openly questioned the logic of growing USTA insistence on accountability for use of grants to sections—that had been building for decades. But just how that was to be done invariably worried sectional leaders. But most of all, the "ownership" of the USTA by its sections seemed threatened. In a quite nonpartisan way, growing sectional discontent was analogous to the never-ending national debate in the United States over the nature of our federal republic: big central government and its promised efficiencies of scale versus more local control with all the confusion and contradictions that went with it. The USTA dynamic was a bit different in that true volunteers played a huge role in moving toward mission accomplishment, but as the debate became more vigorous it often took on the tone of volunteers versus professional staff.

But all that is a bit premature. First came the departure of Marshall Happer and the arrival of Rick Ferman.

The finalists for the job of executive director in 1996 reflected the "who are we" question that Snyder had awkwardly raised. Bob Garry, the chief financial officer, was a long-time senior staff professional who had interviewed before for the executive director position and been acting executive director upon occasion. Rick Ferman, who had been a college tennis player, was a teaching professional and club owner, and coach of a top-ten player (Todd Martin). He had climbed the volunteer ladder, been president of the Midwest (then Western) Section and was nominated a USTA vice president in 1995. Put in overly stark terms, the choice seemed between a full-time professional staff person, and a candidate from the volunteer ranks.

Whatever the other factors involved in the selection of Ferman, it had the appearance of volunteers over professional staff. A comforting decision for the sections and, presumably, for the top national leadership. But, as it turned out, Ferman was committed to a businesslike restructuring of the Association so as to make it better able to deliver tennis programs throughout the United States. That resonated with a number of members of the USTA board, including two who would become president—Judy Levering and Alan Schwartz. The issues were clear: efficient delivery of programs, distribution of money and support to the sections, and "who decides?"

At the January 1996 meeting of the board, Ferman was offered the executive director position, though it took over a month to work out the contract. No details of the job description or of the contract were given in the board minutes. Nor, it seems, did the media pick up on the appointment.[35]

Ferman's presence energized the board, or at least the board minutes. At his first meeting as executive director in March, his agenda of reports kept the board busy with more information than previous minutes recorded for entire meetings. His report had twenty headings, from IHRSA (International Health, Racquet and Sportsclub Association) to marketing of luxury suites at Arthur Ashe stadium, and everything in between. It was a tour de force.

A small ripple, one that would become a tsunami, appeared at the May meeting of the board. Ferman had distributed a vision statement as to where he envisaged where the USTA would be by 2006. Sent to the board, the executive committee, the sections, USTA committee chairs, and the staff, the comments Ferman had received were supportive. Yet, despite the fact that he had just recently been through a series of interviews before being hired, the think piece apparently caught a number of board members unawares. They asked that it not be sent out to the media, then said they would discuss it at a later meeting. Likewise his proposals for a staff reorganization. Why the concern? Staff reorganization could well have been uncomfortable for board members with long standing staff connections (as Happer had ruefully found out). But the vision statement, optimistic and forward looking, spoke to some familiar and comfortable possibilities—"strategic alliances" with other national and international tennis and sports organizations, the routine rhetoric about player development, enhancement of the U.S. Open, "getting closer to the customer" (players and spectators) by creating local tennis organizations. Nothing to raise concerns.

Governance was the fly in the ointment. The most striking and, surely for the board, disturbing statement was that "the primary focus of the Board of Directors will become the creation of policies, goals and priorities"—policy-based governance. A prediction followed that there would (hence should) be a "full-time professional President and CEO." These were highly charged, emotional issues, and a far cry from Snyder's inverted-U, Markin's description of "operating heads of the USTA at board level," or the reasons for repeated rejections of similar proposals in the McKinsey reports. That, followed by suggesting that "standing committees will be streamlined, focused and coordinated with specific USTA staff efforts, objectives, goals and actions plans," drew a line in the sand. Obviously, staff would be in charge. What Ferman and his leadership sponsors envisaged was a significant change in the role of volunteers, and not just at the national level. In language reminiscent of Louis Dailey, Association president in 1930, Ferman predicted "decentralization" in a way that would empower volunteers at the grassroots: "The Association's professional management team will become increasingly results-oriented and accountable. Expert volunteers will supplement the management team and association staff efforts." Middle management would be "realigned" by consolidating the sections "into regional service centers" that would be "drawn along existing state lines."[36] It was a call for the Association's transformation!

At the outset of the vision statement, Ferman cautioned that the Association had "to commit itself to high levels of integrity, trust, creativity and sense of mission." Appealing for integrity and trust betrayed a sense of unease. Part of that related to relationships with other organizations, but it also spoke to a concern that internal politics posed a challenge and that trust within the USTA was lacking. He warned that developing trust will take "time and great patience." How right he was.

If the "later discussions" the board called for ever occurred, they seem to have taken place outside of board meetings.

Ferman's vision statement should not have come as a surprise. Not only did it build on the long train of strategic planning and consultants' reports on management, but in an earlier form it had provided grist for the GAP mill. In June 1993 Ferman and "Skip" Hartman (active in various youth tennis programs in New York) had sent the GAP a paper that suggested most of what later seemed to put much of the board on edge. The most strident emphasis, one that Ferman would endorse throughout his tenure as executive director, was turning "tennis over to the [local] communities, and state tennis associations." The sections simply disappeared. Little wonder that those suggestions, some of which underpinned the GAP recommendations, never made it onto the call of the annual meeting. The purpose was not to eliminate the sections; elimination was rather a byproduct of the creation of "six fairly balanced regional service areas" that could deliver programs and resources from the USTA and help create local and community tennis associations. The sections thought that such was exactly what they were doing, and doing well—just send us the resources.[37]

The Self-Study Solution

This is a small sampling of the long list of reports and studies on just governance (all from the USTA Archive; particularly in box 3523). There are dozens more in the archive, plus a large collection on the multitude of tennis programs generated during the 1990s. The key date was, of course, January 18, 1999, when the charrette was conducted. See also the endnotes:

William J. Pade (McKinsey & Co.), "USTA Delivery and Governance Structure Study Overview, n.d. (ca. 1998?)

Lewis Hartman and Richard D. Ferman, "A Proposal submitted to the USTA Governance and Planning Committee, n.d. (ca. June 8, 1993).

"Second Report of the Recommendations of the Governance and Planning Committee to the Board of Directors," August 1994 (doc. # 2218, box 3523).

Richard D. Ferman, "A Vision of Tennis for the Next Decade," May 16, 1996 (doc. #104, box 2469).

Coopers & Lybrand, "USTA Five Year Strategic Plan," January 1997

Long Range Planning Committee, "Preliminary Report Concerning Sectional Realignment," March 1998 (doc. #111, box 2469).

"USTA Long Range Planning Committee Preliminary Reports," for the USTA Annual Meeting, March 27–April 2, 1998.

USTA Long Range Planning Committee, "Report and Recommendations: USTA Divisions, Division Councils, and Committees," July 1998 (box 3523).

McKinsey and Co., "Summary of Charrette Proceedings, Dallas, TX, 08–10 Jan. 1999" (February 5, 1999)

"Business Plan for Forming State Associations," March 5, 1999 (doc. #102, box 2468), and Levering files, container 7015.

McKinsey and Co., confidential memorandum for Judy Levering and Michael Ainslie, "Strengthening the National Leadership Structure," June 1, 1999 (box 3523).

"Financial Review of Transition Plan: Analysis of Financial Impact of Implementing the Plan," USTA Board of Directors Meeting, September 3, 1999.

Twice in the Association's history secession was contemplated, or at least threatened by the sections. In 1910 Phillip Hawk asked for a "square deal" and warned that the fastest growing regions, the west and the south, would "split" from the Association unless they got what they considered fair treatment. Then, in 1917 Harry Waidner, speaking of the Northeast's control of the Association, warned that the "West won't stand for it."[38] The Association got the message and carefully nurtured good relationships with the sections thereafter. It was more than a tradition, it was a consistent, conscious practice.

Although Ferman's vision statement went off the radar, it was replicated in a flurry of planning by various staff offices and volunteer committees. Those plans and reports and memoranda all hewed to the line set out in the vision statement. What he had suggested clearly had support from board leadership. In fact, state-alignment and governance reform were old refrains, particularly the latter, which came up in the late 1960s when the Association decided not to hire a tennis czar.[39] The vision statement set the agenda for pre- and post-charrette study groups on state alignment and national governance.

In March 1998, the Long Range Planning Committee (chaired by Merv Heller) concluded that "sectional realignment involving the creation of many more new sections in the form of standalone state organizations would be good for the USTA." It warned that existing sections would have to "recognize and accept the benefits" and that "significant incentives" were needed to get sectional support.[40] The committee had a "strong belief" (as opposed to unanimous belief—there were negative opinions) for the chairman's proposal to hold a "gathering of the USTA community" to build a broad-based consensus. That charrette was the byproduct of all the initiatives and plans, boiled down to four overlapping goals: more efficient and effective delivery of programs (six regional service centers); national control and accountability of and for staff and resources at service centers and in the sections (PBIF); elimination of dysfunctional (or less functional) strong sections, a handful of which could frustrate and/or block national plans and decisions—to be accomplished by "transitioning" (state alignment, i.e., replace sections with state units); and restructuring of national governance to put professional staff in charge of operations (reverse roles and titles of CEO-president and executive director). That would culminate in a grand charrette, a populist exercise aimed at demonstrating broad support for proposed reforms. USTA leadership expected such a gathering would endorse changes that would promote its mission to "grow the game."

President Levering and the board agreed and set about planning the gathering, calling on McKinsey and Company to put it all together. The charrette took place on January 8–10, 1999, in Dallas, Texas. Some 120 USTA volunteers attended, plus the seventeen section executive directors—the national and section leadership cadre. The questions, prepared by the consultants, and the break-out comments focused on the issues posed in the vision statement. As the three-day process went on, cynicism appeared, with some attendees guessing as to what the "right" answer would be to various questions. To many it seemed a public-relations gimmick rather than an attempt to take the temperature of the volunteers.

But take their temperature it did, though that did not come through in the summary report. The raw numbers generated by the questions seemed to support state alignment and governance reforms. But the broad overall impact of the proposals did not come through in the disparate, focused queries. To a great degree, the questions focused on soft generalities: e.g., "Is there sufficient benefit to encourage state alignment at either the section or district level?" That vague query got a 75 percent yes vote—"encourage" is a lovely, gentle word. Ninety-seven percent of voters believed program execution and delivery should be an immediate focus; only "Mother" or "The Fourth of July" could have gotten a higher percentage. One section president wrote that "using the same statistics" one could easily make case for keeping "sectional structure unchanged," spending less on national administration and marketing, and increasing the funds sent to "the grass roots level."[41] Nowhere were unintended consequences assessed or even presented. When state alignment was discussed it was always in the future—three or four years away. A memo from the president included in the charrette summary stated that she "was especially impressed with your overwhelming view (93%) that changes need to be made in our governance and delivery structure." That overwhelming support would soon founder on the shoals of the details—where the devil lies.[42]

Most of the reforms proposed by the vision statement and presented to the charrette, were soon rejected, rejected in a forceful, even angry way that had never happened before in the Association's history. Why?

The basic issues at stake were centralization and governance. As the national Association demanded accountability for grants and other monies sent to sections (that is, PBIF), sections had agreed with the concept but pushed back saying the assessment criteria were unfair, the pot of money was too small, and besides, we're the best judge of what's going on in our section. That concern was reinforced by the national Association's insistence that it should control support personnel, provided by USTA funds, in the six new "regions" that would be established—hiring and firing, supervision, performance assessments, job descriptions, in the field or in the office, and so on. The sections responded—that's what we do, and we live here. As for governance, the sections cared less about the national structure than about keeping their political leverage so as to prevent national from ignoring sectional needs and desires. Fifty or so states-as-sections would weaken their overall influence, leaving the national Association to do as it thought best. No one challenged critical need to grow the U.S. Open and to run it almost as a separate business; but were sections able to get their fair share? Was National more concerned about the Open and international tennis than the grassroots? Would/could local community tennis associations fill the gap between six regions and the fifty-odd and fifty oddly shaped and populated states?[43] (See gallery, image 25.)

Following the charrette, the board set up six study groups to analyze the results, the two most crucial being for state alignment and national governance. The state-alignment group's initial report admitted that sections would lose some autonomy, but in May 1999 asked the board to endorse its recommendations: establish an efficient delivery structure for programs, that is, regional service centers; "transition" from section to state associations; increase program-delivery staff (USTA employees at regional service centers); get community tennis associations involved in "state" governance. The report argued that a change to many more state associations and fewer (none at all?) sections would increase a sense of ownership and provide more opportunities for volunteers. The recommendations seemed to go way beyond just state alignment, a recognition that such alignment was necessary for the overall reforms.[44]

By July 17, those study groups had made enough progress for the board to endorse the state-alignment recommendations and implementation of pilot programs and to develop plans for "shared service centers." Left for further study was a recommendation that "all USTA staff become employees of national," delayed so as to take steps to make sure "that volunteer roles remain meaningful." In other words, full speed ahead making the transition from sections to state associations; get the service centers up and running; and cool your jets on the national office managing all USTA staff (even down to the state association level) as that might make the natives restless. On July 20, Levering and her first vice president, Merv Heller, forwarded to the USTA sections and committees the board resolutions calling for state alignment to "strengthen delivery effectiveness of programs and administration." (See box "Board Resolution of July 19, 1999.") Even though pilot programs were proposed, clearly state alignment was the top priority.[45]

The national leadership made a major push to persuade the sections that they would benefit from centralization. The chair of the state-alignment group, Barbara Smith, made Herculean efforts to convince the Southern Section, hefting an eighteen-page set of briefing notes. But to no avail. The largest and arguably best-performing section unanimously rejected the USTA's state alignment transition plan, which was based on an even heftier seventy-five-page McKinsey draft. That report called for USTA staff in the six regions to "ensure that state associations collaborate closely with National." Success depended on good communications and providing high-quality service and "the willingness of states to cede activities that they currently perform." (Clearly the word "sections" should replace "states" in the preceding quotation. The garbled phrasing suggests that McKinsey and Company did not quite grasp the nuances of how the USTA operated.) Such candor was not repeated in the USTA business plan, but the intent was the same. States as sections would vote on major national issues, wrote the consultants, but the key was acceptance of new governance principles—moving away from "managing the association to setting policy and supporting programs." In other words, raising and donating funds and thinking big. The president of the Southern Section, Randy Stephens, reacted bitingly: "Rather than continuing on a divisive course and spending valuable dollars that could better be spent within our existing structure, let's move forward into the new millennium united in our sport."[46]

The other key study group, the one on national governance, moved in much the same direction suggested by the string of reports from McKinsey, backed up by another consultant, Cooper Lybrands. Smart, perceptive volunteers, recruited to those groups after the charrette, endorsed and re-endorsed the concepts behind a policy-based governance system where the chief volunteer was not the CEO. One comment was that change had to mean change of function, not just title, which may have underestimated the emotional power of the title "President of the USTA." The governance study group (the name of which kept changing, ending as the "National Board/Senior Leadership Issues Study Group") dug deep into the details and offered all sorts of wiring diagrams about how real and perceived authority and liaison ought to work, but the fundamental goal never changed—"Our committee is in favor of a paid, full-time CEO."[47]

Until . . . on August 3 President Judy Levering sent a letter to Alan Schwartz, the chair of the governance study group: "In view of the fact that the association is owned by the volunteers I, at this point in time, do not feel it wise to turn over the title of CEO to staff." She suggested that it was merely a matter of titles, and they could achieve their goals without changing them and the bylaws. The key change advocated by the governance study group had been negated. After all, this was the USTA and presidents mattered.

The summary report given by Schwartz at the semiannual meeting on September 10 was a pale shadow of its original form, coming at Levering's strong urging that there be a "watered down" version so that "something could be salvaged from the charrette." The governance study group had wanted to make the change from a volunteer-managed organization to a professionally managed association. Schwartz, who came out of the business side of tennis, firmly believed that was the best way to go. So did the full array of consultants' reports, ever since 1969. But as before, whenever that choice made it to the level of yes or no, USTA presidents said "No!" We must assume Levering meant exactly what she wrote, although growing opposition to state alignment apparently prompted her to conclude that only one big change (state alignment) was all they could hope to get adopted—and state alignment was the key reform. Either way, the USTA president remained CEO, chair of the board, chair of the U.S. Open committee, and the manager of everything. Ferman sensed the issue at hand. Later, after state alignment was withdrawn, he tried to move on, telling the executive committee, "communication is very important to our success and the question is always what do you think instead of who decides."[48] Not really, though perhaps it should be.

The state-alignment "crisis" sprang from an honest conviction on the part of the USTA leadership that the Association needed to adopt better business practices. Calls for an empowered professional staff made sense for a huge business, particularly one that depended on its one golden-egg-laying goose—the U.S. Open—for its revenue. But history and tradition are not easily dismissed, particularly when the changes are extensive and disruptive. When the president of the Southern Section mocked McKinsey for its "tweaking" strategy (a company manual pointed out that "you can 'tweak' your way to your optimum over time") he likely referred to the self-aggrandizing business practices of consultants. But the McKinsey folks were correct. Yet they (and the USTA leadership) failed to follow their own tactics. The so-called transition of sections into state associations (i.e., elimination of sections), creation of a national staff structure (regional service centers) in place of the sections, putting paid professionals in charge of management and operations (nationally and, presumably, at the state association level), and rethinking the role of volunteers in the Association were not "tweaks," they were fundamental sea changes. As a single, all at once package, they never had a chance.

Whether or not the sections owned the USTA, they had the constitutional authority to stop the music if and when they stood together. And together they were. An undated spreadsheet showed the count sometime in late August, early September: seven sections were opposed (including Eastern, Midwest, Southern and Northern California, and Texas). Overwhelming opposition. With five of the largest sections in opposition, state alignment was dead in the water.[49] National governance structure reform was collateral damage. The concept of a professional, full-time CEO may have made sense. But the executive director, Rick Ferman, had become the lightning rod for discontent, for opposition to centralization. Until he left (as he did, though not until January 2003), changing national governance structure was off the table.[50]

The three resolutions confronted at the executive session of the board on September 8 comprised a dramatic turn of events. For thirty years, McKinsey, acting as consultants, had pushed the USTA towards a business model that called for the executive director to have the titles and authority that the president of most corporations possessed. Implicitly and sometimes explicitly, that included a tightening of control by the national body for efficiency in delivering programs to the public. Four major reports and a number of papers repeated the same basic recommendations, however camouflaged by different wording. Responding to the piles of reports from long-range planning and ad hoc committees, the Association leadership routinely agreed with the concepts but pulled back implementation. Why? Partly from concern about alienating its volunteer base, partly because top leadership did not wish to be replaced by what one president called "a hired gun." No one (or at least no one influential) seems to have pointed out that asking the sections to do away with themselves would be like asking the U.S. Senate to conclude, and change, the seeming absurdity that two senators from Wyoming (population 600,000) have the same voting strength as two from California (38.3 million).

The seventeen sections, each represented by its president and its sectional delegate, met and voted "20 for, 12 against, with 2 abstentions," for a blunt resolution: "The Sectional Presidents and Delegates request the USTA Board of Directors to rescind their resolution of July 17, 1999." Six sections—Florida, Northern, Middle States, Missouri Valley, Southwest, Mid-Atlantic—opposed the resolution, Intermountain abstained, all others voted in favor. By a vote of 32–2, a vague amendment that hinted at a lack of consultation with the sections also requested the board "to continue investigations, including sectional involvement, as stated in the document they presented at the joint meeting of Sectional Presidents and Delegates on September 4, 1999." That "document," was the same board resolution of July 17, two months before, which firmly endorsed state alignment and likely establishment of a centralized, unified national staff (after a ensuring effective volunteer roles).

Board Resolution of July 17, 1999

The mission of the USTA is to promote and develop the growth of tennis. The USTA believes that to advance its mission:

1) it is necessary to increase the program resources and marketing effectiveness of the USTA.
2) it is necessary to improve the efficiency and effectiveness of administrative functions of the USTA and by aligning along state boundaries the USTA will strengthen delivery effectiveness of programs and administration.
3) The Board of Directors further endorses the implementation of pilot programs as well as the establishment of leadership teams as set forth in the report of McKinsey and Company dated July 15, 1999.

The Board of Directors has reserved recommendation on the concept that all USTA staff become employees of national but would recommend that the pilot projects be so aligned to permit further evaluation ensuring that volunteer roles remain meaningful in the USTA.

The Board of Directors endorses and approves the concept of a shared service center and implementation of regional support staff and directs the executive director to prepare a comprehensive operating plan for Board consideration.[51]

Anticipating the sectional resolution, the board had tried on September 3 to make a silk purse out of a sow's ear by committing to platitudes: all offered with soft words like "investigate" and "encourage," replacing the strong endorsement of "unified national staff" and of state alignment—perhaps better called the elimination of powerful sections. But it backed off:

> Many Sections have expressed disagreement with changing the Section governance structure. The Board has heard that concern. As a result, the Board has unanimously agreed to remove all consideration of changes to the Section governance structure and any requirement for a unified national staff.[52]

The sections acknowledged that about face, amended their motion so as to support continued "investigations," and sent on their demand that the board formally rescind the July resolution, which it awkwardly did by stating its resolution of the day before had done just that.[53]

The minutes of the executive session of the board on September 8, 1999, were stark and unadorned. Amid some routine business came a surprising statement: "President's Term. Levering announced that she had no intention of running for a second term as President." Since the establishment of two-year terms in 1974, no president ever formally stood for a second term. Some were tempted. Some were encouraged by others to run. Perhaps some were interviewed by the nominating committee, but that committee has routinely refused to disclose the names of candidates not selected. There is nothing in the record to suggest that Levering wished to serve another two-year term, so her firm denial was likely in response to rumors. Still, that recusal, delivered amidst a leadership crisis, hints at the sense of crisis.

After the war of the resolutions, board members presented the semiannual meeting with the recommendations of their study groups, with summary remarks by the president and vice president. The entire program was based on a script of some one hundred pages put together by a communications consultancy and the board. Some of the briefings had been prepared in late August, but the controversial ones—the president's remarks and state alignment—were in multiple drafts dated as late as September 5. The reports put a coda on the state-alignment reform movement. As Barbara Smith (a USTA vice president), who loyally led the fight, put it in her prepared remarks: "State alignment. Now here's a hot potato. But I must tell you it's not a new potato. . . . Lots of questions, lots of opinions, lots of turmoil . . . will make us stronger in the end." With that "off the table" she suggested that they focus on where they agreed. "I believe the burner under the pot has been turned down."[54]

Life did not end for the USTA with the rejection of state alignment. A plan for growth remained on the front burner, the national office was divided into two business groups—professional tennis (including the U.S. Open) and community tennis—each with a director. The Association's first management audit had been conducted, and its first strategic plan was in place—one that called for monitoring progress toward goals using key performance indicators that established specific time and quantitative markers, a well-established business practice but new to the Association. Revenue concerns arose in 2000, when a budget deficit of $13 million appeared. But whatever the intimations of loose spending, the villain was the stock market. The Association quickly changed its investment firm. Loans were restructured. U.S. Open revenues steadily grew. The golden goose continued to lay its wonderful eggs.[55]

But the effects of the dispute left some open wounds that would take time to heal. As ever in such confrontations, sides are drawn, feelings are hurt, and things get personal. That healing process began in earnest in September 2002 with the appointment of a blue ribbon commission set up by president-elect Alan Schwartz in September 2002. The report might well have been titled "A Crisis of Trust." The membership was carefully constructed: Lee Hamilton (Schwartz's candidate to replace Ferman as executive director), Mary Jo Fernandez (a top-ten player whose appointment was clearly aimed at reaching out to the pros), Randy Gregson (a former president who represented the past); Peter Kram (who represented section participation), and Judy Levering (representing not only the present, but a figure respected by all for her dedication to the game). The charge was "to take a hard look at issues of unity, candor and trust within the USTA family."

The findings were fascinating:

1. Low level of unity, particularly regarding how programs link to the mission ("to promote and develop the growth of tennis") and to resource allocation.
2. Low unity around governance roles with many seeing "the Board as a significant contributor to disunity, failing to fulfill its roles as tennis' national governing body and as the linkage with the sections."
3. Low level of candor due to the "volunteer hierarchy and the power and perks that come with advancement" (i.e., climbing the ladder).
4. "Growing pains" from tension between skilled professionals and volunteers, while "tension between "National" and the "Sections" has risen to an unacceptably high level, particularly over "High Performance" strategy.

5. Unity around USTA mission and goals, but "too little awareness of and allegiance to the USTA Strategic Plan."
6. Confusion and misunderstanding about roles and responsibilities largely because the word is not passed down the line because of "a lack of 'trickle down discipline.'"
7. "Concerns about perks, power and a lack of accountability are pervasive."
8. To a degree, "the Executive Director will be, inevitably, a 'lightening rod.'"

The most emphatic recommendation for reform was that board and staff decisions had to revolve around the strategic plan. Not pet projects; no unapproved initiatives. Despite no mention of state alignment and the issues it raised, it was a very positive start to healing the wounds.[56]

Did rejection of state alignment throw the baby out with the bathwater? The trajectory of centralization versus decentralization ("national" versus "grassroots" in USTA terminology; federal government versus state or local control in 2016 political terms) is not an either/or, zero-sum game. National control made sense for much of what the USTA did. The 750,000 grassroots members at the turn of the twentieth to the twenty-first century were motivated by a love for playing the game, a fervor to bring new players to the game, and for watching the U.S. Open on television. Yet they were also motivated by tennis at the section and the local levels (sort of the same in some cases), whether they played or their families played or there was some other connection with the game. Moreover, much of what the reform intended was later, and gently, put into place. The national staff today is larger than it ever was (as of 2016 some 378 employees), without any sign of unrest in the sections.

How the USTA family received that report and its recommendations; how the national leadership handled the "crisis of trust" described in the report; how the forty-plus-year effort to choose between volunteer and professional operational control over what is now a $300 million corporation will end up are all stories worth the telling. Did the "perk" problem go away? Did the Association commit to full and transparent accountability? Whither governance reforms? What about "High Performance" programs?

The blue ribbon report made no mention of social diversity. Why not? Without claiming that the Association had solved the challenges of social discrimination (race, gender, disabilities, et al.), one compelling USTA achievement has been to provide access to leadership positions in a way that has brought social diversity.

Not until 1993, when Dwight Mosley was elected secretary, did a person of color become a member of the Association's board of directors. It is no small irony that the first black (male) board officer came only four years after the first female officer, Barbara Williams. The struggle women fought with the USTA has parallels to what black Americans faced, both on the court and in the boardroom. But the circumstances of the discrimination they faced were quite different. Women were never barred from the game, only from governance of the Association and paid less as professionals until Gladys Heldman came along. Blacks were excluded—period! Althea Gibson's battle was about race, not gender.

Marion Wood Huey became the first woman on the executive committee in 1962, just as that committee (which met only twice a year since 1938) began to have its responsibilities taken up by the administrative committee.[57] She sat there, the only woman, through 1971. Then, in 1973, the damn burst, or at least sprung some leaks when President Joseph Carrico appointed four women to the executive committee. Yet no section had ever sent a woman as its delegate to sit on the executive committee. That changed in 1978 when Barbara Williams became the first woman president of a section, and also served as the Eastern Section's delegate. Williams became the first female officer (treasurer) in 1989—a long eleven years later. Nevertheless, by the time Judy Levering became president in 1999, women on the USTA board had become routine. But selection of a woman as president was as much a definitive, historic decision, as the election of Dwight Mosley as an officer—and it only took 108 years! In 2015 the Association doubled down on both issues by electing Katrina Adams president, a black woman. Moreover, it returned to its leadership roots by selecting a former highly ranked tennis player. After some eighty years (since World War One) of presidents who were, with rare exceptions, from the business world, an "elite athlete" (as designated by USTA bylaws) was once again in charge of American tennis.[58]

Putting Players Back on the USTA Board

In February 1968 the executive committee had recommended, at long last, adding one male and one female "player" to the executive committee, each selected from the appropriate list of (amateur) players ranked in the top twenty. It was a much belated recognition that the Association had lost touch with the kind of top players who had created and led the organization for its first three decades. That provision survived until the turn of the century but became increasingly meaningless as the executive committee lost its role in policy formulation. The Association resorted to subterfuge to avoid the intent of the Amateur Sports Act (1978), by loosely defining "international competition." But in 2000 with the Olympics insisting on effective player representation in governance, the USTA reluctantly reserved three slots on both its board of directors and nominating committee for "elite" tennis players who had competed in certain major international events.

Done under pressure from the United States Olympic Committee, the "change" actually restored a tradition. The Association had been founded in 1881 by the best tennis players in America. For its first three decades the leadership came from national champions and other top players. But by the 1920s, professional managers and businessmen who also played tennis had taken over governance. Part of that may have been cumulative effect of founding father James Dwight's twenty-one years as president. In 1941 *ALT* somewhat ruefully commented that "no one thinks it strange that the players have no part in the government of the game." Players had to be amateurs, but the leadership could not afford that luxury. Neither could the top players who became paid touring professionals.

Of course the ultimate endorsement of re-incorporating elite athletes back into the Association's leadership came in 2015 when Katrina Adams became president. Not only was she the fourth woman and the first African American to hold that post, she initially got on the USTA board of directors as an elite athlete. Champions had returned.[59]

Families are imperfect. Emotion overcomes reason, hurt feelings create jealousies, focused commitments can cloud recognition of the big picture, personality differences can work against cooperation. But families that succeed manage to get past the problems and build on respect, commitment, friendship (love), and togetherness. Since 1881 the Association has managed to succeed, albeit awkwardly at times, in its management. It has helped "grow the game" from just a handful of white men (and women) in white pants at country clubs to a wonderfully diverse population of folks who love the game. With three-quarters of a million members and surely ten times that number of fans in this era of broadband media (estimates of viewers of recent U.S. Open finals are routinely around five million), the Association has been a good steward, whatever the bumps and detours along the way. To repeat myself, Slew Hester would have drawled: *Laissez les bons temps rouler!*

Perhaps it is best to leave any assessment of the USTA in the twenty-first century to other, less involved historians. What is clear is that the USTA family is alive, well, and "growing the game," which is why we're all here.

The role and responsibilities of the executive director have been a matter for near-constant discussion by the Association's leadership since late 1968, when President Robert Kelleher instructed a special committee to study the USTA's long-range financial plan *and* its administrative structure. Well over a half-dozen formal recommendations to make the executive director the chief executive officer were rejected between 1969 and 2002. Given the significance of those discussions for the Association's development, it is necessary to this history to include the following: "At the Association's 2017 annual meeting, the section delegates, by a vote of 16 to 1, adopted bylaw changes that, as of January 1, 2018, shifted the title, authority, and responsibilities of the chief executive officer (CEO) from the USTA president to the executive director."

APPENDIX 1

"The Founding Myth" by E. H. Outerbridge

This lovely speech, given in 1931 when Outerbridge was age seventy or seventy-one, may not be the precise and full truth about the formation of the Association, which is presented in chapter 2. But it is a grand tale that, along with the stenographer's notes of "laughter" and "applause," reveals the awareness of delegates at that annual meeting of the politics that characterized the Association.

Perhaps a few words might interest you regarding the genesis of this organization. In September, 1880, the Staten Island Cricket and Baseball Club, whose grounds were in what was then known as Camp Washington, later on St. George, decided to hold the first open tennis tournament and had notices of it put in all the papers well in advance of the time set for the tournament. The directors were rather timid in authorizing me to undertake this because there were not very many tennis clubs and they were afraid that it might be a disappointment. The entries began to come in very rapidly, however, and among them was a letter from a man in Chicago who said that he was traveling in this country (he was an Englishman) and had seen the notice in the papers that there was to be a tournament and he would like to know if he was eligible to enter. By way of identifying himself he said he was Mr. O. E. Woodhouse of the West Middlesex Club of England. The only way we had of checking up on that was to look it up in the English Field and somewhat to the disappointment of the best players we had then we found he had been the runner-up at Wimbledon some months before and was beaten by Mr. Lawford there.

We accepted his entry of course.

The few clubs where tennis was played then had no uniform rules and no uniform balls. Some of them were playing with uncovered rubber balls. Some were playing with balls made by Wright & Ditson, some with balls made by Peck & Snyder of New York, all different sizes and weights, none of them true. So we gave notice a long time in advance to every entry, as the application came in, that we were going to play under Wimbledon rules and with the Ayers English ball which was then the standard.

We had beautiful weather for the tournament and large numbers of people came down from New York and there were also a good many Staten Island people there. But early in the playing off of the ties a difficulty arose about the balls. Some of the players who were not playing up to what they considered their standard and who were falling behind objected and said they couldn't play with those balls, they were not the ones they were accustomed to. Some of their opponents said, "All right, we will play with any ball you like."

But the Tournament Committee were called and they said that couldn't be permitted, that we would be having a dozen different kinds of balls on different courts, and that the tournament must go on. Some of those players withdrew. However, the tournament was a great success.

Mr. O. E. Woodhouse astonished everybody in the first set he played by developing what had never been seen up to that time and that was the high overhand service. Before that everybody either served what was known as the "Lawford service" from very low down to the ground, with a cut up, this way (demonstrating), or from hip high. But he was like an asparagus stalk, about six feet two or three high, with an enormous reach. And I remember one thing that caused comment immediately he started to play and that was the fact that the center of his racket was quite black, showing that he always hit the ball right in the center of his racket. (Laughter)

He went through all his competition and won the tournament with Mr. Dick Sears in the final with him. Dick Sears played a very pretty game but wasn't at that time at all in the class of Woodhouse. When that tournament was concluded, at the first meeting of the Board of Directors of the Staten Island Club after that, I said, "This is the plainest evidence in the world that we must have a lawn tennis association that will conduct all large tournaments, have uniform rules, balls, and so on."

So they authorized me to go ahead and see what I could do about it.

I happened to know intimately most of the men in the clubs in Boston, Philadelphia, and other places where they played cricket because it was really at the cricket clubs that tennis first got its foothold. So I took it up with those clubs and found they were ready to go into the organization.

There is a little bit of history that particularly applies to the Staten Island Club which necessitated having a good deal of politics about the original organization, which I believe doesn't prevail any more. (Laughter)

We had a somewhat elderly member of the Staten Island Club who wasn't active in any game at all. As a matter of fact he was what might be called a "piazza sport." (Laughter) His principal interest was in the baseball end of the club but when he found there was going to be a national lawn tennis association he had an undying ambition to be its first president. None of us thought he was qualified for that position but none of us wanted to offend him mortally. So a few of us got together and we decided we would meet that situation by electing him temporary chairman and that we would then have all the business of the meeting prepared well in advance—the by-laws and everything that had to be done, the appointment of a nominating' committee, who they should be and who they should nominate. (Laughter)

When it came time for the meeting, the nominating committee retired. The meeting recessed for fifteen minutes. It may have been a half hour. I don't remember. At all events it was time enough not to convey the impression to those present that it was all cut and dried and prepared in advance. (Laughter)

We did not want to elect anybody really from the Staten Island Club. We didn't want to elect anybody from Boston or Philadelphia because we didn't want to have the feeling go out that any one of these three larger centers had been picked out. There was a little tennis club up in Albany and General Oliver of that club, a very delightful and distinguished citizen of Albany and a delightful gentleman, was the man we picked to put on that ticket as the first president and Mr. C. M. Clark of Philadelphia was selected as the secretary. We also had an executive committee nominated.

The proceedings all went through as smooth as glass and the gentleman who had been elected to act as temporary chairman was quite satisfied with the honor that had been given him in launching this organization. Of course, the elections were the last order of business. We saw to that (Laughter).

That is the history of this organization.

I thank you very much, Mr. President. (Applause)

Minutes, 1931 USLTA Annual Meeting, 1–7.

APPENDIX 2

USNLTA *Original Constitution and Bylaws*

Reconstructed from the annual meeting minutes in 1882–83 and the 1884 constitution and bylaws, Official Lawn Tennis Rules *(Boston: Wright & Ditson, 1894), 13–23*

Constitution and By-laws of the United States National Lawn Tennis Association

Organized and adopted at the "Lawn Tennis Convention," held at the Fifth Avenue Hotel, Saturday, May 21, 1881. Revised and Amended at the Third Annual Meeting, held at the Hotel Brunswick, New York, March 7, 1884.

Article I

NAME

This organization shall be known as the United States National Lawn Tennis Association.

Article II

MEMBERS

Section 1. The clubs being members of this Association shall be known as active.

Section 2. *Propositions for Membership.*—Propositions for membership must be made in writing to the Executive Committee, hereinafter provided for, with the name and address of applicant, and signed by the Secretary of the club making the proposal. The Secretary shall have full power to pass upon candidates for membership without a general election.

Section 3. *Dues, etc.*—The annual dues to this Association shall be seven dollars, ($7) subject to change at the discretion of the Executive Committee, as hereinafter provided for. No club shall be considered a member nor be allowed privileges of a member, until its dues have been paid. All future dues shall be payable at the Annual Meeting.

Section 4. *Limits of Payments, etc.*—Any club which shall fail to have paid its annuals dues at the expiration of one month after the annual meeting, may be debarred from the privileges of a member by the Executive Committee, and at their discretion may be dropped from the roll.

Section 5. *Resignations, etc.*—Any club being a member wishing to resign must do so in writing, addressed to the Secretary; and the resignation cannot be accepted until all its dues are paid.

Article III

EXPULSIONS, ETC.

The Executive Committee of this Association, hereinafter provided for, shall have the power to expel or suspend any club which may neglect or refuse a strict and honorable compliance with this Constitution, By-Laws, etc.; or which shall by scandalous conduct, bring reproach of disgrace upon the Association; subject to a right of the said club to appeal to the Association, at its next annual meeting, for reinstatement.

Article IV

OFFICERS

Section 1. The officers of this Association shall consist of a President, Vice-President, Secretary-Treasurer, and an Executive Committee of six members, including the President, the Vice-President, and the Secretary-Treasurer, who shall be *ex officio* members of the Committee.

[The minutes of the 1882 annual meeting, as reprinted in the *OLTB*, 2, no. 3 (March 5, 1896): 40–43, reported this amendment to the constitution: Article IV., Sec. 3. Strike out "five," put "six," and strike out "or in his absence." That clearly referred to the size of the executive committee (section 1 not section 3), which was again enlarged to seven in 1884. There is no way to determine the original location of the phrase "or in his absence." The 1883 minutes do not report any amendments.]

Section 2. *Time and Mode of Election.*—The election of officers shall be by ballot, at the annual meeting in each year. They shall be balloted for separately, and receive a majority of all votes cast to entitle them to an election; and they shall continue in office for one year, or until their successors shall be elected.

Section 3. *Vacancies.*—In case a vacancy should occur in any of the offices, the Executive Committee shall elect a member to fill the vacancy for the unexpired term, in the manner provided in Section 2 of this Article, except that such election may be at a meeting of the Executive Committee, and not necessarily an annual meeting, as therein stated.

Section 4. *Duties of the President.*—It shall be the duty of the President to preside at all meetings, to preserve order, to appoint all committees not otherwise provided for, and to see that the officers and committees perform their respective duties.

Section 5. *The Vice-President.*—The Vice-President shall assist the President in the performance of his duties, and shall exercise all the powers of the President in his absence.

Section 6. *The Secretary-Treasurer.*—The secretary shall keep a roll of all the members, and from time to time amend and correct the same as circumstance may require. He shall notify new members of their election within two weeks thereafter, and shall give notice of all meetings at least two weeks in advance. He shall conduct all the correspondence of the Association, and keep copies of all letters in a book provided for that purpose. He shall keep the minutes of the proceedings of the Association, and a record of such matters of interest as may occur. As Treasurer, he shall keep, in a suitable book provided for that purpose, and account of all moneys received and paid. He shall liquidate all bills against the Association, and shall report in writing the state of finances when required; and at the annual meeting he shall present a written report showing all the receipts and expenditures for the year.

Section 7. *Executive Committee, etc.*—It shall be the duty of the Executive Committee to see that the general provisions of the Constitution and By-Laws of this Association are complied with by clubs being members of the same; to hear and decide all questions submitted by any of the Association clubs for decision, notice of hearing being given to any other club which may be affected by the question; to construe and enforce all the rules of the Association; to fix, at least one month prior to each annual meeting, such assessment upon the clubs as they may deem necessary to cover the expenses of the Association for the ensuing year. All decisions of the Executive Committee shall be complied with forthwith, but an appeal there from may be taken by any club to the Association at the annual meeting, provided the club applying shall file notice of their intention to do so within two (2) weeks after the Committee shall have rendered its decision. The Executive Committee and the Secretary-Treasurer may cause official notices, and such other matters of information that shall deem of interest, to be put in the "Archery and Tennis News," which paper shall be the official bulletin of the Association. All clubs are expected to take notice of official publication therein. The Executive Committee shall have the arrangement and management of any general tournament between the club members of this Association.

No club shall have more than one delegate on the Executive Committee. A majority shall constitute a quorum.

Article V

MEETINGS, ETC.

Section 1. There shall be a stated annual meeting held, on a date to be fixed by the Secretary, between the 1st and 15th of **March**. [The original Constitution stated May.] in each year, at such place as may have been designated at the previous annual meeting. [Bold word added in 1882.]

Section 2. *Proxies, etc.*—Clubs may be represented at any meeting by delegates or proxies.

Section 3. *Special Meetings, etc.*—Special meetings may be called by the Executive Committee at any time, and shall be called by the Executive Committee at the request of any five clubs in the Association.

Section 4. At all meetings of the Association the representatives of eleven clubs shall constitute a quorum.

Section 5. *Votes, etc.*—Each club represented in the Association shall be entitled to one vote only at all meetings, to be cast by its delegate or delegates, **provided such club shall have twenty or more members**.

A delegate must be an active member of a club in good standing in the Association, and present credentials properly certified by the club or clubs he represents.

Article VI

AMENDMENTS, ETC.

Amendments to this Constitution may be made at any annual meeting by a vote of at least two-thirds of the clubs represented. By-Laws may be amended at any annual or special meeting under the same provisions.

BY-LAWS

[The bylaws established *Cushing's Manual* for parliamentary procedures and laid out the then six "Laws of Lawn Tennis." In short, they required that all matches played by members had to follow the Association's rules, only amateurs could compete in Association matches, and that only Americans and Canadians could play in Association matches. Rules about amateurs, which were revised a bit in 1882, came despite there being no tennis professionals then, nor any international definition of an amateur. The International Olympic Committee was not created until 1894.]

APPENDIX 3

The ATA *and Holcombe Ward, 1947*

PRESIDENT WARD: Last summer, late, we received a letter from a man named Richard A. Cohen, a Negro tennis player, who said that he would like to have an interview with the officers of the Association. Cohen lived in Washington and so I suggested to him that he call upon Mr. Lawrence Baker, which he did. Mr. Baker conversed with him and reported to the Advisory and Finance Committee the result of the conversation.

Subsequently, I received a letter from the American Tennis Association requesting an interview, and I arranged an interview, and three of them came to see me: Mr. Baker, their executive secretary, a Mr. Francis, both of whom are high class men, and this same Richard A. Cohen, who is a younger man and a player. I discussed the matter very fully and frankly with them. They appreciate our position, but they would like to better themselves. They would like to gradually have their players permitted to play in tournaments.

I told them that I thought they were making a great mistake if they attempted to force the issue. I said that would merely antagonize people. I said I didn't think we could have any definite, nation-wide rule; that we should continue as we do now, and allow the local tournament authorities to accept Negro entries if they wish to do so, and if they do not wish to do so, they may reject them.

I think the two officials were fairly well satisfied, but I think they are being egged on by some of the players, some of the younger men, who are more radical, and less patient than the older officials. At any rate, Mr. Baker asked if we wouldn't give consideration to their request, and he wrote me a letter which he said he would like to write so as to get the matter before us. Bill, will you read his letter? This is from Mr. Bertram Baker.

MR. KRAFT: This letter is addressed to the United States Lawn Tennis Association:

"Gentlemen: At a recent meeting of our organization, in consideration of a player's petition, it was decided that we take up with your body the matter of the possibility of some of our top ranking players being admitted to your championship matches. As a consequence, a committee representing our players and executives met with your President, Mr. Holcombe Ward, in New York City to discuss the matter.

"Of course, we realize that Mr. Ward could not commit your Association to any change of policy, but it gave us an opportunity to have a frank discussion on the matter. We are aware of the fact that it is a matter that should be carefully considered. We beiieve, however, that our American democratic ideals and way of life should be the guiding influence in your consideration of the matter.

"The relationship between your organization and ours has been most amicable and cooperative, for which we are extremely grateful. Our players represent the very finest class of our group, and they adhere to all of the ethics and ideals of the game, and all we ask is that a wider opportunity of development be afforded them. We trust that some plan can be worked out which will accomplish the desire and without disrupting the very fine relationship which presently exists between us. Very sincerely yours, Bertram Baker, Executive Secretary."

PRESIDENT WARD: Is there any action that you want to take on this, gentlemen?

MR. CUMMINGS: Mr. President, do I understand that in the acceptance of players in any tournament, it is an understood fact that they must be members of member clubs belonging to district or sectional associations, or direct members, which, of course, have to be members of the U.S.L.T.A.? It seems to me, at least, I assume that any one of these players who belong to clubs do not belong to any section or district that is a member of the U.S.L.T.A., and therefore, automatically, they would not be received. Is that correct?

PRESIDENT WARD: That is right. Entries may be refused if the player is not a member of a member club of the U.S.L.T.A.

MR. CUMMINGS: An unattached player, for instance, could be accepted if the club wanted to accept him, for some definite reason.

PRESIDENT WARD: Yes. Negroes have been accepted at several tournaments, one in New York, an indoor tournament in New York, one out in the Middle West.

MR. CUMMINGS: That gives a club a perfectly legitimate "out" for not accepting them.

MR. ALEXANDER: Mr. President, I recall I wrote you a rather lengthy letter about this matter. My recollection is that he wanted Negroes to be eligible to play in the National Championships.

PRESIDENT WARD: I think that would please him very much. I think they would like to have one or two of their players accepted.

MR. ALEXANDER: I thought that was the particular point he made, that they be allowed to compete not only in, their own American Tennis Association (or whatever they call it) but in our National Championships, and I recall that I quoted from the Tournament Qualifications that, "The National Championship Committee handling the event shall have authority to exercise its judgment in accepting or rejecting entries, subject to the following limitations: Entries shall be considered from players in good standing belonging to clubs affiliated with the United States Lawn Tennis Association. . . ."

PRESIDENT WARD: That is right. They understand that.

MR. ALEXANDER: And there are no Negro clubs that belong that–

PRESIDENT WARD: They understand that. We have the right to accept entries of players, if we want to, who are not members of member clubs, public park players, for example. I am not urging that any action be taken. Lawrence, have you any thoughts on this? I promised that I would bring it to your attention, and so I am doing it.

MR. BAKER: The matter as presented to me was one in which they rather sought our cooperation to the extent even of saying that we would reserve one place in the Championship for the best Negro player. I asked whether we ought to reserve a place for the best Chinese player, and for the best Indian player.

I took the position that the Championship had to be a championship of qualified players, and that if a Negro player had demonstrated that he was entitled to play in a championship on the basis of his ability as a player that it would then be soon enough for us to consider whether he was also the character of player that the committee would feel should be admitted.

We have admitted to the Championship the champion of the Public Parks Tournament. He was a player, however, of national ranking, in the first twenty in the country, and a player who deserved to be admitted to the tournament because he was a good player, and not because he was the champion of the public parks.

I think that that position is the position we should continue to take: that if a player is admitted to the Championship who is not of strictly the ranking that entitles him to be there, he at least is a player of such prominence that the committee in its discretion feels that his showing will justify his presence there.

Their objection to that thinking is that they can never hope to qualify a player on that basis until they are admitted to the sectional tournaments and other competition where they can qualify and build up a player who is qualified to play in the Championship.

So it seems to me that we are in the position of moving along with the stream, so to speak, until somebody comes up among the Negro players who shows clearly that he is entitled, by reason of his ability, to contest in our Championships. When we reach that point, if the committee is of the opinion that he ought to be admitted, both because he is a good player and because he is the character of man that should be admitted, I think we shall have great difficulty in saying that that man cannot play. But until we reach that time, I think we would be wise to take no further action.

MR. MAN: May I just remark that Dr. Reginald Weir, who competed in the Indoor Championships, defeated Gladys Ladislav Hecht in that tournament, so he would come close to qualifying in our National Championship, if he made application.

PRESIDENT WARD: I think he is dead.

MR. MAN: Not unless he died very suddenly. He wasn't dead two weeks ago.

PRESIDENT WARD: Maybe I am wrong.

MR. MAN: He is ranked eight or ten in the Negro Association.

PRESIDENT WARD: Don't you think that instead of slamming the door, we can keep it open in some way to show that we are willing to continue to consider the matter?

MR. LEWIS: I think so.

PRESIDENT WARD: Can't we refer it to some committee for study?

MR. TOBIN: I think it might be to the best interests of all to appoint some committee to give the matter study and report at some future meeting.

MR. BAKER: If you appoint a committee, the committee is going to have to report. Then you are going to have a discussion on the report, and you are going to have pressure for action on the report.

PRESIDENT WARD: They don't have to report tomorrow.

MR. BAKER: We are getting along pretty well so far, and I think that if the officers of the Association could continue to take the position in any conversations with these gentlemen that we are in sympathy with their program, we want to help them build up their own association, and that if they are able to produce a player who is qualified for the Championship his entry will be considered, that that is about as far as we can go at this time. And I think you are just pointing up the thing when you decide that you are going to appoint a committee to consider something, which is entirely at variance with all the procedure we have followed in the past, namely, that the man must qualify under our regulations to get into the Championship.

There has been some pressure brought to bear on us to include a certain number of Juniors each year, and that has proven embarrassing frequently to the Tournament Committee.

But, certainly, we can't single out some particular group and say we will admit to the Championship the best person who presents himself from that particular group.

MR. PARRY: Mr. President, would it help any at all for this body to endorse the stand that has already been taken by its President, as long as they raise the question, and say that we are sympathetic towards their program. There are a lot of things involved in connection with our rules, etc., and you can go ahead and negotiate, or wait for further inquiries by them. They raise the question in the letter, as I remember, that you couldn't bind the Association, and I think we could say you can.

MR. BAKER: They are not complaining of discrimination. They are asking for discrimination in their favor, and I don't see where the discrimination in their favor is justified at this point. When their own organization has been built up to the point where they have a sufficient number of tournaments and develop a good enough player so they can come along and present his entry on the ground he is entitled to come into the competition, then I think it will be up to the committee in charge of the tournament to decide whether he is entitled to be admitted. He may be an entirely acceptable entry. He may not be. But we have our regulations and I see no reason why we should legislate in a discriminatory fashion for some particular group simply because they happen to be colored people.

MR. PARRY: Isn't that the position we have taken?

MR. BAKER: That is the position I have taken. This Committee hasn't taken any position. I am saying that this is the position I have taken.

The Committee can do as it likes about it, but I think we are opening the door to all kinds of trouble when we set up standards that are based upon certain groups. We are going to have to rewrite our

Championship Regulations if we do that, and we are going to have to say that the committee in determining who are acceptable entries must take the Junior champion, that they must tab some Negro who is the best Negro player in the country, they must take some player who comes and presents himself as the best player of the public parks group. We have consistently refused to admit the public parks champion just because he was the public parks champion. We have only taken him when he demonstrated that he was qualified to play in the Tournament.

MR. ALEXANDER: Mr. President, I move it lie on the table and we proceed with further business.

The motion was duly seconded, put to a vote, and carried . . .

Source ExCom, January 1947, 132–43.

APPENDIX 4

Membership Statistics, 1958–1992

YEAR	ADULTS	JUNIORS	LIFE MEMBERS	TOTALS	% OF GROWTH
1958	4,470	8,085		12,555	
1959	6,162	10,676		16,838	34%
1960	7,697	13,860		21,557	28%
1961	8,195	16,036		24,231	12%
1962	9,129	18,392		27,521	14%
1963	9,108	19,261		28,369	3%
1964	11,681	23,210		34,891	23%
1965	13,838	23,286	12	37,136	6%
1966	14,656	24,903	160	39,719	7%
1967	15,940	26,260	339	42,539	7%
1968	17,323	26,690	687	44,700	5%
1969	17,170	28,069	1,053	46,292	4%
1970	17,284	31,785	1,334	50,403	9%
1971	19,813	33,057	1,838	54,708	9%
1972	21,908	37,538	2,530	61,976	13%
1973	21,394	37,664	3,405	62,463	1%
1974	30,038	50,677	3,636	84,351	35%
1975	36,944	56,585	3,781	97,310	15%
1976	47,373	59,212	3,931	110,516	14%
1977	57,469	67,333	4,189	128,991	17%
1978	71,489	69,659	4,350	145,498	13%
1979	68,869	74,718	4,503	148,090	2%
1980	82,037	80,901	4,686	167,624	13%
1981	99,724	89,442	4,808	193,974	16%
1982	110,241	88,598	4,928	203,767	5%

YEAR	ADULTS	JUNIORS	LIFE MEMBERS	TOTALS	% OF GROWTH
1983	125,490	92,741	5,344	223,575	10%
1984	135,301	101,044	5,725	242,070	8%
1985	148,510	106,210	6,262	260,982	8%
1986	163,646	115,246	6,667	285,559	9%
1987	181,613	120,558	7,296	309,467	8%
1988	193,751	121,558	8,155	323,464	5%
1989	219,705	119,565	9,879	349,149	8%
1990	244,062	135,871	11,558	391,491	12%
1991	270,850	155,044	13,655	439,549	12%
1992	291,324	165,353	15,997	472,674	8%

Source: USTA Archive, E&R files.

APPENDIX 5

USTA *Senior Staff List, 1916 to Present*

Executive Secretaries, Chief Administrative Officers, and Executive Directors

Field Secretary Paul Williams, 1916–22
Executive Secretary Edward B. Moss, 1923–43
(None), 1943–46
Executive Secretary Edwin S. Baker, 1947–67
(Executive Assistant) Executive Secretary Robert S. Malaga, 1968
Executive Director Robert S. Malaga, 1969–72
Assistant Executive Director Michael Burns, 1972
Executive Secretary Michael Burns, 1973–90 (During 1972–80 and briefly in 1981, Burns was the senior staff person.)
Executive Director Richard O'Shea, 1980
Interim (Acting) Executive Director and Executive Secretary Michael Burns, 1981
Chief Administrative Officer Donald Conway, 1981–83
Executive Director and Chief Administrative Officer Donald Conway, 1983–85
Executive Director and Chief Operating Officer Donald Conway, 1985–86
Executive Director and Chief Operating Officer John Fogarty, 1986–88
Acting Executive Director Robert Garry, 1988–89
Executive Director and Chief Operating Officer Marshall Happer III, 1989–95
Executive Director and Chief Operating Officer Richard Ferman, 1996–2003
Executive Director and Chief Operating Officer Lee Hamilton, 2003–7
Executive Director and Chief Operating Officer Gordon Smith, 2008–

NOTES

ABBREVIATIONS

AdminCom: Administration Committee Minutes

ALT: *American Lawn Tennis*

BOD: Board of Directors Minutes

ExCom: Executive Committee Minutes

GAP summary report, ExCom, September 9, 1994:
Governance and Planning Committee report, ExCom, September 9, 1994, 40–41

Gowen, comp., "USTA National Tennis Center":
George Gowen, comp., "USTA National Tennis Center: A Historical Perspective and Financial Analysis of Lease Terms"

Hester-ExCom, September 9, 1977:
ExCom, September 9, 1977, 55–111

LRP Report, 1969:
Long Range Financial Planning Committee, Report and Recommendations, January 15, 1969

LTG: *Lawn Tennis Guide*

LTLR: *Lawn Tennis Library Record*

MgmntCom: Management Committee Minutes

1985 McKinsey report:
"Strengthening Organization Structure and Management Processes,"
Final Report by McKinsey and Company, October 1985 (USTA Archive)

OLTB: *Official Lawn Tennis Bulletin*

Pollack opinion: U.S. District Court, Southern District of New York, 73 CIV. 162 (MP), opinion of U.S. District Judge Milton Pollack, February 7, 1973

Schwartz notebook:
Alan Schwartz files, USTA Archive, notebook of the National Board/Senior Leadership Issue Study Group, tab 5

USLTA *News*: *United States Lawn Tennis Association News*

USNLTA Minutes: "Minutes of the [founding meeting of the] United States Lawn Tennis Association [1881]"
USTA *Official Encyclopedia:* USTA *Official Encyclopedia of Tennis*

PREFACE

1. Koster, *The Tennis Bubble*, xii.
2. Warren F. Kimball and John T. Moter to the USTA Board of Directors, A Proposal for Establishment of a USTA Records Management System and Archive, March 27, 2004; Winthrop Group report, Information and Archival Services (Deborah Shea), USTA Record Retention and Archives, August 2003, pages 5, 21.
3. Berry, *Top Spin*.
4. Hawk, *Off the Racket*, xiv–xv.

1. ORIGINS

1. The racquet in Tiepolo's painting was spotted by Tim Kent. Whether or not he was the "wag" who joked at the expense of John McEnroe and Apollo remains *in pectoris*. Tiepolo inserted tennis equipment to curry favor with his patron, an avid player. The website http://www.real-tennis.nl/?page=Tiepolo offers more than you could ever want to know about the painting's connection to tennis: for example, a discussion of a mid-sixteenth-century translation of Ovid's *Metamorphoses* in which a discus contest (Apollo versus Hyacinth) becomes a court-tennis match, along with more spicy tales. For a photo of the Tiepolo painting see http://www.real-tennis.nl/?page=Caravaggio#episode3.
2. Lucas Gassel, Brussels, oil on panel, 1538, found in the collection of the International Tennis Hall of Fame. The *Lawn Tennis Library Record (LTLR)* of the Fischer Library asserted that one Jean Margot, a woman, was a famous tennis player in Paris in or around 1427, one who defeated most of the men. Perhaps. Certainly in today's world, women have played tennis well before most other athletic sports. But whatever "her" record, one wonders if "Jean" Margot was a woman, since "Jeanne" (as in Jeanne d'Arc) is the usual French version of that name for women; *Lawn Tennis Library Record* 10 (April 1951)(hereafter *LTLR*).
3. To quote Shakespeare:

   When we have match'd our rackets to these balls
   We will in France, by God's grace, play a set
   Shall strike his father's crown into the hazard.
   Tell him he hath made a match with such a wrangler
   That all the courts in France will be disturb'd with chases!

   For Milton having the opportunity to play "real" tennis during the tennis "craze" of the 1630s, see Skinner, "The Generation of John Milton," 53.
4. For an overview see *Origins of Tennis*, the Tennis Channel, Signature Series, broadcast January 31, 2010. The "real" in real tennis never meant "royal," as is often assumed. It was first used at the end of the nineteenth century as a "retro-

nym" to distinguish it from the then recently invented game of lawn tennis. See "History of the Game," http://www.irtpa.com/history-of-the-game/. "Field" and "long" tennis are mentioned in Paret, *Lawn Tennis*, 5. For additional details and the "never traveled" quote, see Collins and Hollander, *Bud Collins' Tennis Encyclopedia*, 4; and Alexander, *Wingfield*, 96–97. Court tennis is still played. There are nine courts in the United States—only two open to the public; see Tignor, "Not for Crass Lawners," 46–49. Alastair Martin, USTA president 1969-70, was a court-tennis national champion. The Montaigne story is related in Kramer, "Me, Myself, and I," 36.

5. The Major Wingfield Society was formed in 1976 at the initiative of then Association president Stan Malless, with membership by invitation and limited to persons of at least sixty years of age. The society's main accomplishments have been the refurbishing of Major Wingfield's grave in London's famous Kensal Green Cemetery, donation of a commemorative plaque to the National Tennis Center in Flushing Meadows, New York (found, thanks to Antonia Calzetti, but subsequently misplaced again), and installation of memorial plaques at 112 Belgrave Road in London, where Wingfield lived in 1874, the year his lawn-tennis patent was granted, and another at the home he lived in when he died; Alexander, *Wingfield*, 189–91. The dual efforts of George Alexander, the Wingfield Historical Society, and, eventually, the Association, brought about issuance of a U.S. Postal Service stamped envelope commemorating Wingfield (which must have mystified users). *Bicycle Gymkhana* was published in 1897 in London by Harrison and Sons.
6. This charming tale is told without evidence by Potter, *Kings of the Court*, 4–5. Information about Charles d'Orleans is gleaned from various encyclopedias. The name "lawn tennis" may have been suggested by future British prime minister Arthur Balfour, himself an avid player.
7. The major's game was, of course, *lawn* tennis. There are various versions of rules for court tennis, the earliest of which is dated 1592; that information courtesy of Richard Hillway and Attila Szabo. "Sphairistiké" (from the Greek) was apparently coined by Wingfield. It was probably pronounced "sfair-RIST-ik-ee," hence the derisive "sticky." Again thanks to Tim Kent, this time for pronunciation guidance; see also http://www.answers.com/topic/sphairistike. The tongue-twister name was the framework for a clever and amusing radio broadcast by Paul Harvey (NPR, October 13, 2006). Edward Potter, a long-time tennis writer, described Sphairistiké as "a monstrous concoction of badminton, court tennis, fives and racquets, with a few inventions" like an hourglass shaped court; Potter, "The Insulting Tennis Balls," 12–13.
8. The "beneficiary" is identified below, in chapter 6.
9. The tendentiousness starts (and in this book, ends) here. Even the publication date of the major's first book of rules is misstated by the same author, George Alexander. He wrote that "the indisputable date of publication is

February 25, 1874," which may well be technically accurate, yet he also gives the publication date as December 1873. Wingfield dedicated various editions of his book to a group assembled for a country house–warming party at Nantclwyd, Wales, in December 1873, which may have prompted what Alexander has called (according to others) a proof-reading error. But he made the "error" twice, in two books published twelve years apart. See Alexander, *Lawn Tennis*, 16 (the 1874 date), and 109 (the 1873 date), and Alexander, *Wingfield*, 205 (repeating the 1873 date). Moreover, formal publication of the rules is not the same as distribution, and there is no dispute about Wingfield's assertion that "This game has been tested practically at several Country Houses during the past few months." See W.C.W. (Walter Clopton Wingfield), *The Major's Game of Lawn Tennis*, reproduced in facsimile (and dated 1873) in Alexander, *Lawn Tennis*, 109–18 and Alexander, *Wingfield*, 205–14. It is very possible that either draft or prepublication copies of the rules circulated before the official publication date.

10. A guinea would have been worth a little over one pound in today's decimalized currency. Although the guinea had been discontinued fifty years earlier, the name lived on. "The guinea had an aristocratic overtone; professional fees and payment for land, horses and art [and the major's boxes] were often quoted in guineas until decimalization in 1971." It is used today at livestock auctions and horse races; Wikipedia (accessed January 2012). In the 1870s, five guineas or nearly £6 was a tidy sum—over £274 (about $540) in the buying power of 2008 currency; http://www.nationalarchives.gov.uk/currency/results.asp#mid.
11. Just as tendentious an argument as who "invented" lawn tennis is the on-going debate over who was the "first" person to play lawn tennis (i.e., the major's game) in the United States. In Bermuda where the Outerbridge family was so prominent that locals claimed Bermuda was a series of islands connected by Outerbridges, the island's tourist bureau has the Mary Outerbridge story as an article of faith. That tale has her bringing one of the major's boxes from Bermuda to Staten Island, New York, in 1874 in time for it to be used that summer. One Bermuda tennis historian has claimed that Mary G. Gray, the doyenne of Bermuda tennis, wrote that "the first tennis set imported into Bermuda belonged to Mr. Tom Middleton, but as he thought the game would be too undignified for his wife to play, he disposed of his set to my father and we were the first people to have a court in 1873. It was with us that Miss Mary Outerbridge first played." Unhappily, that historian's memory seems faulty. In 1924, Mary Gray published an article in *American Lawn Tennis* (hereafter *ALT*) in which she wrote that lawn tennis came to the island in 1875. See correspondence and clippings from D. Colin Selley to Warren Kimball dated November 8, 2006, and January 12, 2007 (deposited in the USTA Archive) and *ALT*, September 15, 1924. Mary Outerbridge did bring someone's set of equipment in time for early play on Staten Island. If recollections close to the event are the trump card, then a piece that appeared in 1887 has her bringing tennis to Staten Island in 1875, offering the plausible explanation that she spent the winter of 1874–75 in Bermuda hence the confusion over 1874 versus

1875; Clay, "The Staten Island Cricket and Baseball Club," 104. Frank Phelps, former businessman and tennis-baseball historian (ever since 1927, when he was nine years old and saw Babe Ruth play), checked steamship passenger lists and found that Outerbridge returned from Bermuda on January 31, 1874, and that her next recorded trip came in 1877. That would invalidate the Outerbridge claim to have been first in America with a lawn-tennis set, assuming that a) the major's sets were not available before the formal publication date of his book, b) that Mary O did not sail between those two dates on a private vessel, and c) that she arrived in the ports where Phelps checked the records (apparently New York); Phelps, "Unravelling the Myth," 30–31 and his unpublished typescript, "A Tennis Myth: The Outerbridge Tradition" (courtesy of the author), and in Phelps telephone interview (2007). But who knows the truth? Alexander is correct when he wrote that lawn tennis came to the United States in at least six different places, all within a few months. All agree that Mary O was a tennis pioneer, deserving of her election in 1981 to the International Tennis Hall of Fame. The story of her having brought the very first Wingfield set to America resurfaced in 1917 and in the mid 1920s when her younger brother promoted it. For E. H. Outerbridge's recounting, see his "The History of Lawn Tennis in the United States," *Official Bulletin: United States Lawn Tennis Association* (in three installments). Mary's sister Laura wrote in May 1949 (she was ninety-two) that Mary had brought lawn-tennis equipment from Bermuda on February 2, 1874. However unlikely, that is possible since Wingfield wrote of the game being "tested" in late 1873; *LTLR* 28 (June 1955). See also Whitman, *Tennis: Origins and Mysteries*. Mary Outerbridge's grave (she died in 1886 at only thirty-four years old) was found in the early 1980s by a Staten Island golfer, C. J. Hyland, while hitting golf (not tennis) balls on his property. Some local ladies took over care and upkeep of the grave. In October 1985, the USTA donated $1,250 "to provide perpetual care for the gravesite of Mary Ewing Outerbridge"; Alexander, *Wingfield*, 197–98, and Tom Norris (Archivist/Records Manager) to USTA Board, "Report from the Archives—The Final Resting Place of Mary Ewing Outerbridge," August 22, 2005. For a very cautious perpetuation of the Mary Outerbridge myth see Sam Roberts, "On Staten Island, the Earliest Traces of American Tennis" *New York Times*, August 20, 2010, 11:03. Roberts did note that as of 1659, Peter Stuyvesant, the governor general of then Dutch New Amsterdam, had banned tennis play on "days of fasting and prayer." But that was not the game designed by Major Wingfield. A brief summary of all this is in Collins, *Bud Collins Total Tennis*, the opening chapter of which, "Roots of the Game," was drafted by George Alexander and Lance Tingay, then put into cute Collins-ese by the editor.

12. See Alexander, *Lawn Tennis*, 54–57, for an explication of the 1874 versus 1875 dates. In 1876, the Prince brothers and their friends founded the then and still very exclusive Myopia Club in Winchester, Massachusetts, with tennis

as a bonding force: "in this way [playing lawn tennis] I became intimate with the older men who, with my brothers, were soon to form the Myopia Club." The founders included the four Prince brothers who along with some others were "short-sighted"—hence the Myopia Club. Forbes, "Early Myopia at Winchester," 1–2. This was one of the earliest American lawn-tennis "facilities," but it was not a formal "lawn-tennis club" until a decade later, and then under the name Wedgemere Tennis club. See http://www.winchester.us/communityconnection/sports.html#tennis.

13. In 1874 (or 1875), Dr. "Jim" Dwight had laid out a lawn-tennis court on the property of William Appleton in Nahant, Massachusetts, assisted by Frederick and Morton Prince—all of them as much a part of the Boston elite as the Cabots and the Lowells. In the words of Frederick Prince: "At once the game became very popular at Nahant, and we immediately ordered one to be put up on my father's lawn at Winchester. On weekends many Bostonians came down to see the new game." This convoluted story is examined, with evidence, in Alexander, *Lawn Tennis*, 53–58. Dwight's recollections, made four years apart, are quoted. Dwight never claimed to have played the first set of lawn tennis in America, just in New England, which may be an accurate claim—though he added it was the first "I fancy, in the country." See Dwight, "Lawn Tennis in New England," 157. Alexander concludes that 1875 for Dwight's first game is correct because Dwight described that court at Nahant with dimensions that were set forth in the third edition of the major's book of the game, which was not printed until 1875. Dwight was obviously the major figure in the early history of the Association as the following chapter indicates. By the 1880s, the Nahant "first match" story had become the accepted truth, for example, "An Interesting Letter," *Official Lawn Tennis Bulletin* 3, no. 3 (March 5, 1896): 42–43 (hereafter *OLTB*). Richard Hillway contends that the first book published in America on lawn tennis came in 1877; Hillway, "America's First Lawn Tennis Book," 452–85.

14. Although Martha Summerhayes never mentions herself playing tennis, it is clear that she was a dedicated player. The quotations and dating are from Summerhayes, *Vanished Arizona*. Playing tennis from Camp Apache (later Fort Apache) to San Francisco to Nebraska is mentioned, though without details, on pages 39, 110, and 120. Alexander, *Lawn Tennis*, 56–57, summarizes the Summerhayes tennis story, although some of his statements cannot be traced from the notes. Her book is also available at http://www.gutenberg.org/dirs/etext97/varizl0.txt, Project Gutenberg Etext #1049, September 1997.

Hers is a lovely book that still deserves a reading today. She wrote of "simply the impressions made upon the mind of a young New England woman who left her comfortable home in the early seventies, to follow a second lieutenant into the wildest encampments of the American army"; Summerhayes, *Vanished Arizona*, 1. Imagine the culture shock for a young New England woman, well-off enough to have spent a year in Hanover, Germany, as the guest of a German general and his family, who traveled overland across the United States to San

Francisco. Then in 1874 they sailed south and then north into the Gulf of California so they could reach the mouth of the Colorado River where they embarked on a boat and over-the-mountains trek to Camp Apache. Sixteen years later in 1890, the Summerhayes ended up at Fort Slocum in Long Island Sound and lived in New Rochelle, New York. There they met and became friendly with the painter and sculptor Frederick Remington, who played tennis with Teddy Roosevelt.

15. On the matter of court surface, the major's patent and book of rules are quoted in Alexander, *Lawn Tennis*, 18, 113. For the Wedgemere Club see Ellen Knight, "Sports History," in Town of Winchester, Official Website, http://www.winchester.us/communityconnection/sports.html#tennis. *A Centenary of the Russian Tennis Federation*, published in Moscow in 2008, has a photograph of four Russian polar experts playing tennis at the North Pole on a court laid out on snow-covered ice! The major would have been pleased. There is also a photo from 1917 of a racket-wielding former national doubles champion, Fred Alexander, facing an apparent opponent, both standing on ice wearing ice skates; cover photo, *ALT*, January 15, 1917.

16. Whether they had one of the major's boxes is doubtful. The journey from San Francisco to Camp Apache, fully described by Martha Summerhayes in *Vanished Arizona*, 12–37, was long and arduous—by ship, wagons and mules—and there were strict official weight limitations on baggage, although the wives routinely ignored such regulations; *Vanished Arizona*, 30–31. But they could still have played the major's game if they had a copy of his book of rules. Information about the early years of tennis in California is from Yeomans, *Southern California Tennis Champions Centennial, 1887–1987*, 1–23. English businessmen built turf (grass) courts in San Rafael, California, by 1880. There is no mention of tennis at Angel Island, but then that was in northern California, and the rivalry between northern and southern was already strong. See also Baltzell, *Sporting Gentlemen*, 94. The English champion Willie Renshaw built a clay court on the French Riviera in 1880. Boards laid over dirt courts became common enough to warrant a pamphlet on how to build "every kind of 'hard' court" that was available from the magazine *ALT*, February 15, 1910, 369. My thanks to Joseph B. Stahl of the New Orleans Lawn Tennis Club for pointing me in some right directions.

17. The information about Camp Reynolds is from the Angel Island Association website, http://www.angelisland.org/reynld02.html (accessed 2008).

18. The claim of the New Orleans Lawn Tennis Club to be the oldest in the United States was accepted by the USTA in 2005 in response to evidence submitted by Joseph Stahl. See Stahl to Janet Hanasik (with enclosures), November 28, 2005 and Hanasik to Stahl, December 14, 2005, in this author's possession and to be deposited in the USTA Archive. Some forty-five years after the founding of the New Orleans club, *American Lawn Tennis* magazine stated that it was the oldest lawn-tennis club in the United

States, preceding clubs in Boston and other places; *ALT*, May 20, 1930, 127. The Myopia Club may be a contender, but probably not. (See note 12, p. 281) The research of tennis historian Attila Szabo has led him to conclude that staff members at British consulates were *a*, if not *the* primary source of "growing the game" in the Americas. I agree. A British consulate in San Francisco predated by a half-century (when it was still part of Mexico) the presence there of Martha Summerhayes and lawn tennis. As countless writers have pointed out, English sports followed the Union Jack throughout the world.

19. Potter, *Kings of the Court*, 4. The hourglass shape may have made Wingfield's invention unique, but it also shortened the length and weight of the net, making it easier to tighten it, which was probably why the major designed it that way. Fortunately for Ella Bailey, the rule for the service toss to be with the left hand, thus making it a right-handed game, was ignored; Alexander, *Lawn Tennis*, 16. One history states, without evidence, that Wingfield sold the name "Lawn Tennis" to the Marylebone Cricket Club, which then transferred it to the All England Club because women wished to play and the club had women members; Macaulay, *Behind the Scenes at Wimbledon*, 18.

20. The tale of finding the original patent, told in the box "Major Wingfield's Patent" is from a telephone interview with Stanley Malless by the author, February 13, 2007, supplemented by Carr, "Long Missing Wingfield Patent Recovered," 11 (courtesy of Richard Hillway), and telephone interviews with Hillway by author, March 6 and August 27, 2007. Carr claims that the art collector's agent first contacted George Alexander, but in a telephone interview on February 15, 2007, Alexander professed to know nothing of the search for the original patent. Alexander does note in *Wingfield*, 95, that, although "the 'framed patent of Lawn Tennis'" was listed in a 1924 will, "its present [circa 1985] location is unknown." The million-dollar asking price was, according to Carr, offered to the Wimbledon Tennis Museum, which rejected it. Alexander's *Lawn Tennis*, which was published by the USTA's long-time quasi-official publisher, H. O. Zimman, has an introduction written by the then president of the USLTA, Stanley Malless. The Wingfield biography, which is largely an expansion of that earlier book, acknowledges Malless's role in the formation of the Wingfield Society of which Alexander was an honorary member. Alexander, who spent years researching in England on the early years of lawn tennis, found a store of Wingfield artifacts—the major's uniform, sword, and such—but negotiations with the Wingfield family to obtain the items proved unsuccessful. Alexander brought in Malless who eventually arranged to purchase them. The Wingfield heirs also granted Malless ownership rights to the patent, if he could find it. He did.

21. Potter, *Kings of the Court*, 1–14. Potter's emphasis on the connection between money and tennis is not surprising. In 1936 when his book came out, he was a staunch critic of what later became known as "shamateurism." Alexander vigorously defends Wingfield against charges that he "broke the Victorian code for gentlemen by making money from his game." That code was, of course, hon-

ored largely in the breach, and Alexander admits that sales and interest far exceeded the major's expectations; Alexander, *Wingfield*, 94–97. Whether or not he intended to make money, he did so, though he seems not to have defended his patent against infringement. Why? Perhaps the patent, which related to the layout of the court, was more useful for adding a certain gravitas and the appearance of royal endorsement to his "invention" rather than legal protection. Perhaps because the dimensions of his court had changed significantly. In any event, the major let his patent expire in 1877. Maybe, as one writer suggested, when "Wingfield found he was not the only pebble on the beach" he saved the £50 needed for final registration; S. W. Merrihew in *ALT*, September 5, 1931, 30; Collins and Hollander, *Bud Collins' Tennis Encyclopedia*, 6. But that is belied by the fact that when Wingfield died he left an estate of £48,370, which would have a buying power today (2014) of over $6,725,000; Alexander, *Lawn Tennis*, 51.

For a time, the All England Lawn Tennis Club (Wimbledon) tended to treat "pelota" (named after a Spanish ball game) as the direct predecessor of lawn tennis. This was, it seems, largely work of Tom Todd, whose book, *Tennis Players*, 39–46, 56 (at one point calling the major an old rascal), argued strongly that the credit belonged to one Thomas Harry Gem. For a persuasive corrective, see Hillway, "Lawn Tennis Inventor—Wingfield versus Gem," 14–17. Wikipedia, the all too often unreliable on-line encyclopedia in an entry that as of 2007 could not be edited, echoes Todd, describing how pelota came to England in 1856, when Joao Batista Pereira (Perera), a Portuguese (or Spanish) merchant and a friend played on a lawn in Edgbaston Cricket Ground near Birmingham. By 1873 both men had moved to Leamington Spa, southeast of Birmingham, and with two doctors from the Warneford Hospital, played pelota on the lawn behind the then Manor House Hotel (now residential apartments). In 1874 they formed the Leamington Tennis Club, perhaps the first lawn-tennis club in the world. Later that year (and after publication of the major's first book of rules), Harry Gem, another Leamington player, circulated a set of rules for Pereira's game; http://en.wikipedia.org/wiki/Lawn_tennis. See also Alexander, *Lawn Tennis*, 29, and Alexander, *Wingfield*, 96–97, 176.

22. For the Wingfield restaurant, see https://www.fmccatering.co.uk/wingfield-restaurant-reservations/.
23. The phrase of George Adee of the Association's executive committee, as quoted in the "Amateurs May Lose Status," *New York Times*, January 13, 1916.

2. THE FOUNDING GENTLEMEN

1. "So far [between 1876 and 1880] the Staten Island Cricket club had made no attempt to take the leadership as the All England Club had done. . . . In 1880 . . . the Outerbridges, smarting under Dwight's assertion that Appleton's was the first set brought to America, announced a 'championship'

meeting. Dwight found fault with the balls and refused to enter"; Potter, *Kings of the Court*, 55. As plausible as Outerbridge "smarting" may be, I have found no substantiating evidence for Potter's claim. There were at least three other tournaments in 1880 that claimed to be "national" championships, but the Staten Island tournament was the only historically important one; United States Tennis Association, USTA *Official Encyclopedia of Tennis*, 8–9 (hereafter USTA *Official Encyclopedia*).

2. James Dwight described what he labeled "the first set of lawn tennis in New England—indeed, I fancy, in the country," played in summer 1875 at William Appleton's home in Nahant, Massachusetts. They used very light, spoon-shaped rackets, "large, uncovered rubber balls," and a court "narrowest at the net and widest at the base line"—clearly the major's hourglass court. The service line was twenty-six feet from the net as opposed to today's twenty-one feet. As Dwight later pointed out, "What a chance for service . . . if anyone had known how to serve!" Dwight, "Lawn Tennis in New England,"157. Aberdare, *The Story of Tennis*, 114–15, describes similar early courts laid out in America at Newport, Rhode Island, in Plainfield, New Jersey, in New Orleans, and on the Germantown Cricket Grounds in Philadelphia—all based on the original Wingfield and 1875 Marylebone Cricket Club (Lords) rules with the hourglass shape. For the disparity in ball size see USLTA, *Fifty Years of Lawn Tennis*, "Annals of the U.S.L.T.A." ("Annals"), 227. In 1878 the All England and Marylebone Clubs had agreed on a common set of lawn-tennis rules that used a rectangular court. The sketch of the Staten Island court is captioned "The first National Lawn Tennis tournament at New Brighton, Staten Island; from a sketch by H. A. Ogden," Cunningham, *75 Years of the International Tennis Federation*, 4–5. An earlier court, also rectangular, is depicted in an undated sketch captioned "Site of the first Lawn Tennis court in America. Camp Washington, now St. George, Staten Island," in Aberdare, *Story of Tennis*, following page 104.
3. On doubles as more popular in Wingfield's early game, see Scott, "Vantage Point," 8, and "publisher responds," *Tennis Week,* February 15, 2005, 7. Interestingly, when the Young American Cricket Club tennis players challenged the Staten Island Cricket and Baseball Club in autumn 1880, it was to play a "four-handed" (i.e., doubles) match. Slocum, *Lawn Tennis in Our Own Country*, 114. If payments to the USNLTA are an indication of popularity, doubles had an edge as of 1888, when the National Doubles Championships garnered offers as high as $500, while the Singles Nationals at Newport brought in a payment to the Association of only $250; Minutes, 1888 Annual Meeting, and *OLTB* 4, no. 12 (December 1897): 325.
4. Clay, "The Staten Island Cricket and Baseball Club," 107; "Fine Playing at Lawn Tennis," *New York Times*, September 3, 1880; Roberts, "Aces and Diamonds," 89.
5. "Sports at Gilmore's Garden," *New York Times*, December 13, 1878.
6. "The Game of Lawn-Tennis," *New York Times*, June 23, August 15, 1880. The $100 prize would be worth just over $2,000 in 2008 dollars; http://futureboy.homeip

.net/fsp/dollar.fsp. The founding of the Cincinnati Tennis Club (apparently without a "lawn") is in http://www.cincinnatitennisclub.com/history.html.

7. The *New York Times* reported that Sears and Dwight "arrived from Boston early in the day." The same article closed stating that "spectators visited the grounds yesterday" to watch a singles match between Dwight and Woodhouse (the English champion), but Dwight "refused to play on account of the balls not suiting him." "Double Lawn-Tennis," *New York Times*, September 7, 1880; Dwight, "Lawn Tennis in New England," 73. Fifty years later, E. H. Outerbridge claimed that announcements for the tournament had stated that the "Ayers" ball was the official ball; Minutes, 1931 Annual Meeting, 1–7. For similar and more contemporary account see "An Interesting Letter," *OLTB* 3, no 3 (March 5, 1896): 42–43. Wingfield himself called tennis rackets, bats. To decode the scoring (the old "racquets" system): A "set" went to the first player/team to reach 15 points. Two sets constituted a match with "the aggregate number of points instead of number of sets won, deciding who is winner." As quoted in "First 'National' Lawn Tennis Tournament," *LTLR* 9 (September 1950).
8. Slocum, *Lawn Tennis*, 114; "First 'National,'" *LTLR, 9*.
9. "Annals," 227–30. Unfortunately, James Dwight seems not to have left any record about those negotiations, leaving the field to E. H. Outerbridge whose retrospective public remarks were recorded in Minutes, 1931 Annual Meeting, 1–7 and then apparently summarized/paraphrased in the "Annals." Outerbridge's full speech is reproduced appendix 1. His talk was only a bit more candid than the published excerpts from his 1923 letter (not found) to then Association president, Dwight Davis; "The Origin of Lawn Tennis in the United States," continued as "The History of Lawn Tennis in the United States, *Official Bulletin* 2, nos. 10–11 (October–November 1927): 1–2, and 3, no. 1 (December–January and February 1928): 1–2, 10. Joseph Clark's recollections (his brother, Clarence, was the third signatory on the meeting call) were anodyne and uninformative; Clark, "The United States National Lawn Tennis Association," *Official Lawn Tennis Rules* (1889), 45–46.
10. In 1876, baseball's National League had been founded in the same hotel. Like the USNLTA, it too was formed by clubs, not individuals.
11. This and preceding quotations and information comes from "Annals," 227–34; Minutes, 1931 Annual Meeting, 1–7; and "Minutes of the [founding meeting of the] United States Lawn Tennis Association [1881]," retrospectively printed in *OLTB* 3, no. 1 (January 2, 1896): 1–3. That retrospective collection is cited hereafter cited as USNLTA Minutes, plus the year(s) of the minutes being referred to. See "Note on Citations" in the preface and "Research Guide" for details on the collection.

    Lest you get as confused as I did, know that the Association's founding meeting in 1881 was followed in 1882 by the first annual meeting, and so on. Thus the last digit of the meeting number is always one digit less than the final digit of the year; i.e., the fiftieth annual meeting was held in XXX1

(1931 in this case), the seventy-fifth Annual came in xxx6 (1956), and so on. The annual meetings quickly migrated from May back to April, then March, and then settled on February-March where they have pretty much stayed to the present. Eventually, the board of directors (created in 1973) received authority to schedule the annual meeting sometime between January 1 and April 15 of each year.

The lack of original historical records creates problems, in this case none substantive. The three most complete (and most cited) sources for the founding meeting: 1881 USNLTA Minutes, "Annals," 230–33, and "The Origin of Lawn Tennis in the U.S.," 1–2, carry differing club names and numbers. The number of clubs represented by proxy is variously given as fifteen and sixteen; the proxies as thirteen to fifteen. The "Longarm" Cricket Club listed in "Annals" is obviously the Longwood club outside Boston. The Philadelphia Cricket Club is listed having a delegate in one list, as represented by proxy in another. Harry Slocum, writing less than ten years after meeting, took the cautious course, simply stating that "as many as thirty-three clubs were represented." Slocum, *Lawn Tennis*, 116. One hundred years later, then-president Marv Richmond offered "a few historical comments regarding the founding of the Association. 'Of the thirty-nine tennis clubs in the United States at that time, thirty-three had representatives at the first meeting,'" Richmond stated. Management Committee Minutes, May 21–22, 1981 (hereafter MgmntCom). Close enough.

12. E. H. Outerbridge remarks, Minutes, 1931 Annual Meeting, 5. The genealogy is from Crawford, *Famous Families of Massachusetts*, I:243–44; *LTLR*, 11 (June 1951). "Brig, Gen. Oliver Dies in South at 87," *New York Times*, March 17, 1935. Much of the material about Oliver is courtesy of Geoff Felder.

13. Notes for the box "The Founding Father": Potter, *Kings of the Court*, 53–63; Cummings, *American Tennis*, 40–46, and Frank Phelps, "James Dwight" in the *Dictionary of American Biography*, 184–85; Alexander, *Lawn Tennis*, 59–65. A story about Dwight's "sailor's gait" is in Slocum, *Lawn Tennis*, 111. Slocum, the second great U.S. champion after Dick Sears, played in the 1880s and '90s, as did Dwight. One writer described him as a "dapper little cuss"; Myers, "The Americans at Wimbledon," 19. The old-balls trick is from Myers, *The Complete Lawn Tennis Player*, 179–80. An example of contemporary praise for Dwight's teaching skills is Starey, "Some Aspects of American Lawn Tennis." Starey also suggests that doubles (four-handed game) was more popular than singles. Dwight's twenty-one years as Association president (1882–84, 1894–1911) set the unbroken and unbreakable record. Holcombe Ward served for eleven years as president, much of that during the Second World War. No one else served for more than four years. Historical information about the USTA, including the names of officers and lists of champions, in this instance and elsewhere, is from the *2006 USTA Yearbook*. Dwight so regularly wrote "Cases and Decisions" articles regarding rules of play that the practice became institutionalized. The early pages of

Wind, "The Sporting Scene" 142, offer a lovely, typically *New Yorker* look at James Dwight and the early days of lawn tennis in America.

14. 1881 USNLTA Minutes, and "The Origin of Lawn Tennis in the U.S.," 2. The proposed amendments to the original constitution and bylaws are mentioned therein. Amazingly, the original constitution and bylaws of the Association have been lost. No copy or typescript of those documents can be found. Fortunately, USNLTA Minutes (1882 and 1883), plus a published copy of the 1884 constitution and bylaws and the relatively minor amendments made to it by that time, provide a clear template of what the original documents said. See appendix 2.
15. For both paragraphs, "Annals," 232 and 1881 USNLTA Minutes. The 1–15 scoring system could be used, but only if specified for the tournament.
16. "The History of Lawn Tennis in the U.S.," 10. The constant worry about obtaining suitable tennis balls is obvious in the USNLTA executive-committee minutes throughout the 1880s.
17. Dwight, letter to the editor, 5, 9 (courtesy of Frank Phelps).
18. 1886 USNLTA Minutes. The amendment had to do with a struck ball hitting a loose ball on the opposite court.
19. Slocum, *Lawn Tennis*, 205–7. "Tournaments of 1888," *Official Lawn Tennis Rules* (1889), 80. The word "sections" merely described a geographic region, not the organizations called sections that developed later.
20. Joseph Clark's statement, "The United States Lawn Tennis Association," was published in *Official Lawn Tennis Rules* (1889), 45–54. The nationals were officially played at the Newport Tennis Club, which was located at the Newport Casino.
21. Minutes, 1931 Annual Meeting, 6.
22. The U.S. National Championships began for men singles and doubles in 1881, for women's singles in 1887 and doubles in 1889.
23. The amendment even allowed fractional votes for association members beyond ten; that is, an association with twelve member clubs would have 2.2 votes at USLTA meetings. Association Constitution, 1882, 1884, 1889; USNLTA Minutes. Dues were raised correspondingly. Class-one member clubs still paid $7 a year, while associations of clubs were assessed $25 plus $5 for each five, or fraction thereof, additional clubs beyond ten. Association boundaries could not conflict except by either a two-thirds vote of the USNLTA membership or agreement between the associations concerned. Association of clubs could also be formed by schools and colleges.
24. "A Historical Sketch of the United States Lawn Tennis Association," USLTA, December 27, 1955 (copy of a typescript), USTA Archive. The U.S. usage of seventy-five years for a diamond jubilee parts with British custom which designates the sixtieth year of a monarch's reign as the diamond jubilee.
25. Yeomans, *Southern California Tennis*, 20. Two Chicagoans, Robert Wrenn (who would move to New York) and J. P. Gardner joined the executive

committee in 1890. The Californian was F. G. Ryan, of the Brookhurst Club in Anaheim; *1891 Lawn Tennis Guide*, 193; *The American Cricketeer* 16 (January–February 1893): 5; 1887 USNLTA Minutes. The 1894 sampling is from *Lawn Tennis Guide for 1894* (Boston: Wright & Ditson, 1894). See also the *USLTA Yearbooks* for those years, USTA Archive CDs.

26. Tennis in the "sections" is frequently mentioned in minutes of the annual meetings for those years. Wrenn's "reluctance" is reported in "Proposal to Wipe Out Old Custom Strongly Opposed by Players," *New York Times*, January 7, 1912. Champions as president were the norm except for one T. K. Fraser, who served as Association president for two years (1885–86), a time when James Dwight was in Europe. Fraser was from the Northeast and played tennis (in 1895 he lost to tennis writer and historian, J. Parmley Paret, in a tournament at Sleepy Hollow, New York, but his name does not appear in the lists of top players or as an entrant in major tournaments). The *1966 USLTA Yearbook* claimed incorrectly that after the founding year of the Association, every president had been a national men's singles champion or runner-up until 1916. Joseph Clark never got to the national singles final, but did won the national doubles title in 1885. Dwight repeatedly asked not to be nominated, but he never refused to serve. At one point Association leaders told him he would be elected president forever. The shift away from former champions as president and officers began in 1916, with the election of George Adee, just before the era of Bill Tilden and champions who played tennis nearly full-time. See chapter 3.

27. "An Interesting Letter," *OLTB* 3, no. 3 (March 5, 1896): 42–43; *OLTB* 3, no. 4 (April 2, 1896): 55. The "bisque" is described, with its detailed restrictions, in *Official Lawn Tennis Rules* (1889), 10–11. Testimony on today's bisque is in email, Alan Schwartz to author, August 24, 2007.

28. See chapter 6 (USTA League program).

29. Minutes, 1882 Annual Meeting, 41. The provenance of that provision is not clear, but it likely came via the Marylebone rules, which provided the model for the USNLTA's constitution and bylaws. No records of professionals playing for money in the United States in the early 1880s have been found, but I leave what was happening in England to the English. However, concern among Association founders about amateurism may well have been a byproduct of ongoing conflicts in British rugby circles that eventually resulted in formation of "the openly professional Rugby League" in 1895; Guttman, *From Ritual to Record*, 31.

30. http://www.wimbledon.org/en_gb/about/history/history.html (as of January 22, 2011). 1885 USNLTA Minutes, 58; Davenport, "Professionalism in Sports," 66–94; "U.S. National Lawn Tennis Association," *American Cricketeer*, 1890 (Phelps photocopies); *Lawn Tennis Guide*, 1891, 133 (hereafter *LTG*); Joseph Clark, "The United States Lawn Tennis Association," *Official Lawn Tennis Rules* (1889), 45–54. The on-going controversy over amateurism is discussed more fully in chapters 3 and 4.

31. Those sections were listed as having had Championships; *Spalding's Lawn Ten-*

nis Annual (April 1900): 41–42; Wright and Ditson's *Lawn Tennis Guide for 1903* (Boston: 1903). Canadian and Caribbean clubs had been eligible for membership in the USNLTA from the outset. After all, the Association's purpose was to standardize the rules of lawn tennis. The impetus for a non–U.S. club to belong seems to have come from their hosting a tournament that attracted good (and therefore influential) American players, the kind who were usually active in the USNLTA. From the inception of the Association until 1990, when bylaw 6 was amended, member clubs did not have to be within Association, later section, boundaries.

32. The preceding paragraphs about the 1890 annual meeting, including the minutes and summary, the list of challenges, and the article on scoring, are all from *The American Cricketeer*, 1890 (Phelps photocopies). During this early era, national champions "stood out" of the regular rounds of a tournament and then played the challenger—hence the phrase "challenge round," still used in Davis Cup matches. Starting in 1890, the east-west regional winners had a playoff, with the winner getting into the challenge round. By 1907 there were three regions competing, and that number grew as sections came into being. The last challenge round for doubles came in 1919, and thereafter the national doubles was a play-through event; *2006 USTA Yearbook*, 482.
33. Sites and records in the box "Sites of the National Championships" are from various *USTA Yearbooks* plus the Wright and Ditson, *Lawn Tennis Guide for 1936* (with thanks to Richard Hillman, phone conversation with author, September 28, 2104).
34. "Annals," 243. There are only a few references in the minutes and newspapers to the membership drop, but the numbers were clear. The website http://futureboy.homeip.net/fsp/dollar.fsp calculated that $7.00 dollars in 1896 had the same buying power as $174.25 current (2008) dollars.
35. *OLTB*, "Echoes from the Annual Meeting," February 10, 1898, 23.
36. *Outing*, March 1894, 99 (USTA Archive, early minutes CD). The foot-fault controversy would take decades to resolve. The problem was determining whether or not players could step or run forward while serving, and what constituted a "step." See James Dwight letter, March 12, 1897; *ALT*, February 10, 1898, 24, for the debate as of the end of the nineteenth century. At various times the Association constituted a "Committee on Footfaults" (e.g., "Tennis Men Meet To-Day," *New York Times*, December 19, 1913). The two-feet together launch used by the better players today did not become legal until July 9, 1958. In the words of Jack Starr, the most influential tennis rules maven since James Dwight, as of that date a server was permitted "to leap as high as he might wish—and even well forward into the court if he so desires—provided that he hits the serve before either of his feet actually touches the line or the ground inside the line." Starr, *Stahre Decisis*, 7.1. (With thanks to Roy Van Brunt for the citation.)

37. *OLTB* 3, no. 2 (February 6, 1896): 22.
38. The Panic of 1893 was primarily a financial crisis, whatever its root causes and long-term effects. Three major railroads failed, along with tens of thousands of businesses and some five hundred banks. High unemployment (over 15 percent of the workforce) would have had little effect on a game played primarily by the leisure class, but the dramatic contraction of credit (as in 2007–8) probably limited discretionary spending among even the well off.
39. The information in the text and in the box "Dwight Davis—More than a Cup" is taken from Kriplen, *Dwight Davis*, particularly pages 12–58. "The Davis Cup trophy originally cost about $600, and was designed and crafted by the firm of Shreve, Crump, and Low of Boston in 1899 (the first Davis Cup tournament was in 1900). Seven years later, the magazine *American Lawn Tennis* was preparing a story about the Davis Cup and contacted the company with some detailed questions about the cup's manufacture. Shreve, Crump, and Low replied that the firm had made many thousands of sports trophies and that, although they may have made one called the Davis Cup, they certainly could not be expected to remember it! Nowadays, the company proudly proclaims on its website that it was indeed the designer of the Davis Cup trophy"; Tom Norris to USTA Board, October 12, 2005, "Report from the Archives—The US Open Film and Video Collection, and a Davis Cup anecdote."
40. The first match was held in 1900, with Great Britain the only "challenger" for the trophy, which was "held" by the Americans since they had donated it. The United States won the first three of five matches (two singles, one doubles), or "rubbers," hence the phrase "dead rubbers" matches that could not affect the overall outcome. In Davis Cup competition, that referred to matches played after a team had won three (always singles matches since the original format, still used today, called for two singles matches, then a doubles, then two singles). The competition quickly became international, as Davis had intended, when Belgium, France, and Australasia entered challenges to the previous year's winner. The number of challengers rose in erratic fashion, but by 1913 seven challenges came, sixteen in 1923, then into the twenties where it stayed until 1954 when thirty challengers appeared. The final round was against the previous winner, which "held" the cup—hence the phrase "challenge round" rather than "finals." An MA thesis by Elizabeth L. Herritt, "Social Class and the Women's National Tennis Championships in the United States, 1887–1905," belabors the obvious—that women's tennis in those years was very much a social activity and dominated by the "elite" and "upper classes." Nonetheless, the thesis is a gold mine of names and statistics about tennis in the northeastern United States during that period. Richard Olney was an avid tennis player well into his sixties.
41. *ALT*, February 15, 1912, 440. The United States–England match was a preliminary round. The United States went on to play the challenge round against Australasia in New Zealand and won, bringing in additional revenue. The West Side Tennis Club, which became the long-term home for the U.S. National Championships,

began in 1892 on Central Park West (hence "West Side") in Manhattan, and migrated in 1913 to the Forest Hills community in Queens, New York City.

42. "On the Tennis Courts," *New York Times*, July 20, 1902, has "the seal of approval" comment. The same article noted that President Roosevelt intended to attend the Davis Cup matches scheduled for Bay Ridge, Brooklyn, New York, noting, "[Roosevelt] is an ardent admirer of the game and, as was made evident only a few days ago, he likes nothing better than to face an opponent worthy of the name across the white net." Thus, Robert "Bob" Wrenn ("former champion" Wrenn in USNLTA talk) visited Roosevelt's home in Oyster Bay, Long Island. Wrenn had no difficulty winning their match, but the president forced Wrenn to "work in his most strenuous manner for every point." The story went on to relate Roosevelt's earlier assessment that lawn tennis was "more laborious than a bout at boxing or wrestling." I have found no record of him playing with or against Dwight Davis, but if he hit with Bob Wrenn, why not Davis? The White House tennis court built for Roosevelt in 1903 was destined to become a basketball court during the Obama administration. To my dismay, I have not been able to find a photograph of Teddy Roosevelt playing tennis. It seems he meant what told his successor, William Howard Taft: "About your playing golf . . . I have received literally hundreds of letters from the West protesting about it. . . . It is just like my tennis. I never let any friends advertise my tennis and never let a photograph of me in tennis costume appear." A reference, perhaps, to golf and tennis not being seen as "manly" sports; *Time* 100 leaders profile at: http://www.time.com/time/time100/leaders/profile/troosevelt_related7.html. Happily, there is the wonderful cartoon drawn by Roosevelt and sent to his young daughter, Ethel, showing himself with the handwritten comment that "father's shape and spectacles are reproduced with photographic fidelity"; Theodore Roosevelt ("picture letter") to Ethel Roosevelt (his daughter), June 23, 1904, Theodore Roosevelt Collection, Houghton Library, Harvard University, MS AM1454.48 (29). (See gallery, image 8.) Martha Summerhayes's friendship with Remington is mentioned above, chapter 1, note 14.

43. Kriplen, *Dwight Davis*, 23.

44. Baltzell, *Sporting Gentlemen*, 12–13. Club membership numbers are from "Annals," 243. An Association committee stated in 1910 that it had "no statistics as to the average [individual] membership of each club"; *ALT*, February 15, 1910 (misdated in the printed header on page 353), 356. As a comparison, a participation survey by the Tennis Industry Association and the USTA in autumn 2007 indicated there were over 5 million "frequent" tennis players in the country, and some 25 million who play at least once a year (USTA Archive).

45. Membership on the executive committee in this era can be located on the masthead of *ALT*; in this case, February 15, 1912, 440. There is a dramatic difference between the average age of executive-committee members in

the early twentieth century and that of the board of directors since the Second World War.

46. *Spalding's Lawn Tennis Annual,* 1906, 17.

47. "Plan New Tennis Body," *New York Times*, March 13, 1904; "Reforms in Tennis Needed, Say Experts," *New York Times*, February 3, 1905; "Tennis Factions Meet To-Night at Waldorf," *New York Times*, February 5, 1906. The Association did not have a board of directors until 1985. The national singles championship would remain at the Newport Casino until 1915.

48. "Tennis Trophy Challenge," *New York Times*, February 6, 1906. The total amount, $518, had in 1905 had the same buying power as $12,150 in current (2008) dollars. The conversion is from http://futureboy.homeip.net/fsp/dollar.fsp.

49. A good example of such complaints is in "Queries and Opinions" (letters to the editor), *ALT,* February 15, 1908, 387–88. "Indignation on the Pacific Coast" was the header for one letter. For newspaper accounts see the *New York Times*, which usually covered the Association's annual meeting. One such account was credited for generating "much interest" in a ranking committee report; *ALT,* February 15, 1908, 379. Those who did not play the major tournaments in the East were routinely not ranked because of "insufficient data."

50. "Proxies," *ALT*, February 15, 1911, 431.

51. "Annual Meeting of the USNLTA," *ALT*, February 15, 1908, 382. Cragin's motion and his justification for a committee on "representation" (or governance as such committees would later be called) is in his letter to the editor, *ALT*, February 15, 1908, 386. Cragin was a member of the West Side Tennis Club.

52. "Tennis Men May Fight," *New York Times*, January 16,1910, and August 19, 1909. For the dead letters see Hawk letter, February 7, in *ALT,* February 15,1911, 363. Merrihew's wisecracks are in on pages 353–54. Hawk was a physiological chemist at the University of Illinois and became a well-published scientist. Hidden within a maze of titles like *Activity of the Pancreatic Function under the Influence of Copious Water-drinking with Meals* (1911) is his book *Off the Racket: Tennis Highlights and Lowdowns* with an introduction by S. Wallis Merrihew. Hawk later moved to New York and served as president of the West Side Tennis Club.

53. *ALT,* February 15, 1910, 368. Concern about diluting the nationals is on page 358.

54. Notes for "He Carried a Torch for Tennis": Merrihew's run for the executive committee raised questions of a conflict of interest since he received a subsidy from the Association for publishing *ALT* despite his claim that the publication had lost money initially and was, as of 1911, a break-even proposition; *ALT*, January 15, 1911, 399. The clever move is described in "Thirtieth Annual Meeting," *ALT*, February 15, 1911, 416. The self-description of his dedication to tennis is in *ALT*, December 15, 1919, 475. Biographical information on Merrihew (1862–1947) is from Hillway and Felder, "Stephen Wallis Merrihew and American Lawn Tennis," 452–56, and Phelps, "Merrihew, Stephen Wallis," 375–76 (courtesy of Richard Hillway). Phelps states that Merrihew played tennis daily. The February 20, 1944

issue of *ALT* contains a symposium on Merrihew's contributions to lawn tennis.

55. "Tennis Men Meet; Proxies Not Here," *New York Times*, February 5, 1910 and "Tennis Committee on Rotating Plan," *New York Times*, January 2, 1911. All the quotes are the reporters' words. Since the executive committee included the officers, all of whom were easterners, they had a majority of nine to four. From 1891 through 1988, qualifications for the treasurer's position appeared professional rather than tennis abilities or Association politics. Most treasurers served multiple terms and did not move up the ladder to other officer positions. Richard Stevens, for example, served from 1899 through 1916. The notion of governance organized along state lines would come up with a vengeance nearly a century later.
56. Hawk to the USNLTA Officers, February 9, in *ALT*, February 15, 1910, 356; generally see "29th Annual Meeting of the U.S.N.L.T.A.," on pages 353–57. Formation of the Clay Court Association had been reported in "New Tennis Association," *New York Times*, February 13, 1910. Membership would be individual, dues were fifty cents a year, and each member would vote by mail. It would seem that the organization never organized.
57. "Who decides?" was the favorite and cynical query of Gordon Levering, the spouse of USTA president Judy Levering (1999–2000). It neatly captures a dilemma that the Association has faced throughout its existence since 1881. The 1911 revolt is described in some detail in "Thirtieth Annual Meeting of the U.S.N.L.T.A.," *ALT*, February 15, 1911, 415–18. The *ALT* editors ended by noting that there were "some discrepancies" between that summary and the "official, verbatim report submitted by President Dwight." The discrepancies were obvious. The official report provided no indication of the confrontation that took place over the elections to the executive committee, while the word "proxy" never appears; *ALT*, February 15, 1911, 418–20, 435. The "official" minutes contained testimonials for the Newport Casino and various clubs in the Philadelphia area as good sites for the national championships, but "who decides" was conspicuous by its absence.
58. Eastern solidarity on governance was widespread, but not unanimous. There were, for example, New Yorkers like Calhoun Cragin who supported governance reforms. The Merrihew/Hawk vote and the rest of the meeting are from *ALT*, February 15, 1911, 416–17.
59. *ALT*, February 15, 1911, 416–17; "Tennis Committee on Rotating Plan," *New York Times*, January 2, 1911.
60. "Sweeping Reforms in Lawn Tennis," *New York Times*, January 29, 1911.
61. Despite statements that Dwight could be president for life, he had told the 1911 annual meeting that he would accept the presidency for only one more year.
62. "Old Tennis Laws Hard to Wipe Out," *New York Times*, January 7, 14, 1912. By 1932, twenty years later, P. B. Hawk was president of the West Side Ten-

nis Club—the same club to which Cragin belonged. Ah, the small world of lawn tennis, even some decades after the turn of the century.

63. If, to this point, this account seems wedded to the Association's annual meeting, year by year, that is because there is little or no evidence of what was going on between meetings, other than tennis matches. It is likely that people were conniving, planning, and preparing—but they were doing so to get ready for the annual meeting, which is where decisions could be made.

64. All the quotations in the box "The Three-Ring Circus Tale," which has an only slightly fanciful description of the 1911 and 1912 annual meetings, are cited in the main text. "Cushing's Manual" remained the Association's source for parliamentary procedures at meetings until 1933, when the executive committee switched to *Robert's Rules of Order*; Minutes, 1933 Annual Meeting, 19.

65. As late as 1939, the Western Section still complained at the failure of the Association to schedule a major tournament in the West that would attract "the best players." Somehow, the scheduling committee always found it "impossible to change the Eastern program without injury to the old established clubs" *LTG*, 1939, 9–11.

66. "Proposal to Wipe Out Old Customs," *New York Times*, January 7, 1912.

67. *ALT*, January 15, 1912; *ALT*, February 15, 1912.

68. The phrase is that of Baltzell, *Sporting Gentlemen*, 85.

3. EVOLUTIONARY REVOLUTION

1. *ALT*, January 15, 1913, 398. Each of the forty-eight states in the continental United States (Arizona and New Mexico had been admitted as states in 1912) plus the District of Columbia were placed in one of 10 sections: New England (six states); Middle States (New York, New Jersey, Pennsylvania); Middle Atlantic (Delaware, District of Columbia, Maryland, Virginia, West Virginia, District of Columbia); Tri-State (Indiana, Kentucky, Ohio), Southern (Alabama, Florida, Georgia, Louisiana, Mississippi, North Carolina, South Carolina, Tennessee), Western (Illinois, Iowa, Kansas, Michigan, Missouri, Nebraska, Wisconsin), Northwestern (Minnesota, Montana, North Dakota, South Dakota), South Western (Arizona, Arkansas, Nevada, New Mexico, Oklahoma, Texas), Inter-Mountain (Colorado, Idaho, Utah, Wyoming), and Pacific States (California, Oregon, Washington).

2. Unhappily, no minutes have survived for the executive committee or the annual meetings of 1912 and 1913. But the very extensive summary of the 1913 annual meeting in *ALT* (February 15, 1913) gives no indication of any serious disagreements, and does not mention any discussion of the proxy matter. The magazine's editor, S. W. Merrihew, usually reported on controversies, even creating a small one himself by running, again unsuccessfully, for an at-large seat on the 1913 executive committee. In 1916 the executive committee continued Merrihew's *ALT* as the Association's official organ but required "proper supervision" by a

committee "representative"; Executive Committee Minutes, March 17, 1916 (follows 1916 Annual Meeting minutes in Annual Meeting CD) (hereafter ExCom).

3. See above chapter 2. Clark, "The United States Lawn Tennis Association," *Official Lawn Tennis Rules* (1889) 45–54 (emphasis added). The clause about section boundaries first appeared in the 1914 constitution.
4. The 1914 USNLTA Constitution reads: "Article V, Sec. 3. The President, Vice-President, Secretary and Treasurer shall be elected at the annual meeting of the National Association in each year and shall serve until their respective successors are elected. The Sectional Delegates shall be appointed by the active associations of the sections which they respectively represent and shall serve for two years. If a section is not represented by an active association its delegate shall be elected by the National Association at its annual meeting. Each Sectional Delegate must live in the section which he represents. On his removal outside the bounds of such section his place shall become vacant. Sectional Delegates appointed by active associations must present their certificates of appointment to the Secretary of the National Association at or before the annual meeting." *1914 USTA Yearbook*.
5. Minutes, 1915 Annual Meeting, 30–31. The Intermountain area, then and now, comprised states in the Rocky Mountains.
6. Minutes, 1916 Annual Meeting, 11.
7. The wealthy-class argument was, of course, fraudulent and self-deceptive. The "upper" classes earned money by rents, by assessments, and by investing in commerce and production through third parties. They frequently worked hard and were as much capitalists as those they scorned.
8. Much of this background information on amateurism is based on Guttman, *From Ritual to Record*, 26–32. See also *Time*, July 27, 1992.
9. "Tennis Made Good in Critical Season," *New York Times*, January 20, 1907.
10. "An Amateur in Tennis," *New York Times*, February 1, 1913.
11. *ALT*, February 15, 1913, 420. Compare to Davenport, "Professionalism in Sports," 70. Davenport cites the missing 1913 USNLTA Annual Meeting Minutes but could have been quoting from the ostensibly verbatim report of Slocum's remarks printed in *ALT*. There are a few unsubstantial differences in phrasing that could mean that Davenport used the actual minutes, but that it is the solitary citation to any of the missing 1904–13 USNLTA Minutes suggests otherwise. "Class" legislation is also mentioned in *New York Times*, February 14, 1913.
12. "Tennis Men Meet Today," *New York Times*, December 19, 1913, "Tennis Made Good in Critical Season," *New York Times*, January 20, 1907; "American Tennis Team to Meet Britons," *New York Times*, February 6, 1907. In the absence of USNLTA, ExCom and annual meeting minutes, and given limited newspaper coverage, reconstructing details and discussions is difficult. Although *ALT*, February 15, 1910, 354, reported that the annual meeting

easily passed a motion to challenge for the cup in 1910, the discussion indicated that President Dwight Davis and some others thought they should wait until 1911. Money was an issue, although the Association lost only $200 on a trip to Australia in 1909. But no challenge round was held in 1910. Then, in December that year, the executive committee voted not to challenge Australasia (Australia and New Zealand) in 1911, but the United States did so and lost. "Tennis Men in Session," *New York Times*, December 23, 1910. USTA records show that the 1909 Challenge Round pitted Australasia against the United States on November 27–30, 1909. Australasia won 5–0. The 1911 Challenge Round was Australasia versus the United States on January 1–3, 1912. Australasia won either 4–0 or 5–0.

13. Citations for the box "The Handkerchief Dropped" are *ALT*, February 15, 1916, 553, and a lovely article by Allison Danzig, "Repeated History—Tennis and Wars," in "Sports of the Times," *New York Times*, May 5, 1939, written when it appeared possible that Germany and Australia could meet in Davis Cup competition in 1939, once again "with the war clouds gathering."
14. Minutes, 1914 Annual Meeting, 71, 75–76, 106. Thorpe won two gold medals at the 1912 Olympics. The following year, his amateur status was revoked retroactively for accepting pay for playing summer baseball in one of the minor leagues. In 1983, the International Olympic Committee restored his medals.
15. The very sketchy (and presentist) details of the history of the ILTF are uncritically set out in Cunnington, *75 Years of the ITF*. ILTF voting is from Minutes, 1914 Annual Meeting, 106–7. The USNLTA reaffirmation not to join the ILTF is Minutes, 1922 Annual Meeting, 4–7, and in *ALT*, February 15, 1920, 538. The Association likewise rejected involvement in the Olympic games so long as the Amateur Athletic Union was the governing body for Olympic tennis. The amateurism debate along with the parliamentary procedures discussion (which was like swimming in oatmeal) can be followed in Minutes, 1914 Annual Meeting, 57–126. Davis Cup was controlled by the Davis Cup nations, not the ILTF.
16. *ALT*, February 15, 1914, 449, 450. The West Side Tennis Club began in 1892 on rented space on Central Park West in Manhattan. In 1912 it relocated "to a spacious, 12-acre stretch of lawn at Forest Hills": Nancy Gill McShea, "A Century of Eastern Champions," courtesy of the Eastern Tennis Association.
17. Minutes, 1916 Annual Meeting, 23. Up until 1917, the significance of sections was enhanced by the procedures for entering the Association's National Men's Doubles Championships. From 1890 through 1906, "sectional" doubles tournaments were held in the east and the west to determine two winners who then played off, with the victor meeting the "standing-out" (previous year's) champions in a "challenge round." After 1906, the various sections competed in what was called the "preliminary doubles" in order to play in the challenge round against the previous year's champions. The First World War prompted temporary changes, and in 1920 the Association adopted the play-through model (all entrants play from the start) but with entries based on rankings rather than on being designated a sectional champion; *2005 USTA Yearbook*, 465.

18. Minutes, 1916 Annual Meeting, 24–25, 38–39. Missouri Valley was listed as a section with a seat on the executive committee as of 1920.
19. The speech by a "Delegate from Lakewood" (Kroesen) is from Minutes, 1914 Annual Meeting, 43–44. The second speech is from Minutes, 1916 Annual Meeting, 34–36. To sharpen Kroesen's point, it may be that the typist did not know of or how to spell Erie, as in Lake Erie—although, to be fair, the E and W keys on the typewriter are next to each other. His whispered comment is from *ALT*, February 15, 1916, 546.
20. The national championships referred, of course, to the men's singles competition. The labels are from "Hard Problem for Tennis Delegates," *New York Times*, February 1, 1915. The arguments, in the form of briefs, are in *ALT*, January 15, 1915, 523–27, with the financial data on page 527. "A stormy meeting" was described in "Californians First in Tennis Honors," *New York Times*, December 12, 1915. Wrenn's request for counsel is from ExCom, February 5, 1915.
21. The Association's treasury was not in as parlous condition as it might seem. Thirty-thousand dollars came to the tidy sum of about $720,000 in today's (2016) buying power.
22. "Keen Fight for Tennis Players" *New York Times*, January 25, 1915; "Change Philadelphia Vote," *New York Times*, February 6, 1915; *ALT*, February 15, 1915, 555–63, mentions the "big crowd" attracted to David Cup matches at Forest Hills and has a full summary of the annual meeting discussions. The very lengthy debate, which was postponed until after dinner, began at 8:50 p.m. and did not come to a vote until after 11:00 p.m. The full text of the discussions are in Minutes, 1915 Annual Meeting, 39–105, 113. The long article on foot faults is in *ALT*, January 15, 1915, 530.
23. Australasia combined Australia and New Zealand. In over a century of competition, the only non-European Davis Cup winners were Australasia, Australia, and the United States. South Africa was awarded the cup in 1974 when India refused to travel to that country because of its apartheid policies. Other non-European champions appeared thereafter.
24. Minutes, 1916 Annual Meeting, 2. The report is not attached to the minutes.
25. Minutes, 1917 Annual Meeting, 31; ExCom, July 5–6, 1918, 10.
26. "Big Boom in Tennis," *New York Times*, November 29, 1914. A membership report, prepared in November by the Association's secretary, not been found in the USTA Archive. Wrenn's announcement is "Encourage Young Talent," *New York Times*, December 20, 1914. For tennis in public parks see three *New York Times* articles, "Tennis Tourneys in Public Parks," November 28, 1915; "A New Davis Cup," February 29, 1916; and "Booming Municipal Tennis," March 4, 1917. *ALT*, February 15, 1916, 544. For election of a nominating committee see Minutes, 1915 Annual Meeting, 133, and ExCom, December 3, 1915. Also see *New York Times*, February 6, 1915.
27. Umpires Association is in "Booming Municipal Tennis," *New York Times*, March 4, 1917, and *ALT*, February 15, 1917, 542.

28. The interscholastic or junior tournaments were for boys under twenty who were "attending schools preparing for college." The boys' tournaments were for those under seventeen years of age. *ALT*, February 15, 1916, 544, 552. "Players Advocate Tennis for Girls," *New York Times*, May 5, 1918. Before long, "juniors" were designated as those eighteen and under.
29. Minutes, 1916 Annual Meeting, 30–32. The USTA "Schools Program," which aimed at having tennis as part of school physical-education programs, was developed in the 1970s at the Education and Research Center in Princeton, New Jersey. See chapter 6.
30. *ALT*, February 15, 1916, 552.
31. "To Attack Tennis Clause," *New York Times*, February 7, 1917; "Rivalry Brewing for Presidency of Lawn Tennis," *New York Times*, December 31, 1917. Minutes, 1917 Annual Meeting, throughout.
32. "Hardy Tells Stand of West on Tennis," *New York Times*, January 7, 1917. *ALT*, February 15, 1917, 547.
33. Minutes, 1917 Annual Meeting, 127–28. Waidner's emphatic reference to losing the sectional doubles championships likely stemmed from the procedure that gave sectional doubles champions automatic entry into the national doubles championships. See above, note 18.
34. Minutes, 1917 Annual Meeting, 130–31.
35. *ALT*, February 15, 1917, 551, 544.
36. Notes for box, "More Time for Tennis," Minutes, 1917 Annual Meeting, 32. Franklin mused about moving clocks ahead seasonally, but it was an Englishman, William Willett, who worked out a proposal for daylight savings time, in good part because he wanted to play golf (not tennis) in the late afternoon. In 1909 Winston Churchill supported the bill in Parliament; Langworth, ed., *Churchill by Himself*, 410.
37. Minutes, 1915 Annual Meeting, 7;Minutes, 1917 Annual Meeting, 57–58. "Tennis Men Favor Universal Service, *New York Times*, March 25, 1917 (two articles).
38. Williams, *The United States Lawn Tennis Association and the World War*. President Wilson's ambiguous letter (presumably unintentionally so) is quoted on page 14. The Association's campaign for funds was oversubscribed, and monies were eventually returned to the donors; "40,000 Homeless Dollars," *New York Times*, November 26, 1917. The Association dropped the word "National" from its name in 1920.
39. Merrihew's description is from *ALT*, March 15, 1918, 462-66; to enhance readability, ellipses are not used in the quotation. Edwin Torrey of Clinton, New York, was chairing the meeting as secretary of the Association and had been a candidate for president. See also "Major Adee Is Renominated," *New York Times*, January 17,1918; *ALT*, January 15, 1918, 392. Both Merrihew's *ALT* and the *New York Times* state that Dwight Davis was the incumbent vice president. That seems unlikely if not impossible. As of August 1917, Davis was undergoing field training with an infantry unit that was posted in June 1918 to the Vosges Mountains

in eastern France; Kriplen, *Dwight Davis*, 103. Association records do not show Davis as vice president in 1917. Merrihew may have argued that it would be unfair to bypass Adee when he was "mopping up 'jerries' in the Argonne," but it was internal politics that prompted the decision to reelect; Fred B. Alexander in ALT, February 20, 1944, 14.

40. Williams, *The United States Lawn Tennis Association and the World War*, 6; "Makes a Plea for Tennis," *New York Times*, October 29, 1917.

41. Williams, *The United States Lawn Tennis Association and the World War*, 5, 7, 10; "Tennis Body to Go On," *New York Times*, September 9, 1917. The Four Minute Men program was directed by the Committee on Public Information—the famous (or infamous) Creel Committee, named after its chairman, George Creel. To quote Wikipedia at http://en.wikipedia.org/wiki/Committee_on_Public_Information (as of April 16, 2009): "The purpose of the CPI was to influence American public opinion toward supporting U.S. intervention in World War I via a prolonged propaganda campaign. Among those who participated in it were Wilson advisers Walter Lippmann and Edward Bernays, the latter of whom had remarked that 'the essence of democratic society' was the 'engineering of consent,' by which propaganda was the necessary method for democracies to promote and garner support for policy." There were some seventy-five thousand speakers nationwide in the program during the war.

42. ALT, March 15, 1918, 463, 467–69, 474.

43. Minutes, 1918 Annual Meeting, 15–20; ALT, March 15, 1918, 464.

44. Minutes, 1918 Annual Meeting, 75–76. Past presidents would eventually get their wings clipped a bit when, in the mid 1930s, the bylaws were changed to limit the number on the executive committee to no more than five. By the 1950s, all past presidents were members of the executive committee, but their vote was restricted to the lesser of the number present or a maximum of five (pro-rating the five votes if more than five past presidents were there). Past presidents made a small comeback in the late 1970s when the "immediate past president" was added to the board of directors. The executive committee did not die but did become increasingly superfluous, a remnant of a different system of governance. All these changes and matters are discussed more fully in chapter 6.

45. Minutes, 1919 Annual Meeting, 37–38, 100–103. This is not to be confused with the controversial proposals for "state alignment" made in 1999.

46. The Great Compromise set up representation by population in the U.S. House of Representatives, and representation by states (two Senators for each)—aimed at avoiding both a tyranny of the majority and a tyranny of the minority. Inefficient, but efficiency was not its purpose.

47. *1919 USTA Yearbook*.

48. ExCom, August 30, 1919, 9–19. Reconstructing what took place at the crucial executive committee meeting of December 12, 1919, meeting is a bit

dicey. Minutes for the afternoon session, which according to the November 15, 1919, issue of *ALT* began at 4:00 p.m., are not in the USTA Archive CD. Since the important governance and constitutional issues were discussed in the afternoon, historians are left with the November 15, 1919, issue of *ALT*, which was obviously published sometime after December 12. That was not the first time that *ALT* made such dating mistakes. That issue, which also contains incorrect internal page references, is consistent with the subsequent actions taken at the February 1920 annual meeting and it is, therefore, cited.

49. There was a category for "Tennis Center Associations" to take care of groups of clubs that fell outside organized sectional boundaries. This revision of the constitution also addressed foreign clubs, requiring each individual application for membership to be approved by the executive committee. The organized or active sections were New England, New York, Middle States, Middle Atlantic, Missouri Valley, Southern, Western, North Western, South Western, Inter-Mountain, Pacific Northwest, and California. That largely replicates the sectional structure as of 2016. California would divide into north and south in 1952; Texas and Florida would break away from Southern; the Caribbean and Hawaii-Pacific regions would eventually become active sections—making the current (2016) number of seventeen sections.
50. *1920 USTA Yearbook.*
51. *1920 USTA, Yearbook.* There were some temporary exceptions for sections that were not "active" or organized in that manner.
52. ExCom, December 17, 1921, 1–7, which include the financial statistics for 1921. The Association had assisted India financially by waiving the American share of preliminary match receipts because India had sent four men a long distance to play Davis Cup. No such luck for the English since the USLTA had increased Britain's gate receipts by sending teams over for two straight years and received nothing in return.
53. http://www.blacktennishalloffame.org/ (as of June 4, 2009).
54. Ashe, *Hard Road to Glory,* 3: 145; http://www.atanational.com/ (as of April 22, 2009); Gray and Rice, *Born to Win*, 42–43. Because segregation laws and practices extended to most people "of color," I have routinely referred to black Americans or blacks rather than the more exclusive and imprecise phrase, African-Americans. Black and brown and "oriental" diplomats, as well as tennis players, from countries around the globe, were subjected to legal segregation in the southern states until the late 1960s.
55. ExCom, February 4, 1922, 3.
56. ExCom, September 23, 1923, 4.
57. Photograph in *ALT*, April 15, 1924, 37. This is the only photo of a black person I have found in *ALT* up to this issue. However, *ALT* routinely reported on the American Tennis Association (ATA) championships, and photos of blacks appeared subsequently in the magazine, e.g., November 20, 1929, 582. *Time*, August 28, 1939 reported that the "Only Negro ever known to have competed

at Wimbledon is Briton B. M. Clark, member of a Jamaica, B. W. I. tennis club." He lost in five sets in the opening round in 1924. http://joyousjam.googlepages.com/%22bm%22clark (as of August 8, 2009).

58. The box, "Membership for Howard" is quoted from ExCom, February 4, 1922, 3.
59. ExCom, February 4, 1922, 3, 4. The Chicago race riots of July 1919 grew out of tensions caused by a growing migration of African Americans out of the south into Chicago, where the jobs were. That competition was exacerbated by the return of soldiers and sailors who had enlisted during the First World War. For the report of the Chicago Commission on Race Relations, *The Negro in Chicago: A Study of Race Relations and a Race Riot*, which examined the riots, see http://books.google.com/books?id=3kEraaaamaaj&pg=pa6&lpg=pa6&dq=negro+belt,+chicago&source=bl&ots=hzi2rzKru9&sig=de0sgx8w1cUeoBsHaS-6ekhojrI&hl=en&ei=toyssqwljtu_tgequMnoba&sa=X&oi=book_result&ct=result&resnum=2#v=onepage&q=negro%20belt%2c%20chicago&f=false.
60. Minutes, 1922 Annual Meeting, 80. The full joke, which is not worthy of retelling, was related by Abner Y. Leech of Washington DC, the executive committee member who made the motion not to admit Howard University as a member club. He was also the one who raised concern about "negroes" being members of industrial leagues; ExCom, September 15, 1922, 6.
61. Minton, *Forest Hills*, 172–73; *ALT*, May 1948, 10.
62. S. W. Merrihew in *ALT*, December 15, 1923, 582. For an example of coverage of ATA Championships, see *ALT*, November 20, 1930, 582.
63. Minutes, 1920 Annual Meeting, 56–59; letter to ExCom from Paul Williams, February 10, 1920, attached to ExCom, February 15, 1920. For those interested in the history of tennis the game, as played from the late 1880s through 1919, see the fascinating article, Hardy, "Thirty Years of Tennis," 11–16.
64. For the British default see http://cdnc.ucr.edu/cgi-bin/cdnc?a=d&d=su19221212.2.95. Minutes, 1922 Annual Meeting, 106. At the same meeting, the Association voted to affiliate with the National Amateur Athletic Federation (NAAF), a group set up to challenge the AAU's control of amateur and especially Olympic sports in the United States. Within a few years, the NAAF disappeared (despite being supported by a number of prominent figures) page 103. ExCom, September 1922, contains comments about French wishes. Merrihew's comment is in *ALT*, February 15, 1923, 627. The decision to join the ILTF is in *ALT*, March 15, 1923, 692.
65. During 2001–2, the USTA conducted extensive interviews with various American professional tennis players about how to develop high-level players. The one thing they all agreed upon was that competing against the best players was essential; "Recommendations/Report of the High Performance/Junior Reorganization Task Force, July 12, 2002," USTA Archive. Jack Kramer, one of the game's great players and teachers, repeatedly argued that constant competition against the best throughout the country was the best

way to develop great players. In his autobiography he fudged that a bit, asserting that the best players were in southern California, then claiming that the hard courts in California were an even more important major factor in developing his skills. The Association would continue to grapple with the costs and geographic issues connected with trying to arrange constant competition among the nation's very best young players; Kramer, *The Game*, 23 and throughout.

66. Collins and Hollander, *Bud Collins' Tennis Encyclopedia*, 110–12; *2005 USTA Yearbook*, throughout. Deford, *Big Bill Tilden*, 97–105. For a useful corrective to stories depicting Tilden as penniless and pathetic in his final days, see Hillway, "Bill Tilden and his Protégé," 12–15.
67. ExCom, December 17, 1921, 1—secretary's report.

4. THE MONEY

1. The quip is attributed to Tom Pettit, the pro at the Newport Casino, Minton, *Forest Hills*, 189, but it was a commonplace.
2. For an example of the Byzantine efforts to get sectional cooperation, see the long discussion in ExCom, March 15, 1924, 36–48. That long discussion ended when the committee admitted it was unable "to set up satisfactory machinery" for enforcement. This and the next chapter provide a synthesis of the lengthy struggle over amateur rules and with Tilden. The details can be found throughout the minutes of the executive committee, particularly during the 1920s and early 1930s.
3. In 1931 the ever-perceptive Merrihew pointed out the shift away from former champions as Association leaders; *ALT*, November 20, 1931, 36. Perhaps most telling about assumptions regarding the advanced age of Association leaders is a photograph taken at the 1941 annual meeting in New York showing a quite vigorous looking Holcombe Ward about to shake hands with an equally fit former president Julian Myrick. Both been in leadership positions for some twenty-five years, yet each was only just entering his sixties—elderly for previous Association leaders, but in the prime of life for successful adults; *ALT*, February 20, 1941, 20.
4. Deford, *Big Bill Tilden*, 3. Deford clearly shares Tilden's contempt for the Association leadership. Deford's usual reference is to the "mossbacks of the USLTA"; e.g., Kramer, *The Game*, 10.
5. See note 44 below for tennis as an "effete" and "sissy" game. To quote tennis historian Richard Hillway (Hillway email to author of July 14, 2013):

> The Bill Tilden of the 1920s was the Babe Ruth of tennis, its Jack Dempsey, its Bobby Jones, its Red Grange. In fact when the first 50 years of sport in America were viewed by a US poll in 1950 that tallied votes from 391 participants, mainly sports writers, that rated the top players in each of several sports from 1900–1950, for tennis Tilden garnered 310 votes, Kramer 32, Budge 31, Johnston 1, Perry 1 and Vines 1 for the best player of that period. He was the most dominant athlete of any sport, gaining many more votes than Ruth or Cobb, Dempsey, Jones, etc. The 1920's were the first time that

radio covered the sporting events, the first years of the big stadium events in many sports, the newspaper coverage increased and sports really became part of commercialism. So sports were much better covered in the US and more of the public became interested in playing and watching sports. At that very time arose this tennis genius, almost 6 foot 2 inches, long-legged, who hit the hardest serves ever seen up to that point, the cannon-ball, who had every shot and power, who ran like a track star, and had virtually no weaknesses.

6. These background paragraphs on Tilden and the USLTA are taken from Voss, *Tilden and Tennis*; Deford, *Big Bill Tilden*; my reading of *New York Times* reports; and the extensive coverage printed in *ALT*. A typical example of Tilden's omnipresence is in ExCom, February 1924. The commercial connection between Bancroft sporting goods and Tilden is angrily discussed in ExCom, December 1921, 7. At the same time, the ExCom criticized Merrihew and *ALT* for defending Tilden, page 17.
7. The initial player-writer controversy in 1923–24 is examined in Carvalho, "The Banning of Bill Tilden," 122–36. Carvalho did not consult the USTA records or examine the renewal of the controversy in 1928. "Evil influence" is in Voss, *Tilden*, 65. Deford described Ward as "bewildered" in *Big Bill Tilden*, 88. I doubt that. Ward, a former national champion, was an adamant supporter of "pure" amateurism and an implacable foe of Tilden, yet he described Tilden as "not only a great tennis player, but . . . an interesting writer, a lover of music, an actor, and I don't know what all else." Other quotes and comments are from ExCom, June 4, 1924, 6–7; *ALT*, June 15, 1924, 123–24.
8. Myrick's remark that Merrihew made "a comfortable living" out of the subsidy given by the Association to *American Lawn Tennis* was a bit over the top. A decade later Merrihew reported that the subsidy was $600 a year; *ALT*, April 20, 1935, 30.
9. *ALT*, February 20, 1930, 724. The *Official Bulletin* had begun in 1926.
10. The debate about *ALT* as the official organ is in ExCom, February 1, 1924, 49–60; ExCom, March 15, 1924. In December that year, the executive committee agreed to bury a proposal for an official magazine from Allison Danzig, a *New York Times* reporter who covered tennis; ExCom, December 13, 1924, 131. Merrihew's comment is in *ALT*, December 20, 1929, 665. Ten years later, in February 1933, after the Association publication, *Tennis*, had folded, the executive committee considered a proposal to pay Merrihew to print a few pages of "official" USLTA news. No surprise that Myrick buried the idea, explaining that, despite a subsidy from the Association, Merrihew had colored his reports "to suit his own point of view," particularly during the Tilden imbroglio; ExCom, February 10, 1933, 167–75.
11. Merrihew sold *American Lawn Tennis* in 1942 to William Jacobs, a USTA regional vice president from Clinton, South Carolina. Merrihew

remained as editor for a few years. He died in 1947. When Jacobs died in 1948, the magazine's ownership was transferred to the Allegheny Publishing Corporation. In late 1951, the magazine's name was changed to *The Racquet*, covering the three rackets sports of tennis, badminton, and squash. It was purchased by Gladys Heldman in 1953 and incorporated into her new magazine *World Tennis*. See also Hillway and Felder, "Stephen Wallis Merrihew," 452–56.

Merrihew's contribution to tennis in the United States and throughout the world was seminal. Lawn tennis was his passion, and his magazine reflected that commitment. Despite his being nominated at least three different times to the International Tennis Hall of Fame, Merrihew never made it. Why? Rumor has it that voters think the ITHF is already too American. Moreover, go the stories, former players (and voters) often see no reason to enshrine a nonplayer. Whatever the precise truth, those rumors alone justify creation of an American Tennis Hall of Fame, which is what the international one began as; see chapter 5.

12. Englemann, *The Goddess and the American Girl*, 286. The committee of seven was one of a string of committees, subcommittees, special committees, and study groups assigned the task of defining an amateur, or more accurately, of defining what caused a player to lose amateur status. All in addition to the regular Amateur Rules Committee, which had the responsibility for making and enforcing amateur status rules. For an example of the rush to rules see ExCom, December 15, 1923, 2–3.
13. Pyle's flamboyant career is described in Reisler, *Cash and Carry*. The Lenglen story is taken largely from two sources: Englemann, *The Goddess and the American Girl*, 239–87 (a book unhappily devoid of citations, even for direct quotes) and Pileggi, "The Lady in The White Silk Dress." Pyle's troupe is described in Voss, *Tilden and Tennis*, 104–12. Pyle was a hustler, not a tennis enthusiast. According to Pileggi, he was described as "P. T. Barnum with a short attention span." In 1925 he had persuaded Harold "Red" Grange to leave the University of Illinois to play professional football with the Chicago Bears. The Bears set up a special schedule of seventeen games within sixty-seven days. Fans turned out in droves, and the National Football League headed down the path to financial success—though that would be a long haul.
14. Pileggi, "The Lady in The White Silk Dress." For a highly personal account of Lenglen's career and activities, see Tinling, *Love and Faults*, 8–64.
15. Deford, *Big Bill Tilden*, 95; Reisler, *Cash and Carry*, 118. Engelmann, *The Goddess and the American Girl*, 268–69, dismisses Tilden's claim that Pyle made an offer and infers that Tilden made up the story for some news reports "to enhance his own reputation with the USLTA and the public." Perhaps. But with Pyle an avowed liar and Tilden constantly trying to manipulate the Association and public opinion, it's a coin flip. Richards did not get the top ranking from the USLTA in 1926 because he turned pro before the rankings were voted on.
16. "Miss Brown to Sign Pro Contract Today," *New York Times*, September 7, 1926;

Reisler, *Cash and Carry*, 119; obituary for William Pickens (Pyle's business manager), "W. H. Pickens Dead," *New York Times*, July 21, 1934. The flamboyant Suzanne Lenglen seems to have disliked Tilden because she had to share the limelight with him, and when Tilden came to see her at an auditorium where the court was laid down over a hockey rink, she flared: "*Ce pédéraste* comes especially to see me in this igloo!" It seems that neither Association minutes nor *American Lawn Tennis* ever referred to Tilden's homosexuality, but Lenglen's casual, contemptuous dismissal of him as "that pederast" suggests they were well aware of Tilden's behavior. In the social milieu, that surely intensified the dislike USLTA leaders had for him; Pileggi, "The Lady in The White Silk Dress." According to Ted Tinling, Tilden disliked Lenglen with equal fervor. Tinling also asserts without evidence that USLTA leaders feared that the image of tennis as effete could be reinforced "by the world's No. 1 player projecting a homosexual aura." Tinling, *Love and Faults*, 80.

17. ExCom, August 24, 1928.
18. Frank Deford, writing in 1974, expressed amazement that the Association would state the wish that its Davis Cup team had lost; *Big Bill Tilden*, 92. By the time of the third edition of the USTA *Official Encyclopedia* in 1981, the offending sentence had changed to read: "By winning over the Italians, the battling second-line American players had unwittingly kept the controversy alive," 26. It would seem that someone at the USLTA read Deford's book.
19. Citations for the box "Presidents—United States and USTA" are Oliver obituary in the "Brig, Gen. Oliver Dies in South at 87," *New York Times*, March 17, 1935, and *Lawn Tennis Library Record* 11 (June 1951); covers of *ALT*, May 15, 1923 April 15, 1924, April 15, 1926; Kriplen, *Dwight Davis*, 111–20, 144–62; President Harding to Take Up Tennis," *New York Times*, April 23, 1921. Davis referred Harding to the Honorary Membership Committee for consideration, but nothing happened before the president's death in August 1923; ExCom, September 1922, 13. There was no mention of the proposal thereafter. Davis became secretary of war in the Hoover administration. Hoover had his photograph taken with public parks tennis players but seems to have kept his distance from the Association. That is, perhaps, because of Hoover-ball, "once the most popular sport at the White House, played by the President, Supreme Court justices, Cabinet members and other high government officials." Invented by a White House physician for Hoover, it combined tennis, volleyball, and medicine ball. Scoring was the same as for tennis. Hoover played regularly, but when he left office, Hooverball disappeared. http://www.hooverassociation.org/newsevents/hooverball/hooverball_history.php (accessed July 19, 2014).
20. Wightman's resignation is in ExCom, September 14, 1928. Wear's resignation cablegram is printed in *ALT*, August 20,1928, 377. The bizarre story of Tilden's off-again, on-again status for the Davis Cup matches in Paris is

told with full detail and unrestrained sarcasm by Deford, *Big Bill Tilden*, 89–93. "Ringleaders" is his word. The *USTA Official Encyclopedia*, 27, reports the State Department's request.

21. Voss, *Tilden and Tennis*, 162; Deford, *Big Bill Tilden*, 96; *ALT*, February 20, 1929, 715. Unfortunately the Association archive does not have any executive committee minutes for 1929, so the discussion surrounding the decision to have Tilden write for the USLTA is lost.
22. On Tilden turning pro see Deford, *Big Bill Tilden*, 95, 128–30.
23. *ALT*, November 20, 1933, 36.
24. Nor shall I (Warren Kimball) ever forget the look on Billy Talbert's face in 1977 when, during the last U.S. Open played at Forest Hills and in the first year of separate tickets for day and night matches, fans chanted "hell no, we won't go" after tournament officials decided to postpone the scheduled afternoon match that featured the darling of the crowd, Guillermo Vilas. The crowd stayed; the USTA accommodated them. In both cases (the chant and the accommodation), John Tunis's analysis pertained. *ALT*, November 20, 1934, 26, describes "a shower of cushions" at the end of the day's play. The three articles are Merrihew, "The Amateur at Bay," Fred Hawthorne, "The Commercialization of Tennis," and John R. Tunis, "The Lawn Tennis Industry," 289–98 (quote on 290). Tunis later became a quite successful author of baseball books for youngsters.
25. The first U.S. Open Golf Championship was played on October 4, 1895, on a nine-hole course in Newport, Rhode Island. It was a thirty-six-hole competition and was played in a single day. Ten professionals and one amateur entered. The winner was a twenty-one-year-old Englishman named Horace Rawlins, who had arrived in the United States in January that year to take up a position at the host club. He received $150 cash out of a prize fund of $335, plus a $50 gold medal. The U.S. Golf Association, which governed the amateur game, continually wrestled with finely tuned definitions of an amateur, but the "open" remained; http://usga.usopen.com/history/index.html.
26. For a general and sympathetic survey of Association policies by one who viewed the struggle for amateurism as a "noble gesture," see Davenport, "Professionalism in Sports." There is a near-endless array of mind-numbing little fixes to various rules governing amateur status, mostly relating to the details (in excruciating detail) of expenses and limits on travel time outside the United States (Davis Cup, Wightman Cup, and the like were excluded); a classic example is both USLTA and ILTF bylaw amendments and resolutions taken up at the 1935 annual meeting. For further self-punishment, read *USLTA Service Bulletin* 18, which was an impossibly long list of expense regulations consisting of six paragraphs of rules, three long paragraphs of exceptions, and four paragraphs of complex explanations and examples of the rules, printed in *ALT*, February 20 1939, 30.
27. See above, chapter 3, note 16; ExCom, February 1930.
28. *ALT*, February 15 1923, 626–27. The term "Grand Slam," obviously taken from

bridge, and used in golf since 1930, was first applied to tennis by *New York Times* columnist John Kieran (a bridge player) in 1933, according to Collins and Hollander, *Bud Collin's Tennis Encyclopedia*, 53. When Australian player Jack Crawford won the Australian, French, and Wimbledon Championships that year, reporters wrote of him winning the "Big Four" if he could take the U.S. championships. As Kieran put it: "If Crawford wins, it would be something like scoring a grand slam on the courts, doubled and vulnerable." Crawford lost, but the term stuck. Jack Kramer, a bit petulantly, called the Grand Slam "a grand publicity gimmick" and claimed Don Budge "simply made it" up in 1938. (Of course in the world of the twenty-first century, there would have been a huge legal fight over the Grand Slam as a trademark.) Kramer disparaged the French Open, which he never won, and dismissed the Australians as not great Davis Cup champions, conveniently ignoring the six titles won by Australasia from 1907 through 1919; Kramer, *The Game*, 101–2.

29. The "nays" have it is in ExCom, May 1930, 43–44. The lengthy and candid discussion about "open" tournaments is in ExCom, May 1930, 26–39. Louis Carruthers, who would soon become president of the Association, gave a full summary of previous efforts to institute an "open." See also *ALT*, April 20, 1930, 4, and June 20, 1930, 158. The disingenuous language of the official ITF history is that the United States delayed joining the federation since the Americans "had been prevaricating for some time . . . on various subjects." Cunnington, *75 Years of the ITF*, 12–13; in fact, the Association had been direct and candid, not evasive. The ITF takeover of Davis Cup in 1978 is mentioned in a single sentence on page 25.
30. For the International Lawn Tennis Club, see *ALT*, August 5, 1932, 40. Engelmann, *The Goddess and the American Girl*, 213–14.
31. The ILTF resolution is in ExCom, April 8, 1933, 1. The reporter was Allison Danzig, "U.S. Open Tourney in Tennis Is Voted," *New York Times*, February 12, 1933. Interestingly, some seventy years later the Western Hemisphere "bloc" was the response of ITF president Francesco Ricci-Bitti when USTA leaders complained at the end of the twentieth century about the federation's voting structure. For the "multiple voting system," see *ALT*, December 20, 1937, 8. In the early 1960s, the tennis-writers association called the 1933 USLTA stand "a defeat with honor;" Lawn Tennis Writers Association of America (n.d.-1963?), Presidential file, "going open," USTA Archive.
32. *Time* magazine, January 23, and February 20, 1933.
33. ExCom, April 8, 1933, 1–62; *ALT*, February 20, 33, 4–5; *ALT*, April 20, 1933, 22, 26, quotes *Tennis et Golf*.
34. Engelmann, *Goddess and the American Girl*, 323, and Minutes, 1931 Annual Meeting, 9–10.
35. Minutes, 1934 Annual Meeting, 22–23, 107–20; Carruthers is quoted on page 111. For extensive details see Carruthers's report as delegate to the ILTF

meeting in ExCom, April 1934, 1–32. For a summary of *ALT*'s coverage, see Potter, "The Old Question of the Open Tournament," 16–17. Potter wrote the articles on the open tournament debate for *ALT* in 1933 and 1934.

36. Minutes, 1935 Annual Meeting, 19; Allison Danzig, "Eastern Net Body Backs New Rules," *New York Times*, January 20, 1935.

37. Hawk, *Off the Racket*, 187–88. The most recent official ITF history lists Carruthers as having been president of the ILTF in 1934; Bowers, *The International Tennis Federation*, 239. However, Bowers notes that from 1913 through 1938, "a chairman was appointed for each annual general meeting of the ILTF." Election of a president with a term of office began in 1938. Carruthers reported to the USTA that he had been elected chairman of the (annual general) "meeting." The title confusion may have begun with the *New York Times* report "Carruthers Elected Head of Federation, March 17, 1934, that Carruthers "was elected president" of the ILTF after carrying on a battle against granting overly broad powers to the federation. Association leaders seemed singularly unimpressed by ILTF titles, routinely referring to Carruthers as the U.S. "delegate" to the annual general meeting in March 1934, rather than its chairman. According to USLTA records, when the U.S. proposal about "open" tennis came up, he recused himself; ExCom, April 1934, 7. American sources give no indication that he chaired later ILTF meetings. However, the ILTF responded to queries by stating that Carruthers was "principal/chairman, effectively president" of the federation in 1934 for the entire year; L. Skaaren email to author, July 26, 2012. Carruthers's lengthy report and remarks about the annual general meeting are in ExCom, April 1934, 2–47. Chairman or president, he clearly was the go-to person on ILTF matters for the USLTA leadership.

38. ExCom, December 16, 1922. Minton, *Forest Hills*, 108–9.

39. Arthur Ashe Stadium, the site of the U.S. Open Championship since 1997, had some thirty-three thousand seats as of 2010. Its predecessor at Flushing Meadows, Louis Armstrong Stadium (previously the Singer Bowl), had eighteen thousand. The "buzz" was the favorite word of Arlen Kantarian, the Association's director of the U.S. Open event during its dramatic expansion from 2000 through 2008. The eighty-thousand-seat Cowboy Stadium was built in 2009.

40. The shift made no ripples for the Association, although it gave a platform to a staunch critic of Bill Tilden's challenge to amateurism. Williams's resignation came just after death of the elected secretary, and he was immediately appointed temporary secretary, then elected secretary for two years, putting him on the executive committee—the reverse of a pattern that appeared in the 1990s–2000s when two USTA board members resigned to accept the executive-director position; ExCom, December 16, 1922; *ALT*, November 15, 1922, 487, and December 15, 1922, 531. Williams resigned to become editor of the Utica, New York, *Daily Press*. Moss had been general sports editor for the Associated Press. His salary was raised to $6,800 by 1925; ExCom, March 7, 1925.

41. ExCom, September 15, 1922, 2.

42. By the late 1990s, after a half-century of muttering about the matter, a number of special ad hoc committees were created to study a myriad of issues that all boiled down to governance—who decides? Should it be the sections (and did the sectional structure make sense?) or the national association? Of course the sections had no intention of giving their own local "districts" effective autonomy. Much of the tension came from attempts to develop accountability standards for how the sections spent the money they got from the national Association. That is a tale for later chapters, but a marker here might be useful to the reader.
43. ExCom, February 1923, 7. Myrick's support call for "home rule" echoed a call from his own district, the Metropolitan (New York City) district of the New York (later Eastern) Section. In November 1921, that district called for an amendment to the USLTA constitution that would have made the Metropolitan district a separate, "self-governing" section of the Association. The primary issue was control over the scheduling of local tournaments. Nothing came of the proposed amendment, but the story illustrates the decentralizing impulse inside the USLTA; "M.L.T.A. Votes for Tennis Home Rule," *New York Times*, November 4, 1921.
44. Citations "Uncle Mike (Julian Myrick, 1880–1969)" box: General background from Deford, *Big Bill Tilden* and Voss, *Tilden and Tennis.* Details and quotes: "Tennis as a Major Sport," *New York Times*, June 9, 1918 (lifetime sport); "First Tennis Speech by Radio," *New York Times*, June 4, 1922 (radio broadcast); ExCom, September 1922, 1–2 (distribution); ExCom, February 1923, 7–8. For perceptive comments on Myrick's political acumen, see Minton, *Forest Hills*, 80–81, 212. In 1933 Myrick forced Marble to play four matches, eleven sets, and 108 games in day, by indicating she had to play in order to make the Wightman Cup team (which he controlled); Marble, *Courting Danger*, 29–35. A year later, after she played poorly for the USLTA in Europe, "Czar" Myrick berated her for wasting the Association's money, even though it turned out she had pleurisy and perhaps tuberculosis. When she regained her health in late 1936, Myrick and the USLTA refused her entry into the major eastern tournaments on grounds of her poor health. Myrick relented a bit and told her if she could play against men and prove her good health, they would give her a chance. She played, she won, she returned to the competitive courts, winning the national championship in 1936. Marble grudgingly admitted that "the [male] players Myrick found weren't very good"; Marble, *Courting Danger*, 59–62, 74, 93–94, 105; Tinling, *Love and Faults*, 159–68. Since there was talk of the Association being "responsible" for Marble's collapse, Myrick proposed that players sign disclaimers before receiving financial support; ExCom, December 1934, 101–2. Myrick died on January 8, 1969 at age eighty-eight. "He was instrumental in transforming tennis from a rather effete society pastime into a major international competitive sport"; "Julian S. Myrick Dead at

88,"*New York Times*, January 9, 1969. The "effete" reference was earlier used by novelist and sportswriter Paul Gallico in an article for *Liberty Magazine*, which called tennis a "sissy sport" played in "a certain aura of sweetness and lifted pinky," despite the "undeniably masculine young men and women" who played. Written in the age of Bill Tilden and Babe Didrikson Zaharias, the inferences are obvious; quoted in *ALT*, January 20, 1943, 14. Gallico was not alone. Sportswriter Joe Williams, writing about Didrikson in the *New York World-Telegram*, ignored her remarkable talents (Olympic and golf champion): "It would be much better if she and her ilk stayed at home, got themselves prettied up and waited for the phone to ring." Even the USLTA leadership, hardly outspoken champions of tolerance, must have winced; Larry Schwartz, "Didrickson Was a Woman Ahead of Her Time," http://espn.go.com/sportscentury/features/00014147.html.

45. The U.S. national singles championship for men has had only four venues since it began in 1881: the Casino in Newport, Rhode Island (1881–1914), the West Side Tennis Club in Forest Hills, New York City (1915–20, 1924–77), the Germantown Cricket Club in Philadelphia, Pennsylvania (1921–23), and the USTA National Tennis Center in Flushing Meadows, New York (1978–present).
46. ExCom, December 16, 1922, 4–11; "Permanent Tennis Stadium Favored," *New York Times*, December 17, 1922; Minutes, 1923 Annual Meeting, 108–17; *ALT*, May 15, 1923, 80–82. The contract called for the Forest Hills stadium to have at least twelve thousand seats and to be expandable temporarily or permanently to twenty-one thousand. Contract (unsigned copy) of February 20, 1923 between the USLTA and the WSTC (copy in USTA Archive, courtesy of the West Side Tennis Club).
47. *Official Bulletin*, February 1928, 6; ExCom, April 8, 1933, 70–72.
48. Contract (unsigned copy) of May 5, 1925 between the USLTA and the West Side Tennis Club (copy in USTA Archive, courtesy of the West Side Tennis Club); ExCom, December 5, 1931, "Action Digest" and throughout; letter, Philip B. Hawk to Louis Carruthers, October 6, 1932 (copy in USTA Archive, courtesy of the West Side Tennis Club). Stadium construction estimates had been $150,000; actual cost by 1925 was $253,000. By 1932 the WSTC claimed $269,000 plus land costs. The 1932 contract deferred payments, again at favorable interest, and increased the club's share of proceeds from tournament. The target date for repayment of the loans was 1938. The club's annual debt to the USLTA was "wiped out" in 1943, according to USLTA minutes; the WSTC was paid off in 1950; Minton, *Forest Hills*, 212. For the contract discussion and the "loan" to the sections see Minutes, 1933 Annual Meeting, 28–32 and ExCom, February 10, 1933, 75–80.
49. *ALT*, July 20, 1931, 39 and July 5, 1931, 30.
50. ExCom, January 1946, 126. See also chapter 3. The first appearance of geographic distribution requirements for the nominating committee is in *1948 USLTA Yearbook*, 42.
51. Recreating details for events in 1929 and 1932 is difficult since the minutes of all executive committee and annual meetings are missing for those years. *American*

Lawn Tennis fills in some of the blanks but the coverage is vague and spotty. Allison Danzig of the *New York Times* dug deeper, but only occasionally.

52. Allison Danzig, "Tennis Selections Bring Split Here," *New York Times*, January 26, 1930; Minutes, 1930 Annual Meeting, 40. The 1929 nominating committee was making nominations that would be voted on during the annual meeting in February 1930.
53. *ALT*, February 20, 1930, 725.
54. The quite vigorous Myrick-Daley argument is in ExCom, February 14, 1930, 14–21. The deficit is mentioned in *ALT*, February 20, 1930, 723. The 1929 financials looked a bit better with a surplus of some $7,000 once the reserve was replenished to the $90,000 level set by earlier policy decisions; *ALT*, April 20, 1930, 26. As of 1931 the sections were California, Eastern, Intermountain, Middle Atlantic, Middle States, Missouri Valley, New England, Northwestern, Pacific Northwest, Southern, Southwestern, Texas, Western. Each had a delegate on the USLTA executive committee.
55. ExCom, February 13, 1931, 7–8; Minutes, 1931 Annual Meeting, 11–12, which includes Bloem's comments. By 1935, the distribution had dropped a bit, with the "minimum refund" bringing only $9,100; ExCom, February 8, 1935, 1–2.
56. Merrihew's comments on Rickey's address (not printed) are in *ALT*, February 20, 1930, 726. Rickey is best described as a professional baseball executive.
57. Allison Danzig, "Dailey to Retire as Tennis Leader," *New York Times*, December 17, 1930, and "Louis B. Dailey Dies," *New York Times*, February 18, 1932. Similarly, *ALT*, March 20, 1932.
58. Minutes, 1930 Annual Meeting, 10.
59. *New York Times*, February 18, 1932. Dailey's resignation statement is from "Louis B. Dailey Dies," *New York Times*, February 18, 1932.
60. Holcombe Ward letter, ca. November 27, 1931, Committee of One Hundred file, USTA Archive. The voting structure established in the 1920 constitution remained in place with some minor adjustments. See chapter 3; Minutes, 1931 Annual Meeting, 43–44. The "regular" nominee for second vice president was Fitz-Eugene Dixon, of Philadelphia, which suggests intersectional squabbling between Middle States (Philadelphia) and Eastern.
61. A very small cache of papers concerning the Tennis Committee of One Hundred came from William Clothier II to Richard Hillway, who was kind enough to send me copies (now in the USTA Archive). The documents consist of a written call for a meeting of the Committee of One Hundred to be held in New York City on November 13, 1931; a short note dated November 27, 1931 that apparently forwarded an unsigned copy of a letter from Ward (chairman pro-tem of the committee) that was addressed to the Middle States Tennis Association; and two lists of persons who presumably were also sent copies of the same letter. Nearly all the ninety-four names

were from the Northeast, except for three from St. Louis and two from the West Coast—California and the Pacific Northwest Sections. Curiously, only a single section president (Middle Atlantic) was included. The anniversary history was United States Lawn Tennis Association, *Fifty Years of Lawn Tennis*.

For nervous California members, here's the scoop on southern versus northern California in the twenties. In February 1925 the executive committee considered the application of the "Southern Section of the California (sectional) Association" to become a separate USLTA section. Sumner Hardy, the elder statesman from northern California, gave his okay, though grudgingly. He admitted that the California Section itself was divided into northern and southern "sections," which already operated as separate units, but suggested that the increased cost to the national Association (to send sectional winners to the national doubles) was a reason to say no. They had "followed state lines pretty closely in making sections"—pretty closely being a huge loophole. The matter was buried by referral to a committee already studying a realigning of sectional lines. Not until 1952 did northern California and southern California become separate sections within the national Association structure, although one wonders how much they talked to each other in the interim; ExCom, February 6, 1925; *1951 USLTA Yearbook; 1952 USLTA Yearbook*; ExCom, August 1951, 16–18.

62. Ward won a decisive victory, with roughly 9,500 votes to Van Bloem's 2,250; Allison Danzig, "Eastern Net Group Is Headed by Ward," in the *New York Times*, January 10, 1932. For those who wish details: The struggle within the Eastern Section between Van Bloem and Ward, ostensibly over the ranking of Helen Wills Moody the year before, resulted in Ward being elected section president over Van Bloem. In January 1932 it turned into a battle between the "Old Guard" and the "so-called younger element" or "insurgents" and was clearly about control, not rankings. Carruthers attacked Van Bloem as not properly representing Eastern's position. A member of the Eastern Section's executive committee accused Carruthers, who succeeded Dailey as USLTA president, of "stooping to ward politics" (an unintentional play on words) to gain control of the elections that would take place at the Association's annual meeting in New Orleans in February 1932. George Currie, "Tennis," *Brooklyn Daily Eagle*, January 11, 1932; "Politics Enter Tennis Meeting"; Associated Press report in the *Cornell Daily Sun*, 52:75, January 11, 1932. The Associated Press report on that annual meeting, printed in the *New York Times*, was strikingly innocuous, making no mention of the election controversy or the Committee of One Hundred; *New York Times*, February 6, 1932.

The minutes for the 1932 annual meeting and all the executive committee meetings for that year are missing from the USTA archive. Given the election controversy and the actions of the Committee of One Hundred, that is too much of a coincidence not to raise suspicions that those records were consciously removed; for what purpose is not known.

63. Ward, as first vice president, acted as president for all of 1933. The president, Harry S. Knox, who lived in Chicago when he was elected, had to move to

Washington state for business reasons early in his first year. He never attended any executive committee meetings as president. Needless to say he was not renominated. Ward simply noted Knox's absence at each of the meetings; "Hall Is Nominated as U.S.L.T.A. Head," *New York Times*, November 22, 1933; ExCom meetings of April, September, December 1933, and February 1934. Executive committee-meetings were routinely held in April, September, December, and just before the annual meeting in February of the following year.

64. Article 3, section 4 of the USLTA bylaws read: "The Executive Committee of the U.S.L.T.A. shall be the tribunal to decide all questions as to the amateur status or eligibility of a player that may arise" The lengthy discussion on the amendment and political philosophy is from ExCom, February 10, 1933, 80–107. The quotations are on pages 91 and 84.
65. For Carruthers's quite remarkable discourse see ExCom, February 10, 1933, 97. Emphasis added.
66. Notes for the box, "The Bermuda Exception," and the text: The 1924 Annual Meeting (Minutes, 65), voted to require that clubs join the USLTA through their sections. The "tiff" with the British is in *ALT*, February 20, 1937, 11 and ExCom, September 10, 1937, 55–56. The Bermuda Lawn Tennis Club had a formidable advocate—S. W. Merrihew who was the club's official "delegate" to the USLTA annual meeting. In 1932, the Association had eight direct member clubs (i.e., not within a section) in the Bahamas, Cuba, Puerto Rico, Hawaii, Bermuda, and Mexico. As of 1937, only two direct member clubs remained—one in Hawaii, the other in Bermuda, although that number would change. The Bermuda Lawn Tennis Club appeared annually at least since 1923—so long as it paid its dues, which it apparently did not do in 1939. Hawaii, Puerto Rico, and Alaska appeared routinely; Panama and American Samoa sporadically. As late as 1938, the *Lawn Tennis Guide* listed a Canadian "section" comprised of all provinces, including Quebec, although that "section" played no role in governance of the USLTA. Occasional anomalies popped up: for example, in 1949 a direct-member club set up by the Arabian American Oil Company in Saudi Arabia and a club in Jamaica in 1956.

    The Pacific Northwest Section had only seven clubs as of 1935, and four of them were in Canada. Moreover, there were only two grass courts on the entire west coast, both in British Columbia. Without the Canadian members, the section was too small to survive; ExCom, February 8, 1935, 2–3. In 2010, the USTA did away with the exception for British Columbia; the Canadians were no longer needed for survival.

    In 2005 the executive committee (largely sectional delegates) had a thirty-minute preliminary discussion (based on a paper written by the USTA historian) about the anomalous status of the Coral Beach and Tennis Club in Bermuda, but nothing came of it.
67. Intermountain, Western, and Southwest remained "active" but not "char-

tered" members until the distinction disappeared in 1940. The minutes do not reveal the reasons for their recalcitrance, and it seems to have had little practical effect.

68. In 1934, the Westfield, New Jersey, Tennis Club refused to let Eastern count the club's one hundred votes for first vice president nominee Holcombe Ward or for any of the five ex-presidents nominated for the executive committee. The "regular" nominating slate was duly elected, but with those six getting only 10,950 of Eastern's 11,050 votes. Awkwardly, Ward was chairing the meeting in the absence of the president, Harry Knox. When Walter Merrill Hall (he seems to have used all three names) gave a little acceptance speech on becoming president, he began by saying that when it came to Holcombe Ward, "we love him for the enemies he has made." Perhaps a more revealing comment than Hall intended; Minutes, 1934 Annual Meeting, 18.
69. The arithmetic is complicated, and the numbers given are my round figure estimates. What is clear is that being an organized section, and voting as one, paid off in political clout. Merrihew's comments are in *ALT*, February 15, 1923, 611–12, along with a copy of the official list of club and association (section) voting strengths.
70. ExCom, February 4, 1922, 7.
71. *LTG*, 1939, 13–15.
72. ExCom, February 4, 1922, 7; United States Lawn Tennis Association, *Fifty Years of Lawn Tennis*, "Annals," 254–55.
73. The executive committee routinely met the week before the annual meetings, which were already held in places other than New York City. Each section selected its own "delegate" who sat on the national Association's executive committee. As more and more sections voted for all their club members, those section delegates (as opposed to those club "delegates" who attended the annual meeting and voted) became important political players.
74. ExCom, January 14, 1938, 41–44. The officers were president, first and second vice presidents, secretary, treasurer, and four regional vice presidents. The other ExCom members were eight "at large" delegates, and delegates from each of the thirteen sections. The four regions were North Atlantic, Southern, Central, and Pacific. In 1948 when a newly selected regional vice president asked if that post had specific duties or was "of any value," the president dismissively retorted, "I think the man makes the job," then gave a long harangue about what might be done. There was no description of duties anywhere in the USLTA *Yearbooks*; ExCom, September 17, 1948, 67–71.
75. ExCom, February 1933, 29–32.
76. Jones W. Mersereau was the New York (Eastern) Section president and then USLTA president, 1925–27. He was on the committee that negotiated the original contract with the WSTC back in the early 1920s.
77. A harbinger of things to come was the executive committee decision in April 1937 to pursue an offer of ten thousand dollars from the Columbia Broadcasting

System (CBS) to purchase rights to make radio broadcasts of the national (men's) singles and doubles championships. The immediate concern of the committee was sponsorship. The committee claimed it would be ashamed to hear, "The finals of the Amateur Tennis Championships are coming to you through the courtesy of Wheaties." Myrick warned that sponsorship would further "commercialize" the game, something the Association had been criticized for in the past. One proponent quoted a headline from *Variety:* "Radio Crazy over Sports," and pointed out that since CBS had not raised the issue, why should they? In the end, they voted to approve the principle of an "unsponsored program" and to negotiate with CBS and other potential bidders for the best possible deal; ExCom, April 3, 1937, 3–27. They apparently got fifteen thousand dollars, according to later court statements; see "Tax Exemption File," USTA Archive (courtesy of George Gowen). The radio broadcast rights for the nationals never brought in much revenue for the Association—by 1945 the going rate was still ten thousand dollars. As a postscript, the executive committee authorized the Davis Cup team captain to accept an offer of a hundred dollars or so from the *Los Angeles Times* to broadcast "unsponsored" coverage of the United States–Japan Davis Cup matches being held in California.

78. The 1939 television broadcast ("A Glimpse of the Future") is described in *ALT*, August 20, 1939, 20.

79. To the dismay of historians, many organizations (including the USLTA) fail to include reports and attachments with their records. The report of the special committee is, it seems, lost forever. The reconstruction is from ExCom, September 6, 1940, 17–72 (quotations from pages 30, 38, 54–55), and the next ExCom meeting; see the following endnote. The final payment of the stadium loan came in 1942, terminating that contract with the West Side Tennis Club; Minutes, 1943 Annual Meeting Summary of Minutes, 1943, 2. Obviously, other arrangements followed since the U.S. National Championships were held there through 1977.

80. ExCom, February 7, 1941, especially pages 65–66, 97–101. Longwood Cricket Club, just outside Boston, appears to have expressed interest in bidding on the national championship; 65.

81. *ALT*, January 20, 1935, 4–5; *ALT*, February 20, 1935, 4–6; *ALT*, November. 20, 1935; *ALT*, November 20, 1935, 19; *ALT*, 220 February–March 1938, 20; ExCom, February 7, 1941; *Time*, December 18, 1939. The Kovacs comment is in *ALT*, December 20, 1941.

82. ExCom, February 7, 1941, 63. The tournament play limitations were designed to prevent so-called tennis bums from becoming overly "professional" by playing tournaments year-round. Whether for eight, ten, or twelve weeks, the restrictions were unenforceable. International teams were given exemptions, adjustments were made for long-distance travel, and the executive committee could and did grant additional exemptions. See, for

example, the discussion at the 1935 annual meeting, summarized in *ALT*, March 20, 1935, 4–5 and *ALT*, January 20, 1936, 28. Into the early 1940s, *ALT* routinely complained about the absurdity of the rule. Avery Brundage, president of the U.S. Olympic Committee in the 1930s, and later president of the international committee, was an intractable, vocal, and unprincipled opponent of the professionalization of sports.

83. Petition to review "West Side Tennis Club v. Commissioner of Internal Revenue," 111, *Federal Reporter*, 2d series, April 15, 1940, 8–9 in "Tax Exemption File," USTA Archive. The original decision, contained in the file, contains a useful history of the WSTC. The U.S. Supreme Court refused an appeal; "Tennis Club Must Pay," *New York Times*, October 15, 1940. The comment is that of George Gowen.
84. Predictably with the lawyers in charge, Association minutes said little or nothing about the tax case as it worked its way through the Internal Revenue Service and legal system. In January 1942 a rare comment opaquely read: "Mr. Baker was asked to bring the committee up to date on the tax situation." Nothing more. That fall, executive committee delegates greeted the victory of August 11, 1942, in tax court with applause, but no recorded words; ExCom, January 16, 1942, 4 and September 4, 1942, 1.
85. Commissioner of Internal Revenue to the USLTA, November 17, 1943, "Tax Exemption File," USTA Archives. This at a time during the Second World War when the federal government was closing loopholes and raising tax rates in order to fund the economic growth that would make the nation what President Franklin Roosevelt had called for—"The Arsenal of Democracy."
86. The tax tale is neatly summarized in two letters, George Gowen to Robert Garry, November 20, 1996, and in more detail in Lawrence Baker to Lawrence Krieger, January 29, 1964. The detailed story is told in court documents filed together with the letters in the USTA Archive. Later tax cases prompted by Internal Revenue Service rulings included a settlement with the USTA in 1979 that protected U.S. Open income (see chapter 6). A 1991 attempt to declare college football's Cotton Bowl sponsorship money as taxable met with opposition in Congress and ended when the IRS decided to differentiate between "advertising" and "acknowledgment" of sponsor funds. A similar case in 2009 that had congressional support (some members wanted to force colleges to establish a football playoff system) wilted in the economic crisis at the end of that decade.

5. MARKING TIME

1. Epigraphs: ExCom, August 1951, 93 and ExCom, January 1954, 162 (ellipses omitted).
2. *ALT*, November 20, 1939, 18 and December 18, 1939, 1. Stuka's were German dive-bombers. Over three hundred of them were used against Poland in the early days of the war. Slow and vulnerable to fighters, they could be used only when the Germans had air superiority.
3. *ALT*, March 20, 1940, 22–23. The new "law" was described in excruciating detail in the USLTA *Bulletin* of March 1940. For responses to the European war see *ALT*,

March 20, 1940, 12–13 and *ALT*, March 20, 1941, 23. Wimbledon pig keeping is from *ALT*, November 20, 1940, 18.

4. Ward suggested the ILTF management committee should have a single member from England, France, the United States, Canada, South Africa, Australia, South America (Brazil, then Argentina—despite the latter's support for the Axis), Asia (perhaps China), and one representative elected at the annual meeting of the "World Federation"; ExCom, September 1943, 5–8, which also contains the overall discussion; Ward to H. Anthony Sabelli, secretary of the (British) Lawn Tennis Association, August 2, 1943 (appended). See also *ALT*, April 1947, 11. Ward made similar comments at the 1947 ILTF meeting, where he proposed that a minimum of three members of the management committee be from the Western Hemisphere.
5. Minutes, 1942 Annual Meeting, 2.
6. The national championships had slimmed down draws and had a minimalist budget; Allison Danzig, "Tennis Officials Decide to Hold U.S. Tourney," *New York Times*, June 23, 1943, 26.
7. *ALT*, December 20, 1941, 7; ExCom, January1943, 6–7.
8. Ward discussing the "Amateur Rule" in *ALT*, December 20, 1941, 7, 13 and August 5, 1942, 8; Holcombe Ward, "Tennis Head, Points to Game," *New York Times*, January 12, 1942; "Plans Night Tennis," *New York Times*, February 3, 1942. Ward claimed there were some eleven thousand lighted courts in the United States. One wonders about wartime blackout regulations for coastal cities.
9. *ALT*, January 20, 1942, 5 and February 20, 1942, 5; *ALT*, October 20, 1942, 10. The "Victory" ball was made entirely of reclaimed rubber. Ward outlined the USLTA's wartime policies, including those for junior tennis, in *ALT*, December 20, 1941, 22.
10. The special "code" for tennis players in the military is summarized in "Athletes' Status Is Frozen in Army," *New York Times*, June 28, 1942, and mentioned in ExCom, September 1942, 1–2. Joe Louis was the heavyweight boxing champion. He enlisted in the army in January 1942. On Kelly (father of Grace Kelly Rainier), see *ALT*, July 5, 1943, 10.
11. ExCom minutes for 1943 and 1944 are full of discussion about the size of the nationals and the extent of other major tournaments. Kramer, *The Game*, 123–24. See also three articles by Allison Danzig in the *New York Times*, "Title Tennis Voted," January 17, 1943; "Schroeder Added to Tennis Program," June 23, 1943; and "More Title Play Planned," January 16, 1944.
12. *ALT*, February 29, 1944; "Tennis Card Is Set," *New York Times*, January 22, 1944; Allison Danzig, "Schroeder Added to Tennis Program," *New York Times*, January 25, 1944; William D. Richardson, "Budge Beats Kramer," *New York Times*, January 29, 1944. Pauline Betz (women's national champion), Ted Schroeder, and Don McNeill—all well-known players—also played. The later benefit matches are reported in the *New York Times*;

"Sports Will Help," February 16, 1944; Allison Danzig, "Budge Will Fly Here," March 8, 1944; "Tilden Will Play," June 20, 1944. Kramer later claimed he was "lucky" to have eaten "some bad clams a couple of nights before the 1943 finals"; winning too soon could have made him turn pro prematurely; Kramer, *The Game*, 123.

13. In 1944, Tilden arranged a series of matches to entertain members of the armed forces stationed in southern California. As part of the show, Tilden and another male player, both dressed in drag, played a "ladies single" match and then teamed up against Gertrude (later "Gorgeous Gussie") Moran and another woman, Gloria Butler. Described with photos in *ALT*, April 19, 1944, 13, 33; telephone conversation with Richard Hillway by author, January 2012. (See gallery, image 16.) For an inside look at the wartime exhibition circuit see Marble, *Courting Danger*, 211. In 1943 Ted Tinling, the openly gay British tennis enthusiast, who got into the International Tennis Hall of Fame as a fashion designer of women's tennis dresses, asked General Dwight Eisenhower for permission to hold an exhibition match for the Red Cross in Algiers. According to Tinling, Ike replied "No. This is a man's war and tennis is a woman's game." Tinling, *Love and Faults*, 304. Ironically, during the war Tinling was a lieutenant colonel in the British Army intelligence service stationed in Algiers. Whether or not Eisenhower knew that is unclear since it was not made public until Tinling's death in 1990; "Ted Tinling, Designer, Dies at 79," *New York Times*, May 24, 1990 and Robin Finn, "Rebel Recalled in Style," *New York Times*, June 25, 1990, with references to his military service likely taken from the May 1990 obituary in the *Times* (London).
14. *ALT*, September 1, 1944, 21. "*SMASH*," bulletin of the Wartime Tennis Committee, August 1, 1944, courtesy of Steve Gerdes.
15. The Junior Davis Cup program began in 1937 with the goal of producing some one hundred quality players in the fifteen to twenty age group. Tennis centers in various cities would organize teams of talented youngsters who would receive professional instruction using USLTA and sectional funding; "Tennis Plan to Aid Younger Players," *New York Times*, March 28, 1937. A Junior Wightman Cup program would follow. The concept would crop up again and again within the Association, invariably running afoul of the details: how to identify talented youngsters early on, where to situate the training centers (population centers or hotbeds of tennis), and the relationship with existing junior programs in the sections, etc.
16. *ALT*, January 1945, 10–11; *ALT*, March 1946, 39.
17. ExCom, January 18, 1946, 12–56. Ward's long lecture is in Ward, "Amateur Tennis and the USLTA-1," *ALT*, December 1946; five parts followed. Ward routinely capitalized "Tennis" as a proper noun. For an example of "stuffed shirt" see Gene War, "The Open Tennis Tug-o-War," *ALT*, June 1948, 13. "Doddering old fogies" was another epithet used by Californians; *ALT*, February 1949, 10.
18. Kramer, *The Game*, 91; ExCom, September 5, 1947, 16–18; Robin Finn, "Pauline Betz Addie, Banished Champion, Dies at 91," *New York Times*, June 3, 2011. Thorpe had won two gold medals at the 1912 Olympics. The following year his

amateur status was revoked retroactively for accepting pay for playing summer baseball in one of the minor leagues.

19. ExCom, September 5, 1947, 21; Kramer, *The Game*, 70–71. Donald Dell was once briefly suspended for staying too long after playing at Wimbledon—no vacations were allowed when travel expenses were paid by the Association. Kramer recalled that Eugene Scott once stayed in Europe after Wimbledon and played under a false name; Kramer, *The Game*, 69. Hardwick's comments are from *ALT*, June 1947, 9. For additional bizarre stories about making a living as an "unpaid" amateur, see Riggs, *Tennis Is My Racket*, particularly pages 6–131.
20. ExCom, January 17, 1947, 109–19.
21. Minutes, 1948 Annual Meeting, 7–11, quotation pages 9–10.
22. Baker was born in South Carolina in 1890, but lived most of his adult life in the New York area. He became an officer of the Association in 1932, second vice president for four years, and wore out first vice president Joseph Wear in 1942 to become president. He was general counsel of the USLTA from 1952 through 1970. The tax exemption is discussed in chapter 4.
23. Baker speaking to the ExCom, September 1950, 78; *ALT*, January 1945, 10–11.
24. U.S. presidents Wilson, Harding, and not-so-silent Calvin Coolidge (he averaged one broadcast a month, more than FDR) all used the radio, but for speeches and announcements—pronouncements from on high—not for cozy, comfortable chats. For the "Wheaties" story, see chapter 4.
25. *ALT*, August 1, 1947, 36. The semifinals and finals were held on September 13–14, 1947. In 1943, there were lengthy negotiations for broadcast rights, which were all connected up with which company's ball would be used. When Wilson Sporting Goods backed off on a stipulation to use Wilson balls, the committee immediately accepted Wilson's offer to sponsor the broadcast; ExCom, September 1943, 2–4.
26. The 1939 TV broadcast is described above, chapter 4, text box, "A Glimpse of the Future." In 1945 the radio contract was extended for five years, but obviously there were clauses giving Spalding an out since radio revenue dropped from the contractual amount of $17,500 to $5,000 by 1949; ExCom, January 19, 1945, 2–4.

    The revenue numbers for radio and television in 1948–49 are from the 1949 treasurer's report and the discussion that followed. Without the actual report (not found in the archive), it is sometimes difficult to determine which figures and comments were for 1948 and which for 1949; ExCom, September 1949, 33–45.

    According to Wikipedia (as of December 2011): "By June 1939, regularly scheduled . . . television broadcasts were available in New York City and Los Angeles. . . . Television usage in the United States skyrocketed after World War II with the lifting of the manufacturing freeze, war-related technological advances, the gradual expansion of the television networks westward, the drop in set prices caused by mass production, increased leisure time, and additional disposable income. . . . While only 0.5% of U.S. households had a television set in 1946, 55.7% had one in 1954, and 90% by 1962."

27. At the 1954 annual meeting, the Association formally adopted the ILTF amateur rules; Minutes, 1954 Annual Meeting, 96–97. For Myrick-Marble, see chapter 4, note 43.
28. Shields and Bishop are quoted in Roberts, "Aces and Diamonds," 29. Roberts exaggerates the immediate importance of the adoption of ILTF "amateur" rules.
29. All information and quotes in ExCom, September 1953, 31–46; ExCom, January 1953, 3–4, 45, and January 1954, 44–49, 51–53. Similarly, in 1949 the Association called for the Davis Cup nations to not allow anyone who had lost amateur status to be a Davis Cup nonplaying coach; ExCom, January 21, 1949, 2.
30. ExCom, September 1953, 19–21; ExCom, September 1950, 78. From the outset, the international federation had been sanctioning major international tournaments, although early on, "approving" was more gentle word.
31. ExCom, September 1954, 40–46, 59. Only a year earlier, Baker had rushed through an amendment to the Association's constitution on the grounds that a stated purpose was needed to protect its tax status. Conveniently, that statement included "maintenance of high standards of amateurism"; ExCom, January 1953, 21–22; *1953 USLTA Yearbook*.
32. Kramer, "I Was a Paid Amateur," 7–9; Dick Phelan, "The Small Green Empire of Jack Kramer," *Sports Illustrated*, February 24, 1958, http://www.si.com/vault; "Kramer Loses Post," *New York Times*, July 14, 1955; Allison Danzig, "Rain Interrupts Brookline Tests," *New York Times*, August 18, 1955; Kramer, *The Game*, 65. Kramer apparently used the "paid amateur" line routinely; "'I was a paid amateur—well paid,' he said. 'Open tennis is the only way we can regain our honesty.'" *Independent Press Telegram*, December 6, 1967, http://newspaperarchive.com/press-telegram/1967-12-06/page-4.
33. ExCom, March 25, 1927, 40–61, quote on 53. James O. Anderson, Howard Kinsey, and Vincent Richards were to be removed from the list of honorary members. The names of all three were on the last published list; *1941 USLTA Yearbook*. The honorary membership category, emulating that of Wimbledon, was established in 1921. For early details see, *ALT*, May 15, 1923, 96.
34. The full discussion and quotes are in ExCom, January 1954, 64–71. For the cross-outs see archival copy of the *1941 USLTA Yearbook*, 23. No listing of honorary members has been found in the USTA Archive since that 1941 publication. Lawrence Baker wrote the same thing in 1969. During 1967–68, Baker was a one-man honorary membership committee. In 1969 one John L. Brown of Omaha, Nebraska, joined as the only other member. It stayed that way through 1971, when the committee disappeared. Baker's correspondence makes clear that during that five-year period two names—Allison Danzig and William Scripps Kellogg—were added to the list, the first and only additions since the last printed list of 1941; Lawrence Baker papers, ITHF, 6.7.1 USTA Honorary Member-

ship Committee, 1968–1971, Box 15 (courtesy of Meredith Miller, Librarian, ITHF). Baker was succeeded as committee chair by Judge Robert Kelleher and others. In 1980 the committee was reconstituted into a group of heavy-hitting past presidents—W. E. Hester Jr. (chairman), Robert Kelleher, Stanley Malless, and Edward A. Turville. But I have found no recommendations from the committee being taken up by the executive committee in the early 1980s; *1980 USTA Yearbook*, 29. That committee continued for a few years, (adding another former president, Joseph Carrico, as a member), then disappeared in the mid 1980s. Nonetheless, bylaw 9 of the current (2016) USTA bylaws still states that honorary membership may be conferred upon such worthy persons as may be selected by the executive committee.

35. William M. Fischer began collecting tennis memorabilia, from books to newspaper clippings, in 1897. What became a collection of over two thousand items was housed in various locations, finally ending up in 1978 at St. Johns University in Queens, New York. http://www.stjohns.edu/libraries/archives/special-collections#Fischer.

36. Minutes, 1946 Annual Meeting, 34–35; *LTLR*, 29 (August 1955); *ALT*, March 1946, 39. The report touched on efforts to establish an International Hall of Fame containing records of "all the leading men players of the world," but that was thirty years in the future. The National Hall of Fame changed its name in 1975 to the International Tennis Hall of Fame.

37. Van Alen sent two letters to the USLTA president; *LTLR*, 29 (August 1955); ExCom, September 1953, 84–97 and January 1954, 81–82. In 1957 the protected option was extended to ten years, conditional upon the Casino running a grass-court tournament each year, although Lawrence Baker and others spoke of that being temporary awaiting establishment of an Association headquarters, hall of fame, and library; ExCom, January 1957, 108–11. See also Dwight, *Tie Breaker*, 99–111; *Tennis*, September 1992. According to the minutes of the April 18, 1958, meeting of the hall of fame board of directors, "professionalism, as such, was in itself not a deterrent for consideration to enshrinement, but character would also continue to be carefully reviewed." (courtesy of the International Tennis Hall of Fame archive).

38. Harold Rosenthal, "U.S.L.T.A. Lifts Racial Barrier," *ALT*, May 1948, 10. The 1929 Association statement is quoted in therein. See also chapter 3 for a discussion of the 1929 episode.)

39. *ALT*, September 5, 1940, 17. *ALT* reported on ATA championships and on African American college players. For examples see "American TA Championship," *ALT*, September 20, 1932, 24; and "Colored Players and the Colleges," *ALT*, June 20, 1938, 46, both of which covered the exploits of "flashy and flawless" Reggie Weir; and "Ratings of American TA," *ALT*, October 20, 1941, 38.

40. "Budge Sets Back Negro Champion," *New York Times*, July 30, 1940.

For Xavier University tennis, see http://www.xula.edu/athletics/news/2010/0729.html.

41. ExCom, January 17, 1947, 132–43. (See appendix 3 for the entire ten-page executive-committee discussion of January 17, 1947, 132–42.) A small sidebar from personal experience—in the early 1970s, Richard Cohen lived in Plainfield, New Jersey. My dear friend, Fred Crystal, a local player who was on the membership committee at the Netherwood Tennis Club, proposed Cohen be asked to join. The vote was negative, but Crystal persisted and the following year Cohen got in—the club's first black member. The two played singles regularly for years afterwards. Rather what S. W. Merrihew had in mind back in 1923, though it took a long time (see chapter 3).
42. Perhaps the most famous example of a forty-year-old who could beat the best was Pancho Gonzales who, at age forty-one, defeated John Newcombe, Ken Rosewall, Stan Smith, and Arthur Ashe in succession at a tournament in Las Vegas in 1969. (Courtesy of Richard Hillway.)
43. The most complete source for the Weir story is Rosenthal, "U.S.L.T.A. Lifts Racial Barrier," *ALT*, May 1948, 10; see also "Reginald C. Weir," in Caldwell and McShea, *Tennis in New York*, 153–54. Other sources are http://www.blacktennishalloffame.com/; http://www.examiner.com/black-college-sports-in-national/saving-ace-james-mcdaniel-broke-barriers-on-the-court; "Black History Timeline," http://www.bookrags.com/tandf/american-tennis-association-tf/. Weir was eventually appointed to the USLTA Administrative Committee in 1969 and later elected to the Eastern Tennis Hall of Fame; http://ustaeasternhalloffame.com/1999.htm. Oscar Johnson received a "'special award' for outstanding services to the game" from the International Tennis Hall of Fame; "Return to Form: Black Tennis Trailblazer Oscar Johnson Jr.," *Los Angeles Times*, August 27, 1987. Jimmy McDaniel was profiled with honesty and sensitivity in Barry Meadow, "Jimmie McDaniel," 52–57.
44. I found no such mention of Jackie Robinson by Association leaders in newspapers and USLTA records. In fact, the only mention of Robinson I have found in USLTA minutes and meeting records came in 1951 when former Wimbledon champion Sidney Wood offered an example of a fascinating charity event. He made no mention of race but presented the farcical image of Robinson using a racket and Billy Talbert (a nationally ranked tennis player) using a baseball bat to play a tennis match. Fittingly, comedian Milton Berle would be master of ceremonies; ExCom, August 31, 1951, 115–16. Woody Strode and Kenny Washington had "reintegrated" the National Football League in 1946 when the Los Angeles Coliseum Commission made signing black players a condition for the Los Angeles Rams to use of the facility. The league owners had agreed informally in 1933 to ban blacks, who had played occasionally since the turn of the century. Professional basketball began integrating in 1946.
45. "Negress Stars in Eastern," *ALT*, April 1948, 29. A word is in order here about Gibson's strongest supporter and advocate, Dr. Robert Walter Johnson, the

"Godfather of Black Tennis." In the 1950s and '60s, Johnson ran a program in Lynchburg, Virginia, for promising young black tennis players. Gibson was his star pupil, though there were others. In 2009 Johnson was inducted into the International Tennis Hall of Fame; Harris and Kyle-DeBose, *Charging the Net*, 112–13. One "white" facility in Eastern that allowed black players to participate in tournaments before Weir's breakthrough match was the Hamilton Tennis Center on Dykeman Street (now a New York City housing project), though there likely were others. Weir's "friend Ernie Kuhn, whose family built and owned Hamilton's 32 red clay courts, ran tournaments there and told Reggie he'd put him in the draw and see what happens." Apparently nothing; courtesy of Dale Caldwell, email to author of March 26, 2012. A club somewhere in the "Middle West" also permitted a black player to enter a tournament; ExCom, January 17, 1947, 135–36. Dr. Johnson did talk with the chair of the USLTA Interscholastic Committee after watching two of his best players get demolished, "love and love," at an interscholastic tournament in Charlottesville, Virginia. "I never saw tennis played by young people the way those white boys played." Like Jack Kramer, Johnson realized that for raw talent to develop, his youngsters had to compete against the best players; *World Tennis,* July 1965, 32–33.

46. Gibson's biographers give the ATA a good deal of credit for pushing to get her entered into major all-white tournaments, protesting the failure of one venue (Maplewood Country Club, New Jersey State Champs) even to answer a request for an entry application as a "lack of common decency" characterized by "procrastination, evasion, and absolute discourtesy." They assume the ATA was influential in getting Gibson into the nationals at Forest Hills, but offer no evidence; nor is there any in the USLTA records; Gray and Rice, *Born to Win*, 44–57; Caldwell and McShea, *Tennis in New York*, 40.

47. According to Marble's autobiography, her work as an American spy during the Second World War is a bizarre tale of reuniting in early 1945 with her prewar lover, a Swiss banker, who was happily accepting Nazi gold and stolen valuables. After being recruited by an American named "Jones," Marble went to neutral Switzerland, ostensibly to play tennis exhibitions, where she and the banker resumed their affair, allowing Marble to gain access to his personal records of transactions with the Germans. Despite her true affection for the banker, she photographed the records, was detected, and while making her escape, was shot by "Jones" who, it turned out, was a double agent working for the Russians. The Americans (presumably the Army Counter Intelligence Corps which was active in Switzerland), arriving a bit late, shot "Jones" and rescued Marble, who was able to provide from memory (her camera was lost in the chase) substantial data about the stolen hoard. Researchers have found no corroborating evidence for her breathless tale, and since Marble used fictitious names for all the players in the story (including the Americans),

tracing the story is apparently impossible. Her name comes up in the FBI archive site, but those files make no mention of her. But why would she lie? Marble, *Courting Danger*, 242–81; email of July 31, 2015, Hayden Peake (intelligence historian/bibliographer) to author.

48. Alice Marble, "A Vital Issue," *ALT*, July 1, 1950, 14. The publisher of *ALT* (Oliver Rea) backed up Marble's forceful plea with a brief statement that the magazine "wishes to go on record as wholeheartedly supporting the sentiments and opinions expressed by Miss Marble." The campaign continued with a lengthy piece titled "The Gibson Story," that spoke to her talent and potential, concluding that she "hopes to be able to compile a record in USLTA outdoor tourneys—a clear reference to the USLTA nationals; *ALT*, July 1950, 6–7. This was the era when *Brown v. Board of Education*, the Montgomery bus boycott, and the murder of fourteen-year old Emmett Till launched the most active phase of the civil rights movement.
49. Gray and Rice, *Born to Win*, 57, 63–67.
50. In the unlikely event that someone has struggled through all this prose to confront, for the first time, the tennis scoring system, let me try to explain—briefly. Getting past the arcane 15–30–40 in lieu of 1–2–3 and advantage or "ad" for scoring within a game, a set consists of winning at least six games, but as with scoring within a game, the margin must be two. Hence 6–4 or 7–5 or 9–7, etc. until adoption of the tiebreak system in 1970. Most matches consist of best two out of three sets. The most significant exceptions are the men's singles matches in the Grand Slam tournaments and Davis Cup competition where the winner must take three out of five sets. For an amusing summary of the history of tennis scoring, see Stuart Miller, *New York Times*, May, 24, 2013, https://straightsets.blogs.nytimes.com/2013/05/24/quirks-of-the-game-how-tennis-got-its-scoring-system/.
51. Alice Marble, "An Open Letter to Althea Gibson," *ALT*, November 1950, 19, 32.
52. *ALT*, October 1951, 21.
53. Harris and Kyle-DeBose, *Charging the Net*, 59.
54. Sam Pope Brewer, "Clubs Here Face Inquiry on Bias," *New York Times*, July 18, 1959 and Robert D. McFadden, "Dr. Bunch of U.N., Nobel Winner, Dies," *New York Times*, December 10, 1971; Anon., "Segregation: West Side Story," Online Archive of California (July 20, 1959), http://www.oac.cdlib.org/view?docId=hb787009m8&brand=oac4&doc.view=entire_text. A transcript of the telephone call between Bunche and Burglund is in http://www.oac.cdlib.org/ark:/13030/hb4j49p152/; Potter, "Passing Shots," 44–45. Bunche was a long-time tennis fan who wrote happily in his diary about seeing Bill Tilden in 1937 and of being a spectator at the Davis Cup match between Hitler's Germany and the United States. The final match, played at Wimbledon, between Don Budge and Baron Gottfried von Cramm, decided the competition. In the fifth match point of the fifth set, Budge hit a huge forehand passing shot while falling onto the grass—"the greatest tennis match ever." That match was used by Marshall Jon Fisher to juxtapose international tennis and Hitler's persecutions of Jews and homosex-

uals, since Von Cramm was gay and had an affair with a Jewish actor. See Fisher, *A Terrible Splendor*, 154–56. When the Americans went on to defeat the defending British champions, USLTA leaders simply breathed a collective sigh of relief that the United States finally won the Davis Cup without Bill Tilden, who had last led them to victory in 1926.

55. ExCom, September 1961, 111; Hall, *Arthur Ashe*, 38–39.
56. Victor Denny in *United States Lawn Tennis Association News*, 266 (August 1959) (hereafter *USLTA News*). Denny was viewed as a "progressive . . . opposed to the ultra conservative New York clique," but on racial issues east and west saw eye to eye; quotation from *USLTA News* 270 (December 1959): 6; ExCom, September 1960, 5–6. The comment about the racial makeup of Flushing Meadows was reported in Tony Kornheiser, "A Racial Dispute Flares at Forrest Hills," *New York Times*, September 9, 1977, and "Forest Hills Official Resigns," September 10, 1977; see also Steinberger, "Queens Was Burning Too." According to Steinberger, Arthur Ashe, who had "automatically" become a member of the West Side Tennis Club after winning the 1968 U.S. Open, threatened to resign, but the board member beat him to it. The club finally broke the color barrier in 1978 but too late to make peace with the USTA. Slew Hester, then USTA president, refused comment saying "they have enough troubles"; Fred Ferritti, "Black Gains Membership at Forest Hills," *New York Times*, June 27, 1978.
57. ExCom, February 1969, 74–81.
58. Lee Hamilton interview with author, March 11, 2012; email exchanges with author by George Gowen, August 2012. For the confrontation with South Africa generated by Arthur Ashe's request for a visa to play in the South Africa Open, see chapter 6.
59. Harris and Kyle-DeBose, *Charging the Net*, 144–45.
60. Executive director's report (Ferman) ExCom, September 1998, 17–18. See the various files in container 2532 about minority participation, but particularly document 482, "Minority Participation Committee: Progress Report and Funding Request," January 8, 1992, *USTA* Archive.
61. "Russell Kingman, Led Tennis Group," *New York Times*, March 13, 1959; *USLTA News* 262 (April 1959). Kingman was the first American to hold the formal title of president of the ILTF. However, Louis Carruthers was "principal/chairman, effectively president" of the federation in 1934.
62. Myrick warned that the ILTF would make Davis Cup "a European affair"; ExCom, May 1930, 44. In 1963 the USLTA emphatically rejected the idea that the ILTF had any authority whatsoever over Davis Cup. Only the Davis Cup nations had such authority; ExCom, February 1963, 24–25. For the details and other citations for the box "'A European Affair': The International Federation and the Association," see chapter 4.
63. *ALT*, March 1951, 4–5 (ellipses omitted for readability).
64. ExCom, August 1951, 89. The chair was W. Donald McNeill.

65. ExCom, August 1951, 99.
66. ExCom, September 15, 1922, 2; ExCom, January 1957, 7–9.
67. The late 1940s and 1950s offer apt examples. For "national" approaches to junior development see *USLTA Service Bulletin* 139 (January 1949) and *LTLR* 36 (August 1957). For sectional approaches, see *USLTA Service Bulletin* 133 (July 1948) and 246 (December 1957). In the early fifties, Jack Kramer offered to "underwrite" junior development and Junior Davis Cup programs; *USLTA Service Bulletin* 200 (February 1954). The suggestion was sent to a study committee. Given the USTA's later preoccupation with tennis in the schools, it is worth noting that similar efforts were made in the early 1950s, although the focus was on getting tennis moved out of the "minor" sport classification. The Association did call for competition for girls as well as boys. The goal was "to prepare a tennis program which can be used throughout their school system"; *USLTA Service Bulletin* 152 (February 1950). They key, of course, was identifying tennis enthusiasts within each school system. No easy task. Endorsements or quotas are mentioned in ExCom, January 16,1942, 3.
68. Kramer makes that argument throughout his autobiography, *The Game*.
69. The foundation was established by the ExCom late in 1951, and announced to 1952 annual meeting; ExCom, September 1951, 116–21; Minutes, 1952 Annual Meeting, 34–37. The foundation's tax-exempt status per section 101(6) of the tax code was confirmed early in 1953; *USLTA Service Bulletin* 191 (May 1953). (My thanks to George Gowen for helping me navigate the rocks and shoals of tax cases relating to the Association's income tax status.) A life-membership enrollment program instituted in the 1960s that cost only one hundred dollars put only a little money into the foundation, prompting caution about raising the price; ExCom, February 1969, 46. The Association had a different tax-exempt foundation in the early 1970s, but it too failed to take off; see Potter, "Passing Shots," 12. The foundation was rejuvenated in the early twenty-first century as USTA Serve; see chapter 6. Baker's plea to the professionals is from *USLTA Service Bulletin* 240 (June 1967). I found nothing to indicate that anything came of Baker's suggestion. A number of "patrons" organizations at the sectional and local level cropped up at the same time, perhaps on their own, perhaps stimulated by the Association's actions. For example, *USLTA Service Bulletin* 173 (November 1951) and 174 (December 1951), which reported patrons organizations being founded in the Western (in Chicago, Cincinnati, Detroit and Cleveland) and New England Sections.
70. ExCom, August 1951, 124–30. Wood's closing remarks included a reference to the Kefauver Commission, an investigation by a U.S. Senate committee into organized crime and corruption, seeming to hint that the dispute centered on increasing revenue from the national championships at Forest Hills. As usual, the report was not appended to the minutes and is presumably lost. Wood later rejected nomination to the Eastern Tennis Hall of Fame because of what he perceived to be its exclusionary policies.

71. ExCom, August 1951, 91–93, 99,104.
72. Minutes, 1952 Annual Meeting, 13, 26–29.
73. Oliver Rea (publisher of *The Racquet*) to Edwin Baker, November 9, 1951; a handwritten note on that letter provides the date of the transfer to *World Tennis*; *The Racquet*, December 1951, 37. Gladys Heldman was a vigorous and voluble supporter of professional and open tennis, and women's tennis, although Jack Kramer called her an "establishment apologist" who labeled the pros "greedy carpetbaggers." Kramer, *The Game*, 83. Their differences were ones of practicality, not principle (see chapter 6).
74. ExCom, January 14, 1944, 1–4; 1944 Minutes, Annual Meeting, 2.
75. Minutes, 1952 Annual Meeting, 7; Treasurer's Report for 1951, attached to ExCom, January 1953 (six pages plus financial statements).
76. ExCom, January 1952, 52–76.
77. ExCom, August 1951, 93.
78. Minutes, 1952 Annual Meeting, 18–21. ExCom, January 1955, 76–78. Turville to the board and sectional presidents (November 21, 1962, presidential file). The appeal for an executive director came from Martin Tressel; Administration Committee Minutes, December 1966, 2 (hereafter AdminCom).
79. Minutes, 1952 Annual Meeting, 2.
80. ExCom, September 1950, 63–67. The first president of the Florida section was Edward Turville, later president of the USLTA. On the California split, see ExCom, January 1951, 134; ExCom, August 1951, 16–18; ExCom, January 1952, 135–36. Treasurer's Report for 1951 (attached to ExCom, January 1953).
81. "Tennis Players Organize League," *New York Times*, September 3, 1953; "Larsen Beats Kovaleski," *New York Times*, July 31, 1954; ExCom, September 1954, 57–60; ExCom, January 1954, 183. The "Player's Association" discussions are covered in *The Racquet* 46 (May 1952), 4. The player rumored to have asked for excessive expenses was apparently Tony Trabert, the number-one ranked U.S. player, who was curiously one of the early organizers of the Players Association and one of the first forty-five members of the TPL and a member of its executive committee. Trabert vigorously denied the accusations; Allison Danzig, "Tennis Players Plan Round-Robin," *New York Times*, January 15, 1954. Wood later developed and patented the portable playing surface known as "Supreme Court."
82. *USLTA News* 253 (July 1958).
83. *USLTA Service Bulletin* 190 (April 1953).
84. "Tennis Inquiry Started," *New York Times*, August 5, 1954. In September 1957 following a proposal to create an award for the journalist who did the most for tennis, Danzig was the immediate and unanimous selection; ExCom, September 1957, 6–12.
85. ExCom, January 1954, 159–73.
86. ExCom, January 1954, 173–83; "Trabert Subdues Seixas," *New York Times*, January 15, 1954. The first match of the "National" round robin came in

April 26 of that year (1954) with Tony Trabert (who turned pro the following year) playing Vic Seixas. The tournament scheduled play for Monday nights for the next four months. News coverage grew steadily smaller, and after July the tournament seems to have disappeared from the pages of the *New York Times*.

87. Barbara La Fontaine, "Busiest Voice In A Busy, Busy Clan," *Sports Illustrated*, June 22, 1964, http://www.si.com/vault.

88. Misner's performance and the quotes for two paragraphs are from ExCom, January 1953, 212–21. See above, chapter 3 for Dick Kroesen's biting satire (1914 and 1916) and Harry Waidner's angry threat of secession (1917), both in response to what they perceived as discriminatory policies and actions by the northeastern tennis establishment.

89. In 1947 President Harry Truman had appointed Herbert Hoover to head a commission to recommend changes in the administrative structure of the executive branch. Congress was about to create a second version of the commission.

90. Only eight cities had hosted the annual meeting before the San Francisco meeting. New York City of course dominated with fifty-three meetings (1881–1926, 1939–1955). The others were Philadelphia 1927, 1936; Chicago 1928; Boston 1929; St. Louis 1930; New Orleans 1932; Pittsburgh 1934; Miami 1938; and San Francisco 1956; USLTA *Service Bulletin* 222 (December 1955). See "Annual Meeting Sites, 1881-2017," compiled by the author, USTA Archive.

91. ExCom, September 1954, 1; ExCom, September 1955, 17–21. In 1956 Baker reported settlement with New York State on tax liability of just short of ten thousand dollars for the period 1935 to 1946 where the Association had a joint venture with the West Side Tennis Club to share profits and losses for USLTA events held at Forest Hills. New York State won the argument that taxes were due for that period, but since the USLTA signed a new agreement in 1946 whereby the USLTA shared profits but not losses with the WSTC, the liability ended; ExCom, January 1956, 3–5.

92. ExCom, January 1957, 3; *LTLR* 33 (April 1957); USLTA *Service Bulletin* 220 (October 1955); USLTA *Service Bulletin* 233 (November 1956); and USLTA *Service Bulletin* 236 (February 1957). Publication of Cummings, *American Tennis,* was delayed until July 1957, which could not have helped sales; USLTA *Service Bulletin* 238 (April 1957). As of September 1958 there were 34,500 comic books unsold, and *American Tennis* lost only some $10,000, bringing the jubilee in at about $35,000. Making a silk purse out of a sow's ear, the president pointed out that was "only $15,000 over what we originally appropriated," i.e., nearly double the $20,000 budget item; ExCom, September 1957, 12–15; ExCom, September 1958, 22. For a quite lengthy and unfunny description of the comic book, see Howard Tuchner, "Unfunny 'Comic' Books Win Friends for Tennis," *New York Times*, October 21, 1956. One of the comic books will be donated by the author to the USTA Archive.

93. ExCom, January 1957, 10–11; *LTLR* 33 (April 1957). Emphasis added.

94. For just one example see ExCom, September 1954.

95. USLTA *Service Bulletin* 236 (February 1957). The concern over revenue was constant.
96. USLTA *Service Bulletin* 236 (February 1957) and USLTA *Service Bulletin* 238 (April 1957).
97. ExCom, September 1957, 70–162. Turville's comments are on pages 154–55. His "caste system" reference is in Turville to the board and sectional presidents (November 21, 1962, presidential file). "Tennis Officials, Bar Open Event," *New York Times*, September 8, 1957; ExCom, September 1958, 24–25.
98. Potter, "Passing Shots." The official ITF history verifies Kramer's claim that "open" tennis could have come in 1960, though it would have been in a very messy form; Bowers, *The International Tennis Federation*, 54. A vote at that year's ILTF general meeting failed by five votes. The fix was in, wrote Kramer. The ITF history describes the "somewhat farcical circumstances" a bit more fully: one delegate was in the toilet, two were arranging a riverboat cruise for that evening, and another had fallen asleep. No word on the fifth possible voter, no word how each would have voted. Kramer insists that the USLTA voted for the motion, but lobbied against it. USLTA representatives at the ILTF meeting were ambivalent about unrestricted open tennis, but that was not what was proposed. A favorable vote would only have allowed national federations to hold open tournaments, allowing at the same time "designated players," something the USLTA opposed as hypocritical but which seems to have been part of the deal. See below, note 114; Kramer, *The Game*, 253. Asked about the bathroom story, Kelleher sniffed "dubious"; Marmion interviews, "The USTA Interview with The Honorable Robert J. Kelleher," USTA Archive DVD.
99. Kramer, *The Game*, 236; ExCom, January 1960, 36.
100. ExCom, January 1958, 68–70.
101. Citations for the box "Who Decides": ExCom, February 1962, 116–19; Gerald E. Misner, "The Delegates Assembly," *1962 USTA Yearbook*, 43–44, provides unique historical background.
102. Minutes, 1958 Annual Meeting, 164, 169.
103. USLTA *Service Bulletin* 224 (February 1956).
104. The direct member clubs were in Hawaii, which would become the Hawaii State (later Hawaii Pacific) section in 1964; in Bermuda where two clubs have remained (as of 2012) as direct members (see above, chapter 4, "The Bermuda Exception" box); and in the Caribbean, where Puerto Rico became a direct member "district" in 1961, then in 1983 became a section composed of Puerto Rico and the U.S. Virgin Islands so that Puerto Rico could participate in the Olympics and the Pan-American games. That direct member "district" category is unique in Association history. Correspondence with author from Charles (Chuck) Hitt, August 2012; *1960 USLTA Yearbook* and *1983 USLTA Yearbook*.
105. Standing Orders, *1959 USLTA Yearbook*, 231.

106. *1959 USLTA Yearbook*; ExCom, January 1958, 7–10.
107. In Association parlance, anything west of Pittsburgh was "The West." Technically, in 1933, Chicagoan Harry Knox became the first westerner to be president, but in name only, since his vice president served as acting president for the entire year. See chapter 3.
108. Tom Norris (USTA archivist) to Lee Hamilton (USTA executive director), May 1, 2007, "USTA Membership History and Archives Progress Report," USTA Archive. The 1958 membership figures showed 64 percent were juniors (eighteen years old and younger); *USLTA News* 269 (November 1959). See also the reports of credentials committees in the Minutes, Annual Meetings for 1958 and for 1959.
109. ExCom, September 1957, 24.
110. Up through the early 1950s, I have found no one who became a national leader without being either a well-known player or having extensive sectional experience, although some rose to national involvement more quickly than others.
111. Note for "Individual Membership" box: The proposal that "Class A clubs have one (1) vote for each voting member" was in the "call" for the 1959 annual meeting but was deleted from the proposals put before the delegates; Minutes, 1959 Annual Meeting, "Call" (appended to minutes); ExCom, January 1959, 51–52, wherein the president noted that the motion "will not include all of the items in the Call." On voting, see article 3, section 1 of the 1960 USLTA constitution, and following years. For the initial block voting formula see, chapter 3. "Enrollment" cards replaced "registration" cards to enter USLTA sanctioned events. By 1969 they cost six dollars for adults and two dollars for those under eighteen. In 1972 bylaws 11–12 contained the provisions regarding dues and voting strength. As of today (2017), member clubs and organizations add a relatively small number of votes to overall sectional voting strength. On direct member clubs, see above note 104.
112. The *USLTA News* apparently picked up its numbering system from its immediate predecessor, but it was a far different publication. It lasted only until December 1963.
113. Note for "Volunteer Committees" box: ExCom, January 1958, 6–65.
114. "Comes the Tennis Revolution," *Sports Illustrated*, February 24, 1958, http://www.si.com/vault. Denny's comments are in *World Tennis*, February 1960, 33. *USLTA News* 295 (March 1962). The French proposal for "authorized" players is discussed in Potter, "Passing Shots," October 1959, 12 and March 1960, 28–29. Jean Borotra, speaking as president of the ILTF, publicly proposed such a category at a press conference in Chicago on January 19, 1961, to the obvious distress of the Association president, George Barnes. The main purpose was to allow national federations to force their best players to play Davis Cup. A professional could play certain international competitions but only if they were on their nation's list of "authorized players." The USLTA rejected that as a violation of "the spirit and regulations covering Davis Cup play"; Barnes "to various member nations of the ILTF" (March 1960), and "President's Annual Report, 1960," both in presiden-

tial file on "going open." Both warned that the "authorized player" category would "destroy amateur tennis . . . throughout the world."

115. *World Tennis*, March 1960, 29. (E. B.) Potter's perceptive if acerbic column in *World Tennis*, "Passing Shots," covered Association high politics in the 1960s in detail. Self-determination for American tennis to choose open tennis was his avowed crusade from the time he lived and wrote in Paris in the early 1930s. His column was irreverent, personal, and entertaining.

116. USLTA *News* 271 (January 1960).

117. USLTA *News* 291 (October 1961), on the masthead.

118. There are extensive discussions of open tennis throughout the sources. For example ExCom, January 1960, 31–36; Minutes, 1960 Annual Meeting, 13; AdminCom, November 1960, 4–5. Early in 1959 Denny sent a strongly worded letter to all ILTF member nations about the need for a review of amateur regulations. He described the existing rules as "completely unrealistic" and "grossly incorrect," called for avoiding "hypocrisy," and bluntly asserted that current regulations "if enforced, will encourage players to become professionals." Denny to ILTF members, February 27, 1959, presidential file on "going 'open.'"

119. Letter to the editor, *World Tennis*, June 1959, 2. The precise Churchill quote is "I have not become the King's First Minister in order to preside over the liquidation of the British Empire." Myrick's sentiments are forcefully expressed in a letter to "My dear George [Barnes]," January 24, 1961, presidential file on "going 'open.'"

120. AdminCom, June 16, 1962, 5; USLTA *News* 294 (January–February 1962): 4–6; USLTA *News* 295 (March 1962); and USLTA *News* 300 (August 1962). President's Annual Report, 1960, 3, and Barnes, memo to Executive and Administrative Committees, June 15, 1961, presidential file, "going 'open.'" For a gentle plea "that Amateur Tennis should be *kept* amateur," see Howard Ackerman (Middle States Section delegate), *World Tennis*, April 1963, 46. The presidential file on "going 'open'" contains a number of letters and reports that elaborate on the USLTA arguments. For example, Barnes openly worried that "important nations" might pull out of the ILTF "in order to chart their own destinies"; Barnes to the ExCom, February 2, 1962 (for public release); Barnes to Myrick, July 27, 1961, refers directly to reduced revenues. The "rape" charge is in ExCom, January 1960. Despite the Association's request for autonomy, the ITF history simply states that, in 1962 (it was 1963), the USLTA "set back the cause" by voting "to oppose the principle of open tennis." Bowers, *The International Tennis Federation*, 54.

121. ExCom, February 1963, 16–24; Minutes, 1963 Annual Meeting, 58, 72, 90. The precise wording of the resolutions is easily accessed in AdminCom, "miscellaneous materials"; Call of Special Meeting, May 22, 1967. See also "The President's Column (Edward Turville)," USLTA *News* 308 (May 1963):

1–3, wherein he summarized, quite critically, the history of "open" tennis and the USLTA.

122. Allison Danzig, "A Black Eye for U.S. Tennis," *New York Times*, March 1, 1963.

123. AdminCom, June 1964, 2, 65–66. For an example of liberalizing the rules see ExCom, February 1967, re: reinstatement to amateur status. Avery Brundage was a controversial figure. Accused of anti-Semitism for not allowing Jewish members of the 1936 U.S. Olympic team to participate in the Berlin games, he was an autocratic, unsentimental, unswerving, powerful devotee of amateurism in what he perceived as its pure form.

124. The overwrought rhetoric about Tressel is that of Ned Potter, "Passing Shots," *World Tennis*, December 1963, 34. Obviously, Potter supported open tennis. Tressel had earlier offered an apocalyptic nightmare of how open tennis would affect the Association: "as we go from one open tournament nationally, to two open tournaments . . . and so forth, a great share of our income is going to go in the hands of the professionals. . . . That means, at least to me, the death of the United States Lawn Tennis Association"; ExCom, January 1960, 32.

125. Minutes, 1967 Annual Meeting, 64–76.

6. OPEN TENNIS

1. Evans, *Open Tennis*, 12–13, 18–23; Collins and Hollander, *Bud Collins' Tennis Encyclopedia*, 172–73, 516–17. The first open tournament began on April 22, 1968, at the West Hants Club in Bournemouth, England. For a lively description of the challenges the tournament posed for both amateurs and professionals see "Big Bang in Bournemouth: The Open Era Begins," *Tennis* (May–June 2015), 23–24. Lamar Hunt, "the guiding light" of and a partner in, World Championship Tennis also helped found the American Football League and owned the Kansas City Chiefs. Rich Koster calls Hunt "the catalyst of the American sports boom of the 1960s" and offers a perceptive business bio of Hunt in Koster, *The Tennis Bubble*, 53–80.

   Kelleher flatly stated that "the USTA was broke most of the time—Davis Cup saved it. Never could rely on consistent levels of funding"; (phone interview with Kelleher by author, February 10, 2011.) Lance Tingray, a reporter for the *London Daily Telegraph*, wrote in 1966 that elimination of the distinction between amateurs and professionals had been British Lawn Tennis Association policy "for some time now." Letter to the editor, *World Tennis*, January 1966, 4. Wimbledon put on an eight-man professional tournament in August 1967 that proved very successful; Bowers, *The International Tennis Federation*, 56.

2. USTA *Official Encyclopedia*, 58, 64–65. Kelleher supported two year terms for Association presidents but said he laid low on that and open tennis until he was nominated for a second one-year term. Pressure on the ILTF is described in Bowers, *The International Tennis Federation*, 58–61. The Americans raised the threat of resigning from the ILTF. Yet the ITF history suggests that "it all could have come much earlier," quoting Kramer's angry criticism of the USTA for not

supporting open tennis back in the 1930s; Bowers, *The International Tennis Federation*, 61.

3. On the 1963 resolution, see chapter 5.
4. AdminCom, March 1967; ExCom, September 1967, 81–87. Sorlien, a canny grass-court player, qualified repeatedly for the U.S. nationals at Forest Hills and once for the Wimbledon championships.
5. Just before the annual meeting, the Association's executive committee voted to include professional players as members. The search for an effective relationship with professionals would come up repeatedly; ExCom, February 2, 1968.
6. AdminCom, November 1967, 4–5. Evans, *Open Tennis*, 19. Kelleher, in a 1998 interview with the *New York Times* quoted in Robin Finn, "Robert J. Kelleher, 99 Dies," *New York Times*, June 24, 2012.
7. Evans, *Open Tennis*, 21–22 captures the atmosphere but offers quotes I cannot locate. He also wrote that the key meeting was on a Wednesday morning, but the meeting was on Saturday; Charles Friedman, "Approval Seen for Open Tennis," *New York Times*, March 26, 1968. Nevertheless, his tale has a ring of truth. See also Robin Finn, "Robert J. Kelleher, 99 Dies," *New York Times*, June 24, 2012, which likewise contains quotes I cannot verify. In the *Sports Illustrated* article, tennis writer Bud Collins, repeatedly has Kelleher referring to those who opposed him as "old goats," but the only direct quote has him saying he accepted the presidency "primarily to keep the job from going to one of the backward old goats," meaning some dedicated New Englander out of touch with "the sporting picture in America"; Bud Collins, "An Open-Minded Boss for a Bunch of Old Goats," *Sports Illustrated*, February 5, 1968, http://www.si.com/vault. Perhaps Evans saw the transcript of Collins's interview with Kelleher, and some of the quotes ended on the cutting room floor once *Sports Illustrated* editors did their work. The preceding citations were largely provided by George Gowen who, in a letter to Kelleher of September 24, 2009, forwarded a number of news clippings. Gowen was kind enough to copy me as well.

   When Kramer was running the pro barnstorming tour, he one time cussed out Kelleher, a long-time friend, saying he could not compete with the USLTA because it was paying amateurs more than he could pay them. "Trouble was Jack was right," said Kelleher; Kelleher interview with author, December 17, 2010. The Association didn't challenge the players taking money—partly for legal reasons, partly because the leadership had little desire to confront the issue.
8. Notes for "Here Comes the Judge—Robert J. Kelleher" text box: Kramer, *The Game*, 278. ExCom, February 7, 1974 contains the discussion about Jimmy Connors (pages 41–45, 44–48), with the "little white charger" remark (page 44), and the judge's rant against "brass hats" (pages 46–48). That broadside went against the efforts of others, like Stan Malless, that

emphasized taking *control* of the professional game. Connors made no mention of the incident in his memoir, *The Outsider*.

The Ralston affair is described in Robert J. Kelleher, "Dennis Ralston As Captain of the United States Davis Cup Team," typescript memorandum (n.d.), enclosed in Kelleher letter to author, January 25, 2005. ExCom Minutes for September 1972 show one of those presidents referring to Ralston as that year's captain: "I can't say enough for the individual efforts of the players and I can't be too complimentary to Dennis Ralston, who has handled his responsibilities as *captain* and coach very, very well." ExCom, September 1972, 9 (emphasis added); *1993 USTA Yearbook*, 666. The story made the newspapers: Robin Finn, "20-Odd Years Later, Captain Is Removed," *New York Times*, January 11, 1994.

9. Minutes, 1968 Annual Meeting, part 1, 14–29. According to the delegate from Puerto Rico, Chuck Hitt, there were rumors of plans to deny Kelleher a second term: "Though Bob Kelleher was supposed to be a shoo-in, there was a group that asked to meet in a small room which I understood was to promote another candidate. Never heard anything more." Hitt email to author, August 27, 2012.
10. See Minutes, 1968 Annual Meeting, part 1. For the role of the delegates assembly, see chapter 5. According to Richard Evans, Kelleher's cohort consisted of Larry Krieger, Charlie Hare, and Henry Benisch, with Slew Hester as the unobtrusive campaign manager, though it is hard to imagine Hester as unobtrusive. Neil Amdur wrote that Kelleher became so pessimistic about getting approval for open tennis that he told Hester he thought of resigning; "The Man Who Slew Forest Hills," *World Tennis*, August 1977, 37–38. Kelleher later gave Walter Elcock (from Massachusetts) credit for persuading many in New England and the East that open tennis "was the way to go"; Bud Collins, "Walter Elcock, 81; Former USTA President," *Boston Globe*, October 11, 2003. Their most influential opponent was former president Martin Tressel with staunch support from Dick Sorlien; Evans, "An Astonishing USLTA Meeting," *World Tennis*, March 1968, 48–49; Minutes, 1968 Annual Meeting, part 1, 35–37. Alastair Martin's phrase is from Minutes, 1968 Annual Meeting, part 1, 37 and was spoken in response to Sorlien's speech in opposition. See *World Tennis*, April 1968, 4 for one typical misquote.
11. Minutes, 1968 Annual Meeting, part 2, 7–14. (Since the two parts are filed together researchers be aware that part 1 was transcribed in 108 pages; part 2 took 168 pages.)
12. "The Alastair Martin Show" box notes: Amdur, "Alastair B. Martin," 484–86. Kelleher interview with author, December 17, 2010; ExCom, February 6, 1970, 1–2. Martin was regularly praised by players and the media for what *World Tennis* called his "untold generosity to players, tournaments, and Junior development"; *World Tennis*, August 1969, 12. See also, Gowen, *Talk of Many Things*, 69–71.
13. Borotra was president of the French Tennis Federation, but Philippe Chartrier was already the *éminence grise* and would soon replace Borotra before embarking on a fourteen-year-long career as president of the ILTF; Evans, *Open Tennis*, 7–8, 34–36. Borotra was one of the "Four Musketeers" during France's only ride at the top of tennis. During the late 1920s and early 1930s they together won over forty

Slam titles in singles and doubles, and six straight Davis Cups starting in 1927.

14. Kelleher interview with author, December 17, 2010. Evans, *Open Tennis*, 24 claims that the breakfast at the Hilton was the birthplace of the "dreaded authorized player." Not so—a "designated" player category had been bruited about for some time and seems to have been a peculiarly French proposal; see chapter 5. The LTA statement and the Evans quote are from his *Open Tennis*, 25. The details of the breakfast story were not part of Martin's report to the annual meeting. Myrick's prediction is in Minutes, 1928 Annual Meeting, 16. The quote is mistakenly attributed to President Samuel Collom in USTA *Official Encyclopedia*, 62, 65.

    Kelleher later claimed that there were no ILTF minutes for the meeting about "open" tennis. When queried in 2013, the ITF stated that they could find no record of a meeting on April 1 but did have minutes from March 30 of an extensive meeting about "open" tennis, bound in a book and thus "very difficult to copy." (phone interview with Kelleher by author, February 10, 2011; author's email file). The March 30, 1968, date is verified in Lance Tingay, "The Peaceful Revolution," *World Tennis*, June 1968. Tingay stated that there was not a dissenting vote.

15. The late arrival story prompted one delegate at the USTA meeting (William Clothier II, generally known as "the Spy" since all knew he worked for the CIA) to inquire if any of the "Soviet bloc" countries had objections to the changes since the Soviet Union had long opposed open tennis. Kelleher responded that the only comment from any of the "so-called Communist countries" came from the Russian who arrived late. When told of the vote, the Russian commented that while his country still opposed open tennis, he agreed to the change; Minutes, 1968 Annual Meeting, part 2, 36–38. Kelleher interview with author, December 17, 2010.

16. Martin's report is in Minutes, 1968 Annual Meeting, part 2, 14–22. Eight years earlier, Ned Potter commented in "Passing Shots," *World Tennis*, February 1960, 13, that six members of a special ILTF committee looking at the "authorized player" idea, changed from opposition to support. Why they did so is "a mystery," wrote Potter, "perhaps due to the well-known reputation of the French for hospitality."

17. Sportswriter Bud Collins in "Edward Hickey, 88; Helped Found US Pro Tennis Tour," *Boston Globe*, February 14, 2004, credited Hickey with helping to "revive the professional tennis circuit in the mid-1960s" when it nearly went under, all done for fun so his thirteen-year-old daughter could again watch Rod Laver play after he had turned pro. "Aren't we lucky Julie fell for Rod Laver," Hickey later quipped. Hickey's plea is in Minutes, 1968 Annual Meeting, part 2, 60–67. The existing contract with the West Side Tennis Club for the nationals was likely moot since a U.S. Open was a different animal. But that was never argued since the U.S. Open went to Forest Hills.

18. Kelleher had earlier assured the head of the United States Professional Lawn Tennis Association that it had no intention of taking over the teaching organization, whatever the language in the administrative committee's recommendations that were considered just before the annual meeting; ExCom, February 2, 1968, 2.
19. The quotations in the box "The ILTF and Amateur Rules" are from Evans, *Open Tennis*, 22–25. A "perk" is defined in the Urban Dictionary as "a special privilege or a side benefit."
20. Minutes, 1968 Annual Meeting, part 2, 130–33. The threat of a player union (a professional guild) was behind Alastair Martin's battle with the "Independent Pros" in summer 1970 over the Grand Prix men's circuit; see World Tennis, August 1970, 20. The 1985 event—initially called the International Players Champions, later the "Miami Masters"—was a two-week event for both women and men, an attempt by the professional organizations to promote a major tournament rivaling the Slams, thereby gaining leverage for their demands that players in the Slams be paid a larger share of the proceeds. The USTA reacted vigorously to that and similar attempts to challenge the status of the U.S. Open. Prize money consistently rose, accompanied by publicity. Burnishing the image of the U.S. Open as the nation's most prestigious and exciting tennis tournament became a formal part of the Association's strategic mission.
21. The quotes and information about the discussion and decisions made at the 1968 Annual Meeting, Minutes, part 2, are found in pages 23–151. The changes to the bylaws and standing orders made to accommodate open tennis were made a year later with little discussion; Minutes, 1969 Annual Meeting, 58.
22. AdminCom, April 6, 1968. USTA officers had routinely expressed contempt for "cheaters" who ignored rules about extended stays after getting their way paid to one of the Slams, while promoters and clubs running the grass-court circuit in the summer put heavy pressure on the Association to force players to come home.
23. AdminCom, June 18, 1968; 3–5. The story can be followed in four articles: "Pros Barred from Davis Cup," *New York Times*, July 5, 1968; "Aussies Say Davis Cup Should Be Open to Pros," *New York Times*, August 22, 1968; "Boycott Threat in Tennis Lifted," *New York Times*, February 18, 1969; Dave Anderson, "Tennis Pros Accept Year Truce," *New York Times*, February 19,1969.
24. For the extensive and nit-picking discussions see ExCom, July 4, 1968, and February 9, 1969; AdminCom, June 18, 1968; Collins and Hollander, *Bud Collins' Tennis Encyclopedia*, 183–84; Kriplen, *Dwight Davis*, 193–95. Initially, the Davis family was unenthusiastic about the Cup competition being "open"; AdminCom, December 6, 1968, 4.
25. For a chastening summary of politicized Olympics, starting in Greece in 365 BC, see http://www.washingtonpost.com/blogs/the-fix/wp/2014/02/05/machiavelli-meet-the-olympics/. The FIFA statement is quoted in an Associated Press article, "FIFA Rejects Change of Venue," *Post and Courier* (Charleston SC), July 26,

2014. For a participant's perceptive personal comments, see Gowen, *Talk of Many Things*, 73–75.

26. Kelleher's proposal for Ashe to play Davis Cup in South Africa is from an interview with Ashe as quoted in Hauser, *Muhammad Ali*, 205. See also *Kentucky New Era*, July 17, 1969 on Google News http://news.google.com/newspapers?nid=266&dat=19690717&id=eOcraaaaibaj&sjid=v2cfaaaaibaj&pg=3360,1373608. The overall confrontation with South Africa's *apartheid* and sports, with a focus on Arthur Ashe, is extensively covered in Hall, *Arthur Ashe*, chapters 4–6. It is particularly useful for those who wish to follow the South African issue in detail. Hall does not mention Kelleher's scheme for the 1967 Davis Cup, and apparently did not have access to the USTA records.
27. I am indebted to Eric Morgan, not only for his excellent article, "Black and White at Center Court," but for other references he provided.
28. Statement (by George W. Gowen) on Behalf of the United States Lawn Tennis Association before the Subcommittee on African Affairs of the U.S. House of Representatives Committee on Foreign Affairs, February 4, 1970, Gowen files, USTA Archive. Even Ashe's doubles partner, Clark Graebner, said Ashe was only complicating the problems. The two South Africans were Cliff Drysdale and Ray Moore; Parton Keese, "Tennis Pros Hesitant," *New York Times*, February 22, 1970.
29. The "Statement by Robert Colwell, Representative of the USA to the Davis Cup Nations meeting on March 23, 1970, Gowen files, USTA Archive" offered a new regulation aimed at the avoiding being forced to boycott Davis Cup because of South Africa's policies. It called for establishing a special committee to evaluate whether or not to accept a "challenge," with the standard being if participation by that nation would endanger the competition itself. See also, Fred Tupper, "South Africa Barred," *New York Times*, March 24, 1970 and Dave Anderson, "Ashe Scores a Victory," *New York Times*, March 24, 1970. George Gowen, the USLTA general counsel, played a key role in pushing the boycott through both the Association and the ILTF; ExCom, February 1970, 69–73. It says a good deal that the South African boycott was not even mentioned at the 1970 Annual Meeting. For the flavor of tennis public's opinion and racism in America, see *World Tennis*, April 1970, 87–88 and August 1970, 12. The 1975 attempt to expel the South Africans is reported in *Tennis Week*, October 1975, 77–78. The "politics" of the vote were complicated by the Cold War, since the Soviet Union and its satellites routinely supported sanctions against South Africa. The minutes of the Management Committee during the 1970s are replete with Association proposals for disciplining nations that withdrew rather than play the South Africans; e.g. MgmtCom, January 10, 1975, 2.
30. Neil Amdur, "Deep South's Slew Hester," *New York Times*, March 20, 1977 and a series of articles in March 1978 about the Davis Cup; MgmtCom,

September 4–9, 1977 and MgmtCom, February 26–28, 1978. By this time, Davis Cup draws were divided into geographic zones. Because so many European and Asian teams refused to compete with South Africa, the ITF wedged South Africa into the Americas zone. That prompted the Association to support a new ITF regulation that required a two-thirds majority of members of a zone to agree to a new member; MgmtCom, February 26–28, 1978. Association leaders were obviously uneasy about playing South Africa in the United States and worked to ensure a site where civil authority would be supportive; ExCom, September 1977, 50–52.

31. For example, MgmtCom, May 26–27, 1977. Belatedly, the Association realized that South Africa had to change its policies if Davis Cup was to survive; MgmtCom, September 4–9, 1977. Bowers, *The International Tennis Federation*, 110–11 summarizes the South African issue up through the late 1970s. Slew Hester set out the USLTA "principle" in a letter to Jewell Handy Gresham, executive director, Coalition of Concerned Black Americans, May 6, 1977, Gowen files, USTA Archive.
32. Peter Alfano, "Tennis Dispute Is Unresolved," *New York Times*, January 27, 1988.
33. Lawn tennis was an Olympic sport from the start of the modern games in 1896 until 1924 when arguments over amateur rules prompted the ITF to drop out. It had just rejoined in 1988.
34. USTA (David Markin, president) to "Dear American Tennis Player," May 1989 and press release (n.d.), both in S. Box 4103 USTA Archive; *New York Times*, May 10, 1989. Ward's decision is discussed in chapter 5. The Gowen files in the USTA Archive contain a number of letters and statements condemning apartheid while criticizing boycotts that would restrict an individual's freedom to play anywhere. The ITF's refusal to sanction South African tournaments came in an announcement to ITF members, March 17, 1989 Gowen files, USTA Archive.
35. Board of Directors Minutes, October 1988 (hereafter BOD). The club's president, Eugene Scott, was less than receptive to the USTA letter, using the phrasing of the Association's oft-stated "principle" that individuals should decide for themselves where they would play. Scott ended his response by pointedly alluding to politics: "I sympathize with your difficult conflict and trust that you equally empathize with mine"; Scott to Gordon Jorgensen, October 25, 1988, Gowen files, USTA Archive.
36. ExCom, February 1969, 174–87. Gene Scott was particularly vocal. The "Lawn" was mowed down, so to speak, on March 28, 1975.
37. ExCom, February 1969, 166–69 (emphasis added; ellipses omitted for clarity).
38. Long Range Financial Planning Committee, Report and Recommendations, January 15, 1969 (hereafter LRP Report, 1969), "Background." The committee was composed of eight long-term national volunteers, including Richard Sorlien and two men who would become president of the Association, Joseph Carrico and Stanley Malless; ExCom, September 6, 1968, 2 (emphasis added). One section had the promising title "Social Responsibility of the USLTA." It spoke of "these

troubled social times," but that was merely a veiled jab at "big-time" tennis and assumed professional players would not support recreational tennis. The comment is from a past president's email to the author, July 18, 2013

39. LRP Report, 1969; Tom Norris, "Report from the Archives," November 29, 2005; ExCom, February 1969, 12–13. The inaugural (1968) U.S. Open grossed $432,289 with the Association's share coming to $91,000. One unverified estimate of attendance at that tournament was "probably" thirty thousand, which was more than the national singles championship for 1967. That, even though only a few of the big names touring professionals played in 1968 because of contract restrictions—restrictions that frightened USLTA leaders but which the players themselves soon refused to accept. Early in 1970, Alastair Martin headed off to Europe to negotiate with tour promoters about letting their players enter the U.S. Open; ExCom, February 1970. Martin also proposed a "self-determination" amendment to the ILTF rules accompanied by an effort to rally newspaper reporters to support that amendment and one allowing the tie-break system to be used. See USLTA press release of April 14, 1970, appendixes A and B (record # 4907, item 1386). In essence, U.S. restraint of trade legislation would provide the self-determination sought by the USLTA.
40. "National volunteers" refers to the ever-expanding coterie of volunteers leading and serving on the growing array of USLTA committees. Similar cohorts had developed at the sectional level as well. The role and the effect of "perks," particularly among national volunteers, has long been controversial. Perks, real or perceived, created resentment and jealousy, yet also motivated and rewarded. The only record found of a formal effort to deal with the distribution of perks came in the "Report to the President" of a Blue Ribbon Commission, December 20, 2002 (doc. #22, container 2469). That report is without details (presumably included as exhibits, but not attached to the report), but does twice express brief concern about the effect of perks on morale and trust. Without any definitions of just what constitutes perks or analysis of just how they challenge or benefit the Association, the report blandly suggests that "some volunteers may be unusually focused on perks because they have not been sufficiently challenged with meaningful committee assignments." No mention of how the lack of perks affected those who did not get them or did not get what they felt was their fair "share." A vast business and scientific literature exists about motivation, but there is no reference to such information in the report.
41. Richard Goldstein, "Alastair Martin, 94," *New York Times*, January 20, 2010.
42. Minutes, 1962 Annual Meeting, 47–48; *World Tennis*, February 1962, 56–57. The report has not been located in the USTA Archive. The ideas it contained may have percolated within the USLTA committee structure, but I found no further mention of it.
43. "Strengthening Organization Structure and Management Processes," McK-

insey and Company, 1969. Quotations are from a summary of the report made by McKinsey representatives before the executive committee; ExCom, September 1969, 2–49. Kelleher later wrote that Martin had provided "financial assistance" for retaining McKinsey and Company; Kelleher to author, letter of January 25, 2005.

44. McKinsey report, Excom, September 1969, 9–10.
45. McKinsey report, Excom, September 1969, 11.
46. McKinsey report, ExCom, September 1969, 14–15. *World Tennis*, February 1967, 13 is one example of calls for a tennis commissioner. Another is Bob Briner, "Can the USLTA Be Saved?," *World Tennis*, April 1974, 78–81. An amusing article in *World Tennis* on the Association's dilemma is an extensive interview with Donald Dell. Dell played Davis Cup and later captained the team, but his successes came as an agent for a number of the most famous professional tennis players. He commandeered the interview in which he promoted himself, slammed Robert Malaga, the Association's executive secretary, as an overpaid fund-raiser (not what Malaga did), and declared that the only hope for tennis was the World Tennis Championship tour, which, not so coincidentally, had his "best clients" under contact. In Dell's words, "in big-time spectator tennis, the USLTA is fast becoming passé." Of course the real challenge for Dell, and other promoters, was that the U.S. Open had quickly become the most powerful spectator attraction in U.S. tennis; *World Tennis*, March 1971.
47. An expansion of Thomas Norris, "Report to the USTA Board of Directors on the Executive Director Position," August 13, 2007, USTA Archive. Quotation marks omitted. A list of US(L)TA executive secretaries and directors (i.e., the senior/top staff person) is in appendix 5.
48. Letter-contract, Kelleher to Malaga, March 23, 1967; Anna Schmelzer to Robert Malaga, October 18, 1967, forwarding an excerpt of ExCom, September 1967 (executive session), concerning the retirement arrangement with Edwin Baker. The names of retired General Maxwell Taylor, Sargent Shriver (a government official in the Kennedy and Johnson administrations), Frank Pace (former secretary of the army), and one "General Terry," were all mentioned for the executive director position; AdminCom, March 1967, 2. Kelleher phone conversation with author, February 10, 2011; interview with Kelleher, Marmion interviews. Malaga had been an active volunteer and tennis promoter in Cleveland. Initially his USLTA title was executive secretary, but that soon changed to executive director. If Kelleher's recollections are any guide, he said Malaga was just a promoter who handled the press well and did logistical arrangements for various presidents. Asked if Malaga was given enough authority to be an executive secretary or director, Kelleher simply said, "No! I did it all myself." According to Kelleher, Malaga's job just "ended" in 1972–73, since he thought he was worth more than the Association was willing to pay. As a reference point, Malaga's annual salary as of 1969 was $32,000; ExCom (executive session), February 1969, 31–36.

49. 1969 LRP; ExCom, September 1969, 88–89; USLTA press release of April 14, 1970, appendix C, which was not released to the media (records 4907, item 1386).
50. ExCom, February 1970, 22–31.
51. *World Tennis*, January 1972, 83.
52. ExCom, September 1969, 52. For yellow tennis balls, see ExCom, February 1972, 214. The USLTA decision followed an ILTF rule change allowing colored balls. Historically, balls were either black or white in color, depending on the background color of the courts. Meanwhile Wimbledon continued to use the traditional white ball, not adopting yellow balls until 1986; http://www.itftennis.com/technical/balls/other/history.aspx. It would take the USLTA nearly a decade and competition from the ATP to get computerized rankings, and then only for the United States; Eugene Scott, "The 'Why' behind the Tennis Wars," *World Tennis*, 1976, 52–53. See Evans, *Open Tennis*, 113–16 for a defense of the mystique of the ATP computer ranking. There is little doubt that control of the rankings gave the ATP great leverage with professionals, an opportunity missed for both the ITF and the USTA. The women professionals were, of course, hardly relevant to the ATP. See also Bowers, *The International Tennis Federation*, 65.
53. ExCom, February 1969, 20–25. A good, brief summary of the professionalization of tennis umpiring is in Bowers, *The International Tennis Federation*, 90–95.
54. BOD, March 23, 1986, 2. Professionally trained officials helped improve behavior, but the most effective improvement came in 2006 with Hawk-Eye, a system of six or more computer-linked television cameras providing views that are read by computer and that together generate a representation of the ball's path. It had a remarkable calming influence on player behavior; http://www.topendsports.com/sport/tennis/hawkeye.htmtime. See also http://www.si.com/tennis/2013/08/26/tennis-innovations-hawk-eye. Hawkeye took a long time coming. "An automatic line calling machine" that showed promise was mentioned as early as November 1977; MgmtCom, November 11–12, 1977, 5.
55. ExCom, February 1969, 53–58; MgmtCom, October 21–22, 1985, 1–2. Those rewriting the Association's governing documents followed Martin's injunction about not messing with the nominating committee. As of 1971, amendments to the constitution (article 8) called for a vote of two-thirds of the "*total voting membership*" to change the composition or method of election of the nominating committee. Previously it took only a two-thirds vote "of all the votes cast," which could be significantly different since a quorum was only a simple majority of the total. That heightened requirement exists today (2015). The nominating process was and remains a very sensitive matter. See also, text box "Individual Membership," chapter 5.
56. McKinsey report, ExCom, September 1969, 29; Gowen email to author,

February 14, 2014; Statement by Gowen on incorporation, ExCom, September 1973, 130–34.

57. ExCom, February 1971, 2–23. The debate over "amateur" followed, pages 23–41. There was long discussion about changing the dues structure so that voting would be "on a dollar basis not a club basis," ExCom, February 1971, 60–69.

58. *1976 USTA Yearbook*, 468; Minutes, 1977 Annual Meeting, 35–36; Gowen's statement is in Minutes, 1977 Annual Meeting, 37–39. In the 1990s, commercial clubs controlled the Northern California (NORCAL) Section, causing some distress among USTA leaders and staff. Whatever the details, in retrospect it appears that the deeper cause of tension came from the USTA push for centralization. In 1994 the governance and planning committee expressed concern that at the section level and lower, "voting strength is in the club and member organizations. . . . We have over a half million individual members . . . that need possibly to have a say-so"; ExCom, September 9, 1994, 31–45. In 2014 the bylaws were amended to cap at 40 percent the voting strength of any single section, regardless of the number of USTA members. As of this writing (2016), "collaboration" between the national Association and the sections to ensure sectional constitutions and bylaws are "in accordance with" those of the USTA, remains an ongoing process. Apparently the sections are still "catching up."

59. ExCom, September 1970, 16–41 and ExCom, February 1971, 78–79. Turpin offered a twenty-year lease at nine thousand dollars a year, with the Association paying maintenance, insurance, and taxes—the intimation was the lease could be broken without penalty. He would build the building (ten thousand square feet). It would be near the airport being constructed (Dallas/Fort Worth International Airport), noting that nearby freeway "the LBJ Freeway, pardon the name—is the main artery into the new 'regional' airport." Turpin served on the Texas Tennis Association board, 1959–65.

60. Robert Colwell speaking to the executive committee; ExCom, February 1972, 12.

61. Neil Amdur, "Tennis Dispute Flares Anew over Structure for Opens, Boycott Likely at Forest Hills, Pro Consider Scheduling Major Tournament Here at Time of U.S. Open," *New York Times*, February 7, 1970.

62. Evans, *Open Tennis*, 81. For a succinct summary of the "brave new world" of pro tennis, albeit focused on the ITF, see Bowers, *The International Tennis Federation*, 62–69. See also Hall, *Arthur Ashe*, chapter 6.

63. The short-lived National Tennis League (NTL) in the late 1960s had a handful of top men and women players. They played for salaries, not prize money. The International Lawn Tennis Federation imposed suspensions, and the women were not allowed to play in the Wightman Cup in 1968 and 1969. The USLTA excluded Casals and King from their rankings for those years. The WCT men's tour bought the NTL in 1970, leaving the women adrift. http://en.wikipedia.org/wiki/National_Tennis_League; http://en.wikipedia.org/wiki/Women%27s_Tennis_Association#History.

64. It was a bit more complicated than that. As tennis historian Donn Gobbie explains: "[Stan] Malless' solution was to grant the sanction on the condition that the prize money in Houston could not be publicized—in other words, they could run an 'amateur' tournament, and the prize money could quietly be paid under the table as expenses." Kramer's tournament was the Pacific Southwest Open, played at the Los Angeles Tennis Club; Donn Gobbie email to author, July 14, 2014. For the observer's comments, see Gowen, *Talk of Many Things*, 72.
65. "CDC-Surgeon General's Reports-2001-Marketing Cigarettes to Women-Smoking & Tobacco Use" as quoted in Wikipedia, "Virginia Slims."
66. Quotes and details from Robson, "The Doyenne of the Dollar Bill." For the iconic photograph see gallery, images 19.

    Other details from U.S. District Court, Southern District of New York, 73 CIV. 162 (MP), opinion of U.S. District Judge Milton Pollack, February 7, 1973 (hereafter Pollack opinion); *World Tennis*, July 1979, 6.
67. The discussion over the 6 percent sanction fees for the Association took up twenty-three pages of the minutes! Whether or not USLTA leadership truly wanted a successful women's circuit outside its control, there is no question that the money really mattered; ExCom, February 1971, 12–16, 104–27. The Virginia Slims story can be followed in sarcastic and bitter detail in the pages of Heldman's magazine, *World Tennis*, from 1969 through 1972 (when she sold the magazine) and after. For unexplained reasons, a supposed 12 to 1 ratio at Kramer's tournament became the assumed wisdom. The actual ratio of total prize money between women and men was 7 to 1—$51,500 to $7500; Donn Gobbie email to author, July 14, 2014. Much of this discussion of women's professional tennis in the early 1970s comes from correspondence and conversations with Gobbie. He speculates that Heldman believed the 6 percent fee went to support the official Association magazine, then *Tennis USA*, which competed with her magazine. He also asserts that USTA president Robert Colwell wanted the Slims to succeed.
68. The reasons for Heldman's resignation were a major issue in the USLTA defense against her lawsuit. It clearly did not help her credibility to admit that her publicly stated reasons for resigning her USLTA post were "in some ways 'a white lie.'" Judge Pollack's dismissal of the complaint came in no uncertain terms, referring to "issues of credibility" on the part of the plaintiff. Moreover, the court found "substantial indication of violation of fiduciary duties of good faith and fair dealing" on Heldman's part; Pollack opinion, 13, 27–28, 33.
69. Notes for text box on "Five Sets on Clay": Quotes and details from Robson, "The Doyenne of the Dollar Bill." There is near-unanimous opinion that Heldman was extraordinarily difficult to deal with. Certainly that is how USLTA officials described her.
70. ExCom, September 1974, 4. The *New York Times* routinely reported on the

on-again–off-again negotiations in 1973 between Heldman and Elcock, during April and May 1973. Bud Collins called Evert "that delightful scab." Charles Friedman, "Elcock Inherits Hatful of Woe," *New York Times*, July 16, 1974, and "Elcock, Head, Healing Wounds in International Tennis." *New York Times*, November 6, 1974. Evert and the other women players did play some Slims tournaments in 1971–72; Gobbie email to author, July 19, 2014.

71. ExCom, September 1973, 3–39 contains a full report from USTA general counsel George Gowen and Roy L. Reardon (routinely misspelled in the minutes as Riordon) of the New York law firm of Simpson, Thatcher and Bartlett. (An interim report had been presented earlier; ExCom, February 9, 1973, 7–9.) They advised against continued litigation. The Association filed a countersuit, apparently as a ploy to pressure Heldman to negotiate. Judge Pollack's opinion stated that there were "close and complex" issues for a full trial, particularly regarding antitrust claims. The threat to ban Billie Jean King is in *World Tennis*, April 1973, 100 and is referred to in the Pollack opinion, 26, 27. The story is a bit complicated since King was reinstated as an "amateur" more than once. According to Donn Gobbie, "Alastair Martin said in an interview that the USLTA cannot keep reinstating a player who frequently becomes a contract pro"; Gobbie email to author, July 14, 2014. For what promises to be the definitive study of the women's professional tennis world in the early 1970s, see Gobbie, "Gladys Heldman and the Original Nine."

72. See above, chapters 3, 4, and 5. The World Team Tennis scheduling problem is in ExCom, February 8, 1974, 110–13.

73. See Chandler, *Television and National Sport*, 158–59 and Koster, *The Tennis Bubble*, 14–20, 75–76. Unlike golf, where the Professional Golfers' Tour appeared before competing tours established a series of businesses, professional tennis developed much more slowly. A side note, in the early 1990s, the Association's executive director, Marshall Happer, negotiated an agreement with the amateur U.S. Golf Association regarding the ownership and joint use of "US Open." The USTA used it first in 1968, but the USGA registered it first in the United States, while the USLTA registered it first in a number of countries; Happer email to author, June 2015.

74. *World Tennis*, March 1972, 72–82. The associations were the Middle States Section, and the districts of Philadelphia and Delaware. Their concern was the Philadelphia Pro Indoor Tennis Championship, a major tournament. The USLTA threat to move the Open out of Forest Hills is in ExCom, February 1972, 192–96. That problem dissipated when Bill Riordan filed an antitrust suit against the WCT and ILTF, both of which had in 1972 agreed to divide the men's calendar between the ITF Grand Prix and the WCT. As a result, the U.S. Open at Forest Hills in September 1972 was the major tournament actually open to all—since the various disciplinary suspensions and bans had been lifted. For instructive insights into the politics of international tennis in the early 1970s, Koster, *The Tennis Bubble*, particularly chapters 1–3, is indispensable. There is no straight-

forward month-by-month, year-by-year tale of this ban, account of that suspension, this pro tour, that pro circuit; but try the bits and pieces scattered throughout Collins and Hollander, *Bud Collins' Tennis Encyclopedia*, 177, particularly pages 204–10 in which he summarizes 1973—"the game's most peculiar year." All this confusion is likely to be explained definitively in a history (working title "Pioneers of Tennis") of the Men's Tennis Council (previously the Men's International Professional Tennis Council) being prepared by Marshall Happer.

75. Riordan claimed the Association planned to make him "player coordinator" but that he ended up as "the sacrifice in the Hunt-ILTF agreement"; Koster, *The Tennis Bubble*, 39.
76. Amdur, "The Man Who Slew Forest Hills," 37–38. Bud Collins earlier reported that Hester had voted against the arrangement, the only negative vote; *World Tennis*, July 1972, 36. The management committee minutes for 1972–74 have not been located in the USTA Archive making it difficult to verify the reportage; yet it has a ring of truth. Requests to ear witnesses have been unrewarding. For the IPA, see Connors, *The Outsider*, 79–82.
77. In 1973 a special meeting of the membership could be called by the management committee, or if sections with one-third of the total vote requested such a meeting. The record is unclear, but it appears that Riordan had widespread sectional support. Neil Amdur reported that there would be a special meeting of the membership on June 20 to discuss withdrawing from the ILTF (no mention of the Riordan controversy); "U.S. to Weigh Quitting International Tennis Unit," *New York Times*, June 3, 1973. Apparently, cooler heads prevailed and got the special meeting postponed until after that summer's ILTF meeting in Warsaw.
78. The full minutes of the "special meeting" are in ExCom, September 7, 1973, 139–74. Some have suggested that Slew Hester was the "decider," ensuring that Southern's vote (the largest section) would be against the Riordan motion. I have found no documentation verifying that assertion. The "voice" who reflected the opinion of most of the delegates at the special meeting, was that of J. Howard "Bumpy" Frazer; ExCom, September 7, 1973, 149.
79. In 1974, Connors was refused entry into the French and Italian Opens after he had signed a contract to play WTT (World Team Tennis). The ILTF was not directly involved. Connors and his manager-promoter, Bill Riordan, began a series of lawsuits against the French Federation, the ATP, Arthur Ashe (then president of the ATP), Jack Kramer, Donald Dell, and the Commercial Union Assurance (which sponsored the Grand Prix) and others. According to news reports, the claims totaled $10,000,000 (Connors wrote "$30 million), for restricting Connors's freedom to play professional tennis—"in restraint of trade." The complaint accused Dell and Kramer (though not the ATP, which had taken a neutral stance) of having "participated in a scheme to exclude plaintiff Connors and other WTT players from

competing in major European tennis championships and said defendants have been successful in that plaintiff Connors was prohibited from entering the Italian and French national championships during 1974." (The wording of the action is courtesy of Marshall Happer, who has a copy of the full complaint.) See also, Koster, *The Tennis Bubble*, 7–8. Shortly after the legal combatants met in the 1975 Wimbledon final (with Ashe winning), Connors dropped the suits; Connors, *The Outsider*, 114–17; http://www.atpworldtour.com/Tennis/Players/Co/J/Jimmy-Connors.aspx, which says what every other website says about the lawsuits; Evans, *Open Tennis*, 130, 137; Kramer, *The Game*, 283–85.

In the words of tennis writer (and player) Gene Scott, "stripped of nasty name-calling, the ATP properly backed down and agreed to restrict its activity to customary labor union functions"; *World Tennis*, January 1976, 50. That raises an ancillary question beyond the scope of this study. The ATP has carefully avoided the label of "labor union" but calling itself a professional guild does not change the fact that it engaged in collective bargaining. For a useful discussion see Gibson, "The Association of Tennis Professionals," which examines the legal and antitrust elements of the progression of the ATP from a quasi-union (player association) to an independent business corporation. It is a complicated legal matter but not complicated in terms of its real role. Eschewing careful legal language, the ATP bargained with promoters, including the USTA, on behalf of its members. If that's not a "labor union," then it's at least a reasonable facsimile thereof.

80. ExCom, September 1973, 3–39; Gowen email to author, March 1, 2014; *New York Times*, April 29, 1973; Bud Collins, "A Card-Carrying USLTA Member to our dear leaders—'We're thinking of you, fellows,'" *World Tennis*, February 1973, 62–66. Gobbie concludes that Heldman felt "betrayed" when the top women players compromised with the Association; Gobbie email to author, July 14, 2014.
81. Connors, *The Outsider*, 169.
82. 1975 Annual Meeting, 38–55. The quoted material is on pages 54–55.
83. New York District Director, IRS to USLTA, April 20, 1975; Gowen to Raymond P. Hernacki (IRS), April 23, 1975, both in USTA Archive; MgmtCom, miscellaneous correspondence, 1974.
84. *1976 USTA Yearbook*, 467; *2015 USTA Yearbook*, 85.
85. ExCom, September 5, 1975, 21. Hester's refusal to serve on the ITF management committee is from interviews with George Gowen and Marshall Happer by the author. Hester suffered from severe rheumatoid arthritis, which likely reinforced his unwillingness to travel to ITF meetings. In 1992 the ITF added a seat on its management committee for the western hemisphere region north of the Panama Canal. That seat increased the chances for the USTA to have two members but hardly answered the Association's concerns about inadequate representation; BOD, October 1992. Effective with the 2015 constitution, the ITF made very minor adjustments to the voting strength allocation but soundly rejected (by a two-thirds vote) a proposal from the Grand Slam nations that they have

increased voting strength. The Federation did limit the terms of the president to a total of twelve years. See Dave Haggerty and Jon Vegosen, Report (to the USTA) on the ILTF Annual General Meeting of September 16–18, 2014.

86. ExCom, September 1973, 139–235; ExCom, September 1974, 52–57. Even the current (2016) ITF constitution is a variation on the controversial FIFA voting structure of the one-country–one-vote system that ignores that "5,257 times more people play soccer in Germany than in Bhutan, but both Germany and Bhutan each get one vote." Francisco Torojune, "How to Clean Up FIFA," *New York Times*, June 2, 2015. The ITF formula purports to consider the membership of national federations but adjustments are, according to some observers, politically difficult. In addition, the ITF can award additional voting strength for certain actions that demonstrate an increase or have the potential to increase tennis play, for example, statistics showing greater participation in international play.

87. Note for box "The ILTF Wars": The federation timeline, excerpted from information in the 1988 ITF history, Cunnington, *75 Years of the International Tennis Federation*, was posted at http://www.itftennis.com/about/organisation/history.aspx. In 2013 a quite different and less combative ITF timeline was published; see Bowers, *The International Tennis Federation*, 6–7.

88. Gowen email to author of March 17, 2014; *New York Times*, July 20, 1973; Memorandum, Tom Norris to L. Hamilton, March 1, 2006, regarding (in part) "Equal Prize Money," USTA Archive. Neil Amdur, "Tennis Near Peace Pact for Women," *New York Times*, April 10,1973; "Women's Tennis Nearing a Truce," *New York Times*, April 28, 1973; "Women Players Agree to Peace Pact," *New York Times*, May 1, 1973; Parton Keese, "Tennis Decides All Women Are Created Equal, Too," *New York Times*, July 20, 1973.

Billie Jean King praised Elcock who was Association president at time; Bud Collins, "Walter Elcock, 81; Former USTA President," *Boston Globe*, October 11, 2003. Virginia Slims was listed as a sponsor in the USLTA *Official Championships Magazine* for the 1973 U.S. Open. http://www.huffingtonpost.com/2013/09/10/billie-jean-king-prize-money-wta-riggs_n_3898790.html. Collins, *The Bud Collins History of Tennis*, 10, 452, 454.

89. "The New Faces of Women's Tennis," *Wall Street Journal*, June 20, 2014. "You've come a long way," ("baby" was often tagged on) was the slogan for Virginia Slims cigarettes (Phillip Morris Company), in an advertising campaign that began in June 1968. The sponsorship for the Virginia Slims circuit rescued the women's professional game and became a national catch phrase; see Brian Horrigan, http://the1968exhibit.org/covering-1968/2011-07/youve-come-long-way-campaign-launched-july-22-1968.

90. Phillips quote from BBC Sport, February 22, 2007, http://news.bbc.co.uk/sport2/hi/tennis/6385295.stm.

91. Evans tells the story, *Open Tennis*, 77–79, as does Kramer, *The Game*, 104–

21. According to Evans, Elcock told Dennis Ralston that Heyman had phoned to reassure the USLTA there would be no boycott. Interestingly, Philippe Chartrier, then French Davis Cup captain but soon to become Federation president (1977–91), supported the boycott.

92. ExCom, September 1973, 5–6, 109–10; ExCom, February 8, 1974, 152–75; ExCom, September 1974, 5–7. Two-year terms for officers went into the bylaws in 1974 but actually started with the first odd-numbered year. When Elcock resigned, the first vice president, Stanley Malless, automatically took over. Malless was subsequently elected to a two-year term starting in 1975. The conflict-of-interest argument surfaced when a proposed bylaw included a prohibition against the USLTA president from being a member of the ILTF committee of management. It was not adopted, but Elcock nevertheless resigned. Elcock was not appointed by Malless to the Association's management committee. The *1975 Yearbook* did not list the Association's representative on the ILTF management committee (Elcock, who was ILTF president) as done previously. For Haggerty's election, see "American Will Lead I.T.F.," *New York Times*, September 26, 2015. On the evolution of the ITF president's position see Bowers, *The International Tennis Federation*, 26.

93. Collins and Hollander, *Bud Collins' Tennis Encyclopedia*, 204–5. Given Riggs's reputation as a hustler, little wonder that rumors abounded that he lost on purpose so as to pump up sales for a rematch.

94. MgmtCom, April 6, 1975; Minutes, 1975 Annual Meeting, 118–20. Botsch's statistics bring to mind the old saw that 78.7 percent of all statistics are made up. The game's inventor, Major Wingfield, referred to setting up a court "on a lawn, on ice, or in any suitable sized space either in or out of doors." "The ground need not even be turf," he wrote, "the only condition is, it must be level." See chapter 1. A federation history describes the decision to drop "lawn" from its name as "A sad moment in some people's minds." http://www.itftennis.com/about/organisation/history.aspx.

95. "USTA Individual Membership-1958–1992," USTA Archive, E&R files. See appendix 4 for the full document. The vast numbers for tennis players throughout the United States were "calculated" by the Tennis Industry Council, frequently based on tennis ball sales.

96. There is a small literature on the broad aspects of sports in America: see, for example, Guttman, *From Ritual to Record*. More specific to tennis is the perceptive and somewhat elitist study, Baltzell, *Sporting Gentlemen*. The tennis boom is addressed perceptively in "Tennis," American Decades. 2001. Retrieved December 13, 2011 from Encyclopedia.com: http://www.encyclopedia.com/doc/1g2-3468302912.html. I have borrowed liberally from this analysis. Wind, *Game, Set, and Match* is essentially a collection of his articles in the *New Yorker* magazine. For colorful players and mass appeal, see Neil Amdur, "U.S. Open Symbolic of Spectator Boom," *New York Times*, August 30, 1981. Jimmy Connors describes, in his brash, entertaining style, the marketing shenanigans that

he and his manager, Bill Riordan, concocted to stimulate public interest. The walk-up to the Laver-Connors exhibition in Las Vegas early in 1975 is a classic. With $100,000 as the winner's take (Connors won the 1974 U.S. Open and received only $22,500 as prize money), the match captured headlines and top TV ratings. Laver pocketed $60,000—so much for Riordan's patently false claim that it was a winner-take-all match; Connors, *The Outsider*, 137–42. No memoir by a top-ranked tennis player in the "boom" era better captures the excitement and colorful controversy that put tennis in the headlines than Conners's memoir (even if the index "accidentally" omits any entry for "U.S. Open, 1977" where he was at his most obnoxious). It is a delight to read. Writing of his most notorious temper tantrum, the 1984 Davis Cup match in Sweden, he almost manages to place the blame on the USTA and Davis Cup officials for making the mistake of asking him to play and for not defaulting him "immediately" before he went on to alienate the crowd, his teammates, and the USTA president; Connors, *The Outsider*, 285–87. The Connors quote is on 383–84.

97. For the earlier "boom" see chapter 3; *ALT*, February 15, 1910 (misdated in the printed header on page 353), 356.

98. The few studies of the "boom" came from management consultants with a vested interest in making the USTA happy or from firms selling tennis equipment—which the Association curiously viewed as disinterested. All made assumptions about the "boom" that were not validated by academic, scientific studies. Such studies, which might explain what happened, are missing. A summary of four years of the Plan for Growth dated October 2001 makes no reference to the "boom" years and contains no historical analysis; doc. # 1112, container 4685.

99. Dave Haggerty (USTA president) to USTA Family, email of June 27, 2014, subject: "Membership Innovation Study Group Update."

100. The only history of the remarkably successful USTA league program is a short "table-top" book, heavy on pictures but with some useful short essays about the early league organizers. Long and Rennert, *USA League Tennis: A Celebration of 25 Years*. That is, perhaps, because the bulk of the legwork, administration, and recruiting for the leagues was done at the local level with sectional support. The national office ran the national championships, developed astoundingly complex rules, hunted for sponsors, and held lots of meetings. The initial league pilot programs came in the late 1970s in four sections; Southern (Pat DeVoto as coordinator), Western (Genie Gengler and Sheila Collolpy), Mid-Atlantic (John Embree), and Middle States (Jackie Kimball). See also Barry Meadow, "The Leagues Are Coming," *World Tennis*, February 1980, 34–38. Individual members statistics are from "USTA Individual Membership 1958–1992," USTA Archive, E&R files. See appendix 4.

101. Gordon Jorgenson (treasurer) to the Management Committee, July 25,

1980, forwarding financial data and projections, 1975–1984, in Mgmt Committee Misc. Correspondence, 1974_12t, USTA MgmtCom CD.

102. Attendance at meetings before the 1980s is nearly impossible to determine since apparently there was no registration process until sometime well after the Second World War.

103. Gowen email to author, December 8, 2016; Schwartz email to author, February 3, 2017. See also "Annual Meeting Sites, 1881-2017," USTA Archive.

104. 2004 Yearbook, 161. The precise origins of the semi-annual meeting are lost in the fog of history. It was functioning by 1970 when Robert Garry began his long career with the USTA [e-mail, Garry to Kimball, February 10, 2017]. No mention of it has been found in the USTA records until the 1980s.

There are three (and only three) September executive committee meetings titled "executive committee and semi-annual meeting." All were held in the 1990s in New York City during the US Open.

105. Estimates by long-term USTA staff based on records in the office of the executive director indicate that from the 1980s to mid-1990s, the annual meeting had some 500-600 registrants. By 1999 that had risen to about 900. Not surprisingly, there were over 1,000 registrants for the 2006 annual meeting held at the Disney World resort in Florida. By the 1990s, the semi-annual meeting ran a tad larger, with about one thousand registrants.

106. See chapter 5.

107. Curiously, in 1982 another of the consultants reports that the Association seemed addicted to suggested that the USTA should choose between: (1) not supporting recreational players and focusing on tournament players or (2) committing to providing effective service to recreational players and to trying to bring that large group into the USTA. An uncomfortable, stark choice. The draft minutes stated that the recommendation was "on target," but someone (higher authority?) disagreed. Hence the big X drawn across that paragraph and the later instruction to delete it from the minutes. Perhaps the draft minutes inaccurately portrayed the committee's reaction to the recommendation. More likely the president or one of the officers objected, since the entire subject was not mentioned in the summary of the minutes. MgmtCom, September 5–12 1982 (draft), 3. The final version of the full minutes is not in the archival file.

108. Other E&R initiatives and interests include wheelchair tennis and promoting USTA cooperation with both Special Olympics and the National Junior Tennis League. Henry Talbert organized the writing of a short history of the E&R office where he worked. In the words of that report, "Perhaps the single major impact of Princeton was to broaden the thinking of the USTA . . . to actual tennis participation for everyone"; undated draft of "USTA Princeton Office: June 1973–January 1993." The draft will be deposited in the USTA Archive. Hopefully that draft will someday be completed. In an obvious expression of concern about E&R's autonomy, USTA treasurer Julius Hoyt recommended in 1981 that the management committee "should offer greater guidance and supervision to

its [E&R's] director Mrs. Kraft. Also, there is a feeling that a review of Mrs. Kraft's involvement in international junior tennis is in order"; MgmtCom, August 6–8, 1981. At the beginning of 1989, responsibility for E&R moved to the director of recreational tennis, while Kraft was kicked upstairs to an advisory position. A year later, the Princeton office closed and responsibilities were distributed to various USTA departments; BOD, February 1989; Tom Norris, "Archive Report," December 1, 2006, USTA Archive.

109. Kurt Kamperman email to author, November 8, 2014.

110. *ALT*, August 10, 1942, 10; Ward's annual report, 1943 *Official Guide*, 5; and *ALT*, 20 January 1943, 5; Decision of the Tax Appeals Board, 1943, "Tax Exemption File," USTA Archive. See also chapter 4.

111. For coverage of presidential participation see *ALT*, September 1942, 3; *ALT*, October 20, 1942, 9; *ALT*, August 5, 1943, 23; *ALT*, April 19, 1944, 12. For Truman and the Davis Cup draw see *ALT*, March 1947, 10, 20. If George Marshall counts as (almost) president, see him as secretary of state drawing Davis Cup pairings in *ALT*, March 1948, 8. Nixon's letter if from *USLTA News*, 263 (May 1959). Reagan's message is in MgmtCom, May 21–22, 1981. See also http://www.whitehousemuseum.org/grounds/tennis.htm. According to biographer Lon Hamby, when Truman was courting Bess, his future wife, he laid out a tennis court on the lawn of his farmhouse. Hamby drily commented, "It's unclear whether that actually lured her out there." For Carter's controlling of the court see Fallows, "The Passionless Presidency." For Obama's decision see http://www.whitehousemuseum.org/grounds/tennis.htm. Donald Trump's connections with tennis (before his presidency) are surveyed in http://www.ubitennis.net/blog/2016/11/09/is-the-election-of-donald-trump-an-unlikely-victory-for-tennis/.

112. *New York Times*, March 11, 1925; *New York Times*, March 20, 1926. Bowers, *The International Tennis Federation*, 32, states that it is difficult to understand why the IOC treated tennis "so shabbily" at the 1924 Olympics, "but politics were involved." Certainly the USLTA was publicly furious.

113. Gowen emails to author, April and October 2010.

114. For examples of Association rejections of Federation control, see chapters 3 and 4.

115. ExCom, September 1978.

116. Citation for "Davis Cup – Championship Patterns": Cunnington, *75 Years of the ITF*, 25.

117. The decisive ITF General Meeting was held in Gstaad, Switzerland, on July 8, 1981. According to the ITF, they cannot determine who cast the American vote. Both Malless and Carrico were on the ITF management committee and were renominated by the USTA; MgmtCom, January 15–16, 1981. The details of the USTA response and counterproposal are in "Gowen to the Management Committee," January 11, 1982, "Davis Cup Proprietary Rights," page 5, container 3314, USTA Archive. The 1984 trademark agreement is

attached to Gowen to Heller, January 8, 2001, "Davis Cup/ITF" container 3314, USTA Archive. That letter also contains Gowen's perceptive historical analysis on USTA/ITF relations, including this comment: "Any of us who worked with the United Nations and the International Olympic Committee know that the ITF shares with those organizations a degree of suspicion and a reluctance to accept things American." Gowen followed by calling for "patient negotiation," which had been successful in the past. See also MgmtCom, January 14–16, 1982, 8–9.

118. Gowen to Author, emails, April and October 2010; *Seattle Times*, April 7, 1991; Wirtschafter, "Fourth Quarter Choke." The description of the "acknowledgments" (not advertising) in the TV broadcast of the 1994 Mobil Cotton Bowl is hilarious. In the words of one corporate official, "The bowl is an extraordinarily efficient media buy. It would cost us a great deal more money to help influence sales by normal advertising," page 1481; the quote about Texans in Congress is on page 1494.

Walter Byers, the NCAA president at the time, later wrote: "We crafted the term student-athlete, and soon it was embedded . . . as a mandated substitute for such words as players and athletes." Editorial, *New York Times*, August 13, 2014; obituary, *New York Times*, May 27, 2015. See also, Byers, *Unsportsmanlike Conduct: Exploiting College Athletes*. Sports have been the beneficiary of other curiously favorable legal decisions. The most curious came in 1922 when the Supreme Court unanimously agreed (Oliver Wendell Holmes wrote the decision) that baseball was not "interstate commerce," even though teams crossed state lines to play. As one historian put it: "Preposterous as this ruling seems in retrospect, it appears to have accorded with contemporary public sentiment" Buhite, *The Continental League*, 75.

119. For those who are fascinated (morbidly or not) by the arcane language and tortured logic of the U.S. tax code and IRS rulings as they relate to various tax-exempt statuses, curl up with a few beers and read the twenty-nine pages of Memorandum to John Fogarty, Exec. Director, Robert Garry, Dir. of Finance and Admin., (Bill) Weimer, Controller, from Stanley S. Weithorn and Rochelle Korman (Baer Marks and Upham law firm), dated May 14, 1987, RE: *Analysis of the Structure, Activities and Operations of the United States Tennis Association and the National Tennis Center* (doc. #96, box 4685). Crucial reading for leadership and financial personnel since the Association's financial well-being is overwhelmingly dependent on its tax exempt status. As for me, I learned the meaning of UBTI.

120. The transgender controversy came when Renée Richards, who as Richard Raskin had played high-quality tennis, including being captain of the Yale tennis team and playing in two of the Slams, chose to have gender-reassignment (sex change) surgery in 1975. Her skills and love of tennis did not change. When the USTA, with the support of the ITF and the Women's Tennis Association, refused to let her enter women's draw of the 1976 U.S. Open, she sued the USTA, winning a decision that the refusal constituted unlawful discrimination. The Association lost its case with Richards's lawyer musing aloud during the court case that it

wasn't that she had the body of a male, the real question was "What bathroom is she to use?"; Gowen, *Talk of Many Things*, 76. The judge issued an injunction that forced the USTA and the ITF to allow her to play in the U.S. Open where she lost in the first round, though she got to the finals of the doubles. The affair was noisy, generating rude and crude comments, but Richards carried herself with dignity throughout. The media and the public soon lost interest while she went on to have a productive if brief professional career, retiring in 1981. Her "male body" wasn't enough to get her ranked any higher than twenty-second, but then she started her pro career at age forty-three. What sports leaders in tennis and the Olympics, women and men, had feared would change their sport did nothing of the sort. The USTA "male body" argument is presented in MgmtCom, March 25–26, 1977, 2. "Gender verification" continues to concern sports administrators, although the cases are infrequent. For a summary see http://en.wikipedia.org/wiki/Gender_verification_in_sports.

121. See chapter 4.
122. ExCom, February 1972, 192–98.
123. The various quotations and numbers are from Robert Lipsyte, "Backtalk; Last Rites for a Tennis Shrine: Good Riddance," *New York Times*, August 23, 1998, who also quotes Billie Jean King from the *New York Times*, March 17, 1977; Gowen, *Talk of Many Things*, 82–83. My (Warren Kimball's) personal experiences at various tournaments at the West Side Club were the same as those of the critics, particularly at the 1977 U.S. Open, the last held at Forest Hills.
124. "Heads of U.S.T.A., West Side Club, Volley Charges," *New York Times*, July 26, 1977; see chapter 5.
125. I have tried my best to compare Hester's harangue to the facts as I have dug them out of the archival record. He avoided specific dates, but his chronology seems spot-on. His oration is in ExCom, September 9, 1977, 55–111 (hereafter Hester-ExCom, September 9, 1977).
126. Kelleher to Hester, June 30, 1977; Gowen to Kelleher, July 5, 1977; both in George Gowen, comp., "USTA National Tennis Center: A Historical Perspective and Financial Analysis of Lease Terms" (hereafter Gowen, comp., "USTA National Tennis Center")(courtesy of George Gowen). By 1977 the executive committee had become advisory, limited to two meetings a year.
127. MgmtCom, February 9–11, 1977, 1–2. It is unclear from the minutes whether the meeting concerning the U.S. Open site was on February 9 or 10. Either way it was before the executive committee met; ExCom, February 11, 1977.
128. Hester-ExCom, September 9, 1977, 63. Kelleher did not attend the September 1977 executive committee meeting in New York City.
129. Elk Murray as secretary of the WSTC, Lindley Hoffman was president, Dick Miller was on the negotiating team.
130. "What the hell is that," Hester asked himself; Hester-ExCom, September

9, 1977, 69. "That" was a stadium located at the north end of a 1,200 acre public park (actually about 875 acres if roads are excluded). Robert Moses, New York's "master builder," developed it from a dump into the site for the 1939–40 World's Fair, and the 1964–65 World's Fair was also held there. He had brokered the deal for building Shea Stadium, which housed the New York Mets and Jets, and later provided parking for the U.S. Open; Broadcast Excerpt (WCBS TV), U.S. Tennis Open, September 10, 1978, in Gowen, comp., "USTA National Tennis Center." See also Tignor, "Ashes to Ashes." The time of that plane ride is difficult to determine. It would take a forensic audit to figure it out from Hester's rambling explanation to the ExCom in September 1977. My surmise is late December 1976, but see Ed Fabricus, "The USTA National Tennis Center Is Born," *1978 US Open Tournament Magazine*, and Lachman, *Mr. New York*, 85. During talks with the USTA, Parks Department and city officials routinely called the stadium the Singer Bowl despite its name change on July 4, 1973.

131. Rudin's biographer says that Hester called Rudin, but no matter, contact was made; Lachman, *Mr. New York*, 85. For a biting attack but informative look at the USTA and the stadium decision see Tignor, "Ashes to Ashes."

132. Specter, "A Stadium Is Born,"10.The observer was Randy Gregson, a friend of Hester's and later USTA president; Robert McG. Thomas Jr., "William (Slew) Hester, 80," *New York Times*, February 10, 1993 (Hester obituary).

133. Twenty years later the architect, Specter, wrote that Hester contacted him on Friday afternoon, not a Wednesday. George Gowen firmly agrees. Whether or not the architect and the USTA had just an evening and a day to prepare the site plan or six days is unimportant. Either way it was "how quick we were." Specter, "A Stadium Is Born," 10; Gowen email to author, March 18, 2016.

134. Bids are used to narrow down competition to those who offer plausible tentative plans. Negotiations on specifics came next. Gerald Eskenazi, "City Approval Expected," *New York Times*, April 7, 1977. Leasing park land required permission from the New York State legislature, but the city could grant a "permit" for up to fifteen years. Asking for bids to use the Armstrong Stadium was likely a routine for the Parks Department, unsuccessful up to that point. Player complaints about the noise from aircraft taking off from LaGuardia Airport finally prompted Association concern. Early in 1980, Hester, no longer president but still running the U.S. Open, told the management committee that once they had full information about the take-off patterns they would consult with the relevant authorities about alleviating the problem. But it took until 1990 and heavy pressure from then New York City mayor David Dinkins—a tennis fan—along with talk of the USTA moving elsewhere when its lease expired in 1994, for the authorities (FAA et al.) to agree to noise abatement measures for the full fourteen days of the tournament; MgmtCom, February 17–20, 1980; Robert McG. Thomas Jr., "Quiet Please," *New York Times*, August 17, 1990.

135. "Sports World Specials," *New York Times*, February 27, 1978. The same article reported planned seating of 14,974 regular seats, and 641 boxes seating another

3,976. The grandstand had another 6,000 seats. Four months after the first U.S. Open was held at the National Tennis Center, the estimate of initial construction costs "would not exceed $12,500,000"; MgmtCom, January 11–12, 1979. The only significant costs for the city were connected with infrastructure—mainly roads. The USTA gained exclusive use of the stadium and tennis center for one month a year, otherwise the National Tennis Center ran public-tennis programs and rented out the courts. A comparison prepared in 1978 of the net (cash) benefit/loss to New York City for its three major stadiums showed Yankee Stadium $7.3 million loss, Shea Stadium $2.15 million loss, Louis Armstrong (NTC) Stadium, $2.975 million benefit. The comparison and the various documents that constituted the agreement are in Gowen, comp., "USTA National Tennis Center."

136. Whenever architect David Specter bridled at cost-cutting measures, Hester would mutter, "Whatcha think you're doin', building the Taaj Mahaal?" always drawling the vowels. Specter later gave Hester bumper stickers that read: "USTA Taj Mahal"; Specter, "A Stadium Is Born," 12.

137. Unattributed quotations for this entire discussion of the NTC are from Hester-ExCom, September 9, 1977, 55–111. For the WSTC complaint, see "Sports World Specials," *New York Times*, July 26, 1977. The Eastern Tennis Association, which included the WSTC, forlornly requested the USTA to pay a "sanction fee" for the 1977 U.S. Open. The Association, as usual, rejected the request pointing out that the tournament was for the benefit of the entire USTA; MgmtCom, January 4, 1978.

138. Steinberger, "Queens Was Burning Too."

139. Specter, "A Stadium Is Born," 15. A sensitive and positive look at the change from Forest Hills to the NTC is Barry Lorge, "A Last Late-Summer Night's Dream at Forest Hills," *Tennis Week*, November 1977, 22–23.

140. Some additional color-commentary from Hester's speech (Hester-ExCom, September 9, 1977): "We have appeared before more damn people than you can imagine, nine boards, the only fear that any of them have is that the City would end up operating the property." "The other day, I was mad. I said I want the damn thing finished. Give me a fast track schedule and what does it cost." "This one guy who is going to blow up the seats [the old seats in Armstrong stadium], the demolition. There is another one who is going to do the cosmetic refurbishing . . . rebuild, get rid of the pigeons and the sea gulls." "There are certain things in here that fascinate me and there are certain things that scare hell out of me." "If it *is* built and ready . . . it would be some name like USTA National Tennis Center. If it is not ready, it will be known as the Hester Memorial. (Laughter)." "The press has been wonderful. If we want a story killed, we get it killed. If they want an answer, I give it to them."

There are other stories. Don Conway told of a struggle to prevent telephone lines to the NTC offices from being routinely cut just after installation (to keep the work going?). Conway also wanted to put furniture into those offices, but the union rep wouldn't give him the keys. He got a locksmith who worked for the Mets to put in all new locks. Next morning the union guy complained he couldn't get into those offices, whereupon Conway said give me the master key to all the other spaces in the NTC, I'll give you the master to those offices. No more phone lines were cut; Conway had access; Donald Conway telephone interview with author, September 5, 2014.

141. The Gowen quotes are from "Risks and Rewards," Gowen to Judy Levering, email of March 31, 2000, Gowen files, USTA Archive; and draft comments of November 1, 2012, Gowen email to author, December 30, 2013.

142. "Strengthening Organization Structure and Management Processes," Final Report by McKinsey and Company, October 1985 (USTA Archive) (hereafter 1985 McKinsey report), 3-11; emphasis as in the report. Rick O'Shea was fired in 1981; see below.

143. 1985 McKinsey report; *1986 Yearbook*, 535; *1985 Yearbook*, 592. Conway telephone interview with author, September 5, 2014. As of the *1973 Yearbook*, committees took up 10 pages (41–51), compared to 1.5 pages in 1920. By 2000, that had slid to 24 pages.

144. MgmtCom, October 21–22, 1985, 2–3. Conway interview with author. President Randy Gregson remarked that the McKinsey study was expensive: "The cost will be close to a quarter of a million dollars. We had a report from McKinsey in 1969. The cost then was $60,000, and it was not nearly as expensive as this report. . . . That report was paid for by the then president [Alastair Martin]. This one will not be paid by your current president. That is a lot of money"; ExCom, January 1986, 5. Whatever the precise cost of just the 1985 McKinsey report, it was "a lot of money."

145. O'Shea, then forty-two years old, had spent the preceding five years as executive director of the Young Presidents Organization (a professional organization for young executives); Lawrence van Gelder, "Calling the Shots," *New York Times*, June 22, 1980. MgmtCom, May 8–9, 1980; MgmtCom, December 11, 1980; MgmtCom, May 21–22, 1981. The legal actions dragged on unresolved before disappearing from the minutes after December 1981; MgmtCom, December 1–2, 1981. The misunderstanding between O'Shea and the management committee is odd, since shortly before he was hired, the management committee held a lengthy discussion that emphasized the importance of its role in guiding implementation of policies; MgmtCom, November 1–4, 1979.

146. Note for box "The Elusive Executive Director": See appendix 5. No formal changes in the executive director's title or responsibilities have been made in the constitution, bylaws, or standing orders since 1986, although the practical and contractual authority and management activities of the executive director have expanded steadily. Employment contracts cannot be examined since according to the USTA legal department such contracts with its executive directors have not been retained in the files once the employment ended. Fortunately a number of position descriptions survived in the archive and personal papers, making

it possible to assess changes. The added title of chief operating officer (1986) indicated the "operating role of the executive director," making evident the business-management structure recommended by the USTA's consultants; 1985 McKinsey Report, 3–10. Marshall Happer, who became executive director in 1989, was also interviewed in 1970 for the position.

147. MgmtCom, May 21–22, 1981; Conway email to author, August 11, 2014; MgmtCom, October 21–22, 1985, 2; Conway interview with author. The downgrading of the position was forecast in January 1981; MgmtCom, January 15–16, 1981, 1.

148. William M. Powers to the Executive Committee, January 3, 1986 (Rick Ferman files, box #3523).

149. ExCom (special meeting), January 1986, *passim*. Quotations on pages 6, 17 (emphasis added), 24, 46. Slew Hester's comment was classic Hester—"if it ain't busted, don't fix it. And I think that we have got an organization who claimed we were amateurs. We went from a $250,000 organization to a $35 million organization with amateurs. I think we have to take into consideration that the brains of this organization has been trained by 15, 20, 25 years of coming up through the sections, coming up through the various chairs at the management level"; ExCom (special meeting), January 1986, 55. The "buffer" role for the executive committee was again suggested in 1994 by the Governance and Planning Committee; ExCom, September 9, 1994, 31–45.

150. *1986 Yearbook*, 1 (emphasis added), 641; ExCom (special meeting), January 1986, 1–2; see also, MgmtCom, October 21–22, 1985, 2–3.

151. BOD, May 29, 1986, 1–2; anonymous source. Fogarty is mentioned in the December 1987 BOD minutes, but there are minutes for only one of the board meetings in 1988, and those (for October) contain a reference to the acting executive director (presumably Robert Garry). After board meetings, Fogarty wrote what he called "national updates," which were sent out to the sections and others in the USTA family. Unfortunately, those summaries have not been found in the USTA Archive. Fogarty's salary is estimated in Gene Scott, "Vantage Point," *Tennis Week*, October 27, 1987 http://www.10sballs.com/2014/05/23/tennis-needs-a-commissioner-by-gene-scott-the-man-with-a-crystal-ball/. It appears that the USTA made no public announcement of Fogarty's hiring or departure, or at least no announcement the *New York Times* found fit to print. A draft press release stated that his resignation came on June 6, 1988. The quotation is from an anonymous source.

152. ExCom, 1969, 60–68; Richard Sandomir, "ESPN Set to Take Over Full Coverage," *New York Times*, May 17, 2013; various USTA sources.

153. 1985 McKinsey report, 2–10. The initial Caulkins report on staff compensation was given to President Marvin Richmond in 1982. In September 1996, Ferman reported that was preparing a "thorough study of our Compensation and Performance Management Systems;" ExCom, September 1996, 2. That report, presumably, is the one in box 2469, USTA Archive.

154. 1985 McKinsey report.

7. WHO DECIDES?

1. Alexander and Associates, "Report: Recommended Program for Involvement of Minorities for the United States Tennis Association," July 1989, 50.
2. BOD, November 1989; BOD, January 1991. Markin himself promoted a "Chicago bid" with the help of Chicago billionaire magnates Jay Pritzker and Jerry Wexler. Likewise, Markin encouraged an Atlanta bid, all the while believing the right place for the U.S. Open was New York City; Schwartz email to author, March 9, 2015.
3. Runway 13 takeoffs had always gone straight out over Great Neck, Long Island, and did not affect the NTC until the takeoff pattern was changed at the request of the residents of Great Neck, sending the planes over Flushing Meadows. So returning to the original takeoff pattern for three weeks was actually safer. The final noise abatement compromise called for modest fines for each violation after a set minimum number (excluding safety issues, such as a conflict with airplanes backed up from nearby Kennedy Airport). Eventually, to avoid delays and limit costs, Arthur Ashe Stadium was built without the pilings needed to support a roof in the future. The U.S. Open lease is between New York City and the NTC, with the USTA's commercial use of the property limited to sixty days per year, a limitation that made it difficult to use the U.S. Open outdoor facilities during the most of the year; Happer email to author, January 22 and 23, 2015; Marmion Interviews, USTA Archive.
4. Anonymous source.
5. For example, see Jodie Adams/Sandy Coldsnow to MVTA Management, et al., May 29, 1991, Doc. # 481, Box 2472.
6. The fiscal analysis of the U.S. Open project is in container 2472, doc. # 481. This is an extensive collection of documents, some of which go beyond 1991. "Revenue excess" was a politically slippery phrase. Some might call it a WAG. Boiled down it meant running a tight budget, which might have had an effect on the distribution to the sections, as they feared. However, USTA leadership was careful not to let that happen, as the business plan and assumptions made clear. The final cost of the new stadium was some $266 million; BOD, March 8, 1997.
7. Catherine Madegold, "The Games Dinkins and Giuliani Play," in the *New York Times*, September 5, 1993. Dinkins was New York City's first and, to date, only African American mayor.
8. Tim Whitmire, Associated Press, August 31, 1997, http://www.apnewsarchive.com/1997/New-Ashe-stadium-s-first-matchup-City-Hall-vs-tennis-fans/id-15f2f50af1887b11a62e0e7171dc213c. "Tennis Center Scores Again," *New York Times,* January 25, 1994, Richard Sandomir, "City Gets Higher Profit on Tennis," *New York Times,* August 26, 1997, "Bonus Season for Baseball," *New York Times,* January 17, 2002; Gordon Smith email author, December 23, 2014, stated no fines have been paid. Arthur Ashe Stadium was completed in time for the 1997 U.S.

Open; the full renovation of the NTC (the Billie Jean King National Tennis Center since 2006) took until 1999.

9. BOD, May 5–6, 1995; BOD, January 5, 1997 (executive session); and BOD, February 16–17, 1997 (executive session). One USTA member wrote the president saying naming it the "USTA Stadium" was "one of the dumbest and most disconnected non-decisions I have ever witnessed"; Phil Davis to Harry Marmion, February, 17, 1997. Page Crossland, the Association's public-relations director, warned the fallout would be devastating. Gene Scott, a recent board member and editor of *Tennis Week*, consistently needled the USTA about the decision; container 2314, Levering/Marmion archives box.

10. To be fair, the Mitsubishi Forklift label is for a football club in the Netherlands, while Middlefart is a town in Denmark. Moreover, in Danish *fart* has to do with motion—no wordplay intended. Hunky Dorys Park in Drogheda, Ireland, is another contender.

11. The *New York Times* reported that "[President Randy] Gregson has been pushing for the U.S.T.A. to become a type of national federation, handpicking talented youngsters and overseeing their development, the way it is done in West Germany, Czechoslovakia, Sweden and France. He has waved the American flag in support of the Davis Cup effort now that it has become an event of international scope"; "Give McEnroe a Chance to Play," *New York Times*, September 11, 1986. The USTA goals statement is from a report of the Project 2000 project; BOD, August 21–22, 1997.

12. BOD, December 1987, 1–3. The board discussion focused exclusively on identifying and training "top players." In a report submitted two months earlier, a broadly based special committee set out a quite different single goal of attracting "more young people to tennis—and keeping them playing." After a quick genuflection to developing players who will have a chance "to win the U.S. Open," the report became a potpourri of all the popular causes—recreational tennis, minority "encouragement," public relations, junior team tennis, even short-court tennis. No one seemed to notice the disconnect between those programs and the tight board focus on the "top players." See "Taking Care of Tomorrow," Report of the USTA Special Committee on Player Development, September 10, 1987 (doc., #82, box 2473). See also, for example, BOD, May 1989, 5–6, about "regional training centers"—part of the attempt to identify talent. In March 1989, Nick Bollitieri, a successful coach for young professionals, became USTA adviser to player development, a clear indication of what the board intended; Executive Director's Report, September 1998, 16; Richard D. Ferman, "USA Tennis Player Development, 2001 Review: Key Findings," July 21, 2001 (doc. #80, box 2473).

13. Doug McCurdy speaking to the board; BOD, October 8–10, 1999, 7.

14. BOD, January 1997 and August 21–22, 1997. One USTA president from that era asked a crudely phrased but valid question: "Who wants to watch a US

Open final between two Lithuanians with names like [fill in with names that sound 'funny' to Americans]?" To be fair, the Project 2000 study recommended the program "be discontinued and a new program and committee be established to foster the advancement of players desiring to advance beyond the Junior Competitive area of tennis"; "Final Report, Project 2000," August 10, 1997 (doc. #91, container 2469). The board endorsed that recommendation. Yet the association's 2000 strategic plan had as a goal to "Help American players reach the highest levels of professional tennis." In July 2001, player development underwent another of its periodic housecleanings with the firing of two professionals who essentially were codirectors of the program; *Sun Sentinel* (Broward/Palm Beach FL), July 28, 2001. Even amidst the state-alignment crisis during the 1999 U.S. Open, the executive director could get applause by asking the executive committee, "How would you feel about two all-American finals this weekend?"; ExCom, September 10, 1999, 21. For a positive assessment of recent USTA efforts at player development, see Juliet Macur, "U.S. Tennis Association's New Executive Waits Patiently for American Boys to Fill a Void," *New York Times*, September 1, 2015.

15. The USTA Circuit was put together largely through the efforts of Marshall Happer; Murray Janoff, "How USTA Satellite Circuits Were Combined," *Tennis Week*, September 10, 1979, 28–29. The USTA Circuit eventually evolved into the ITF Futures and ITF/USTA Pro Circuit.
16. *USA Today*, May 14, 2014, and January 25, 2015; USTA sources.
17. BOD, August 27, 1989. Bob Garry was acting executive director.
18. All quotations in this and the preceding paragraph are from "Position Description, Executive Director," updated May 1993, attached to Happer to Les Snyder, May 1, 1995 (emphasis added.) Happer's initial job description was equally limiting for the COO, although the language seemed to give the board more joint authority with the CEO/president; and from "Draft Job Description for the Executive Director," David Markin (president) to the Board of Directors, October 21, 1988 (in possession of the author).
19. 1985 McKinsey report, 3–11. On the executive director being bypassed by board members and senior staff, see Happer to Robert Cookson (USTA past president), August 29, 1995 (in possession of the author).
20. Summary (by C. Morris) of the second Governance and Planning Committee report, ExCom, September 9, 1994, 40–41 (hereafter GAP summary report, ExCom, September 9, 1994). Snyder speech to ExCom, September 1996, 38. The two-year legacy lurch has not disappeared. A *New York Times* article about Katrina Adams becoming USTA president in January 2015 included the comment that "Two years may not be much time to create a legacy, but Adams may come to the position readier to 'reach back and pull someone else up' than her predecessors were." Harvey Araton, *New York Times*, January 16, 2015.
21. BOD, January 1995. Happer believed that the USTA staff had never been properly managed. None of his predecessors had the authority to create management pro-

cedures that would encourage more efficient and productive performance. Rather, the long-term staff focused on taking care of their volunteer "protectors" and each other. Supervision of the staff was made more difficult by having USTA staff in three locations—Manhattan, Princeton (New Jersey), and Jericho (Long Island). As byproduct of the search for a new NTC site in Westchester County, Happer identified an office site in Harrison, just outside White Plains, New York, where the USTA headquarters moved to in 1992. That move not only fit in with cost effectiveness (the Manhattan site had become inordinately expensive) but provided an opportunity to bring national staff under the eye of the ostensible "boss." Moving membership offices to White Plains bothered no one, but moving E&R—a grassroots operation—seemed to some a bit too controlling. The work done and personnel in that Princeton office were popular with the sections, although its director, Eve Kraft, had aggravated a good many board members with her outspoken candor. No one from the USTA showed up at the closing party in Princeton. Within a few years, E&R would disappear with its work either dropped or reassigned to other USTA departments, including Key Biscayne, Florida, where sports science, medicine, and player development ended up. So much for consolidation; Happer emails to author; anonymous sources; Happer to Cookson, August 29,1995 (in possession of the author).

22. Happer to Snyder, May 1, 1995; Happer emails to author, October 24, 2014.
23. Flink, "The White Plains Incident," 14; Williams, "Time to Reform the USTA," 12–13.
24. ExCom, September 1996, 39–41.
25. Addition to MgmtCom, May 21–22, 1981; BOD, January 16–17, 1986, 3. No report from the 1986 study turned up in the archive.
26. Strategic Planning Subcommittee on Recreational Tennis: Preliminary Report, March 1988, page 24 (doc. #69, box 3689); BOD, October 18–19, 1988, 2–3 (punctuation added for clarity). The chair of the committee, Merv Heller, would become a staunch, stubborn proponent of "state alignment" throughout the 1990s.
27. J. Howard Frazer (USTA president) to USTA Voting Delegates, November 16, 1993; Julia B. Wrege (Georgia Tennis Association president) to USTA board of directors, December 6, 1993; both in container 2262.
28. BOD, August 1992. The *1992 Yearbook* contains the first mention of the Sectional Presidents Committee in the bylaws, but only in a negative sense, i.e., the bylaws stated that the USTA president did *not* appoint the chair or members of the committee. No mention of the committee's purpose. It took time before it became a "standing committee" in the bylaws.
29. "Second Report of Recommendations of the Governance and Planning Committee (GAP, second report) to the Board of Directors," August 1994 (doc. # 19, container 2469) 17 (emphasis added); see also GAP summary report, ExCom, September 9, 1994, 31–45.

30. Minutes, 1994 Annual Meeting, 27–61; GAP summary report, ExCom, September 9, 1994, 31–45; anonymous source. The initial GAP report is not listed in the archival records. It obviously raised state alignment, but precisely what "state alignment" meant to the committee is unclear.
31. GAP summary report, ExCom, September 9, 1994, 31–45 and GAP, second report, August 1994. Intriguingly, but probably unnecessarily, in 2014, the USTA approved a bylaw change that capped any section's voting strength at 40 percent of the Association total.
32. BOD, February 16, 1995. The minutes of the 1995 annual meeting are missing, but call items had to go through the executive committee. GAP was succeeded by the Member Organization Relations Committee (MORC), charged with reviewing items tabled at the 1995 annual meeting, examining the roles of the sections vis-à-vis the national association, and reviewing the sectional distribution and the purchasing of memberships by sections; BOD, February 11–12, 1996. MORC's records have not been located in the USTA archive.
33. See chapter 4.
34. Notes for "The Owners" box: Mike Mee to the (USTA) Board—"an open letter of appeal," February 20, 2003, USTA Archive, container 4229. For the earlier references to the role of sections in governance, see chapter 3.
35. Google searches and the *New York Times* articles archive yielded no hits. Ferman's salary was not disclosed at the time of his hiring but was reported as over $600,000 annually at the time he resigned in early 2003; *Sports Business Journal,* January 13, 2003. The USTA legal department stated that such contracts were "not available."
36. BOD, May 1996; Richard Ferman, "A Vision of Tennis for the Next Decade," May 16, 1996. Ferman's vision statement owed much to the USTA mission statement—"To Promote and Develop the Growth of Tennis"—drafted in 1995 by Alan Schwartz at Snyder's first board meeting as president. For Louis Dailey's call for decentralization, see chapter 4.
37. Lewis "Skip" Hartman and Richard D. Ferman Jr., "A Proposal Submitted to the Governance and Planning Committee," attached to Ferman to Charles Morris, June 8, 1993. Les Snyder, then first vice president, was copied. The CTA (community tennis associations) concept was largely the brainchild of the E&R office; see "A Plan for Community Tennis Development," Education and Recreation Committee, January 11, 1991, (doc. #1092, container 2543).
38. See chapters 2 and 3.
39. See chapter 6.
40. Long Range Planning Committee, "Preliminary Report Concerning Sectional Realignment," March 1998; memorandum, Merv Heller to Rick Ferman, re: "Preliminary Report Concerning Sectional Realignment," "Chairman's Overview," March 17, 1998, page 5, (doc. #177, container 2468).
41. Memorandum from Randy Stephens (STA Board Chair/President) to Sectional

Presidents, USTA Board of Directors, et al., RE: USTA Business Plan and Transition Plan, August 27, 1999, container 2468.

42. McKinsey and Company, "Summary of Charrette Proceedings," January 8–10, 1999, box 3111. The memo from the president (Levering) is on pages 116–17. Impressions and recollections of the charrette were gathered personally and in a number of interviews.

43. This analysis is gleaned from all the documents, but the most convenient summary is in Stephens memo RE: USTA Business Plan and Transition Plan, August 27, 1999, container 2468.

44. "Initial Report," State Alignment Study Group, May 1, 1999 (Michael Ainslie, general chair; Barbara Smith, study group chair), Alan Schwartz files, USTA Archive, notebook of the National Board/Senior Leadership Issue Study Group, tab 5 (hereafter Schwartz notebook).

45. BOD, July 17, 1999. Memorandum from Levering and Heller to Exec. Committee, section presidents/exec. Directors (et al.), July 20, 1999, Schwartz notebook. With Levering's support, Merv Heller had bounced back from not being renominated to the board in 1995 to becoming first vice president in 1999.

46. "State Alignment Overview," (annotated) for Southern Management Meeting, August 13, 1999," attached to Memorandum, Barbara Smith to Rick Ferman, RE: Scripts for Southern Meeting, container 2468; McKinsey and Co., "Business Plan for Forming State Associations," March 5, 1999, (doc. # 102, container 2468); memo from USTA/Southern Section Board of Directors to Sectional Delegates & Sectional Presidents, August 15, 1999; Stephens memo RE: USTA Business Plan and Transition Plan, August 27, 1999, container 2468. Messages from other sections reporting non-support for the proposals are in container 2468.

47. Moter to Schwartz, May 17, 1999, Schwartz notebook, tab 14; "Third Draft," July 6, 1999, 1 (emphasis in original), Schwartz notebook, tab 15. In a "pragmatic" decision lest higher priority changes be put "at risk, the nominating committee should stay as is." No surprise. For Ferman's input see Ferman to Schwartz RE "optimum roles," July 24, 1999, Schwartz notebook, tab 15. Ferman had recognized the politics of governance and withdrew from the discussions lest his participation "cause some people to be uncomfortable." Ferman to Levering and Schwartz, April 26, 1999, Schwartz notebook, tab 14.

48. Levering to Schwartz, August 3, 1999, Schwartz notebook, attachment; Schwartz email, March 9, 2015. The letter is apparently Levering's draft and has annotations making changes to the original. The quotations were not deleted. The original date of July 3 seems an obvious error and was crossed out; USTA Study Group Recommendations: presentation order, September 6, 1999, (doc. #101, container 2468), Schwartz presentation. Ferman speaking to ExCom, September 10, 1999, 25.

49. "Stephens memo RE: USTA Business Plan and Transition Plan," August 27, 1999, container 2468. State Alignment Resolutions," n.d., container 2468. This matrix

is likely the one distributed to the board at its September 3 meeting—just before voting to pull back on state alignment. Only two sections had passed resolutions of support while eight had not responded. But the "nays" had it.

50. There were desultory discussions about the governance study group recommendations, but nothing seems to have come from them. Making the executive director the CEO/president was not on the agenda; BOD, October 9–10, 1999 and November 19–20, 1999. A number of the volunteer leaders likewise were "lightning rods" or so the subsequent nominating committee slates suggest. At least two USTA presidents (and likely more) spoke "privately" of becoming the executive director once they left office. That seemed the only way in which the executive director would become the chief executive officer.

51. For the text of the board resolution of July 17, 1999, see text box "Board Resolution of July 17, 1999."

52. The full text of the Board resolution passed September 3, 1999, read:

> Over the past year, the Board of Directors has sought positive ways to meet the challenges tennis is facing and has examined ways to improve the delivery of tennis programs and the effectiveness of our administrative functions. A course of action was considered and proposed. Many Sections have expressed disagreement with changing the Section governance structure. The Board has heard that concern. As a result, the Board has unanimously agreed to remove all consideration of changes to the Section governance structure and any requirement for a unified national staff. The Sections also expressed an interest in pursuing ways to improve USTA effectiveness. Again, the Board has listened. In response, the Board seeks to move forward in the following ways:
>
> —Investigate ways to create efficiencies and more consistent professional staff coverage through shared services.
>
> —Investigate and experiment on a voluntary basis by Sections of ways to improve the delivery of programs and services to the community level.
>
> —Encourage Section self-determination to align along state boundaries both internally and with adjacent Sections.
>
> —Provide reasonable, equitable and prudent support for the Sections' efforts to improve how they operate.
>
> —Investigate ways to increase play opportunities by reducing residency barriers.
>
> —Continue to create meaningful, impactful and rewarding roles for talented and committed volunteers.

Moving forward under volunteer leadership teams, the Board reaffirms its commitment to open and interactive communications.

53. The War of Resolutions was played out in the two BOD meetings of September 3, 1999 (one an executive session) and two meetings on September 8, 1999 (one an executive session). None of the minutes for those meetings provide any sense or flavor of the discussions.

54. USTA Study Group Recommendations: presentation order, September 6, 1999, (doc. #101, container 2468), Smith presentation, 2–3. (Heller's remarks and Levering's closing remarks are missing. Surely changes were made after September 6, but, unfortunately, neither the final script nor the minutes of that September 1999 semiannual (special) meeting were found in the files.)
55. *New York Times*, April 21, 2000. Michael Kohlhoff, who served on the board from 1997 to 2004, deserves major credit for reshaping Association thinking on assessing progress toward goals and for putting the initial strategic plan and KPIs in place. Between 2000 and 2003 the Association, guided by Alan Schwartz, upgraded its credit rating from B to A and refinanced loans for Arthur Ashe Stadium at a significantly lower interest rate, paying off the original loans and funding a new indoor facility that met the requirements of the lease with New York City. In March 2000, Arlen Kantarian became the USTA's chief executive of the U.S. Open and professional tennis. In his own words, "I saw a tremendous opportunity to take an incredible sport and market it and add a little fun to it." He turned "tennis into an 'Event,'" in the phrase of one reporter. Kantarian's efforts ensured that the golden goose would continue to lay even larger eggs, but that success came largely after the scope of this history; Dan Markowitz, "Turning Tennis Into an "Event,'" *New York Times*, September 9, 2001.
56. "Blue Ribbon Commission, Report to the President," December 20, 2002, (doc. #22, container/box 2469). As had become traditional, the nominating committee got off scot-free of any blame or responsibility for the mess. Yet that committee had hardly followed the classic description of a proper internal nominating committee: "The Nominating Committee members are elected to elective positions and are expected to perform their responsibilities in a neutral, wholly objective manner, without regard to personal preferences, favored policy positions, or preconceived agendas."
57. Huey received the ITHF Tennis Educational Merit Award in 1973.
58. The comments of George Gowen are, as ever, worth including: Gowen to Barbara Smith, December 17, 1998 (commenting on compliance with the Sports Act): "Two years ago cries of lament were heard because one professional athlete [Pam Shriver, elected in her own right] was joining the Board. Today there are more cheers than tears over that election. Two more should not be considered the end of the world. Hopefully the integration of Sports Act requirements with traditional USTA governance may not be as earth shaking as feared." Gowen to William Simon, April 19, 1999: "USTA Board members bristled with varying degrees [of] intensity by what they perceived to be the USOC dictating to them USTA governance structure and how the USTA officers and board members were to be nominated and elected." Both from the Gowen papers.
59. Notes for "Putting Players Back on the USTA Board": *1968* and *2000 Yearbooks; ALT*, April 20, 1941, 18.

RESEARCH GUIDE

The two indispensable sources for this study were the minutes of various Association meetings and committees, and, for the first seventy-five years of the Association, the magazine *American Lawn Tennis* (ALT).

Edited by Stephen Wallis Merrihew, *American Lawn Tennis* provided uniquely candid and critical assessments of Association meetings and discussions. The journal lost its status as the official organ of the Association after 1923, following a dust-up between Merrihew and the USLTA leadership, but continued publication for some twenty-five years under his editorship. Merrihew, who died in 1947, was an accomplished player, chairman of the Tennis Committee at the Plainfield Country Club in New Jersey, and author of a number of instructional books on lawn tennis. Bound volumes of *ALT* are available in the USTA Archive. Citations are to the date and page numbers rather than volume number, since consecutive pagination was not used for each volume. Beginning in April 1944 (volume 38), *ALT* publication data used only the year and month, not the date. Late in 1951, *ALT* was folded into a four racket sports magazine, *The Racquet*. It was purchased by and incorporated into Gladys Heldman's new magazine, *World Tennis*, in October 1953. For more on Merrihew see text box, "He Carried a Torch for Tennis," chapter 2.

The "official" Association magazine and/or newsletter changed frequently, especially in the early years. By 1900 it had shifted at least ten times, and continued to do so for decades after: *The American Cricketeer, Archery and Tennis News*, *The Cyclist and Athlete*, *The Official Lawn Tennis Bulletin*, *Lawn Tennis Guide*, *Lawn Tennis Rules*, *Outing Weekly Tennis Record*, *Golf and Lawn Tennis*, *American Lawn Tennis*, *U.S.L.T.A. Service Bulletin*, *The Official USLTA News* (which picked up the sequential numbering of the *Service Bulletin*), and—most delightful of all—*Sport, Music and Drama* (which could well be the name of today's U.S. Open program). Various short-lived "official" newsletters came and went until *World Tennis* became the official magazine in 1979. It had that status until 1989, and apparently ceased print publication in 1991. *Tennis USTA* became the official magazine in 1990, changed its name to *USTA Magazine* in 1999, and ceased publication at the end of in 2011. Since then there has not been an official USTA print magazine.

Invaluable as *ALT* was, the key source for this study were the minutes of the executive committee and its successors—the advisory and finance committee, the administrative committee, the management committee, and the board of directors. Association minutes for its annual meeting proved very useful, particularly when used in conjunction with executive committee minutes. The advisory and finance committee, set up in the 1950s, was authorized to act for the executive committee, which after the Second World War had moved to meetings only twice a year (ostensibly a cost-cutting move, since bringing delegates in from all the sections was expensive). No minutes for that advisory committee have been found. It seems to have become the administrative committee that slowly absorbed some of the policy-making responsibilities of the executive committee. No minutes for that committee have been found in the USTA Archive for before 1960. Fortunately, those committees (formally subordinate to the executive committee) reported major actions to the executive committee, although the discussion-deliberation thread is lost.

Once incorporation took place in 1973, a management committee (which became a board of directors in 1986) replaced the executive committee as (which continued, largely as a vestigial remain of bygone days). The official minutes of the management committee and board of directors became routinely minimalist, as the same financial success for the US Open tournament that generated incorporation gave the Association "deep pockets" and the concomitant fear of financial liabilities. "Risk assessment" was the lawyers' caution. Board minutes became more and more circumspect and cautious; separate and secret "executive session" minutes became common (some were accessible, others were closed by the legal department for no apparent reason). By the twenty-first century, the public minutes were so anodyne as to be little more than public-relations statements. The argumentation and maneuvering of earlier days, often presented in verbatim minutes, disappeared. Major reports (usually not retained) can provide valuable insights, but until creation of the executive director's office-secretariat in the 1990s, the historian has to rely heavily on interviews, newspapers, and other media, which are as much gossip and speculation as they are news. With the exceptions described above and some unexplained gaps (see below), all those various minutes are available on CDs at the USTA Archive.

Fortunately, the minutes for the first century of the Association's life are relatively full and complete. A retrospective collection of USNLTA annual-meeting and executive-committee minutes from 1881 through

1885 was printed in the *Official Lawn Tennis Bulletin* in 1896 and 1897. The originals appear to have been lost or destroyed. For decades thereafter, minutes were routinely printed in the various USNLTA official organs, although there are gaps. The minutes for 1881 to 1885 were published in the *Official Lawn Tennis Bulletin*; 1886–87 were published in the *American Cricketeer*; 1888 was published in the *Official Lawn Tennis Bulletin*; 1889–91 and 1893 were published in *American Cricketeer*; 1895–99 and 1901–3 were published in the *Official Lawn Tennis Bulletin*. Minutes for 1900 have not been found in the USTA Archive nor in any official Association publication. The minutes for 1892 and 1894 also appear to be missing. Where those magazines contain minutes and/or summaries of early Association annual meetings, they are available in the USTA Archive on CDs. Some executive committee (ExCom) minutes are also on those annual meeting CDs. Early ExCom minutes sometimes included substantive discussions but often merely recorded votes and decisions. The retrospective records were, for the most part, received by the USTA Archive as photocopies of pages in the original publication. Therefore, a photocopy of the retrospective minutes (e.g., 1885, printed in an 1896 issue of the *Official Lawn Tennis Bulletin*) may contain letters or articles written in 1896. Many of these early records were found and copied through the courtesy of the late Frank Phelps. Occasionally, photocopies of publications contain multiple years of minutes and articles on the same pages, making precise citations difficult. The photocopies I and my research assistant, Lorna Skaaren, found in our research will be deposited in the USTA Archive.

Full citations to that retrospective collection would create a nightmare of differing years and missing specific dates. Fortunately, the USTA archivists (Tom Norris, Brent Stauffer) sorted this out and included that material in the above-mentioned CDs. It is an excellent and extensive collection, although specific citations to the original publication are occasionally obscure, and a few pages and some meeting records are missing. My citations are to USNLTA minutes (and the CD) with the year of the meeting, not the year or name of the retrospective publication. Besides printing both current and retrospective official Association records, those magazines frequently carried articles about tennis and summaries of USTA annual meetings. Citations to then current minutes or to then current articles include whatever publication data is available. Lest the reader get confused, know that the Association's founding meeting in 1881 (the Association did not exist until *after* that meeting) was followed in 1882 by the first annual meeting, and so on. Thus the final digit of the meeting number is always one less than the final digit of the year, i.e., the fiftieth annual meeting was held in "xxx1" (1931, in this case), the seventy-fifth came in "xxx6" (1956), and so on. Fortunately, the Association soon stopped making such references to annual meetings, using the year date instead.

Adding to that date confusion is that the annual meeting was held early (or too late, if you prefer)—between February and April. Thus information about one year is published in the yearbook of the following year. For example, to find reports about 1955 one must look in the 1956 yearbook, for 1956 in the 1957 yearbook, and so on for each year. This, plus occasional brain cramps, may have prompted a few citations that are off by a year.

There are some gaps. For the early era, minutes for 1900 have not been found in the USTA Archive or any official Association publication. The minutes for 1892 and 1894 also appear to be missing. The largest apparent gap is the lack of official annual meeting minutes 1904 through 1913. That may be because, as the former USTA head archivist, Tom Norris, suggested, the Association's secretary saw no need to keep the minutes once they were summarized and excerpted in *American Lawn Tennis*, a policy that began in 1907 and included some executive committee minutes. In a few cases, the actual minutes are printed in *ALT* (e.g., 1910). Curiously, there is a citation to the USNLTA annual meeting minutes for 1913 in Joanna Davenport, "Professionalism in Sports: The History and Interpretation of Amateurism in the United States Lawn Tennis Association" (PhD dissertation, Ohio State University, 1966), 70. Davenport could have been quoting from the ostensibly verbatim report of Slocum's remarks, printed in *ALT* 6, no. 14 (February 13, 1913): 420; but there are a few quite insubstantial differences in phrasing that could mean that Davenport used the actual minutes. That hers is the solitary citation (that I have found) to any of the 1904–1913 minutes suggests otherwise. (As an aside, in 1975, Davenport, who died in 2004, alleged that the USTA *Official Encyclopedia* printed, without her permission, verbatim portions of her work—presumably her unpublished 1966 doctoral dissertation, "Professionalism in Sports." Later editions carried a fulsome acknowledgment of Davenport's cooperation, which presumably settled the matter. See the correspondence of George Gowen to John Taylor Williams, Esq., and to Robert Scharff, both dated April 24, 1975. The responses are not in the file.)

By 1920s to the later delight of historians (at least this one), the minutes of the Association's executive committee and its annual meeting were verbatim, apparently recorded by professionals. But that was, of course, before incorporation and the arrival of the lawyers. There are no annual meeting or ExCom minutes for 1929 or 1932. No one has offered any explanation. That both types of minutes are missing for both years suggests misfiling, but not in the conspiratorial sense as with the monk-librarian in Umberto Eco's *The Name of the Rose*. The administrative-committee minutes end in mid 1969. The management committee began in 1970 or 1971, but there are no minutes in the archive until 1974. For 1988 only the October minutes of the board of directors are available. ExCom minutes for 1991 and 1993, and annual meeting minutes for 1989, 1995, and 1999 are missing from the records available to me.

Also routinely missing are the many reports submitted to the annual meeting and to the ExCom and other governing committees (management, board, etc.) Unfortunately, that includes reports from the treasurer and the secretary, even though the minutes often indicate "(Here insert Treasurer's or Secretary's report)." See, for example, 1915 Annual Meeting, p. 3. Thus key evidence regarding Association finances and membership is missing.

Neither the original nor any copies—printed, published, or archival—of the initial USNLTA constitution and bylaws (1881) have been found. See appendix 1 for a "reconstructed" version of the first constitution and bylaws. Since 1884 the USTA Archive has published copies of those documents for most years, usually taken from that year's "official" USNLTA yearbook, magazine, or newsletter. Again, many of the early versions were found courtesy of Frank Phelps, though precisely where he found them is unclear. The entire collection is cited as Constitution or Bylaws plus the year(s), without citing the specific publication, and is available from the USTA Archive on a series of CDs. The contents of each year's "Guide" or "Laws" or "Yearbook" and the publisher varies, sometimes from year to year. To minimize clutter, they are cited as *USTA Yearbook* (year). Those who wish to identify or look at the actual publication should contact the USTA Archive.

The "Annals of the U.S.L.T.A.," an appendix to the USLTA's Golden Jubilee book, *Fifty Years of Lawn Tennis*, may have been the last publication to have access to some of the missing early minutes of the USNLTA, but that is uncertain. Most of the information could have been gleaned from such sources as *ALT*, which reported extensively on the Association's annual meetings. There is no archival record related to the compiling and editing of *Fifty Years of Lawn Tennis*, nor any introductory information about the sources in the "Annals" appendix.

Unhappily, in 1951 the executive committee considered a proposal to clean out the files by destroying all bills and vouchers that were seven years old or older. That raised the question of keeping other records, particularly correspondence. All agreed that the key to determining whether to keep or destroy a record was the "subject matter," which was a judgment call. They decided to "serve notice" of the intent to "get rid of some of that old material" and to leave it up to executive-committee members and anyone who cared to contact the Association if there were records they wished to save. President Lawrence Baker unceremoniously dumped it all in the lap of Vice President Russell Kingman. Attendance at the meeting was unusually large: voting members of the executive committee, some of the committee chairmen and the principle officers of some of the sectional associations, some members who were particularly active on important association committees. Nonetheless, there is no sign of any save-the-record requests. Good-bye historical record, or at least much of it! [ExCom, January 1951, 6–8, 2.]

There are no specific files for the early professional staff leaders (executive secretary, etc.). Even with the appearance of an executive director in the 1970s, there seems not to have been a formal secretariat-style executive-director's office (with staff to keep records) until after 1995—at least no such records have been located. Fortunately, the general files of the executive directors after 1989 are voluminous. Queried about a formal executive director's office or secretariat, Marshall Happer responded:

> When I got to the USTA there was no central filing system and indeed no filing system at all. Each employee just maintained their own files. Naturally, I made files for my work and I guess that when I left, Dario [Otero] just boxed them up and labeled them Happer Files. I actually hired a professional company to devise a central filing system at a hefty fee, but did not have time to get it implemented before I left. This was before the invention of a computerized document system and its implementation by the USTA later. (Happer to Kimball e-mail, April 29, 2016)

Unfortunately, those records could not be archivally processed fully in time for the research required for this project, making it difficult to conduct a full search. Nevertheless, Lorna Skaaren and Brent Staples somehow managed to dig out invaluable material from the 1990s, material that made it possible to trace events despite the lack of detail in board minutes. The only restrictions on my access was to personnel records (including salaries) and to a file containing some executive (closed to the public) sessions of the board of directors held during the late 1990s. However, a number of those executive-session minutes were available in files I did access—all the information was innocuous.

Between 2005 and 2007, the Association adopted a well-articulated records-management and collection policy (as described in the preface). Just in time, as space considerations brought the temptation to discard much, if not all, of everything but the most recent records.

That said, archivists, records managers, and particularly lawyers complain that by the end of the twentieth century, the volume of records routinely generated had become overwhelming. Creation of records by electronic means (computers, word processing, photocopying, etc.) threatens to bury us all. Recent updates to the Association's initial records policy have developed it into one that could serve as a model for other organizations. The practicality and effectiveness of the Association's policy regarding electronic records remains to be tested, but, as of this writing (May 2016), it appears to be way ahead of that of the U.S. government.

Club and sectional histories are understandably self-absorbed. Even for clubs whose histories were closely intertwined with that of the national Association (including the West Side Tennis Club in Forest Hills), they rarely offer any substantive comments or details about that relationship. Thanks to Jean Frangos, the WSTC was kind enough to provide a few useful documents, but none of the sections indicated that they had a significant collection of historical files.

Please note that unambiguous typographical errors in the various association minutes are silently corrected.

BIBLIOGRAPHY

MANUSCRIPTS, ARCHIVES, AND OTHER UNPUBLISHED SOURCES

Clark, Joseph S. "Life History of Joseph S. Clark, Sr.," 65 page typescript, undated (1953 or 1954). USTA Archive.

Gowen, George, compiler. "USTA National Tennis Center: A Historical Perspective and Financial Analysis of Lease Terms," containing copies of key documents and press reports related to the construction and history of the National Tennis Center (courtesy of George Gowen).

International Tennis Hall of Fame Archive (Newport, RI).

Phelps, Frank. "A Tennis Myth: The Outerbridge Tradition." Unpublished manuscript (courtesy of the author).

Selley, D. Colin, letter to author, dated November 8, 2006 and January 12, 2007.

Stahl, Joseph B. "Survival of the Oldest: Fate of the Hemisphere's First; The New Orleans Lawn Tennis Club" (2005). USTA Archive.

Talbert, Henry, Beth Brainard, et al. USTA Princeton Office: June 1973 to January 1993 (undated). (Copy with notation "Supercedes all others/ Big change to Pgs 6–7.")

U.S. District Court, Southern District of New York, 73 CIV. 162 (MP), opinion of U.S. District Judge Milton Pollack, February 7, 1973 (Pollack opinion).

USTA *Yearbook* and "annuals" (e.g., "Official Lawn Tennis Rules," 1884–present (on CD).

U.S. Tennis Association Archive (White Plains NY). See "Note on Citations" in preface.

Winthrop Group Report, Information and Archival Services (Deborah Shea), "*USTA Record Retention and Archives.*" August 2003.

PUBLISHED WORKS

Aberdare, Lord (Morys G. L. Bruce). *The Story of Tennis.* London: Stanley Paul, 1959.

Alexander, George E. *Lawn Tennis: Its Founders & Its Early Days.* Lynn MA: H.O. Zimman, 1974.

———. *Wingfield: Edwardian Gentleman.* Portsmouth NH: Peter Randall Publisher, 1986.

Amdur, Neil. "Alastair B. Martin." In *The Fireside Book of Tennis*, edited by Allison Danzig and Peter Schwed, 484-86. New York: Simon and Schuster, 1972.

———. "The Man Who Slew Forest Hills." *World Tennis*, August 1977, 37–38.

"An Interesting Letter." *Official Lawn Tennis Bulletin* 3, no. 3 (March 5, 1896): 42–43.

Ashe, Arthur R., Jr. *A Hard Road to Glory*. 3 vols. New York: Amistad Press, 1993.

Baltzell, E. Digby. *Sporting Gentlemen: Men's Tennis from the Age of Honor to the Cult of the Superstar*. New York: Free Press, 1995.

Berry, Eliot. *Top Spin*. New York: Henry Holt, 1996.

Bowers, Chris. *The International Tennis Federation: A Century of Contribution to Tennis*. New York.: Rissoli International Publications, 2013.

Buhite, Russell D. *The Continental League*. Lincoln: University of Nebraska Press, 2014.

Byers, Walter. *Unsportsmanlike Conduct: Exploiting College Athletes*. Ann Arbor: University of Michigan Press, 1997.

Caldwell, Dale G., and Nancy Gill McShea. *Tennis in New York: The History of the Most Influential Sport in the Most Influential City in the World*. N.p.: Intelligent Influence Publishing Group, 2011.

Carr, Bob. "Long Missing Wingfield Patent Recovered," *Wingfield Family Society Newsletter* 13, no. 2 (Spring, 1999).

Carvalho, John. "The Banning of Bill Tilden: Amateur Tennis and Professional Journalism in Jazz-Age America." *Journalism and Mass Communication Quarterly* 84, no. 1 (Spring 2007).

Chandler, Joan M. *Television and National Sport: The United States and Britain*. Urbana: University of Illinois Press, 1988.

Chicago Commission on Race Relations. *The Negro in Chicago: A Study of Race Relations and a Race Riot*. Chicago: University of Illinois Press, 1922.

Clark, Joseph. "The United States National Lawn Tennis Association." *Official Lawn Tennis Rules* (1889).

Clay, Charles E. "The Staten Island Cricket and Baseball Club." *Outing* 11, no. 2 (November 1887).

Collins, Bud. *The Bud Collins History of Tennis*. 2nd ed. New York: New Chapter Press, 2010.

———, ed. *Bud Collins Total Tennis*. Toronto: Sport Media Publishing, 2003.

Collins, Bud, and Zander Hollander, eds. *Bud Collins' Tennis Encyclopedia*. Detroit: Visible Ink Press, 1997.

Connors, Jimmy. *The Outsider*. New York: Harper, 2014.

Crawford, Mary Caroline. *Famous Families of Massachusetts*. 2 vols. Boston: Little Brown, 1930.

Cummings, Parke. *American Tennis*. Boston: Little Brown, 1957.

———. "Major Walter C. Wingfield, Inventor of the Game." In *The Fireside Book of Tennis*, edited by Allison Danzig and Peter Schwed, 9-14. New York: Simon and Schuster, 1972.

Cunnington, Dennis, ed. *75 Years of the International Tennis Federation*. London: International Tennis Federation, 1988.

Davenport, Joanna. "Professionalism in Sports: The History and Interpretation of Amateurism in the United States Lawn Tennis Association," PhD dissertation, Ohio State University, 1966.

Deford, Frank. *Big Bill Tilden: The Triumphs and the Tragedy*. Wilmington DE: Sport Media Publishing, 2004.

Dwight, Eleanor. *Tie Breaker: Jimmy Van Alen and Tennis in the 20th Century*. New York: M.T.Train/Scala Books, 2010.

Dwight, James. "Lawn Tennis in New England." *Outing*, May 1891, 157ff.

———. Letter to the editor. *The Amateur Athlete and Archery and Tennis News* 2, no. 44 (October 23, 1884): 5, 9.

Engelmann, Larry. *The Goddess and the American Girl: The Story of Suzanne Lenglen and Helen Wills*. New York: Oxford University Press, 1988.

Evans, Richard. *Open Tennis: The First Twenty Years*. London: Blooms Publisher, 1988.

Fisher, Jon. *A Terrible Splendor: Three Extraordinary Men, a World Poised for War, and the Greatest Tennis Match Ever Played*. New York: Crown Publishers, 2009.

1891 Lawn Tennis Guide. Boston: Wright & Ditson, 1891.

Fallows, James. "The Passionless Presidency." *Atlantic Monthly*, May 1979.

Flink, Steve. "The White Plains Incident." *Tennis Week* 19 (October 19, 1995): 14.

Forbes, Allen. "Early Myopia at Winchester." *Essex Institute Historical Collections* 78, no. 1 (January 1942).

Gibson, Amy D. "The Association of Tennis Professionals: From Player Association to Governing Body." N.d., ca. 2010. www.na-businesspress.com/jabe/Jabel05/GibsonWeb.pdf.

Gobbie, Donn. "Gladys Heldman and the Original Nine: The Visionaries Who Pioneered the Virginia Slims Tennis Circuit." PhD diss., Purdue University, 2015.

Gowen, George W. *Talk of Many Things: Law, Sports, Politics, Nature*. Bloomington IN: Xlibris, 2014.

Gray, David. "Gray's Anatomy of How It All Happened." *World Tennis*, June 1978.

Gray, Frances Clayton, and Yanick Rice. *Born to Win: The Authorized Biography of Althea Gibson*. Hoboken: John Wiley & Sons, 2004.

Guttman, Allen. *From Ritual to Record: The Nature of Modern Sports*. New York: Columbia University Press, 1978.

Hall, Eric Allen. *Arthur Ashe: Tennis and Justice in the Civil Rights Era*. Baltimore: Johns Hopkins University Press, 2014.

Hardy, Samuel. "Thirty Years of Tennis." *Spalding's Lawn Tennis Annual 1919*. New York: American Sports Publishing company, 1919.

Harris, Cecil, and Larryette Kyle-DeBose. *Charging the Net: A History of Blacks in Tennis from Althea Gibson to the Williams Sisters*. Chicago: Ivan Dee, 2007.

Hauser, Thomas. *Muhammad Ali: His Life and Times*. New York: Simon & Schuster, 1992.

Hawk, Philip B. *Off the Racket: Tennis Highlights and Lowdowns.* New York: American Lawn Tennis, 1937.

Hawthorne, Fred. "The Commercialization of Tennis." *North American Review* 223, no. 4 (December--February 1926–27): 614–21.

Herritt, Elizabeth L. "Social Class and the Women's National Tennis Championships in the United States, 1887–1905." Master's thesis, Pennsylvania State University, 1977.

Hillway, Richard. "America's First Lawn Tennis Book." *The Journal of the Tennis Collectors of America* 31 (Spring 2014): 452–85.

———. "Bill Tilden and his Protégé, Art Anderson." *The Tennis Collector [The Journal of the Tennis Collectors' Society]* 72 (Summer 2011): 12–15.

———. "Lawn Tennis Inventor—Wingfield versus Gem." *The Tennis Collector* 68 (Spring 2010): 14–17.

———. "Frank Phelps: #1 Tennis Historian." *The Journal of the Tennis Collectors of America* Special Number 1 (Summer 2010): 1–15.

———. "Origins of Tennis," *Colorado Tennis* (part 1, December 2003–January 2004; part 2, February–March 2004; part 3, April–May 2004).

———. "Sphairistiké." *The Tennis Collector* 48 (Summer 2003): 10–11.

Hillway, Richard, and Geoff Felder. "Stephen Wallis Merrihew and American Lawn Tennis." *The Journal of the Tennis Collectors of America* 29 (Autumn 2013): 452–56.

"The History of Lawn Tennis in the U.S." *Official Bulletin* 3, no. 2 (February 1928): 10.

Koster, Rich. *The Tennis Bubble: Big Money Tennis: How It Grew and Where It's Going.* New York: Quadrangle/New York Times Book Company, 1976.

Kramer, Jack. "I Was a Paid Amateur." *This Week Magazine*, May 15, 1955, 7–9.

Kramer, Jack, with Frank Deford. *The Game: My 40 Years in Tennis.* New York: Putnam's Sons, 1979.

Kramer, Jane. "Me, Myself, and I." *New Yorker*, September 7, 2009, 36.

Kriplen, Nancy. *Dwight Davis: The Man and the Cup.* London: Ebury Press, 1999.

Lachman, Seymour P. *Mr. New York: Lew Rudin and His Love for the City.* Albany NY: State University of New York Press, 2014.

Langworth, R., ed. *Churchill by Himself.* London: Ebury Press/Random House, 2008.

Lawn Tennis Guide for 1894. Boston: Wright & Ditson, 1894.

Long, Barbara, and Rick Rennert, eds. *USA League Tennis: A Celebration of 25 Years.* White Plains NY: United States Tennis Association 2005.

Macaulay, Duncan, as told to John Smyth. *Behind the Scenes at Wimbledon.* New York: St. Martin's, 1965.

Marble, Alice. *Courting Danger.* New York: St. Martin's Paperbacks, 1992.

Meadow, Barry. "Jimmie McDaniel: Never Allowed to Be a Legend." *World Tennis*, October 1979.

Merrihew, Stephen Wallis. "The Amateur at Bay." *Atlantic Monthly,* October 1924, 497–502.

Minton, Robert. *Forest Hills: An Illustrated History*. Philadelphia: Lippincott, 1975.

Misner, Gerald E. "The Delegates Assembly." *1962 USTA Yearbook*, 43–44.

Morgan, Eric J. "Black and White at Center Court: Arthur Ashe and the Confrontation of Apartheid in South Africa." *Diplomatic History* 36 no. 5 (November 2012): 815–41.

Myers, A. Wallis. "The Americans at Wimbledon." *The Sportsman*, July 1927, 19.

———. *The Complete Lawn Tennis Player*. Philadelphia: George W. Jacobs, 1908.

Nixon, Rob. "Apartheid on the Run: The South African Sports Boycott." *Transition* 58 (1992): 68–88.

"The Origin of Lawn Tennis in the U.S." *Official Bulletin* 2, nos. 10–11 (October–November 1927): 1–2.

Outerbridge, E. H. "The History of Lawn Tennis in the United States." *Official Bulletin: United States Lawn Tennis Association* 2–3 (October–November 1927; December 1927–January 1928; February 1928).

Paret, J. Parmley. *Lawn Tennis: Its Past, Present, and Future.* New York: Macmillan, 1904.

Phelps, Frank. "Unravelling the Myth: The Traditional Tale of How Tennis Came to America" *Tennis Week* 11 (March 2003): 30–31.

Phelps, Frank V. "Merrihew, Stephen Wallis." *Biographical Dictionary of American Sports,* edited by D. Porter. Westport CN: Greenwood Press, 1988.

Pileggi, Sarah. "The Lady In The White Silk Dress," *Sports Illustrated*, September 13, 1982. http://www.si.com/vault.

Potter, E. C., Jr. *Kings of the Court: The Story of Lawn Tennis.* New York: Charles Scribner's Sons, 1936.

Potter, Edward. "The Insulting Tennis Balls." *World Tennis*, May 1956, 12–13.

Potter, Ned. "The Old Question of the Open Tournament." *World Tennis*, January 1956, 16–17.

Potter, Ned. "Passing Shots." *World Tennis.*

Reisler, Jim. *Cash and Carry: The Spectacular Rise and Hard Fall of C. C. Pyle, America's First Sports Agent.* Jefferson NC: McFarland, 2009.

Riggs, Bobby. *Tennis Is My Racket*. New York: Simon and Schuster, 1949.

Roberts, Joshua. "Aces and Diamonds: The USLTA Celebrates its Seventy-fifth Anniversary," *Town and Country*, August 1956, 29ff.

Roberts, Randy, and James S. Olson. *Winning Is the Only Thing: Sports in America since 1945*. Baltimore: Johns Hopkins, 1989.

Robson, Doug. "The Doyenne of the Dollar Bill." *Tennis Magazine*, May 2008. http://www.douglasrobson.com/tennis-blog-page/2015/4/27/the-doyenne-of-the-dollar-bill.

Scott, Gene. "Vantage Point." *Tennis Week,* November 30, 2004.

———. "The 'Why' Behind the Tennis Wars." *World Tennis*, 1976, 52–53.

Skinner, Quentin. "The Generation of John Milton." In *Christ's: A Cambridge College over Five Centuries*, edited by David Reynolds, 41–72. London: Macmillan, 2005.

Slocum, H. W. *Lawn Tennis in Our Own Country*. New York: A. G. Spalding & Bros., 1890.

Specter, David Kenneth. "A Stadium Is Born," *Tennis Week*, February 20, 1997, 10–15.

Starey, A. B. "Some Aspects of American Lawn Tennis," *The Cosmopolitan* 7 no. 2 (June 1889).

Starr, Jack. *Stahre Decisis*. 5th ed. N.p.: Tennis Ink, 1976.

Steinberger, Michael. "Queens Was Burning Too: The Chaotic Spectacle of the 1977 U.S. Open." *New York Times Magazine,* August 26, 2012.

Summerhayes, Martha. *Vanished Arizona: Recollections of the Army Life by a New England Woman*. Teddington, Middlesex, England: The Echo Library, 2006.

Tignor, Steve. "Ashes to Ashes." September 16, 2014. http://www.tennis.com/pro-game/2014/09/ashes-ashes/52675/#.vvtlnjn_tnp.

———. "Not for Crass Lawners," *Tennis* 45, no. 2 (March 2009): 46–49.

Tinling. *Love and Faults*. New York: Crown Publishers, 1979.

Todd, Tom. *Tennis Players from Pagan Rites to Strawberries & Cream*. Guernsey, UK: Vallancey Publisher, 1979.

Tunis, John R. "The Lawn Tennis Industry," *Harper's Magazine,* February 1928, 289–98.

United States Lawn Tennis Association. *Fifty Years of Lawn Tennis in the United States*. Edited by O. D. Ellis. New York: United States Lawn Tennis Association, 1931.

United States Tennis Association. *USTA Official Encyclopedia of Tennis*. Edited by Bill Shannon. New York: Harper & Row, 1981.

———. *USA League Tennis: A Celebration of 25 Years*. Edited by Barbara Long and Rick Rennert. White Plains NY: United States Tennis Association, 2005.

Voss, Arthur. *Tilden and Tennis in the Twenties*. Troy NY: Whitson Publishing, 1985.

Whitman, Malcolm D. *Tennis: Origins and Mysteries*. Detroit: Singing Tree Press, 1968.

Williams, Paul B. *The United States Lawn Tennis Association and the World War*. New York: Robert Hamilton, 1921.

Williams, Roger M. "Time to Reform the USTA." *Tennis Week*, October 19, 1995, 12–13.

Wind, Herbert Warren. "The Sporting Scene: The Tennis Championships, 1881–1981" *New Yorker*, October 19, 1981.

———. *Game, Set, and Match: The Tennis Boom of the 1960s and 70s*. New York: E. P. Dutton, 1979.

Wingfield, Walter Clopton. *The Major's Game of Lawn Tennis*. London: Harrison and Sons, 1873 or 1874.

Wirtschafter, Nathan. "Fourth Quarter Choke: How the IRS Blew the Corporate Sponsorship Game." 27 Loy. L.A.L. Rev. 1465 (1994) available at http://digitalcommons.lmu.edu/llr/vol27/iss4/7.

Yeomans, Patrick Henry. *Southern California Tennis Champions Centennial, 1887–1987.* N.p.: Southern California Committee for the Olympic Games, 1987. (Courtesy of Richard Hillway.)

INDEX

Page locators in italics refer to illustrations.